Florida Theme Issue

The Journal of Decorative and Propaganda Arts is published by The Wolfsonian–Florida International University and The Wolfson Foundation of Decorative and Propaganda Arts, Inc. Rates per issue including shipping and handling, US: individuals $30, institutions $35; foreign (payable in US dollars): individuals $35, institutions $40. Back issues available at $30 US, $35 foreign (payable in US dollars).

Send address changes to *The Journal of Decorative and Propaganda Arts*, The Wolfsonian–Florida International University, 1001 Washington Avenue, Miami Beach, Florida 33139 USA or fax 305/531-2133.

For advertising rates and schedules, write to *The Journal of Decorative and Propaganda Arts* or call 305/535-2612.

Printed in Singapore by CS Graphics.

Cover: Florida promotional brochure, cover, c. 1920. Florida Collection, Miami-Dade Public Library. (See page 32.)

23

The Journal of Decorative and Propaganda Arts   1875–1945

Publisher and Editor-in-Chief
Cathy Leff

Senior Editor
Andrea Gollin

Editorial Assistant/Sales
Francis X. Luca

Consultants

Guest Editor
Beth Dunlop

Design Director
Jacques Auger

Designer
Frank Begrowicz,
Jacques Auger Design
Associates, Inc.

Acknowledgments

By Cathy Leff

The journey through our home state — "land of sunshine and happiness," of orange blossoms and orange juice, of dreamers, schemers, visionaries, and inventors — has been a particularly enlightening and delightful discovery of modern Florida. Fortuitously, the publication of the Florida Theme Issue coincides with the formation of a permanent partnership between *The Journal of Decorative and Propaganda Arts*, The Wolfsonian, and the state university system at Florida International University, thereby celebrating not only the patrimony of the state but also our official entry into the state's patrimony — and culminating the vision of our founder, Mitchell Wolfson Jr.

Through this volume we gain new appreciation for the individuals who shaped the state during the years 1875 to 1945, and we extend our appreciation to the individuals and institutions who shape Florida today and who made this issue possible.

We are indebted to the Governor and First Lady of the State of Florida, Lawton and Rhea Chiles (native Floridians), who, recognizing the importance of documenting and preserving the state's cultural heritage, have been enthusiastic about this project from its inception. We are grateful for their letters of support, for their commitment to and love of the state's history, and for their friendship. We also acknowledge Joseph F. Pena and Kim Orr of the Governor's office.

Lieutenant Governor Buddy MacKay, born into an Ocala citrus family, has encouraged our examination of the importance of citrus to the state's economic and aesthetic development. We thank him, Jean Sadowski in his office, and Susan Vodicka, director of the Florida Partnership of the Americas, for assisting us.

Producing a volume of this size and scope would not have been possible without the leadership of Secretary of State Sandra B. Mortham and the funding provided by the Florida Department of State, Division of Historical Resources. We owe profound thanks to her and to George Percy, director of the Division, for their collaboration on this project. We also acknowledge the exceptional assistance we received from Vicki Cole, historic preservation planner in the Bureau of Historic Preservation, and we extend our appreciation to Fred Gaske, supervisor of the Bureau, for his support.

The support from the Florida Tourism Industry Marketing Corporation has facilitated our exploration of the state's development. We thank in particular Austin Mott, president and CEO; Bud Nocera, executive vice president and chief operating officer; Dee Ann Smith, vice president for marketing; and Arthur Hertz, vice chairman.

Special accolades to Charles Dusseau, who generously responded to our numerous and constant requests for help and advice.

The grant provided by the Miami-Dade County Cultural Affairs Council and the Board of County Commissioners helped support the research for this issue. We thank Michael Spring, executive director, and his staff, and Alejandro Aguirre, chairperson, and his colleagues on the Council.

The American Express Company recognizes the importance of protecting and preserving the natural and built environment. We are grateful for its contribution towards our Florida project. We especially thank Mabel Vincent, senior manager, community relations, in the Miami office.

As evidenced in the seventeen articles in this volume, Florida's early boosters were masterful in the ways they packaged and promoted the state for travel, investment, and development. So, it seemed not only natural but apropos — and in the spirit of state — that we "package" *The Journal* to further promote its appeal. When we approached Leonard A. Lauder, chairman of the Estée Lauder Companies, to sponsor an orange-blossom "peel-and-sniff" souvenir item, he immediately agreed. The scented reproductions of historic postcards inserted in each issue are a result of his generosity and that of Roger Barnett, president of Arcade and creator of the DiscCover® Sampling Technology. We also extend special thanks to Karyn Khoury of Estée Lauder and Sonia Milfort and Alice Sciortino of Arcade.

SunTrust Bank generously agreed to sponsor this publication, and we recognize Melissa Gracey, marketing manager, and Michael Lehn, regional executive vice president and manager, for their participation.

We thank BellSouth for its contribution, and we acknowledge Don Sadler, area director of corporate and external affairs, for his support.

We gratefully thank Penny Morford, president and CEO of Exhibit Builders, Inc. (EBI) of DeLand, who made available the archives on the firm's participation in the U.S. world's fairs — and then donated those archives to The Wolfsonian, enriching our Florida holdings. We also recognize Ann Aptaker and Ruth Stanley, and other friends associated with EBI, Jim Burkhalter, Linda Colvard Dorian, and Bob Mauk, for sharing with us their Florida histories.

Others to whom we express appreciation: Ray Arsenault, Sam Boldrick, Myrna and Seth Bramson, William Brown Jr., Brenda Burnette, Victor Diaz, Wayne Drummond, Ann Henderson, Jorge Hernandez, Dawn Hugh, William Kearns, Dona Lubin, Bruce Matheson, Clemmer Mayhew, Joan Morris, George Neary, Alison Nordstrom, Elizabeth Plater-Zyberk, Susan and John Rothchild, Leo Sandon, Mark Schimmenti, Vincent Scully, Herschel Shepard, Senator Ron Silver, Mark Silverstein and Colonial Bank, Becky Smith, Karen Stein, Robert A. M. Stern, Merrett R. Stierheim, Ellen Uguccione, Richard Guy Wilson, Rocio Paola Yaffar, Barry Zaid, and Carl F. Zellers Jr.

We express our sincere appreciation to: Beth Dunlop, who helped shape the content of this issue and consulted throughout the editorial process; Claudia and Jacques Auger, Frank Begrowicz, and Donna Carter of Jacques Auger Design Associates for their continuing friendship and collaboration and for once again delivering a superbly designed publication; and Pedro Figueredo, associate librarian at The Wolfsonian, who assisted in the selection and photographing of images and illustrations.

And finally, I thank my colleagues, Andrea Gollin and Francis X. Luca, who took on this enormous project and performed so brilliantly to bring it to print. □

Introduction

By Cathy Leff

Florida witnessed amazing growth and development from the late nineteenth to mid-twentieth centuries. Anything and everything was possible as the state attracted entrepreneurs and developers driven by grandiose dreams and the creative schemes to sell them. No other state mastered the "arts of propaganda"— the ability to invent and promote itself — as well as Florida. It was the era when the state entered national consciousness. Thus, out of a pristine peninsula emerged a land of wonder, which is the focus of this issue of *The Journal of Decorative and Propaganda Arts*.

Though the site of the oldest European settlement in the United States, Florida of the imagination only began to take real form more than three hundred years after Juan Ponce de León came searching for the mythical Fountain of Youth. In the early nineteenth century the state was a mecca for Northern invalids; with the introduction of steamships in the 1820s, inland travel increased; following the Civil War, waterways were used more extensively for travel and commerce. The land sales of the 1880s and the advancement of the railroad further primed the state for tourists and settlers. And they came — in droves — for fun, fortune, property, health, and oranges.

The orange was central to Florida's identity, as it was the state's agricultural potential that attracted the first wave of investors. Fertile soil precipitated fertile advertising copy and once the word got out, the cash arrived, and a real estate frenzy began.

The following essays document the genius of Florida's entrepreneurs and developers in promoting the myth and romance of the state and capturing the imagination — and checkbooks — of the nation. Michael McDonough explores the invention, development, and exploitation of the Mediterranean-inspired architectural motifs used to market boom-time Sarasota. As he notes, powerful images and advertising appealed to the masses and spawned unprecedented real estate speculation.

Helen L. Kohen's essay illustrates how the orange, though not native to the state, became its most recognizable symbol. It seduced early investors, shaped landscape and architecture, and served as an icon for promoting the state, as well as inspiring the blossoming souvenir industry.

Florida's participation at the U.S. world's fairs and expositions is the subject of Joel M. Hoffman's research, which begins with an examination of the state's first serious world's fair presence at Chicago's 1893 World's Columbian Exposition. Early boosters recognized the importance of exporting propaganda as a means of promoting the state's image and encouraging tourism and investment. The real estate bust and hurricane of 1926 and the stock market crash of 1929 reversed Florida's good fortune, but high-profile pavilions at Chicago's 1933 A Century of Progress Exposition and the 1939 New York World's Fair — produced through the acumen of promoter extraordinaire Earl W. Brown — restored the state's reputation.

Propaganda extends to Michael L. Carlebach's article on William Henry Jackson, the country's preeminent landscape photographer. Jackson's images of natural beauty served the intentions of hoteliers and developers of the Florida railroad who employed him to help market the state as a tourist destination.

And as the tourists arrived, they created the demand for grand resort hotels. Thomas Graham introduces us to industrialist Henry Morrison Flagler and his motivations for constructing the luxurious Ponce de León and Alcázar hotels in St. Augustine. Graham further explores the introduction of a Spanish-inspired architecture and interior decoration, which was deemed appropriate by the hotels' New York-based architects, John Carrère and Thomas Hastings, to fulfill the expectations of prospective patrons.

The extension of Florida's transportation systems radically altered the face of the state. Seth Bramson surveys the contributions of three pioneering Henrys — Henry Flagler, Henry Plant, and Henry Sanford — whose railroad, steamship, and hotel networks triggered enormous growth within the peninsular mass. The arrival of Flagler's train in Miami in 1896 allowed for that city's development.

William E. Brown Jr. introduces another transportation pioneer, Juan Terry Trippe, founder of Pan American Airways. First based in Key West and later in Miami, Pan Am changed not only the nature of travel but also the way people viewed themselves and the world. From the design of its Clipper ships and facilities to its promotional brochures, Pan Am understood the power of creating an image of modernity that corresponded to travel in the modern age.

Catherine Lynn explains how themes were invented to promote new communities, looking at the motifs inspired by *The Arabian Nights* for Glenn Curtiss' planned city of Opa-locka. Competition among developers was fierce, and Araby-inspired buildings were capable of luring buyers. The hurricane of 1926 cut short Curtiss' dream for the "City Substantial" and marked the end of Florida's real estate frenzy.

The invention of an architectural style that communicated Old World allure is the focus of Beth Dunlop's investigation. The construction of Spanish-Venetian-Moorish-inspired Mediterranean Revival buildings precipitated the need for furniture and other decorative elements with centuries-old appeal. Coral Gables' developer George Merrick and Palm Beach's Addison Mizner were the primary proponents of this evocative new style, which flourished in Florida between the two world wars.

The themes of fantasy and invention continue in Michael D. Kinerk and Dennis W. Wilhelm's survey of the elaborate motion picture theatres that proliferated throughout Florida in the first half of this century. Kinerk and Wilhelm discuss the architects responsible for these entertainment palaces and the history and motivations of the studios that built them.

Selling fantasies was not restricted to Florida's boom-time developers. As Margot Ammidown's essay reveals, the small tourist attractions delivered the legendary images Florida's road-bound travellers craved. Ammidown steps back in history, tracing the sources of these mythical references and showing how they were present in early attractions.

Joanna Lombard's article discusses the profound landscape designs of William Lyman Phillips. A disciple of Frederick Law Olmsted Sr., the United States' most renowned nineteenth-century landscape architect, Phillips collaborated with Frederick Law Olmsted Jr. on a number of memorable gardens and public parks in Florida, most significantly the Mountain Lake Sanctuary in Lake Wales, and Greynolds Park, Matheson Hammock, and Fairchild Tropical Garden in Miami.

The economic crisis resulting from the Great Depression gave rise to a number of federally sponsored programs under President Franklin Delano Roosevelt. In 1935 the Works Progress Administration was established along with its subsection, Federal One, through which the Federal Writers' Project and other arts-related work-relief programs were created. James A. Findlay and Margaret Bing examine the exceptional output of the Florida branch of the Federal Writers' Project. Directed by Carita Doggett Corse, the program produced a number of important travel guides, providing a portrait of the state's social and artistic history.

Thomas E. Low explores the intellectual principles of the Chautauqua movement and its impact on Florida towns, beginning with the development of its Southern outpost in the planned town of DeFuniak Springs at the end of the nineteenth century. This New York-based movement influenced John Nolen, one of the Progressive Era's most important planners, who was responsible for designing numerous Florida cities.

Dorothy Jenkins Fields documents the contributions of Miami's early black settlers, who provided the labor force to accommodate the city's burgeoning tourist industry, while creating their own community and rich cultural identity. Fields introduces Overtown's key figures and the architectural legacy they left.

Creating an architecture for Florida living was the aim of Igor Polevitzky, who worked from the 1930s to 1970s. Allan T. Shulman examines the buildings of this prolific architect, including some of Miami and Miami Beach's exceptional early Modernist landmarks.

John A. Stuart's interview of Paul Silverthorne reveals the motivations and memories of one of South Florida's most successful interior designers, active in Florida in the 1940s. Silverthorne's interiors and murals reflected the fantasies of tourists and residents drawn to South Florida — like others who preceded them — in search of sunshine and happiness.

Florida's myths, ambitions, and realities unfold in the pages that follow. Our exploration concentrates on the years between 1875 and 1945, the pivotal period during which Florida's destiny was determined. We invite you to put on your sunscreen, get out your "shades," grab a large glass of orange juice, and enjoy this journey through the Sunshine State. □

Fig. 1. A. M. Griffin, Atlantic Coast Line Passenger Station, completed in 1925.

Photograph by San Leon Studio. Sarasota County Archives.

Fig. 2. Dwight James Baum, Sarasota County Courthouse, completed in 1927.

Photograph by Samuel Gottscho. Syracuse University collection.

Selling Sarasota: Architecture and Propaganda in a 1920s Boom Town

By Michael McDonough

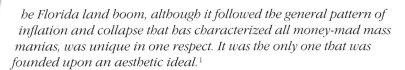

Michael McDonough is a principal in Treu Design, a multidisciplinary design firm in Sarasota, Florida. He has served as curator for both the John and Mable Ringling Museum of Art and the Chicago Architecture Foundation.

he Florida land boom, although it followed the general pattern of inflation and collapse that has characterized all money-mad mass manias, was unique in one respect. It was the only one that was founded upon an aesthetic ideal.[1]

In the last days of the 1920s Florida land boom, three new buildings of peculiar magnificence were completed in Sarasota: the Atlantic Coast Line Passenger Station, the Sarasota County Courthouse, and the Hotel El Vernona (figs. 1, 2, and 3).[2] Each embodied "all the beauty of Old Spain and every comfort of the twentieth century."[3] The train station resembled a Spanish mission; the courthouse complex comprised a pair of imitation palaces that flanked a 116-foot observation tower; the hotel was proclaimed a "modern reproduction of a medieval palace of the Dons."[4]

The architectural style of these landmark buildings was known variously at the time as Mediterranean, Mission, and Spanish and expressed the myth that Sarasota was glamorous yet stable. The broader term, Mediterranean, acknowledged the entire range of influences from the Mediterranean basin that inspired the architecture of Florida's mid-1920s boom period.[5] In civic, commercial, and residential buildings across the state, the Mediterranean style reinforced the fantasy that Florida was an established yet carefree place. As one Sarasota lecturer stated in 1926: "luxuriant Florida is not puritanical New England….Most everyone will agree that…Mediterranean architecture, goes best with palms, bamboos and brilliant sunshine."[6]

Romantic notions about Florida's three-century history of Spanish rule inspired the state's reinvention as a Mediterranean-looking playground in the

Fig. 3. Dwight James Baum, Hotel El Vernona, completed in 1926. Photograph by Samuel Gottscho. Syracuse University collection.

1. Burton Rascoe, introduction to *Boom in Paradise,* by T. H. Weigall (New York: Alfred H. King, 1932), xi.

2. The use of the word "boom" originated during the Southern California "land rush" of the 1880s. This land boom, in which values and prosperity quickly escalated, was the prototype for later American land booms like that of 1920s Florida. See Daniel Boorstin, *The Americans: The Democratic Experience* (New York: Random House, 1973), 274.

3. *El Vernona, Aristocrat of Beauty* (Tampa: Florida Grower Press, n.d.).

4. Ibid.

5. In 1928 architectural historian Rexford Newcomb defined Mediterranean style: "Spanish, Italian, Moorish, Byzantine — Mediterranean types generally — instead of being archeologically segregated, are under the orchestral process merged, as were those golden threads long ago, into a new, sun-loving style which, while eminently American in its plan and utilities, is never-the-less distinctly Mediterranean in its origins and spirit." Rexford Newcomb, *Mediterranean Domestic Architecture in the United States* (Cleveland: J. H. Hansen, 1928), iv.

6. "Mediterranean Type Architecture is Suited to the State," *Sarasota Herald*, 16 February 1926.

twentieth century. Though a few Spanish colonial structures were still standing in northern Florida in the 1920s, there was no evidence of a permanent Spanish colonial settlement in or near Sarasota. The conception of Sarasota as a Mediterranean city was based on pure fantasy. It was a myth invented to influence a mass audience to buy real estate. Overnight Sarasota became an instant paradise with a ready-made history.

In the early 1920s Sarasota still had an extensive, relatively unspoiled coastline on the Gulf of Mexico. It was a quiet town consisting mostly of wood-frame cottages, with a few notable houses and villas, and was favored by Midwestern industrialists. Real estate developers realized the potential of this beautiful place as a resort that could be marketed to Northern tourists and speculators. Between 1924 and 1926 the number of real estate firms in Sarasota increased from fifteen to more than two hundred.[7] One 1926 magazine article stated: "The smell of money in Florida, which attracts men as the smell of blood attracts a wild animal, became ripe and strong last spring. The whole United States began to catch whiffs of it. Pungent tales of immense quick wealth carried far."[8]

One popular 1926 guidebook to boom-time Florida claimed that "probably nowhere else in Florida has there been so much real estate activity in so concentrated a territory as in Sarasota since the beginning of 1924."[9] The city's unique site conditions and the work of one major developer accounted for much of its drawing power. Of greatest importance was the city's extensive, undeveloped coastline. With its numerous barrier islands and beaches, and expansive bayfront (all in close proximity to the town center), Sarasota held an edge over other cities in the state.

Circus magnate John Ringling (1866–1936) was the city's other major asset. His capital and promotional expertise allowed him to set high standards with his many Sarasota real estate development projects. Ringling's circus background taught him the value of presentation and fanfare. Like many others, he discerned a Mediterranean pulse on the Sarasota landscape, and he developed and promoted this aspect in his real estate projects. He commissioned nationally known New York architects Warren and Wetmore and Dwight James Baum to design fantastic Mediterranean-style buildings in Sarasota.

Sarasota was one of many Florida boom towns in which buildings and drawings of buildings were used as propaganda, as direct appeals to the emotions of the public.[10] Propaganda was not a negative word to Sarasota's boom-time boosters; they were proud to be part of the comprehensive program that was luring people to their city. As one promoter stated: "Both the Atlantic Coast

7. *Sarasota, Fla. City Directory, 1923–24* (Asheville: The Miller Press, 1923), 191; and *Polk's Sarasota City Directory, 1926* (Jacksonville: R. L. Polk and Co., Publishers, 1926), 406–412.

8. Gertrude Mathews Shelby, "Florida Frenzy," *Harper's Monthly Magazine* (January 1926): 177.

9. Frank P. Stockbridge and John Holiday Perry, *Florida in the Making* (New York: The de Bower Publishing Company, 1926), 266.

10. Propaganda was defined in 1942 by the Institute for Propaganda Analysis as "the expression of opinions or actions carried out deliberately by individuals or groups with a view to influencing the opinions or actions of other individuals or groups for predetermined ends and through psychological manipulations." Since the "Cold War" the term propaganda has taken on more negative and political connotations. In the 1920s it was considered less threatening, and its main emphasis was on the "manipulation of psychological symbols having goals of which the listener is not conscious." Jacques Ellul, *Propaganda, The Formation of Men's Attitudes* (New York: Vintage Books, 1965), xi, xii. For a period definition of propaganda as it relates to advertising see Harris Wescott, "Just What is Propaganda?" *The Poster* (November 1925): 7–8.

WHISPERING SANDS

Fig. 4. Dwight James Baum,

"Whispering Sands, a Proposed

Development at Sarasota,

Florida." From *The American

Architect* (20 August 1926).

Fine Arts Library collection,

University of Virginia.

Line and the Seaboard [railways] have issued booklets for 1924 carrying propaganda for Sarasota—glowing but truthful—I know for I wrote the dope."[11]

Rail lines, automobiles, advertising, and mortgages facilitated the boom in Sarasota and throughout the state. Florida propaganda targeted a growing segment of consumers in the United States — a newly mobile middle-class audience conditioned by increased mass-media advertising, and empowered by extended credit systems. One 1920s journalist defended propaganda as the "most potent force in World civilization, and in America! Without it starvation would stalk the land."[12] Sarasota's propaganda informed and motivated an audience of eager consumers. Billboards, signs, and subdivision gateways along Sarasota's sunny avenues beckoned to tourists and real estate speculators from the North.

However, many of the promises were empty. The subdivision gateways were often gateways to nothing. Many of the streets in Sarasota's new subdivisions were lined with mature palm trees native to India and South America, but in most of these developments one would have seen only a few modest Spanish-type residences and hundreds of empty lots. Dredging and filling operations were often not finished, and sometimes building sites were still under water when buyers signed purchase agreements. In many subdivisions, little had been done to improve the land except for the grading of roads and the surveying and platting of building lots.

Since only fragments of Sarasota's Mediterranean landscape were completed, promoters used advertisement illustrations and other drawings, subdivision plans, and carefully contrived site tours to communicate what was being offered for sale. An example of this kind of merchandising aid is a drawing of an aerial view of Whispering Sands, one of many Sarasota subdivisions that never evolved beyond the planning stage (fig. 4). A 1927 report described this phenomenon: "Lots are bought from blueprints. They look better that way. Then the buyer gets the promoter's vision, can see the splendid curving boulevards,

11. *Secretary's Report*, Sarasota Chamber of Commerce (2 November 1923).

12. Wescott, "Just What is Propaganda?" 8.

the yacht basin, the parks lined with leaning coconut trees and flaming hibiscus….To go see the lot—well it just isn't done."[13]

An economic crisis, brought on by the excessive ambitions of promoters and speculators, coupled with the devastating hurricane that hit Miami in September 1926, marked the end of Florida's speculative real estate spree. The great Florida land boom waned as quickly as it began. Anti-Florida sentiment was intensified by an embargo on the shipment of building materials from the North, unethical real estate sales, and other controversial conditions. Northern banks and other businesses, which had been losing revenue because of the boom, helped spread this feeling. The full transformation of Sarasota into a Mediterranean resort was to remain unfinished. The master plan for the city by eminent city planner John Nolen (1869–1937) was not implemented. The big harbor for international traffic was never built. In most of Sarasota's boom-time subdivisions, few houses would be built until the next major period of construction—the post-World War II boom.

The collapse of the boom left fragmented landscapes throughout Florida. As one 1925 aerial view of Sarasota poignantly shows, the thriving Mediterranean resort did not completely replace the sporadically developed wood-frame fishing village (fig. 5). For Sarasota—and many Florida cities—advertisements and other propaganda promoted a vision that was never realized fully. On paper, however, Sarasota's Mediterranean transformation was extensive and well documented. In addition to the built projects of the mid-1920s, one must look at the promotional literature and drawings of the period to understand the scope of the vision that developers had for the new Sarasota.

The Mediterranean-style architecture of boom-time Florida derived from many sources. In the 1880s America's burgeoning entertainment and leisure-travel industries began to construct pseudo-historic Mediterranean buildings, which were used to promote attractive images of certain places to large audiences. This phenomenon was especially popular in regions with Spanish colonial histories. In Florida several luxury resort hotels were built that were fanciful interpretations of Spanish and Moorish buildings. These hotels appealed to

13. Homer B. Vanderblue, "The Florida Land Boom," *The Journal of Land and Public Utility Companies* 3 (May 1927): 118.

Fig. 6. A. Page Brown,

California Building, World's

Columbian Exposition, Chicago,

1893. Photograph by George

Glessner. Chicago Historical

Society collection.

the Northern patron seeking an exotic vacation destination. The most elaborate of these retreats were the Ponce de León (1885–1887), Alcázar (1887–1889), and Casa Monica (1899) hotels in St. Augustine, and the Tampa Bay Hotel (1888–1891).[14]

In the 1890s and 1900s world's fairs exposed Mediterranean architecture to an even larger audience. California was one of several states that used architecture at expositions to exploit its Spanish heritage, part of a coordinated campaign that also employed graphics and printed messages to promote tourism and real estate investment. Visitors at Chicago's 1893 World's Columbian Exposition saw the California Building, which was an imitation of a Spanish mission (fig. 6). This building embodied romantic ideas about California's past and helped to promote a glamorous image of the state. The success of the California Building started a trend that exhibitors at other fairs soon followed. Between 1893 and 1915, versions of Mediterranean prototypes were built for every major American exposition.

The highly popular Street of Cairo exhibit at the World's Columbian Exposition established a model for a themed attraction in which architecture from the Mediterranean basin was used purely for entertainment. In this exhibit in the Midway Plaisance, visitors experienced an exotic place without suffering the inconvenience of international travel. Regularly, colorful street scenes were staged by natives, and a risqué dance was performed by a young beauty named Little Egypt.[15]

Following this example, amusement parks across the country began to build Mediterranean-style structures to house a variety of activities. With these buildings, Mediterranean architecture was seen by an even more diverse audience

14. See Rafael Agapito Crespo, "Florida's First Spanish Renaissance Revival" (Ph.D. diss., Harvard University, 1987); and Susan Braden, "Florida Resort Architecture: The Hotels of Plant and Flagler" (Ph.D. diss., Florida State University, 1987).

15. For a description of the Street of Cairo see David F. Burg, *The White City* (Lexington: The University Press of Kentucky, 1976), 220–223.

Fig. 7. Fontaine Ferry Park Entrance Building in Louisville. Designed by architect John Miller, this imitation of a Spanish mission was completed in 1905. From a postcard. Author's collection.

►

Fig. 8. This still from the hit film *Thief of Bagdad* (1924) shows one of the lavish sets that predisposed a popular audience to the charms of the architecture of the Mediterranean basin. Academy of Motion Picture Arts and Sciences collection.

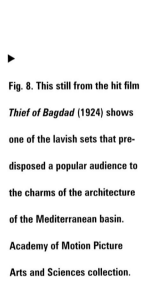

than that of the world's fairs and expensive resort hotels. Instead of promoting a glamorized history of a particular place, Mediterranean buildings at amusement parks simply represented a good time and a diversion from more serious concerns. Typical of many amusement parks of the period, Louisville, Kentucky's Fontaine Ferry Park completed a new entrance building in 1905, with a design inspired by a Spanish mission (fig. 7).

Mediterranean architecture reached its largest audience with the artful movies and opulent movie theatres of the 1920s. By 1925 weekly paid admissions to cinemas in the United States had risen to more than forty-five million.[16] The

16. Richard Koszarski, *An Evening's Entertainment: The Age of the Silent Feature Picture 1915–1928* (New York: Charles Scribner's Sons, 1990), 26.

film industry became a popular tastemaker on a scale previously unknown in any medium. Around 1919 art direction in general, and set design in particular, emerged as important aspects of film production.[17] Architects began working in this field, where previously carpenters and scene painters had been in charge. Critiques of motion picture set design began to appear in professional journals. The *American Architect* commented in 1920 that "the men who design the sets are constantly striving for the better effect of actuality."[18]

With the films *The Birth of a Nation* (1915) and *Intolerance* (1916), D. W. Griffith introduced the historical spectacle — a genre that was to reach the peak of its popularity in the 1920s. Each year between 1922 and 1926, at least one of the five most popular films in the United States had a historic Mediterranean or Middle Eastern setting. Films like *Blood and Sand* (1922), *The Ten Commandments* (1923), *The Thief of Bagdad* (1924), *Don Q, Son of Zorro* (1925), and *Ben-Hur* (1926) exposed mass audiences to pseudo-historic Mediterranean sets, which were constructed in Sarasota and throughout Florida (fig. 8).[19]

By the mid-1920s most Americans had strong, positive associations with the architectural styles of the Mediterranean basin since they had seen them almost exclusively in entertainment, recreation, and travel environments. Like movie producers, Sarasota real estate salesmen sold atmosphere and romance. Illusion was Sarasota's main staple. Here, for the price of a modest down payment, the visitor from a small Northern town could buy a piece of a grand Mediterranean fantasy. The windshield of a Model T was like a movie screen for the real estate buyer touring Sarasota.[20]

Mediterranean architecture was used to construct and promote a place that did not look like the neighborhood back home. This architecture — along with the subtropical climate — reinforced Sarasota's isolation from the rest of the mundane workaday world, aligning Sarasota with the fantasy world of the movies. The scenographic quality of the vision for Sarasota's boom-time transformation is evident in a drawing by Asa Cassidy, a former movie set designer, of a proposed bridge to Siesta Key, which was inspired by Spanish ruins (fig. 9).

An audience conditioned by mass advertising and mass communication responded to architectural images that could be communicated graphically

17. Ibid., 120.

18. Ibid.

19. For a ranking of the most popular film attractions in the United States between 1922 and 1927, see Koszarski, *Evening's Entertainment,* 33.

20. The comparison of the automobile windshield to a movie screen is made by Chester H. Liebs in his book *Main Street to Miracle Mile: American Roadside Architecture* (Boston: Little Brown and Company, 1985), 4.

and quickly. Mediterranean tableaux, like the Siesta Key bridge and its adjacent landscape, were designed to be viewed largely from automobiles and in fanciful illustrations and photographs. Graphic impact and curb appeal were primary considerations for the designers of the buildings and landscapes that comprised these tableaux. The details and elements of the Mediterranean buildings were more important as parts of picturesque compositions than as components of functional designs. Exotic-looking facades, like that of the beachfront Gulf View Inn, served well as backdrops for romantic rendezvous (fig. 10).

Though they may have looked like fanciful movie sets, it was also important that Sarasota's new buildings appeared substantial. The new, more glamorous Sarasota needed an image of stability to attract serious investors. Mediterranean-style buildings provided such an image for a place with an economy that was actually rather unstable. The solid masonry construction of the Mediterranean buildings imparted an appearance of permanence. Various finishes, like rough stucco and paint washes, simulated the patinas of historic buildings. A description of the interior of one "Spanish-type home" appeared in an April 1925 Sarasota newspaper article: "The color effect of the reception hall and living room, as well as the entire stairway hall, is on the two-tone shade of browns with the effect of 100 year old walls and ceilings giving the appearance of being smoked with age….the ceiling is of the wide pecky cypress planks, chemically burnt to give the same old Spanish castle appearance."[21]

Sarasotans were conscious that the new way of building transforming their city signified a break from the past, and they welcomed it. As one October 1925 newspaper article proclaimed: "The type of building being done in Sarasota has changed radically within the last three months, and citizens are now building for permanency and beauty."[22] The article from April 1925 stressed the

21. "Sarasota Awakening to Newer Era of Advancement in Architectural Perfection…," *This Week in Sarasota*, 16 April 1925, 11.

22. "City Building Better Homes," *Sarasota Herald*, 4 October 1925, sec. 4, 3.

importance of solid masonry construction: "Sarasota is now awakening to the newer and greater era of advancement — supplementing temporary structures of purely frame material for homes and residences of a more substantial and more attractive character."[23] Mediterranean-style architecture bestowed on Sarasota the respectability of a venerable older city, a city built to endure.

A new, old-looking Mediterranean image for Sarasota was marketed in countless numbers of illustrated advertisements that promoted the area's seventy-odd boom-time subdivisions. The Mediterranean architectural language was easy to identify and memorize. As visual propaganda it was very persuasive. Its vocabulary was distinctive, simple, relatively limited, and graphically bold. Fragments — such as the wall segments with arched openings, pottery, and window grille in a 1926 Whitfield Estates advertisement illustration — had the power to suggest an entire Mediterranean landscape (fig.11). In an advertisement illustration or at the entrance to a new subdivision, a glimpse of a bougainvillea-draped gatepost or an arched doorway provided provocative images that offered the opportunity to fill in the visual blanks and complete the picture of a Mediterranean Sarasota.

The floor plans of most of Sarasota's Mediterranean-style houses were not responsive to the subtropical climate, nor were they based on Mediterranean prototypes. Amenities like cross-ventilation and generous shaded outdoor living spaces (so pervasive in pre-1920s Sarasota houses) were not of primary importance. The fast-track construction schedules of the boom period were not conducive to the development of a new house plan. In boom-time Sarasota—and throughout Florida — Mediterranean skins were applied to modest house forms that might have been seen anywhere in North America.

Though many of Sarasota's Mediterranean houses were new from the ground up, the photographs of one period renovation project reveal the superficiality of the Mediterranean theme (figs. 12 and 13). Here, a simple wood-frame structure was instantly glamorized by being enclosed in a stuccoed masonry envelope with a few arched openings. A barrel-tile roof and a miniature mission-type gable completed the composition. In houses like this, a functional site-specific plan was less important than its appearance from the street. The facades of these houses were important as civic art in that they reinforced the larger vision of a Mediterranean Sarasota.

The Mediterranean house could be built with a modest budget — an important factor since the target audience for most of Sarasota's propaganda was the middle-class investor. Contractors could quickly and affordably build this house. The stuccoed wall was forgiving; even sloppy work could be concealed easily. The arched openings, the barrel tiles, and the architectural details (such as wrought-iron work and precast plaster ornaments) made up a simple kit of parts of a mythical Mediterranean city. Either built or drawn, no matter how modest the production budget, one or more of these parts could be used to represent the larger vision.

Transplanted Northerners were the dominant figures in the creation of the new Sarasota. These capitalists, who started coming to Sarasota in the 1910s, had discovered rich resources such as climate, waterfront views, and history — all intangible, but nevertheless resources that could be exploited with the help of clever real estate marketing and financing strategies. By the mid-1920s

Fig. 11. Artist unknown, Whitfield Estates advertisement, detail. From *Sarasota Herald*, 4 February 1926. Sarasota County Archives.

23. "Sarasota Awakening," 10.

BEFORE. CHATEAU PETIT

AFTER CHATEAU PETIT

Fig. 12. Photograph of
the F. A. De Canizares residence before its enclosure
in a Mediterranean skin
in the mid-1920s. Sarasota
County Archives.

experienced entrepreneurs and design professionals from Northern cities were directing Sarasota's development plans and the propaganda that promoted them. A survey of the backgrounds of the directors at one influential Sarasota organization exemplifies this point.

At the height of the boom the Sarasota Chamber of Commerce had forty-five directors, only one of whom was a native-born Floridian. More than half of the group had come to Sarasota from large Northern cities. Real estate was the main source of income in Sarasota for at least half of them. Several of the directors had come to Sarasota with experience in promotional campaigns for large audiences: Asa Cassidy had been a set designer and an artist for Griffith's film *The Birth of A Nation*; Ralph Caples ran Warren G. Harding's campaign train for the 1920 presidential election; Samuel Gumpertz managed amusement parks throughout the country, including Coney Island's Dreamland; John McGraw was the manager of the New York Giants baseball team; Charles and John Ringling were famous for their circus.

A high percentage of the people living in Sarasota in the mid-1920s were former Chicagoans.[24] As of 1925 at least fourteen of the directors of the Chamber of Commerce had spent significant time in Chicago prior to coming to Sarasota. Several of them continued to maintain residences, club memberships, and offices in Chicago through the mid-1920s.

Fig. 13. Photograph of
the F. A. De Canizares residence after its enclosure
in a Mediterranean skin
in the mid-1920s. Sarasota
County Archives.

Former Chicagoans influenced the scope and intensity of Sarasota's boom-time development and promotional programs. These transplants had firsthand knowledge of such important large-scale projects as the 1893 World's Columbian Exposition and Burnham and Bennet's *1909 Plan for Chicago*, both fountainheads for the City Beautiful movement.[25] The objective of this movement was the transformation of the chaotic and inefficient American industrial city of the early-twentieth century into a cultured, organized metropolis. In the City Beautiful, large-scale planning integrated the work of artist, architect, landscape architect, and urban planner. In order to gain public acceptance of its goals, the City Beautiful movement developed its own sophisticated propaganda system.

The 1893 fair had given America a vision of an ideal city that was both practical and beautiful. Sanitation, traffic circulation, and utilities were handled efficiently and without marring the beauty of the White City.[26] With its uniform cornice line, all-white Court of Honor buildings, and predominance of Neoclassical architecture, the fair also had been a model of aesthetic unity. The fair showed that great civic projects could be built if individuals suppressed their private motivations and focused on common goals. At least seventeen of the directors of the Sarasota Chamber of Commerce were in or near Chicago during 1893. It is unlikely that they would not have attended the fair.

Ordered growth and the creation of grand civic spaces were important in 1920s Sarasota. The city planner John Nolen was commissioned to produce a design

24. For a description of the importance of Chicago as a center for civic consciousness see Carl W. Condit, *The Chicago School of Architecture* (Chicago: The University of Chicago Press, 1964) and Harold M. Mayer and Richard C. Wade, *Chicago: Growth of a Metropolis* (Chicago: The University of Chicago Press, 1969), 272–280, 290–300.

25. For a thorough discussion of the City Beautiful movement see William H. Wilson, *The City Beautiful Movement* (Baltimore and London: The Johns Hopkins University Press, 1989).

26. The 1893 World's Columbian Exposition was popularly known as the White City primarily because of the color of the buildings in its main Court of Honor. The image of the gleaming "White City" contrasted with the "Black Cities" across the country that suffered from the grime and chaos that late-nineteenth-century industrialization engendered.

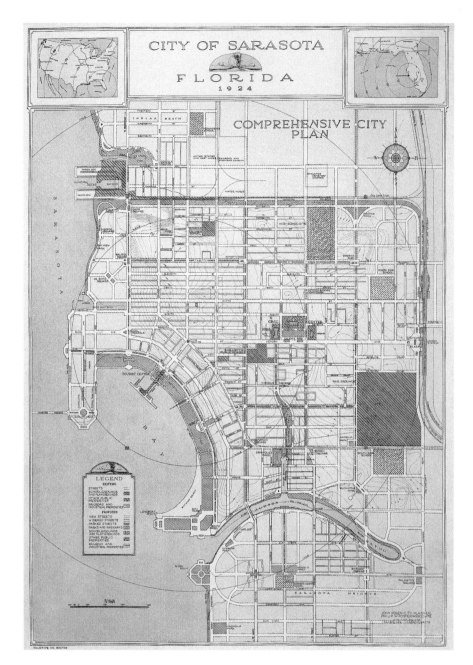

Fig. 14. John Nolen, "Comprehensive City Plan, Sarasota," colored engraving, 21 x 65", 1924. John Nolen Papers, Department of Manuscripts and University Archives, Cornell University Library.

for planned growth for Greater Sarasota (fig. 14). Like Chicago, Sarasota was a rapidly expanding waterfront city seeking to shed its image as a grubby backwater town. The reformed city would be much more marketable than its predecessor. Daniel Burnham (1846–1912), an early proponent of the City Beautiful movement, stated that "beauty has always paid better than any other commodity and always will."[27]

Transplanted Chicagoans knew, from experience, how to plan and promote a new, bigger, more attractive Sarasota. In the 1893 fair and in Burnham and Bennet's *1909 Plan for Chicago*, they had seen the value of a grand cohesive

27. Thomas S. Hines, *Burnham of Chicago: Architect and Planner* (New York: 1974), 316, quoted in Wilson, 29.

vision. The predominance of Mediterranean-style buildings from Sarasota's boom period indicates a high level of agreement about the value of aesthetic unity, an important aspect of the vision of the City Beautiful movement. This kind of unity of vision is not what one might expect in an era of free enterprise and architectural eclecticism. In most of America during this period, architectural variety was the norm. But, as Sarasota — and most of Florida — realized, a cohesive vision had great marketing potential. Coordinated Mediterranean imagery was easily exploited in a powerfully efficient propaganda campaign. The Chicagoans in Sarasota had the expertise to implement such a large-scale transformation.

John Ringling was one famous native of the Midwest who had a particularly big vision for Sarasota, and he was able to market it to a vast national audience. He claimed to be "known in two hemispheres as one of the greatest showmen of all time and in Sarasota as the man whose foresight and confidence has perhaps done more toward the beautification and development of this district than any other individual."[28] At the height of the boom, Ringling's holdings in Sarasota included two luxury hotels (one open and running, one under construction), more than thirty thousand acres of undeveloped land in eastern Sarasota County, and several thousand acres of land on the barrier islands of Lido, Longboat, and St. Armands keys that he was in the process of transforming into residential enclaves that he promised to be "such places of beauty as will be unsurpassed anywhere."[29]

The crown jewel of Ringling's Florida empire was his thirty-seven-acre estate that contained an elaborate art museum and his private Venetian palazzo, Ca' d'Zan. This showplace on Sarasota Bay functioned as more than just a home for John Ringling and his wife, Mable. It was the seat of their Sarasota empire and one of the city's greatest pieces of architectural propaganda. Published descriptions, drawings, and photographs of this house proclaimed the glamour of Mediterranean Sarasota to an international audience (fig. 15).

Though Ringling aggressively improved, subdivided, and promoted a large amount of real estate, the collapse of the boom precluded his financial success in this realm. By the time of his death in 1936, only a few houses had been constructed on his vast subdivided lands on the barrier islands.

John Ringling and his fellow boosters developed and promoted a new, Mediterranean Sarasota for a national market of prosperous middle-class consumers. They used the expanding mediums of mass advertising and mass communication to cultivate this market. Illustrated advertisements for Sarasota appeared in the Ringling circus programs that were distributed from New York to San Diego. During 1925 and 1926 developer C. Roy Kindt erected a large billboard on Chicago's busy Michigan Avenue which advertised Sarasota real estate with the image of a Mediterranean-style building overlooking a waterfront lined with graceful palm trees.

Newspapers throughout the country printed editorials and paid advertising promoting Florida. In February of 1926, for instance, the Marion, Indiana *Chronicle* printed a highly complimentary article on Sarasota, which it described as the "busiest little city in the world." Curious to see for themselves what all the hoopla was about, thousands of people from towns like Marion came to

28. *Sarasota Herald*, 10 January 1926.
29. *Sarasota Herald*, 13 February 1927.

Fig. 15. Norman Reeves, "Venice in Florida." This color illustration of Ca' d'Zan was published in the British magazine, *Country Life* (October 1927). Designed by architect Dwight James Baum for John and Mable Ringling, Ca' d'Zan was completed in 1926. Fine Arts Library collection, University of Virginia.

Sarasota. The thriving paradise city they came to see was not yet finished, but it was lavishly displayed in the pages of the Sarasota newspapers, in beautifully illustrated advertisements.

During World War I, patriotic advertisements had helped to legitimize advertising as a source of responsible information. A wartime federal tax break, which classified advertising expenses as exemptions, further enhanced the climate for promotion. Spurred by a booming economy, the momentum that was generated during the war continued into the 1920s.[30] National magazine advertising, for example, increased six hundred percent between 1916 and 1926.[31]

Print was the primary media in which Florida and its real estate were promoted during the 1920s. In 1925 the *Miami Herald* had the largest advertising linage of any newspaper in the country. One 1925 edition of the *Miami News* had 504 pages, containing mostly advertisements and articles promoting real estate.[32] The 15 January 1926 edition of the daily *Sarasota Herald* had forty-four

30. For a thorough discussion of the changing advertising industry in the United States during the 1920s, see Roland Marchand, *Advertising the American Dream* (Berkeley: University of California Press, 1985).

31. Ibid., 7.

32. Charlton W. Tebeau, *A History of Florida* (Coral Gables: University of Miami Press, 1971), 383–384.

Fig. 16. Advertisement for

Wrigley Engraving Corp.

From *This Week in Sarasota*,

2.1 x 3.6", 21 January 1926.

Sarasota County Archives.

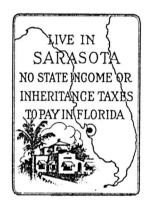

Fig. 17. Artist unknown, Ringling

Trust and Savings Bank Check,

detail, c. 1925. Formerly at John

and Mable Ringling Museum of

Art, currently lost. Photocopy

from author's collection.

display advertisements for real estate, which took up a total of 1,626 column inches, many of which were illustrated. On the same date six years earlier, the city's weekly newspaper had only one small display advertisement for real estate.

Advertisers in the mid-1920s realized that the emotional appeal of an illustration had more influence than a rational text. As one advertising manager stated in 1926: "Advertising isn't read much anymore....It is seen."[33] Illustrations met little psychological resistance.[34] Many of Sarasota's boom-time real estate advertisements were illustrated. Artwork was provided by firms like Wrigley Engraving Corporation of Jacksonville, which itself advertised in Sarasota newspapers (fig. 16). In many cases artists who had never been to Sarasota invented images to promote the city and its subdivisions. These illustrations usually bore little resemblance to the projects they were promoting. Often, the same drawing of a Mediterranean house or landscape was used to promote two or three different and unrelated projects.

In the 1920s the range of goods merchandised on the basis of style expanded enormously.[35] Increasingly, advertising copy and illustrations emphasized romantic associations. Sarasota's typical boom-time real estate advertisement urged the consumer to look beyond the utilitarian aspects of the commodity and reflect on aesthetic and lifestyle issues. Even bank checks could be stylish real estate advertisements. The Ringling Trust and Savings Bank issued checks imprinted with the image of a Mediterranean-style house set in a tropical landscape (fig. 17). The accompanying caption read "Live in Sarasota No State Income or Inheritance Taxes to Pay in Florida." This check was a subtle piece of propaganda that implicated both the payer and payee as subscribers to the prevailing vision of Sarasota as a lucrative Mediterranean paradise. Illustrated advertisements, like the bank check, reinforced a vision of an ideal Sarasota in which one could have an elegant and carefree lifestyle.

Sarasota's real estate advertisements of the boom period reveal why the Mediterranean-style building was so effective as propaganda. It lent itself well to clear representation with a simple, graphic language, which was easy to memorize, and easy to build with. It symbolized the spirit of a carefree, fanciful place, yet it appeared sound because it was of masonry construction, and it looked old, contributing to a stable image of Sarasota. The Mediterranean style offered a landscape and a consciousness that was at once old-fashioned and futuristic, its accessibility and enjoyment enhanced by the burgeoning automobile culture.

An illustration from a 1926 Whitfield Estates advertisement contains all of the components of the typical pseudo-historic landscape that emerged in Florida in the early 1920s (fig. 18). In this illustration, a svelte young woman stands in the foreground surveying an enchanting subtropical scene. Having just alighted from her sporty new coupe, she is elegantly dressed for an afternoon tea or bridge party. The scene she views contains a coconut palm tree, a portion of a new structure that resembles a Spanish hacienda, and an old brick gatepost. The crisp lines and perfectly aligned roof tiles of the house indicate a newly constructed building. A small, two-dimensional arched opening incorporated in its parapet suggests a bell tower.

33. "Minutes of Representatives Meetings," 23 December 1930, J. Walter Thompson Archives, quoted in Marchand, *Advertising the American Dream,* 153.

34. Marchand, *Advertising the American Dream,* 154.

35. Ibid., 120.

Yet the gatepost with its crumbling stucco finish looks like part of a ruin — perhaps the remains of an older hacienda. This fragment indicates a long and noble history of human habitation on the site. The mature coconut palm and the lush jungle-like backdrop represent the primal, Edenic character of the Florida setting. The woman, the car, and the new house are counterpoised with the ruin and the jungle. The automobile has brought this woman to a private place in which she is able to have a private experience — no doubt the contemplation of the beauty of the landscape — a landscape that bespeaks natural simplicity, historic tradition, high fashion, and sound investment potential.

The Whitfield advertisement promoted a certain lifestyle. Architecture helped to delineate this lifestyle. This is exemplary of a fundamental shift in product advertising during the 1920s. The utilitarian, practical aspects of a product became subordinate to what might be called more emotional, romantic attractions. A typical automobile advertisement, for instance, might depict a glamorous setting, like a country club, and the message was that the product (in this case a car) gave access to an exclusive world. Sarasota real estate advertisements, such as the one for Whitfield, promoted the idea that if one bought a lot here one became part of a hedonistic society.

A 1925 advertisement for the Gulf-Bay Estates subdivision communicated the same messages. Owned and developed by two Chicago Pierce-Arrow dealers and marketed by former Chicagoan C. Roy Kindt, this proposed 480-lot subdivision was being laid out on Siesta Key, adjacent to Sarasota. The advertisement copy outlines only the practical aspects of buying a lot in Gulf-Bay Estates and mentions nothing about houses or architectural style. The illustrations, however, depict Mediterranean houses in picturesque landscapes. The developers were marketing lots only. The illustrations suggest the kind of dream house that could be built on one of the subdivision's fifty-foot-wide lots.

The small illustrations from the Gulf-Bay Estates advertisement are loaded with information about style and social status. In one of the illustrations a fashionably dressed man and woman are strolling on a path in front of a charming bungalow, which is situated on a bluff overlooking the sea (fig. 19). A sailboat floats on the calm water, and a gathering of puffy white cumulus clouds serves as a backdrop for the house's observation tower. Two tall coconut palms tower over the residence, and a cluster of low tropical plants frames the scene in the foreground. The house is small. It is one story tall, and appears to contain only about one thousand square feet of living space, but its setting is that of a grand estate. A few select details from traditional Spanish buildings give the house an exotic charm: an arched opening, barrel tiles, stuccoed walls. There is no record of any houses being constructed in Gulf-Bay Estates. Only 196 lots were ever platted in this development. The owners of the property vacated the plat in 1936.

Like the Whitfield advertisement, the Gulf-Bay Estates advertisement uses graphic cues to symbolize everything the developers promised. In these cues the artist created valuable propaganda — more enticing than all of the facts about the soundness of investing in Gulf-Bay Estates. Such inventions were drawn and presented in printed form. Sometimes they actually were built. In these environments, buildings, gardens, and vistas defined places that appeared to be glamorous, historic, and stable. Here one's new 1920s prosperity was given an old, dignified appearance. Modest homebuyers from the growing middle-class market could envision themselves as persons of established means in one of Sarasota's many new subdivisions.

"Move in Tomorrow!" is the heading of a 1926 advertisement for the Homecroft subdivision. The illustration of a Mediterranean house in this advertisement is identical to the one used in the Gulf-Bay Estates advertisement six weeks earlier. The advertisement implies that in Homecroft bits of theatrical fantasy could be purchased as easily as movie tickets. But, like the illusion of many a movie romance, the reality of Homecroft fell far short of the advertisement's promises. Unlike Gulf-Bay Estates, which was on the waterfront, the site of Homecroft was totally landlocked. Since the subdivision was more than two miles from Sarasota Bay, a water view could not have been part of its real landscape. Contrary to the illustration, no house in Homecroft had an observation tower.

The plat map of Homecroft shows a grid of mostly fifty-foot-wide rectangular lots lined up along straight streets on a perfectly flat site, nothing like the picturesque composition depicted in the advertisement. As was the case with many of Sarasota's boom-time subdivisions, advertisement illustrations were the only manifestations of a proposed romantic Mediterranean landscape. In reality, several portable wood-frame bungalows were built on a few of Homecroft's 360 narrow lots.

The illustration in a 1926 advertisement for The Garden of Allah subdivision reveals a small fragment of the vision of Sarasota as the City Beautiful (fig. 20). The advertisement invites the reader to "Study the drawing — you can have a Home on Mecca Boulevard." The drawing depicts the one-hundred-foot-wide boulevard that is lined with coconut palms and picturesque houses. Each house is set in its own "Garden of Allah." Curbing, sidewalks, street lights, water fountains, and a rotary circle with a sunken garden complete the picture of a modest, subtropical version of the kind of neighborhood that might have been illustrated in Burnham and Bennet's *1909 Plan for Chicago*. In the center of the drawing a perfectly straight avenue disappears in perspective into the distant horizon, across an imaginary landscape that contains countless other proposed "Gardens of Allah," which comprised the City Beautiful in paradise.

Fig. 19. Artist unknown, Gulf-Bay Estates advertisement, detail. From *Sarasota Herald*, 27 December 1925. Sarasota County Archives.

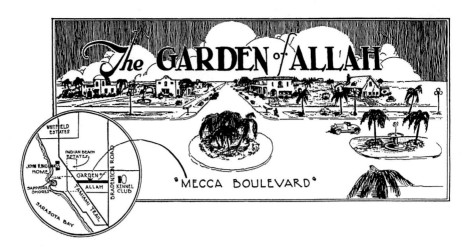

As of the date of this advertisement, these ambitious plans had not yet been completed in the Garden of Allah. However, a previous advertisement had promised: "Every improvement is unconditionally guaranteed and investors and homeseekers who buy in the Garden of Allah are assured of the completion of all of these improvements."[36]

The four houses shown in the Garden of Allah advertisement represent four different architectural styles, evidence of the inclusiveness of the Mediterranean theme in boom-time Florida. The house on the far left is an amalgamation of a fortress and a domed tholos, next-door is a copy of a Spanish mission with a porte-cochere, across the avenue is a palazzo with a porch, and next to that is a quaint English cottage. The only signs of human activity are a convertible heading west on Mecca Boulevard and what appears to be an Arab studying a street sign. A mountain of cirrus clouds serves as a background, giving the entire subdivision a heavenly aura.

On 4 February 1926 the owners and developers of the Garden of Allah advertised a sales event in which the fifty lots that comprised the subdivision would be sold on a "cost-plus basis." The *Sarasota Herald* reported that a "great number of people" attended this event, which included a picnic and band concert, and a Ford car and other prizes were given away.[37] Subdivision sales events like this were popular across Florida during the mid-1920s, as a photograph of one in Hillsborough County illustrates (fig. 21). The 1925 Broadway musical *The Coconuts* contained a scene of such a Florida real estate event in which Groucho Marx played an auctioneer. Though many of the lots in the Garden of Allah were sold and resold, there is no evidence that any construction took place there in the 1920s.

Each of these typical Sarasota boom-time real estate advertisements reinforced and nurtured the idea of Sarasota as a Mediterranean city or — more accurately — as a collection of Mediterranean neighborhoods that were part of a City Beautiful. No ordinance mandated a specific architectural style for new construction, but there was tremendous consistency in the Mediterranean look of almost all of the buildings proposed or built in Sarasota at this time. The vision of a stable, progressive city that offered an old-fashioned but glamorous lifestyle was easily communicated with Mediterranean buildings either drawn or built.

36. Garden of Allah advertisement, *Sarasota Herald*, 15 January 1926, sec. 1, 12.

37. "Marked Demand for Allah Lots," *Sarasota Herald*, 6 February 1926, sec. 1, 7.

Fig. 21. Crowd of prospective buyers at real estate subdivision promotion for Golden Hills, rural development in citrus groves northeast of Tampa, Hillsborough County, Florida, 21 x 26 cm, 1 March 1925. Photograph by Burgert Brothers. Courtesy of Tampa-Hillsborough County Public Library System.

Much more was planned than was actually built in Sarasota. One must study the newspaper advertisements and other extant documents of boom-time Sarasota to understand the full scope of the collective vision for what was promoted as the "fastest growing city in America if not in the civilized world."[38]

When the collapse came, an elaborate multimedia work-in-progress was frozen in time. The fragmented landscapes and the drawings of unbuilt projects that are the legacy of the era reveal more about Sarasota's transformation process than would a completed city. They are reminders that Mediterranean Sarasota existed first and foremost in the imagination. The visions of the city's designers and eager developers were amazingly vast and complete, promising more than just architecture. Land was going to be reshaped. Dreams were going to come true. This was the American Dream set to the speed and jazz rhythm of the new modern age.

Most importantly, the vision of Mediterranean Sarasota was driven by the imaginations of the newly mobile, suddenly credit-empowered middle class. The new Sarasota was possible because of the unprecedented influence of the media in the 1920s — media that planted ideas and expectations in the minds of both the naive and the sophisticated consumer. Throughout the United States the fantastic was made to seem easily accessible in elaborately illustrated print advertising in the home and in lush movie melodramas in the neighborhood theatre. A new lifestyle might be purchased. Florida advertisements suggested that one might easily live a fantasy, become a member of a community where tea dances and romantic trysts took place in the shadows of Spanish arches.

For several decades after the collapse, curiosity-seekers crossed Sarasota Bay on a wobbly wooden causeway to see the haunted barrier islands that John Ringling had once tried to transform into an American Riviera. Lined only with deteriorating sculpture, and overgrown with native vegetation, the empty boulevards of Ringling's subdivision on St. Armands Key met at a mysteriously quiet rotary circle. Nearby, at the southern tip of Longboat Key, the shell of Ringling's

38. "Sarasota Awakening," 10.

Fig. 22. Warren and Wetmore, view of the Ritz Carlton Hotel in a state of ruin (never completed), Longboat Key, 1950. Sarasota County Archives.

Ritz Carlton Hotel stood raw and unfinished (fig. 22). The animated waves on the sugary white sand contrasted with this lonely ruin. Both the empty St. Armands Circle and the Ritz Carlton Hotel were monuments to Sarasota's boom period, pieces of a grand vision. The careful observer sees the individual buildings, landscape features, and drawings of Mediterranean Sarasota as components of a logical diagram of a magical paradise of the imagination.

Very few of the blueprints for Sarasota's unbuilt boom projects survive. Indeed, the best extant documentation of Mediterranean Sarasota is the city's extensive promotional material from the period. The new city needed to be built and sold quickly, so ephemera such as newspaper advertisements become serious artifacts of an aspiring culture.

But Mediterranean Sarasota was not just a city on paper. The Mediterranean vision was realized in several key public buildings. The Atlantic Coast Line Passenger Station, the Sarasota County Courthouse, and the Hotel El Vernona were three landmarks that were particularly effective in establishing the new look of Sarasota. They were important reference points for a city that was struggling to create a new identity for itself.

Of these three landmarks, perhaps the Hotel El Vernona served the needs of the aspiring new citizen most completely (fig. 23). Like the train station and the courthouse, thousands of visitors and speculators passed through this building in a ritual that included arriving, touring the city, and purchasing property. With its integration of public and private spaces and its complete commitment to the Mediterranean theme, it embodied and prefigured the new dream city that was being built around it.

To the arriving winter guest from the North, the new Hotel El Vernona appeared to be an accretion of additions completed over many generations. Part hacienda, part mission, and part palace, it truly resembled a set from a Hollywood movie. With its interior and exterior walls painted and glazed to give them aged patinas, the hotel looked like a ruin that had been discovered by a magician and turned into a glamorous fortress.

Upon entering the hotel, one stepped from the "hustle and bustle of the twentieth century into the soothing quiet of Andalusia's yesteryear."[39] The lobby

39. *El Vernona, Aristocrat of Beauty*.

Fig. 23. Earl Purdy, detail from brochure *El Vernona, Aristocrat of Beauty*, Florida Grower Press, c. 1925. Lillian Burns collection.

floors and walls were covered with glazed tiles brought from Central America and Spain. Antique bronze and iron lanterns hung from the ceilings. Tea would have been served on the hotel's third-floor patio on tables shaded by multicolored parasols.

The elevation of the patio afforded a fine bird's eye view of Sarasota's skyline. For the guest standing in the arched opening of the loggia that enframed the view, the sunshine and warm breezes, and the trickling Spanish fountain nearby reinforced a sensation of being in a paradise far away from the cold gray North. In the mind's eye the landscape of wood-frame bungalows and empty lots below became — as all the promotional material had promised — a pastel Mediterranean resort where one would find true happiness and prosperity. □

FLORIDA

"Land of Sunshine and Happiness"

Fig. 1. Florida's natural allure, personified as a vision bearing palm and oranges, conveys the message of plenty on an early promotional brochure, cover, c. 1920. Florida Collection, Miami-Dade Public Library.

Perfume, Postcards, and Promises: The Orange in Art and Industry

By Helen L. Kohen

"Oh love, what hours were thine and mine…in lands of palm, of orange-blossom…and vine."

– Alfred Lord Tennyson (1809–1892)

Helen L. Kohen is an art historian and former art critic for the *Miami Herald*. She has written and lectured extensively on art and architecture.

Of all blooms celebrated in Florida, the state named for flowers, none has done more to define it (fig. 1), build it (fig. 2), and sell it than the orange blossom. As prelude to the golden fruit, the glorious white petals deliver what they promise: beauty, aroma, and a cash crop that almost never crashes. The orange is Florida, and it made Florida, providing an authentic Fountain of Youth with its vitamin highs, supplying the legendary gold that the state's explorers and settlers lusted after. Florida's history consistently adds gloss to ancient legends of renewal. The earliest most tempting portraits of the state featured oranges in all their pure round perfection and abundance (fig. 3). The first advertised land sales were for orange groves, and the first sales pitches for those Edenic gardens employed a quasi-religious vocabulary consistent with the offering of paradise.

None of this changed much over the near-century it took Florida to evolve from a wilderness territory into a popular destination for work and play. The gated golf (tennis, equestrian) communities that have become the latest lifestyle panacea in Florida are the natural progeny of nineteenth-century orange-grove communities — minus the groves and their once-commercial aspect (fig. 4). When the initial group of Florida entrepreneurs went to work seducing folk from elsewhere to buy into a way of life totally different from the one they knew, the promoters tapped into a preexisting body of orange-related sentiments, concepts knowingly borrowed or subliminally gleaned from religion, art, fact, and language. Very old patterns of thought about oranges continue to reverberate.

Consider the familiar-sounding sell message only slightly submerged in the lilting cadences of a typical how-to book on orange culture published in 1886 by the Reverend Theophilus Wilson Moore. A grower himself, Moore was not above offering lots on his own development at Fruit Grove, Florida. He warms to his subject by warning of the overwhelming love lying in wait for the "aesthetic cultivator," who is sure to look upon an orange grove "as a relic and reminder of paradise." And paradise is only part of it. For, he continues, "this beauty is accompanied with useful, golden, and gold-bearing fruit, affording a living, and promising all other material luxuries."[1] That takes about a decade, Moore admits, years spent in hard work. The get-rich-soon-if-not-quick message poured out of other slim volumes like Moore's. From the biblically oriented boosterism of Helen Harcourt came this heaven-sent narrative: "There are

Fig. 2. Sheet music cover for *Down Where The Orange Blossoms Grow*, words and music by J. Fred De Berry, © 1904. Florida Collection, Miami-Dade Public Library.

---

1. Theophilus Wilson Moore, *Treatise and Hand-Book of Orange Culture in Florida, Louisiana and California* (New York: E. R. Pelton and Co., and Jacksonville: Horace Drew, 1886), viii.

thousands of young men in the inclement North toiling wearily along through the years in the hope of ultimately winning a home for some dear one....Let these, and such as these, turn their faces southward, and in less than 'seven years,' amid the Florida fruits, they will have won independence and their Rachel."[2]

Work and be rewarded, Harcourt stresses, and don't worry much about com-petition. There is no such thing as too many growers, too many groves, or too

2. Helen Harcourt, *Florida Fruits and How to Raise Them* (Louisville: John P. Morton and Company, 1886), 26.

many oranges. While the Englishman Iza Duffus Hardy might disagree (his book begins with the words, "Florida is the best lied-about State in the Union"),[3] he nonetheless makes promises of his own, using the same persuasive syntax as his peers in the United States. "There is room here — room for the willing hand to work, room for the strong heart to hope, room for wealth to find a new and promising field and room for youth and vigour and energy to spend themselves in building up homes…amongst the golden orange-groves."[4]

Thus, amid the hyperbole, Florida's future was not overlooked. Most come-on-down books paired the grove with the homestead, the workplace with a settled way of life. There is even the suggestion in one of the most practical of the late-nineteenth-century guides to Florida that oranges do better on domestic lots. "The orange…is sociable," writes George M. Barbour in *Florida for Tourists, Invalids, and Settlers*. "[It] appears to like human companion-ship; it is a noticeable fact that those trees that are nearest inhabited dwellings are usually the largest and most prolific."[5]

Fig. 5. Early botanical rendering of an orange branch, from Mattioli's *Commentaires*, Lyons, France, 1579. From Ernst and Johanna Lehner, *Folklore and Symbolism of Flowers, Plants and Trees* (New York: Tudor Publishing Company, n.d.), 75.

The grove as the enchanted garden has been lauded nowhere more convinc-ingly than in the compelling prose of Marjorie Kinnan Rawlings, who lived, wrote, and grew oranges at Cross Creek, Florida from 1928 to the start of World War II. The place provided a series of struggles with killer snakes, isola-tion, hard freezes, and soft minds. Even so, she makes her Florida as irresistible as a moonlit dance. For her, the act of stepping into the shade of her orange grove was bewitching: "to walk under the arched canopy of their jadelike leaves; to see the long aisles of lichened trunks stretch ahead in a geometric rhythm; to feel the mystery of a seclusion that yet has shafts of light striking through it. This is the essence of an ancient and secret magic. It goes back, perhaps…to an atavistic sense of safety and delight in an open forest."[6]

The creation of a mystique of that sort was possible because oranges and groves come into the human mind already wrapped in romance. The orange is a celestial fruit, associated with hospitality, benevolence, and wisdom (fig. 5). Its gem equivalent, the near-orange-colored jacinth, is believed to indicate modesty and to cure heart ailments. The very words "orange" and "grove" yield symbolic antecedents. The orange and its blossoms are especially blessed. In the East oranges are a popular gift at festivals, expressing wishes for good fortune.[7] In the West the white orange blossom is a symbol of purity, associated with the virginity of the Madonna, which is the reason the flowers are tradi-tionally carried by brides. It also explains the superstition in Germany that an impure woman could kill an orange tree.[8]

3. Iza Duffus Hardy, *Oranges and Alligators: Sketches of South Florida Life* (London: Ward and Downey, 1887), 1.

4. Ibid., 18 ff.

5. George M. Barbour, *Florida for Tourists, Invalids, and Settlers* (New York: D. Appleton and Company, 1882), 241.

6. Marjorie Kinnan Rawlings, *Cross Creek* (New York: Touchstone Books, published by Simon and Schuster, 1996), 16.

7. Henry Dreyfuss, *Symbol Sourcebook: An Authoritative Guide to International Graphic Symbols* (New York: McGraw-Hill, 1972), 234.

8. This bit of orange lore as well as a mass of information about the fruit comes from the single most significant modern work on the subject, by John McPhee. His serious and delightful *Oranges* (New York: Farrar, Straus and Giroux, 1967) has been indispensable to the research and writing of this article.

L-17—Florida Southern College, Administration Bldg. Lakeland, Fla.

The Oxford English Dictionary defines the grove as an area planted in honor of a deity to serve as a place of worship. So the sacred nature of groves is a given, spilling over to the products of specific enclaves: the holy wisdom imparted in the Groves of Academe; the paradisiacal qualities of groves (versus plantations or farms in general). Perhaps that is what drew Frank Lloyd Wright (1867–1956) into the unlikely scheme of designing a "great education temple" in a Florida orange grove on the sandy Lakeland acreage of Florida Southern College (fig. 6). Summoned to the task by a telegram sent in 1938 by the institution's nervy president, Ludd Myrl Spivey, Wright intended that his ensemble of buildings, his "child of the sun, the first truly American campus," sit naturally and comfortably in the orange grove, that the trees be kept up to envelop the buildings, absorb and deflect the heat, give shade, and lend their aroma to the atmosphere. He even specified the use of an organic burnt-orange color trim in his plans. Though only seven of the eighteen buildings in his scheme were completed, and though the campus and buildings have been alarmingly altered, Florida can still boast the largest collection of Wright structures on one site: seven would-be temples in a once-sacred grove.[9]

Some of the exoticism associated with the orange has its source in the virtual mystery surrounding the fruit's origins. Professional citrus explorers have yet to pin down the precise spot on the globe where the first tree bore what is thought to be the earliest sort of citrus fruit, the ancient and highly sour citron. It is generally agreed that the orange plant or its seeds made many voyages en route to Europe, and that its ancestor, the citron, was carted along with human migrations, wars, and trade from somewhere in India to Mesopotamia and Persia.[10] It reached Palestine during the Roman period and was later cultivated in the Mediterranean basin. When the Roman trade routes

9. There is a good deal of material on Frank Lloyd Wright's Florida Southern College. The volumes consulted here include Hap Hatton, *Tropical Splendor: An Architectural History of Florida* (New York: Alfred A. Knopf, 1987); and Brendan Gill, *Many Masks: A Life of Frank Lloyd Wright* (New York: Ballantine Books, 1988).

10. There is mention of the citron as a medicine on the clay tablets found at Nineveh, according to William C. Cooper, *In Search of the Golden Apple: An Adventure in Citrus Science and Travel* (New York: Vantage Press, 1982), 107.

were taken over by the Arabs, citrus culture spread with their civilization. China had the finest oranges, which is probably why the modern botanical name for the sweet orange is *citrus sinensis*. Etymology helps trace the path of the English word "orange." It is derived from the Sanskrit *nararunga*, which became *naranj* in Persian, which translated to *aurantium* in Latin, which is the *naranja* of Spain. It was via Spain — by Columbus, in fact, on his second voyage — that oranges were introduced to the Americas. By 1579, the Spanish admiral Pedro Menéndez de Avilés sent home reports that orange trees in St. Augustine were bearing fruit.

Oranges were always considered luxury goods. Confucius writes circa 500 B.C. that oranges were sent as tribute. Europeans coveted them even before they cultivated a type that was edible. In 1529 the Archbishop of Milan is reported to have given a sixteen-course dinner party with a menu that showcased his enormous wealth. Among the rich dishes were "caviar and oranges fried with sugar and cinnamon, brill and sardines with slices of orange and lemon, one thousand oysters with pepper and oranges...fried sparrows with oranges... orange fritters."[11] It is notable that oranges were purely ornamental on that table, used for looks and aroma, for seasoning, and as status symbols.

This ability to confer status led to the development of a distinctive and telling architectural form, the orangery. Designed to house orange trees in climes where they could not be cultivated outdoors, the orangery was the structural sign and symbol of enormous wealth and power. It was Charles VIII of France who was the trendsetter; his attempt to conquer Italy was diverted by his falling in love with Italian art and horticulture. Along with heady concepts, the would-be tyrant brought home the basic necessities for growing oranges: the citrus fruits, the gardeners familiar with their care, and the architects capable of designing houses in which the plants would flourish. When his orange trees arrived from Italy, they were treated as treasures by the royal gardeners, who reportedly bathed their roots in milk and honey — a holy watering.

Orangeries, those emblems of dominion in which Nature was both tamed and beautified, added luster to the fruit tended within them. Great architects designed them for European palaces: Louis Le Vau at Versailles in 1663; Jules Hardouin Mansart at Versailles in 1684; Christopher Wren at Hampton Court in 1689; Nicholas Hawksmoor at Kensington Palace in 1704 (Wren and John Vanbrugh were consultants on that one); Matthaus Daniel Poppelmann at the Zwinger at Dresden in 1709. America's own George Washington built one at Mt. Vernon in 1784–1787, based on the design of the one at Wye House, in Talbot County, Maryland, built in 1781–1784. By then the orangery had fully evolved into a kind of playhouse, a place for promenading and entertaining, a pleasure pavilion in which all sorts of tender plants were housed in winter. The Wye House orangery had a billiard room on the upper floor. Though orangeries lost their regal associations and thus their prime place as status symbols with time, oranges remain an exotic crop in the human consciousness.

The fruit has been represented as mysterious and slightly unearthly, thanks to a host of painters from the late Gothic period through the Renaissance and beyond, artists whose works have been popularized through illustrations in texts, in coffee-table books, and on greeting cards. In the center predella painting of Gentile Da Fabriano's *Adoration of the Magi* (1423) there's a depiction of the Holy Family's "Flight into Egypt" along a road in what is obviously a

---

11. McPhee, *Oranges*, 64.

Fig. 7. Sandro Botticelli,

Primavera, panel, 6′8″ x 10′4″,

1482. Uffizi Gallery, Florence.

Fig. 8. John James Audubon's

Ground Doves (Plate CLXXXII),

depicted on the branches of a

wild orange tree, 1831.

Historical Museum of Southern

Florida.

Florentine landscape. Their way is miraculously flanked by orange trees. Or visualize the more famous *Primavera* by Sandro Botticelli (1482), where Venus is shown in an enchanted garden under a bower of oranges (fig. 7). (Flora is there too, forging Florida's connection with paradise.) There is also Andrea Mantegna's *Enthroned Madonna and Child with Saints* (1456–1459) (a.k.a. *S. Zeno* altarpiece), with its cornucopias of oranges and citrons spilling in profusion over the scene, and Paolo Uccelo's *Battle of San Romano* (1445), where the foreground image is separated from the background by a screen of fantastic orange trees.

Most of the fifteenth-century artists cited for painting oranges where none were expected worked for the Medici family. Western museums offer enough examples of the images of oranges in sacred pictures to make one believe that oranges were truly cultivated in the Arno valley, whether they allude to the myth of Heracles, one of whose labors was to gather the "Golden Apples" of cloud-less Hesperides even as he continued to hold up the world (thus conflating the Medici family name with Olympian strength and prowess), or whether the Medicis dictated that oranges were the fruits of choice (in the neo-Latin of the Renaissance, oranges were sometimes called *medici*). It is clear that the trees, groves, and fruit garlands rendered heavy with oranges have allegorical meaning in this body of work, that, as the Renaissance scholar Frederick Hartt so poeti-cally put it, "Before the dark green leaves and giant golden fruit of the grove that shuts out the world…the circumstances of real existence no longer apply."[12]

The wonder of Florida was that it proposed a real existence for real people, built on "the profits and delights of orange culture" that collective memory as well as then-current books and pamphlets touted. All kinds of people came. John James Audubon (1785–1851) arrived in St. Augustine in 1831 to hunt birds in the northeast corridor of Florida, and, on a later voyage, in the Keys. His *Palm Warbler* and *Ground Doves* are both depicted on orange tree branches (fig. 8). There were thousands of trees to be seen in St. Augustine itself,

12. Frederick Hartt, *History of Italian Renaissance Art, Painting, Sculpture, Architecture* (New York: Harry N. Abrams, Inc., 1979), 334.

Fig. 9. Poster advertising the Savanna Line, taking passengers to Florida and the South, c. 1900. The Mitchell Wolfson Jr. Collection, The Wolfsonian, Florida International University, Miami Beach, Florida.

according to Audubon, each loaded with oranges for sale at two cents apiece. It is a wonder that Jesse Fish, purported to be Florida's first orange baron, could make his millions at that rate. He grew sweet oranges off the coast of St. Augustine, where he settled to escape a bad marriage. The writer and abolitionist Harriet Beecher Stowe (1811–1896) came in 1868 and ran a successful grove in Mandarin for seventeen years. Composer Frederick Theodor Albert Delius came in 1884, ostensibly to manage an orange grove at Solana Grove, but actually to study music with a Jacksonville organist. His was a brief stay, but both his *Florida Suite* (1886–1887) and his *Appalachia* (begun in 1896) came of his Florida experience. Aside from attracting these "middle-aged pioneers,"[13] by the end of the 1880s the tourists were coming, travelling in stern-wheelers on the St. Johns (fig. 9), moving west to Pinellas Point on the Gulf via Peter Demen's Orange Belt Railway, and, after 1893, going south on Henry Morrison Flagler's (1830–1913) Florida East Coast Railway. It looked as if everything the promoters said about Florida was true.

13. "Florida was the only wilderness in the world that attracted middle-aged pioneers." McPhee, *Oranges*, 91.

G37 AN ORANGE GROVE IN SUNNY FLORIDA.

Fig. 11. View of a commercial grove. From a postcard, c. 1942. Historical Museum of Southern Florida.

Fig. 10. Map showing commercial citrus plantings in Florida in 1941. From *Citrus Industry of Florida* (Tallahassee: Department of Agriculture in cooperation with University of Florida, 1944), 10.

Then came the killing frosts of 1894–1895, which devastated the citrus industry in Florida. The first phase of post-Civil War orange fever was over, stopped cold. The Orange Belt Railway went bust, though the bathing pavilion built on its terminal pier in the newly founded St. Petersburg continued to be a star tourist attraction for years. More to the point were the great changes faced by the orange growers, the epic shifts ahead. Citrus production before the disaster had reached five million boxes a year, an amount not reached again until 1910. The positive result of the damage was that the brave deserted their ruined trees and moved south to the sandy ridge areas of Central Florida, where the commercial citrus industry we know today began (fig. 10). But this time it was actual industry. Real science entered the game, as did corporate labor, official legislation, hardball competition, and even true cooperation: the growers formed cooperatives at the end of the 1920s for marketing purposes and to protect themselves against unscrupulous dealers.

The big business of orange production and distribution accelerated the economic life of the state without much marring its beauty. Bigger groves, more carefully planned and planted, resulted in gorgeous and colorful geometric landscapes (fig. 11). In addition, the packing houses in which the fruits were cosmetically altered and made ready for shipment — in Mr. E. Bean's labeled wooden crates, invented in 1875 and still the gift box of choice — did little to insert themselves into the visual environment (fig. 12). Built in the byways, near railroads, highways, or waterways, the processing plants were based on the Roman basilica, the earliest structures developed for maximum interior space (fig. 13). A religious form derived from Roman law courts, the basilica found new application in factory and other secular use.

The maturation of the orange industry was accompanied, naturally, by a new measure of the already expertly evolved hard sell, luring tourists — orange juice drinkers all — and developers to the Sunshine State. Despite that sunny tribute, the orange is really Florida's top-ranking icon, with a preeminence altered to suit. Postcards dating from the turn-of-the-nineteenth century often featured families in their groves, all ages working together to gather the crop. Sometimes several generations were shown in a lean-to, a domestic kind of packing shed, preparing the choicest fruits for on-site sale or shipment. The

Fig. 12. The Adams Packing Company, Auburndale, Florida. From a postcard. Florida State Archives.

Fig. 14. Roadside citrus ship-

pers, Miami, Florida, 1922.

Florida State Archives.

quality of the picture, or the beauty of the setting were not factors, for the folks were plain, the groves set out in seemingly random patterns, the business strictly a Mom-and-Pop enterprise (fig. 14). The story told on the postcard had to do with oranges and homesteading. All that changed when orange growing itself changed, when the industry took off, defeating even so tough a pioneer woman as Majorie Kinnan Rawlings. In the end her writing proved much more lucrative than her top-notch grove. For the new Florida, the orange moved from the personal to the public, from a way of life to a state symbol.

To this day, you can buy a postcard featuring a couple of oranges and the word FLORIDA. It says it all, passing on the magic, passing on the place. The San Francisco-based Gump's (purveyor of "The Rare, The Unique, The Imaginative since 1861," according to a current catalogue) offers a solid gold charm bracelet with a choice of travel charms. Florida's is an orange crate, as certain an emblem as Seattle's Space Needle or Philadelphia's Liberty Bell. The magical ability of the orange to invoke dreams is paid homage, whether the fruit is being manipulated by account executives or citrus professionals (fig. 15). Even the state officialdom is not above inserting some of that old-time religion into otherwise dry, informative publications about oranges. From a 1944 Department of Agriculture book comes this amazing sentence: "Perhaps as big a factor [in the development of the Florida citrus industry] is the fact that [the orange] has been featured in the thinking of people for many generations as a romantic fruit coming from distant lands with a little more glamour than the ordinary fruits of temperate climes."[14] That might account for the fact that the jeweler Peter Carl Fabergé chose an orange tree in full bloom as a model for the most beguiling of the famous Imperial Easter Eggs designed for the family of the last Czar of Russia, Nicholas II (fig. 16). It was the only tree in Fabergé's bejeweled repertory of fifty-three Easter fantasies, and among the most spectacular.

Images of oranges in all their inflated glory have carried the message of the promised land on all sorts of print material, including postcards, orange crate

14. *Citrus Industry of Florida* (Tallahassee: Department of Agriculture in Cooperation with University of Florida, 1944), Part 1, "Citrus Growing in Florida" by A. F. Camp, Vice-Director in Charge, Citrus Experiment Station, 6.

Fig. 16. Peter Carl Fabergé, *Orange Tree Egg*, 1911. Gold, enamels, precious stones, hardstones, pearls; height 10 ½″ closed, 11 ¾″ open. The FORBES Magazine Collection, New York.

labels (fig. 17), promotional brochures and other forms of publicity, sheet music, and the cover of at least one theatrical journal. Sometimes nothing more is required than the word "orange" itself. It has worked in the creation of one of the most prestigious private clubs in the social world, in the success of a now legendary crack train, and it made an annual football festival famous.

The Orange Court at the Everglades Club on Lake Worth in Palm Beach, based on one by the same name at the Mosque in Seville, was the creation of no less a dream merchant than Florida's most significant "social" architect, Addison Mizner (1872–1933). The Court and its arched surround and tower figured in his earliest sketches for the club, when the structure was envisioned as a wartime hospital and convalescent center for World War I officers. Writing to his partner in the enterprise, the equally colorful Paris Singer, Mizner saw the creation as, "something religious…a chapel built into the lake, with a great cool cloisters and a court of oranges." And he meant the real thing, orange trees actually growing in a mini-grove, a caprice set down amid a complex of fictions where a person might take in a bit of spiritual refreshment with a breath of fresh air. As the story goes, the opening night of the Everglades Club coincided with a freeze, and all the trees went bare of fruit. Not to worry — oranges from the kitchens were wired in place, and the magic show went on as planned.[15]

If Mizner's outwitting of nature is the stuff of myth, the story about the Seaboard Air Line Railway luring fares away from the railroad of the pioneering Flagler is fact. It was done, initially, with little more than an auspicious name change, some staged fanfare, and a giant-size bottle of (what had to be) common orange blossom perfume. The train so cheaply if aptly christened — the Orange Blossom Special — was the brainchild of S. Davies Warfield, president of the Seaboard line. Running from the Northeast to both coasts of Florida, the special sections of the luxury carrier did much to attract wealthy visitors and investors to the

15. Christina Orr, *Addison Mizner: Architect of Dreams and Realities 1872–1933* (Palm Beach, Fla.: catalogue of an exhibition organized by the Norton Gallery of Art, 5 March–17 April 1977), 18. Additional information about the Orange Court comes from a conversation with Christina Orr Cahall, current director of the Norton Museum of Art, held 19 March 1997.

Fig. 17. Orange crate label,
Saint John's River Fruit,

1935. Historical Museum

of Southern Florida.

▼

Fig. 18. The Orange Blossom

Special travelling through tropi-

cal Florida. From a postcard,

Curteich-Chicago, 1939. Myrna

and Seth Bramson Collection,

Miami, Florida.

TROPIC
GOLD
BRAND

SAINT JOHN'S
RIVER FRUIT

Mc BRIDE PACKING COMPANY
SEVILLE ▼▼▼ FLORIDA

By "Streamliner" Thru Tropical Florida

9A-H1340

Fig. 19. Cover of a luncheon menu from the Orange Blossom Special, 1948. From Theodore Shrady, *Orange Blossom Special: The Story of Florida's Distinguished Winter Train* (Valrico, Fla.: Atlantic Coast Line and Seaboard Air Line Railroads Historical Society, Inc., 1996), inside front cover.

ORANGE BLOSSOM SPECIAL

state, beginning with its inaugural run in 1925 (fig. 18).[16] The joke is that for more than the first year of its run, the deluxe train that was supposed to insure gilt-edged service for its riders did not exist. The Orange Blossom Special was old equipment with a new name, and lots of hype for what the Pullman Company would be delivering in good time. That included well-appointed passenger accommodations, gourmet food, and such extra amenities as space for business deals (bring your own secretary), the services of an on-board barber, valet, ladies' maid, and manicurist, and baths for men and women (fig. 19). It was red carpet all the way, with views of Florida's bustling orange groves for scenery as the cars ran through the state's central ridge section.

The most famous of Florida's orange-named extravaganzas is Miami's Orange Bowl, the football game traditionally (but alas, not forever) staged there at New Year's, and the parade that ushers in the occasion. Here is perhaps the best example of the orange word sufficing to carry the spirit and substance of a previously failed circumstance.[17] In the aftermath of the hurricane of 1926,

16. The train did not run during Word War II, and was permanently discontinued in 1953. For the most complete story of the train and its routes, see Theodore Shrady with Arthur M. Waldrop, *Orange Blossom Special: The Story of Florida's Distinguished Winter Train* (Valrico, Fla.: Atlantic Coast Line and Seaboard Air Line Railroads Historical Society, Inc., 1996).

17. The source for Orange Bowl material is Loran Smith, *Fifty Years on the Fifty: The Orange Bowl Story* (Charlotte, N.C.: Fast and McMillan Publishers, Inc. in association with the Orange Bowl Committee, 1983).

Fig. 20. Claes Oldenburg and Coosje van Bruggen, *Dropped Bowl with Scattered Slices and Peels*, fountain, installed in Open Space Park, Miami, 1990. Metro-Dade Art in Public Places collection.

Fig. 21. Silver spoon, souvenir of Winter Park, c. 1920. From Becky Karst, David Stark, and Jacob Stuart, *More Than a Memory* (Orlando, Fla.: Robinsons, Inc., in association with the Orange County Bicentennial Committee, 1975), 200.

when people were desperate for ways to bring back the tourist season, the social director of Coral Gables' Biltmore Hotel came up with the idea of a post-season football game, complete with attendant events. That first end-of-year sports-centered celebration was called "The Fiesta of the American Tropics" and there was never another. Then, in 1929, a civic group coming together to revitalize the University of Miami and its football program founded the fore-runner of the Orange Bowl Committee, the Greater Miami Athletic Association. Though the clues as to what they should have called themselves were already there — there was a Rose Festival; the University of Miami Hurricanes wore the orange, green, and white of orange groves — the boosters staged a "Palm Festival." There were two of those, in 1932 and 1934, cheered on by the slo-gan, "Have a green Christmas in Miami." Then the Chamber of Commerce stepped in, and the glory for finally getting the name straight goes to its 1934 president, W. Keith Phillips who, with the help of radio personality Dinty Dennis, called the Orange Bowl the Orange Bowl. In December 1936 the offi-cial Orange Bowl Committee was chartered, and at the 1936 game, the first ever King Orange Jamboree Parade honored the citrus industry.

And though it is not part of the orange story, not even part of the time frame set up to tell the orange-in-Florida story, the monumental, ironic send-up of the Orange Bowl dedicated in mid-Miami in 1990 cannot go overlooked. Created by the artist team of Claes Oldenburg and Coosje van Bruggen, the sculpture/fountain *Dropped Bowl with Scattered Slices and Peels*, a Metropolitan Dade County Art in Public Places commission, comments on the randomness of the city's development and on its multicultural, fractious nature. It is all done with a Pop Art spin, including allusions to comics and the low-art craft of kitschy souvenirs, but *Dropped Bowl* is nonetheless wounding, if penetrat-ingly correct. It smashes the icon, fools with the community's affection for its Orange Bowl, and trashes its image as the Big Orange (fig. 20).

Still, no icon in our culture is ever so debased that it cannot be cloned for adaptive reuse — someday. The orange still means something philosophically, but in the face of the total industrialization of the citrus business its entertain-ment value as a symbol has melted into the preserve of nostalgia. Orange

Fig. 22. Juicer, aluminum, c. 1935. The Mitchell Wolfson Jr. Collection, The Wolfsonian, Florida International University, Miami Beach, Florida.

souvenirs are collectibles (fig. 21); orange squeezers have become ubiquitous in the design holdings of museums (fig. 22). As a fresh fruit, the orange is no more revered than the imported apple, and even Florida children no longer know that if the Temples are getting seedy, the season for Valencias is at hand. What was once a bad thing in orange growing — coming up with a thin-skinned fruit — has been a good thing since the perfection of FCOJ, known familiarly since 1948 as frozen concentrated orange juice. That would-be miracle, and today's more common carton-packed "fresh squeezed" juices, depend solely on orange solids. The thick orange zest, so well manipulated into metaphor by copy writers selling the Florida story since the 1880s, has been a detriment to orange production for a full half-century.

All of which leaves only the beginning to contemplate: Genesis, Chapter 3, verses 2–6; The Fall of Man. The name of the forbidden fruit in the Garden of Eden is not specified in the Hebrew texts.[18] However, rabbinical commentaries on the fruit of "the tree of good and evil" speculate that it might be one of several species, including the fig, grape, wheat, carob, or citron. Each of these is grown in the subtropics, the hot places of the Bible, and each is considered a likely plant to have graced paradise. In addition, each of these varieties has been accorded symbolic meanings relating to such concepts as desire and doing the wrong thing. It is with the King James Bible that things get more specific, that the apple is named the culprit, probably because *ra*, the Hebrew word for evil, is *malum* in Latin: the same word as apple. So the orange escaped negative associations from the start. Accentuating its positives made all the difference for Florida. □

18. Conversations the author had with Rabbi Gayle Pomerance of Temple Beth Sholom, Miami Beach, Florida, in March 1997, yielded this interpretation.

Fig. 1. Florida Building, World's Columbian Exposition. From *The Book of the Fair* (Chicago: The Bancroft Co., 1895). The Mitchell Wolfson

From Augustine to Tangerine: Florida at the U.S. World's Fairs

By Joel M. Hoffman

Joel M. Hoffman is associate director of academic programs and administration at The Wolfsonian, Florida International University, Miami Beach, Florida. He holds a Ph.D. from Yale University, where he wrote his doctoral thesis on visual culture in the turn-of-the-century garden community of Bournville, England.

From the middle of the nineteenth century, world's fairs provided exhibitors with an unparalleled opportunity to reach a global audience of prospective consumers. Primary participants included countries, corporations, and cultural organizations, and the fairs based in the United States drew regular contributions from the states. Florida was no exception. Driven by growth, the state's boosters strove to develop tourism, production, and investment. During the past century Florida's involvement in the U.S. world's fairs helped put the state on the map and in the minds of millions of exposition visitors. Perhaps more than any other mode of expression, world's fair exhibits reveal not only how the state was perceived but how it was packaged for consumption. Considering the relationship between explicit and implied constructions of state identity, this essay interprets Florida's world's fair exhibits in the context of broader state history and as they relate to the exposition presentations of other states.

It appears that Florida's pavilion at the World's Columbian Exposition of 1893 was the state's first major contribution to a U.S. world's fair. The 1893 fair was the most elaborate and extensive public exhibition mounted in the United States in the nineteenth century, and was known as the "White City" for its profusion of art and architecture in the Beaux-Arts tradition. Thematically conceived as a celebration of the four-hundredth anniversary of Christopher Columbus' "discovery" of the New World, the fair served as a showcase of American progress and prosperity, although it was held during a worldwide economic depression.[1]

In the state division Florida erected a reproduction of St. Augustine's historic Fort Marion at a cost of $20,000 (fig. 1).[2] There was no state appropriation for Florida's participation in the World's Columbian Exposition, setting a precedent for the state's appearance in subsequent fairs. Instead funds were raised by private enterprise.[3] The ambitious scope of the project, however, reflected strong support from Florida's state board for the fair, whose members included Governor Henry Mitchell (1831–1903, served 1893–1897) and former governors Francis Fleming (1841–1908, served 1889–1893) and William Bloxham (1835–1911, served 1881–1885 and 1897–1901).[4]

1. Reid Badger, *The Great American Fair* (Chicago: Nathan Hall, 1979), xi–xiii.
2. Illinois spent $250,000 on its pavilion, a few other industrialized states dedicated in excess of $50,000, and several spent less than $20,000 on their pavilions. *The Economizer: How and Where to Find the Gems of the Fair* (Chicago: Rand, McNally and Co., 1893), 54–55.
3. Hubert Howe Bancroft, *The Book of the Fair* (Chicago: The Bancroft Company, 1895), 797.
4. John McGovern, *Halligan's Illustrated World: A Portfolio of Photographic Views of the World's Columbian Exposition* (Chicago: Jewell N. Halligan Co., 1894), 97.

Exactly why Florida decided to participate in some fairs and not others remains a topic for speculation. Several of its exposition absences and presences are more logical than others, and it is not at all surprising that Floridians were active in the World's Columbian Exposition. Global depression no doubt left many states scrambling for funds to join the 1893 fair. But in the end, approximately forty states were represented by free-standing pavilions, so participation was the norm rather than the exception. Moreover the 1890s were years of tremendous growth for Florida, making the World's Columbian Exposition an irresistible opportunity for promotion of the state's amenities and resources. Henry B. Plant (1819–1899) and Henry Morrison Flagler (1830–1913) had already initiated their ambitious programs of railroad construction, priming various quarters of Florida for dramatically increased development, industry, and tourism.

The replica of Fort Marion was a star-shaped structure, measuring 137 feet along each side and resting within a cluster of pavilions at the northern end of the state area. One-fifth the size of the actual St. Augustine fortress, the building was surrounded by a "moat" of cacti and palms, and it enclosed a courtyard with more palms, flowers, and other Floridian vegetation. In the place of the dungeons, the ersatz fort contained a series of rooms, accommodating offices and the exhibits. At the entrance, orange, pineapple, lemon, and other plants "expressive of [Florida's] commercial hopes" were arranged in an ornamental pattern, and a fishing exhibition within the building "gave the corridors and courts a strong odor."[5] Also on display were mosses, ferns, shells, fruits, minerals, photographs, infant alligators and chameleons, cotton, sponges, an explication of turpentine processing, and cabinets containing samples of native woods. The effect of curio-shop-meets-natural-history-museum is clearly illustrated in an installation photograph from the fair (fig. 2). Most descriptions of the building emphasize its historical significance, variously

5. Ibid., 213.

Fig. 3. Florida Agricultural Pavilion, World's Columbian Exposition. From *Halligan's Illustrated World: A Portfolio of Photographic Views* (Chicago: Jewell N. Halligan Co., 1894). Otto G. Richter Library, University of Miami, Coral Gables, Florida.

referring to the actual Fort Marion as "the centre of Spanish power on the Atlantic seaboard" or "the oldest building in North America."[6]

In addition to its main exhibition at the World's Columbian Exposition, Florida erected a large display in the Agricultural Building (fig. 3). Accompanied by a promotional exhibit from the Okeechobee Land and Drainage Company, this indoor pavilion was bombastic, as were those of many other states around it, characterized by a flamboyantly French mansard roof and a peripheral arcade with turned-wood columns. At the pavilion's entrance was an archway of russet oranges; nearby a coconut palm rose nearly to the ceiling; and belying the Continental aesthetic of the exterior, the walls were lined with gigantic palm fronds and rows of coconuts and pineapple plants. Within were photographs, subtropical plants, and a wide array of Floridian agricultural goods, including rice and cassava products, sugar, palmetto tapestry and fiber, tobacco, and sisal plants. Florida established the advantages of its Southern climate having "sent the first peaches to the Exposition, with a small collection of early tomatoes, cucumbers, and other fruits and vegetables out of season in the north and west."[7] While demonstrating the diversity of Florida's farm industries, the French-inspired Agricultural Pavilion also provided a semantic complement to the Fort Marion Pavilion, implying that Florida's cultural heritage extended beyond its Spanish roots.

The reproduction of Fort Marion established a precedent for Florida's participation in other fairs. Time and again, Florida's promoters developed exhibits that were in one way or another unusual, if not bizarre, when compared with those of other states. As a view of the Chicago fairgrounds reveals, the majority

6. Descriptions from Ibid.; Bancroft, *The Book of the Fair*, 797–798; and *The Dream City: A Portfolio of Photographic Views of the World's Columbian Exposition* (St. Louis: N. D. Thompson, 1893), no. 17.

7. McGovern, *Halligan's Illustrated World*, 97; and Bancroft, *The Book of the Fair*, 442–443.

Fig. 4. General view of

state buildings, World's

Columbian Exposition.

From W. Walton, *Art and*

Architecture (Philadelphia:

George Barrie, 1893). Avery

Architectural and Fine Arts

Library, Columbia University.

of state buildings followed the Neoclassical model predominant at the fair (fig. 4). Most of the state pavilions had two stories, an abundance of windows, and resembled gracious residential buildings. Exemplifying this aesthetic were the Kentucky and Missouri buildings on either side of the Florida Pavilion. With their Palladian motifs, each evoked an ornate manse.

Why did Florida choose a pavilion so outrageous compared to those of its neighbors? Writing in general terms about the design of state pavilions, William Walton, author of a three-volume set of books on art and architecture at the 1893 fair, noted that the safest and readiest way of "crystallizing in concrete architectural shape all that the State means" was "to select the typical, natural architectural style of the commonwealth."[8] If indeed operating under this principle, those responsible for the Florida Pavilion apparently believed that Spanish colonial military architecture captured the spirit of their state. The state's 1893 building was, of course, the perfect response to an exposition attributing America's origin to Spanish-financed exploration, and set the stage for Florida's Spanish-inspired pavilions at subsequent fairs. To be Spanish was to be legitimate. This attitude was exemplified in a reproduction of the Franciscan monastery of La Rábida on the Chicago fairgrounds. The original was reputed to be the place "in which Columbus found shelter and encouragement when his fortunes were at their lowest ebb."[9] The historically referential edifice was constructed by the Columbian Exposition's board of directors to house a collection of objects pertaining to Columbus and his time. As one critic wrote of the Florida Building: "This structure probably outranks any other building at the Fair, except the Convent of La Rabida [*sic*], in the antiquity of its historic interest."[10] Fort Marion symbolized legitimacy in other respects

8. William Walton, *World's Columbian Exposition: Art and Architecture* (Philadelphia: George Barrie, 1893), 1:xii.

9. Ibid., xlv.

10. William E. Cameron, ed., *History of the World's Columbian Exposition* (Chicago: Columbian History Co., 1893), 199.

Fig. 5. Florida Building, World's Columbian Exposition, print. From W. Walton, *Art and Architecture* (Philadelphia: George Barrie, 1893). Avery Architectural and Fine Arts Library, Columbia University.

as well. St. Augustine was the oldest European settlement in what is now the United States, and Fort Marion, originally known as Castillo San Marcos, had the distinction of protecting the city and Spanish Florida from English invasion in both 1702 and 1740.[11] Fort Marion therefore alluded to a strong and proud chapter of Florida history. The implications of the Florida Building are suggested in a period print that appeared in William Walton's aforementioned work of 1893 (fig. 5). Signed with the initials "G.W. B.," the image creatively exaggerates the relationship of the Fort Marion replica to neighboring state pavilions. Despite the leisurely strollers depicted in the foreground, the Florida Building is shown quite literally as a fortress. It encloses and protects neighboring pavilions, most notably Pennsylvania's replica of Independence Hall — a recognizable icon of U.S. history and national origin. The image seems to imply that Florida is older, stronger, and culturally distinct from the rest of the nation. It remains somewhat paradoxical, however, that a fortress renowned for its ability to repulse invasion by others would represent a state desirous of attracting tourism, new settlers, and outside investment.

Despite this heady start, Florida's participation in world's fairs during the next forty years was definitively lackluster. The state did not succeed in developing an independent exhibit again until Chicago's 1933–1934 Century of Progress Exposition. Florida did participate in the centrally organized thematic buildings of several fairs — for example, at both the 1895 Atlanta and Cotton States International Exposition and the 1901 Pan-American Exposition in Buffalo, Florida had a nominal presence. The Atlanta exposition was organized to showcase the "Cotton States" and to stimulate trade with Latin America. Seven states built their own pavilions while thirty other states and U.S. territories participated in the collective exhibit halls. Florida submitted a total of forty-four exhibits, with representation in the so-called Negro Building, the Woman's Department, and the Agricultural Building.[12] Among Florida's agricultural

11. Charles W. Arnade, "Raids, Sieges, and International Wars," in *The New History of Florida*, ed. Michael Gannon (Gainesville: University Press of Florida, 1996), 100–104.

12. Walter G. Cooper, *The Cotton States and International Exposition and South* (Atlanta: The Illustrator Company, 1896), 57–82.

exhibits was a display of mangoes, oranges, and vegetables from Julia Tuttle of Miami. It is common lore that, during the widespread frost of 1894–1895, Tuttle had convinced Henry Flagler to extend his railway to Miami by sharing with him a healthy citrus blossom from her balmy hometown.[13] The 1901 Buffalo fair boasted a mere handful of free-standing state pavilions. The only evidence of Florida exhibits was in the Horticulture Building, which was dominated by California displays.[14]

Florida was conspicuously absent from some of the best-known fairs of the early twentieth century: St. Louis' 1904 Louisiana Purchase Exposition, San Francisco's 1915 Panama-Pacific International Exposition, and San Diego's 1915 Panama-California Exposition. It is, of course, understandable that the state did not jump on the bandwagon for every single fair. Unlike other established and affluent states, Florida was young at the turn of the century, with a population as sparse as its financial resources. As major fairs occurred nearly every year, Floridians had to plan their participation strategically. While the Spanish inspiration of the World's Columbian Exhibition was a perfect fit for Florida's colonial past, one wonders if the French associations of the Louisiana Purchase Exposition seemed a mismatch. The fact that Florida was recurrently represented at fairs in cities with residents who would most likely travel to, settle in, or buy products from the state is less a speculation. This would have motivated Florida's prominent participation in the Chicago and then the New York City fairs, given the climate and culture of these cities. Similarly, Florida's absence from the Spanish-inspired San Francisco and San Diego fairs of 1915, 1935, and 1939 makes sense. Like the 1909 Seattle fair, from which Florida abstained, the California expositions were quite simply very far away. Moreover, California was a stiff competitor, offering its residents and other world's fair visitors temperate weather and natural resources comparable to those of Florida. In the first decade of the twentieth century, Florida's progressive government was also more inward looking than that of previous administrations. Governors William Sherman Jennings (1863–1920, served 1901–1905) and Napoleon Bonaparte Broward (1857–1910, served 1905–1909), for example, were focused on railroad reform, enhancement of basic education, and the formation of universities — suggesting that national publicity might not have been essential to their goals.[15]

Then came the 1920s land boom and its concomitant boosters. Although Florida did not erect a pavilion at Philadelphia's 1876 Centennial Exhibition, there were ambitious plans for the state's participation in the same city's 1926 Sesquicentennial International Exposition. A celebration of 150 years of U.S. independence, the Sesquicentennial was not considered a great success. Late planning led to weak participation and incomplete buildings on opening day.[16] But Florida held an unusual place in this picture.

The blind optimism of fair officials led to the production of an official Sesquicentennial Exposition postcard that seems to document the state's success (fig. 6). On the face of the card is a color rendering of the lavish Florida Building and on the reverse is printed text that deceptively describes

13. Michael Gannon, *Florida: A Short History* (Gainesville: University Press of Florida, 1993), 58.

14. *The Rand-McNally Hand-Book to the Pan-American Exposition* (Chicago: Rand, McNally and Co., 1901), 82.

15. Samuel Proctor, "Prelude to the New Florida," in *The New History*, ed. Gannon, 278.

16. David Glassberg, "Sesqui-centennial International Exposition," in *Historical Dictionary of World's Fairs and Expositions, 1851–1988*, ed. John Findling (New York: Greenwood Press, 1990), 246.

Fig. 6. Florida Building, Sesquicentennial International Exposition, Philadelphia (unrealized). From a postcard, c. 1926. Myrna and Seth Bramson Collection, Miami, Florida.

the extensive pavilion as if it were up and running: "The Florida building with 100,000 square feet of floor space, cost about $500,000. Built in the form of a V, surrounds a beautiful court with fountains, and orange trees charge the air with their fragrance. Within the building is a color organ."[17] But no such pavilion was ever erected. Thanks to bad luck, bad timing, and what appears to be incompetence on the part of the state's appointed commissioner, Florida would fail miserably in its endeavors to join the fair.

No state appropriation was made for participation in the Sesquicentennial Exposition. In the middle of 1925, exposition organizers from Philadelphia selected Fred K. Ricksecker to serve as commissioner. His duty was to secure contracts from Florida's civic and commercial enterprises for participation in the fair. Ricksecker hailed from Bethlehem, Pennsylvania, where his family sold musical instruments.[18] He was joined by A. T. Corbett, Senator N. J. Wicker, and Charles F. Hall as officers in the organization identified on its letterhead as "Committee for Florida Palace Building." At the foot of this same letterhead was a menacing message: "GOVERNOR MARTIN SAYS: The Eyes of the World are trained upon us, Florida must not take a back seat at this Exposition, we must be in the front row."[19] The motivation for participation in the Sesquicentennial Exposition was clear. Florida was in the midst of a major boom, but as the

17. Postcard, "Florida Building, Sesqui-Centennial International Exposition, Philadelphia, PA," c. 1926, Myrna and Seth Bramson Collection.

18. J. E. Mathews, letter to D. C. Collier, 7 August 1925, Sesqui-Centennial Exposition Association records, RG 232, City Archives of Philadelphia (hereafter cited as RG 232).

19. Charles F. Hall, letter to Alex Mahm, 2 June 1926, RG 232.

Philadelphia fair was being planned there were signs of imminent bust. Real estate values reached their peak in 1925, and Florida began to draw negative press around the country. The state was condemned for the fraudulent transactions surrounding its rampant development and because other states desired to slow the flow of money and people into Florida.[20] Floridians retaliated by generating positive press, and what better place to do so than a world's fair?

The argument in favor of Florida's participation in the Sesquicentennial Exposition was feverishly voiced in an anonymous press release, presumably from 1926:

> The State of Florida cannot remain aloof from an exhibition of national character such as the Sesquicentennial without inviting a deluge of criticism and propoganda [sic] greater and stronger than any yet experienced. With Florida in the spot light of popular thought at this time, the State must adequately demonstrate in a concrete manner to its critics, and the thousands of doubting Thomases throughout the United States the fallacy of the propoganda [sic] which has been spread like a great fan over the country, to the effect that Florida is not of a sound foundation and that its chief assets are confined to real estate promotion and the entertainment of tourists.[21]

At this desperate point, conceivably when the prospects for a Florida pavilion were already looking dim, it was further argued that all "sectionalism and competition between its cities and counties" be banished for the good of the state.[22]

As evidenced by the above-mentioned postcard, Ricksecker and his colleagues did make some progress in planning a Florida building. Preliminary sketches were done by A. Lowther Forrest, a Baltimore architect who was acquainted with Ricksecker, but by early September 1925 Roy A. Benjamin (1888–1963) of Jacksonville was appointed architect for the project.[23] On 3 November Senator Wicker visited the Philadelphia exposition grounds and selected a site for the Florida Building.[24] By late November plans were well underway for the Spanish Revival palace intended to accommodate Florida's exhibits. The renderings appear not to have progressed between November 1925 and the publication of the postcard in 1926. At this time it was optimistically estimated that the building would cost $500,000 to erect, but in the face of unrealized financial commitments, by early 1926 this figure dropped to $200,000.[25]

Florida's boosters followed in the footsteps of their 1893 forebears in looking toward Spain at a fair that would be dominated by British-inspired Colonial Revival architecture. The building they proposed eclectically combined the clerestories, pitched roofs, and arcaded aisles of an Early Christian basilica, ornate Spanish Baroque entry portals, and squat Neoclassical domes, creating a somewhat dizzying mixture of messages. The domes suggested a link to

20. Charlton W. Tebeau and Ruby Leach Carson, *Florida: From Indian Trail to Space Age* (Delray Beach: The Southern Publishing Company, 1965), 2:59–62.

21. Press release, c. 1926, RG 232.

22. Ibid.

23. F. K. Ricksecker, letter to D. C. Collier, 14 August 1925, RG 232; and F. K. Ricksecker, telegram to D. C. Collier, 7 September 1925, RG 232.

24. A. L. Sutton, letter to R. A. Benjamin, 4 November 1925, RG 232.

25. "Florida Palace for Sesqui-Centennial International at Philadelphia Next Year Planned at $500,000 Cost," *Tampa Sunday Tribune*, 29 November 1925, RG 232; and Charles E. Harris, letter to all posts of the American Legion and Chambers of Commerce, 4 March 1926, RG 232.

Jeffersonian America, pertinent for the sesquicentennial celebration. The dominant Spanish component, on the other hand, exploited the same historical tradition as that of the Fort Marion pavilion. But while an ancient fortress might have suggested repulsion of "foreigners" at the Florida shoreline, the ecclesiastical character of the 1926 structure well reflected the boom state's missionary zeal for attracting the masses. Many of the best-known examples of 1920s Florida development had, of course, already invoked a Spanish aesthetic, including Addison Mizner's (1872–1933) Palm Beach villas and George Merrick's (1886–1942) Coral Gables community; and Benjamin's proposed pavilion is more than slightly reminiscent of Phineas Paist's (1875–1937) Colonnade Building (1925–1927) in the latter of these cities.

The Philadelphia exposition was to operate between June and December 1926. Relative to the planning for Florida's major participation in other world's fairs, that for the Sesquicentennial Exposition started late and went nowhere fast. By the end of 1925 A. L. Sutton, the Sesquicentennial Exposition's director of domestic participation, criticized Ricksecker for having neglected and alienated the Florida State Chamber of Commerce, thereby jeopardizing participation by chambers statewide. In January Sutton wrote: "Naturally I am becoming somewhat alarmed over the fact that you seem to be making so little progress in your Florida program."[26] And during the following months he repeatedly accused Ricksecker of ineffective communication and sales. On 9 April, for example, Sutton sent a telegram noting that Ricksecker had not passed on any news in several weeks and that "to date no positive information relative to any exhibitor has been given." He ended his missive on a threatening note: "I must have definite proof that there will be a Florida building or send our sales force into Florida to sell space in exhibits palaces."[27]

Whether Ricksecker was fully to blame is unknown. By 1926 the real estate boom was losing its wind, as buyers withdrew from deals and failed to make payments.[28] No doubt this state of affairs did not create a favorable climate for his cause. But criticism from prospective participants, in addition to that of Sutton, suggests that Ricksecker was not truly competent. The Philadelphia officials nonetheless remained resiliently optimistic, continuing only to threaten Ricksecker with termination of his agreement as late as May, noting that there was still no evidence of exhibit space sold or money raised. In fact, on 22 May 1926, just ten days before the Sesquicentennial Exposition opened, Sutton naively wrote to a prospective exhibitor: "Up until yesterday we had anticipated that Florida would have a building for her State exhibitors, but the Commissioner, who arrived yesterday, stated that the building is quite impossible."[29]

As the prospects for an independent Florida pavilion fell through, fair officials made plans to accommodate exhibitors in the centrally organized theme buildings. They also engaged in dialogue with two organizations that had planned national train exhibits intended to counteract Florida's worsening public image. The Florida Good Will Tour gathered the West Palm Beach Municipal Band, Florida mayors, and other state boosters for a two-week rail excursion to New England and the Midwest in July 1926. Sutton enthusiastically endorsed the

26. A. L. Sutton, letter to F. K. Ricksecker, 22 December 1925, RG 232; and A. L. Sutton, letter to F. K. Ricksecker, 15 January 1926, RG 232.
27. A. L. Sutton, telegram to F. K. Ricksecker, 9 April 1926, RG 232.
28. Tebeau and Carson, *Florida*, 2:62.
29. A. L. Sutton, letter to F. K. Ricksecker, 3 May 1926, RG 232; and John Burns, letter to D. W. Fairservis, 22 May 1926, RG 232.

creation of a Florida State Day to coincide with the Good Will Tour's arrival in Philadelphia.[30] The Florida Exposition, presided over by Governor John Martin (1884–1958, served 1925–1929), had the more ambitious mission, broadcast on its letterhead, of "Sending Five Florida Exhibit Trains to 26 States in the Heart of National Population." Clearly targeted to prospective Florida investors, the five trains were bound for major metropolises from the Atlantic seaboard west to Memphis and Des Moines. Again fair officials sanctioned collaboration with this group, and although plans were made to accommodate a Florida exposition train near the Sesquicentennial Exposition's Transportation Building in November 1926, storms in the South delayed the project beyond the end of the fair.[31]

Shortly after this Philadelphia world's fair flop, the Florida real estate market collapsed and a major hurricane slammed the Miami coastline and the Everglades. In 1928, two years later, another hurricane struck the state at Palm Beach, and in 1929 a Mediterranean fruit fly infestation devastated the citrus industry. Then the stock market crashed.[32] Emerging from this climate of economic despair, Florida mounted a series of exceptionally well-organized and fantastically creative world's fair exhibits between the Great Depression and World War II. This phase of ambitious participation no doubt exemplified a broad-based attempt to revitalize the state's reputation as a tourist and investment mecca.

Florida's aggressive achievements in the 1930s fairs are attributable to the work of a non-profit organization that came to be called Florida National Exhibits (FNE).[33] It is no coincidence that the group's influential officers included Edward Ball, brother-in-law of Alfred I. DuPont and one of Florida's most powerful citizens, and Nathan Mayo, Florida's commissioner of agriculture (1876–1960, served 1923–1960, making him Florida's longest-serving cabinet member). But FNE and its predecessor, the Florida Commission, were truly led by Florida booster extraordinaire Earl W. Brown (1890–1963). Under his leadership, the DeLand-based organization choreographed Florida's exhibits at Chicago's 1933–1934 Century of Progress Exposition, at Cleveland's 1936–1937 Great Lakes Exposition, and at the New York World's Fair of 1939–1940. FNE likewise created and capitalized upon opportunities to showcase the state at other available venues, engineering Florida exhibits at Radio City (now known as Rockefeller Center) and the International Sportsmen's Show at Grand Central Palace in New York, at Pennsylvania Station in Philadelphia, and at the Steel and Heinz piers in Atlantic City.[34]

Earl Brown, the remarkable force behind this program, was born in Milford, Pennsylvania, in 1890. At the age of eighteen he settled in DeLand, becoming a city council member in 1911, city commissioner thereafter, and mayor of DeLand from 1924 to 1932. With investments in real estate, a DeLand hotel, one hundred acres of citrus groves in nearby Pierson, and a fifty-three-hundred-acre cattle and timber ranch in Flagler County, Brown had adequate personal

30. Karl Lehmann, letter to Management Sesquicentennial Celebration, 1 May 1926, RG 232; and A. L. Sutton to Karl Lehmann, 26 May 1926, RG 232.

31. Memorandum, 10 September 1926, RG 232.

32. Gannon, *Florida: A Short History*, 80–85.

33. During the Century of Progress Exposition, Brown's team was organized as the Florida Commission, an antecedent of FNE.

34. "Men Who Make Florida," *Miami Herald,* 18 December 1938, from a scrapbook in the collection of Linda Colvard Dorian (hereafter cited as LCD).

motivation to promote Florida as a center for development, tourism, and agriculture. From 1922 to 1932 he was general manager of the Volusia County Fair and Citrus Exposition, apparently rated the greatest county fair in the South.[35] Following his leadership at the New York World's Fair of 1939–1940, Brown was elected vice president of the Pavilionaires, a group consisting of distinguished exhibitors from the New York exposition and intended as a permanent advisory board for future fair organizers.[36]

Brown's commitment to various cultural and political causes is well documented in two scrapbooks of ephemera and newspaper articles.[37] Invitations, for example, reveal that Brown hosted a 1937 victory dinner for Franklin Delano Roosevelt (1882–1945) and a 1942 dinner in honor of Senator Claude Pepper (1900–1989) at his Putnam Hotel in DeLand. Brown's civic involvements are many. In 1943, while serving as chairman of the board of the Babcock Aircraft Corporation in DeLand, Brown was named as Florida director of the federal government's Smaller War Plants Corporation by Pepper.[38] Following the war, Brown acted as a consultant to Governor Fuller Warren's (1905–1973, served 1949–1953) Florida Industrial Development Council, as a director of Florida Citrus Mutual, and as president of the Florida State Chamber of Commerce.[39]

The primary objectives of FNE's exhibition program were to increase tourism, the consumption of Florida products, investment in the state — and by the 1940s — the number of national defense facilities in Florida. According to one source, tremendous growth in Florida's transportation revenues, race-track returns, construction industry, tourist expenditures, industrial product sales, and citrus values between 1933–1942 could be attributed to the efforts of FNE, beginning with the Century of Progress Exposition. The same author claimed that, during this decade, Florida exhibits gave rise to 3,300,000 column inches of printed news material, twenty-nine newsreels, and $2,150,000 of free radio time.[40]

For their success, Brown and his office inspired wild adulation from many quarters. Rufus Dawes, president of the 1933 Chicago fair, is said to have stated publicly that "due to the ability and showmanship of Earl Brown, Florida's Exhibit at the Century of Progress Exposition was unquestionably the greatest participation of any state in the History of Expositions."[41] Of Brown the *Miami Herald* similarly wrote in 1938:

> He is considered the foremost commonwealth promoter of his day by authorities in the exposition field. Florida's reputation has been built up in competition with exhibits from other states, foreign governments and great industrial corporations at but a fraction of their cost.[42]

John Ringling (1866–1936), with tongue-in-cheek, supposedly went as far as attributing the Florida land boom to Brown's first out-of-state exhibit at Madison

35. Ibid.; "Southern City Builders," *Southern City* (November 1931); and curriculum vitae of Earl W. Brown, c. 1943, all from LCD.

36. *The Sanford Herald*, 9 November 1940, LCD.

37. These scrapbooks were graciously made available by Earl Brown's granddaughter Linda Colvard Dorian.

38. "Named to Post," *Florida Times-Union*, 25 May 1943, LCD; and "Pepper Names Heads of SWPC," *St. Petersburg Times*, 16 June 1943, LCD.

39. "Too Late to Classify," *Floridian*, 19 December 1949, LCD; and Betty-Lou Ewing, "Florida's Super Salesman," n.p., n.d., LCD.

40. "Florida, America's Furlough Land," *Florida Highways,* September 1942, LCD.

41. Typewritten biography of Earl Brown, n.d., LCD.

42. "Men Who Make Florida."

Square Garden in 1922.[43] Following the 1935 Radio City exhibit, John D. Rockefeller (1874–1960) reputedly offered Brown the position of promotional director for Rockefeller Center.[44] And of the Florida Pavilion at the New York World's Fair, FNE's most sophisticated piece, the journal of the Made in America Foundation proclaimed:

> To visit the New York World's Fair and not see the Florida building is like a trip to Rome without seeing Saint Peter's. The Florida exhibit is one of the most attractive and enchanting of the whole Fair. Visit it once and it becomes a habit.[45]

Brown and FNE distinguished themselves from other world's fair exhibitors in a number of ways. Decidedly talented at galvanizing financial and media support, Brown was a tireless showman with a keen eye for administrative detail. The New York Public Library's records on the 1939–1940 world's fair reveal the extent of his scrupulousness. The amount of correspondence between Brown and fair officials — addressing such things as promotion and visibility of the Florida exhibit — is perhaps as great as that generated by all the other states combined![46] Relative to their content, the exhibits created by FNE were known for evoking the spirit of Florida through their creative use of mixed media at the dawn of television and prior to the advent of big-business theme parks:

> When a person enters a Florida Exhibit he is transplanted for the time being into Florida. He sees the State as he could never see it through the printed word or over the radio....The visitor walks beneath moss-hung oaks, among orange trees hung with ripe fruit and looks upon vistas of Florida. All around him is movement and animation. Dioramas, spectoramas and rotoramas depict scenes in Florida. Boats speed over the water, planes hurtle through the air, automobiles dash down the highways as they used to do in the good old days. Such oddities as live parrots and macaws who say, "Come to Florida," Henry, the pole vaulting black bass of Wakulla Springs, the catfish parade and a mechanical mocking bird, whose song makes everyone think him alive entertain the crowds.[47]

If at all exaggerated, this exuberant description makes the point.

FNE was most renowned as the master of the diorama and its variants, the spectorama and rotorama. By the 1950s, in fact, it was said that the firm was turning out more dioramas than any other company in the country. Charles E. Plastow, Gale McAlexander, B. Frederick Grantham, and Margaret Humphreys were among the artists responsible for FNE's sophisticated models of the 1930s. The trademark dioramas were miniature, three-dimensional representations of Florida life, applauded for their uncanny verisimilitude. Often mechanized and incorporating light and sound, the dioramas featured sloping floors and flora hewn from manila fiber.[48] The spectoramas were larger, perspectival

43. "Florida's Master Showman: The World Heard about Sunshine and Citrus," *Florida Magazine, Orlando Sentinel*, 12 March 1961, 7, LCD.

44. George Byrnes, letter to Dennis Nolan, 21 January 1937, Box 92, New York World's Fair 1939–1940 Records, Manuscripts and Archives Division, New York Public Library (hereafter cited as NYPL 39–40, Box 92).

45. F. X. A. Eble, "The Spirit of Florida," *America First: The Voice of the Made in America Foundation*, July 1940, 3, LCD.

46. See NYPL 39–40, Box 92.

47. "Florida, America's Furlough Land."

48. B. F. Grantham, "The Case for Animation," *Midwest Museums Quarterly* 18, no. 3 (1958); and Lillian Blackstone, "Experts in Illusion," n.p., 8 August 1954, archives of Exhibit Builders, Inc., DeLand, Florida (hereafter cited as EBI).

Fig. 7. Court of States. From

A Century of Progress World's

Fair Souvenir Book (Chicago:

The Regensteiner Corp., 1934).

The Mitchell Wolfson Jr.

Collection, The Wolfsonian,

Florida International University,

Miami Beach, Florida.

constructions, often with figures decreasing from life-sized in the foreground to a quarter of an inch in the rear. The less common rotoramas consisted of scenes on turntables, with the sky and far distance revolving slowly, the middle ground moderately, and the foreground quickly.[49] One of the firm's travelling exhibits from c. 1940 featured a rotorama that traced the railroad trip from New York to the Florida border and down to Miami.[50]

In 1931 the state legislature created the Florida Commission to oversee participation in Chicago's 1933–1934 A Century of Progress International Exposition. The commission was led by Governor Doyle Carlton (1887–1972, served 1929–1933) (later by Governor David Sholtz [1891–1953, served 1933–1937]), Nathan Mayo, and a number of other political luminaries. Impressed by Brown's stunning success with the Volusia County Fair and related expositions, Carlton invited the DeLand promoter to manage the Florida Commission and its world's fair exhibits. To assume these duties, Brown retired as mayor of DeLand in 1932.[51]

A Century of Progress commemorated the centennial of Chicago's 1833 incorporation and "the rise of mankind during the last hundred years," particularly in the fields of science and industry.[52] Florida's participation was predicated upon the desire to show the exposition visitor "why he or she should invest, settle or come to enjoy the wonderful climate or take advantage of the countless opportunities for rest, recreation or restoration to health."[53] But before committing to the exposition, representatives from Florida visited Chicago to determine whether A Century of Progress "was to be a real world's fair, or a real estate promotion,"[54] an ironic concern given their home state's tattered reputation. The cost of exhibits was estimated at $250,000. There was no state legislative appropriation and, as of November 1932, it was expected that $100,000 would be raised through county taxes or a percentage of the racing fund, that the commissioner of agriculture would donate $100,000 from inspection revenues, and that the remaining $50,000 would be contributed by private industry.[55]

Florida's general exhibits were housed in the Court of States, a V-shaped structure with a large inner court from which one entered the individual state exhibits (fig. 7). The Florida Hall was designed by Phineas Paist and Harold Steward (1896–1987). Paist had served as associate architect of Miami's Villa Vizcaya (1914–1917) and then as chief architect of the emerging city of Coral Gables in the 1920s. His other works include the Colonnade Building and San Sebastian Apartments (1925) in Coral Gables and, in partnership with Harold Steward in the 1930s, the U.S. Post Office and Courthouse (1931) in downtown Miami and the Coral Gables Police and Fire Station (1938).[56] The firm would later design the elaborate Florida Pavilion at the 1939–1940 New York World's Fair.

The Florida exhibits at A Century of Progress were arranged on two levels, with dioramas and larger sculptures on the ground floor and a cycle of murals

49. Ibid.

50. "Florida State Exhibit" (newspaper article), n.p., n.d., LCD.

51. "Florida's Master Showman," 7; and Florida Commission, *Florida's Part in the International Exposition*, Chicago, 1933 (n.p., 1932).

52. *Official Book of the Fair: Giving Pre-Exposition Information, 1932–1933 of A Century of Progress International Exposition* (Chicago: A Century of Progress, Inc., 1932), 5.

53. Florida Commission, *Florida's Part*.

54. Ibid.

55. Ibid.

56. *From Wilderness to Metropolis* (Miami: Metropolitan Dade County, 1992).

above (fig. 8). The entire exhibit created the impression of a plaza or court-yard surrounded by two distinct Mediterranean Revival buildings. The structure on one side of the hall possessed a heavy rounded arcade and masonry balustrade, the structure on the other side consisted of stacked, rectangular columns and wrought-iron railings beneath a pitched, wooden roof. Like Florida, many exhibitors in the Court of States presented an array of murals, dioramas, and other objects from floor to ceiling. Florida's exhibition was unusual for its architectural and spatial complexity — transcending the exhibit hall aesthetic and inviting visitors to circulate through the loggias and walkways on two levels.

The Florida exhibits were numerous and varied. Ground-floor dioramas featured animated figures and machines and depicted industrial, agricultural, recreational, and touristic scenes, including Bok Tower (1929) and the Ringling Art Museum (figs. 9, 10, and 11). One diorama, entitled "Sunset on the Suwannee River," commemorated the Stephen Foster song, showing fields of cotton and cane, "while a band of plantation hands croon negro melodies to the tune of a banjo played by one of them" (fig. 12).[57] For the exhibit's organizers, Florida's antebellum tradition strongly pervaded its twentieth-century sense of identity. Given that many of Florida's blacks were still suffering under forced labor conditions through the mid-twentieth century, the exact implications of looking back via the deceptively leisured Suwannee River scene are not entirely clear.[58] Murals on the mezzanine level were painted by different artists and told in sequence the stories of "Discovery," "Exploration," "Christianization," "Colonization," "Seminole War," and "Reconstruction," oddly terminating the state's cultural history well in the past. A taste of the present came in the mezzanine lunettes of Coral Gables' planner Denman Fink, depicting the

57. Florida Commission, *Florida's Part*.
58. Gannon, *Florida: A Short History*, 86.

Fig. 9. Phosphate mining in Florida, A Century of Progress, diorama (all dioramas by Florida National Exhibits). From *Florida's Part in the International Exposition, Chicago* (1932). Historical Museum of Southern Florida.

above,

Fig. 10. Dairying in Florida, A Century of Progress, diorama. From *Florida's Part in the International Exposition, Chicago* (1932). Historical Museum of Southern Florida.

left,

Fig. 11. Bok Tower, A Century of Progress, diorama. From *Florida's Part in the International Exposition, Chicago* (1932). Historical Museum of Southern Florida.

Fig. 12. Suwannee River, A Century of Progress, diorama. From _Florida's Part in the International Exposition, Chicago_ (1932). Historical Museum of Southern Florida.

skylines of Florida's larger cities.[59] At the center of the Florida Hall stood George Etienne Ganiere's (1865–1935) statue _The Spirit of Florida_, a female figure in a diaphanous gown grasping or maybe harvesting an oversized orange above her head (fig. 8). Ganiere had gained renown as the sculptor of several memorials to Abraham Lincoln. In 1932 he sat on the faculties of Stetson University and Rollins College.[60] Elsewhere in the Florida Hall were exhibits of Florida fauna, while several thousand specimens of indigenous flora were on display in an adjoining space.

Despite its innovative components, the overall character of the Florida Hall was conservative. The state had already expressed its identity through Spanish-inspired design in 1893 and 1926. By entrusting Phineas Paist with the exhibit's overall aesthetic scheme, Brown and his colleagues on the Florida Commission gazed back nostalgically upon Coral Gables' moment of glory and the Florida boom. In so doing they seemed to imply that Florida's future would rest in its past — a message not particularly compatible with the themes and aesthetics of A Century of Progress.

In stark contrast to the backward-looking Florida display in the Court of States was Robert Law Weed's Florida Tropical Home, erected in the Chicago fair's Home and Industrial Arts exhibit (figs. 13 and 14). Weed's pavilion, constructed in association with Paist and Steward, is probably Florida's most renowned world's fair submission; ironically it is antithetical to anything else the state exhibited before World War II. Consisting of Modern and other more conventional model residences, the Home and Industrial Arts exhibit may be considered a diluted reinterpretation of such expositions as the Deutscher Werkbund's 1927 Weissenhofsiedlung, a forum for International Style architecture. Residential structures at the Chicago fair site included the House of Tomorrow, with glass walls, steel frame, and concrete floor slabs; the Stran Steel-Irwin Modern Town House, a blocky building with massing that vaguely recalled Josef Hoffmann's Palais Stoclet; and the Cypress Log Cabin, sponsored by the Southern Cypress Manufacturers' Association of Jacksonville, Florida.[61]

59. Exhibit descriptions from _Official Directory of Florida Exhibit, World's Fair, Chicago, 1934_ (Tampa: Tampa Chamber of Commerce, 1934).

60. Florida Commission, _Florida's Part._

61. Dorothy Raley, ed., _A Century of Progress Homes and Furnishings_ (Chicago: M.A. Ring Company, 1934); and _Two Century of Progress Homes: The Stran Steel-Irwin Houses_ (Chicago, 1934). In the spring of 1935 several of these model residences, including the Florida Tropical Home and the House of Tomorrow, were moved to form the Beverly Shores Century of Progress Architectural District at Indiana Dunes park in Porter, Indiana. "National Register of Historic Places Inventory — Nomination Form, Beverly Shores," 21 October 1985, in Robert Law Weed vertical file, The Mitchell Wolfson Jr. Collection, The Wolfsonian, Florida International University.

GOVERNOR SHOLTZ' MESSAGE

FLORIDA is pleased to cooperate with its sister states as well as with the nations of the earth in presenting, for the entertainment and information of the world, this great Century of Progress exposition which will be a vivid panoramic picture of the progress made during the past 100 years along all lines—including art, science, industry and agriculture in all their respective branches. Progress as the word is generally understood has been registered by Florida in no uncertain manner in every decade of the century just closing. Florida is a land of specialized production and her fruits and vegetables, produced in profusion all the year-around, contribute much to the health of the world and the wonderful all-the-year-around climate of the state adds years to the lives of those who find rest and recreation under her sunny skies. Though Florida is represented in this great exposition by many exhibits in many parts of the grounds, they are but the "Show Rooms" of the state. We invite you to inspect them and if you are pleased and interested, as we hope you will be, we further invite you to visit the "Play Ground of the Nation, WHERE SUMMER SPENDS THE WINTER."

Dave Sholtz

Fig. 14. Robert Law Weed, Florida Tropical Home, rear elevation. From *The Florida Tropical Home at A Century of Progress 1933* (New York:

Kuhne Galleries, 1933). The Mitchell Wolfson Jr. Collection, The Wolfsonian, Florida International University, Miami Beach, Florida.

Fig. 15. Florida Tropical Home, living room. From *The Florida Tropical Home at A Century of Progress 1933* (New York: Kuhne Galleries, 1933). The Mitchell Wolfson Jr. Collection, The Wolfsonian, Florida International University, Miami Beach, Florida.

Exactly how the Florida Tropical Home was conceived is unclear. Based in Miami, Robert Law Weed (1897–1961) began his career as an architect of extravagant Florida homes, but he eventually built his reputation on stripped Neoclassical, International Style, and Streamline Moderne structures. His commissions included the Miami Shores Elementary School (1930), the Royal Palm Club (1937), numerous buildings at the University of Miami, and a residential aviation community near Miami's airport (1947).[62] His Florida Tropical Home was a modest and more moderate reinterpretation of Europe's International Style villa, endowed with cantilevered shades and large windows appropriate for Florida's climate. Among its amenities were gracious rooftop decks and a double-height living room. The masonry house was filled with a relatively sparse selection of modern furnishings by such national manufacturers as the John Widdicomb Company, the Mueller Furniture Company, and the McKay Company (fig. 15). Floor coverings were decidedly geometric and walls were lined with plate-glass mirrors and Vitrolite (a patented colored glass).[63]

62. *From Wilderness to Metropolis*; *American Architect and Architecture* 151 (August 1937): 57–59; *Interiors* 107 (August 1947): 88; and *Architectural Forum* 90 (June 1949): 70–75.

63. *The Florida Tropical Home at A Century of Progress 1933* (New York: Kuhne Galleries, 1933).

Fig. 16. Florida Tropical Home, living room. From *A Century of Progress Homes and Furnishings* (Chicago: M. A. Ring Co., 1934). The Mitchell Wolfson Jr. Collection, The Wolfsonian, Florida International University, Miami Beach, Florida.

In a 1933 volume dedicated to the Florida Tropical Home, brimming with enthusiastic essays by the building's vendors and designers, it is enlightening to read Earl Brown's entry. Understandably, Brown focuses primarily on the Florida attractions depicted in his own dioramas. Revealing sentimental feelings for the architecture and ambiance of the old South, like those in the Suwannee River diorama, he opens with a discussion of "the productive plantations of north Florida, with fields of cotton, corn, tobacco, and other staple crops overlooked by the colonial plantation homes of the owners."[64] His words on the tropical home seem less heartfelt: "Nowhere in America has architecture been so thoroly [*sic*] adapted to local conditions as it has in Florida, and the 'Florida Tropical Home' is the last word in the small home architecture of Florida."[65] If Brown did not embrace the rigorously Modern aesthetic of this Florida pavilion, he was not alone. For reasons unknown, Chicago interior decorator Marjorie Thorsch was engaged to refurnish the house (fig. 16). Turning the original design on its head, she employed the "modernized Victorian," importing Venetian blinds, heavy chairs with fringed borders, floral papers and rugs, crystal chandeliers, and a decorative, over-mantel panel with white monkeys among white tropical foliage.[66] Despite contemporary design developments on Miami

64. Earl W. Brown, "Florida," in *The Florida Tropical Home*.
65. Ibid.
66. Raley, ed., *A Century of Progress Homes*, 54–60.

Fig. 18. Florida Manor House. From *Great Lakes Exposition Official Souvenir Guide* (Cleveland: Great Lakes Exposition, 1936). The Mitchell Wolfson Jr. Collection, The Wolfsonian, Florida International University, Miami Beach, Florida.

Fig. 17. Great Lakes Exposition, label, 1936. The Mitchell Wolfson Jr. Collection, The Wolfsonian, Florida International University, Miami Beach, Florida.

Beach and the state's enthusiasm for A Century of Progress, it would seem that Florida was not quite ready for the modern world.

This theme rings redolent in the state's pavilion at Cleveland's 1936–1937 Great Lakes Exposition. In the year preceding the Cleveland fair, the Florida Keys endured a major hurricane; nonetheless the winter of 1935 was Florida's best tourist season yet recorded, with some two million visitors spending $625,000,000 in the state.[67] Though not technically a world's fair, the Great Lakes Exposition was developed in the spirit of A Century of Progress. The project celebrated Cleveland's centennial; the region's civic, business, and cultural life; and what its promoters oddly dubbed "the romance of iron and steel." The fair's somewhat sparsely dispersed structures ranged from Modern to futuristic, with streamlining and illuminated pylons galore (fig. 17).

Florida was clearly determined to capture Cleveland, for it was the only state other than Ohio to erect its own pavilion. Smack in the middle of the fairgrounds, in close proximity to the Hall of Progress and the Automotive Building, FNE constructed a $250,000 Florida Manor House through public subscription (fig. 18).[68] Measuring 106,000 square feet, the building was characterized in one souvenir guide as the "Mammoth Florida Exhibits."[69] Consistent reference to the structure in fair ephemera portrays it as a highlight.

Compared to the residence exhibited by Florida at A Century of Progress, the antebellum, Neo-Colonial mansion house is a semantic shocker. While nostalgia for plantation life was latent at the 1933 fair, erupting merely in a diorama and a written comment by Earl Brown, it was everything in 1936. Despite the shift from Spanish Colonial to British Colonial, FNE recycled many of its Chicago exhibits for use in the Great Lakes Exposition. A view of the pavilion's interior reveals the murals and the *Spirit of Florida* statue created for A Century of Progress (fig. 19). But on another level the entertainment within the Florida

---

67. William W. Rogers, "*The Great Depression*," in *The New History*, ed. Gannon, 319.

68. *Great Lakes Exposition Official Souvenir Guide* (Cleveland: Great Lakes Exposition, 1936), 25 and map. The 1937 edition places the cost at $500,000.

69. *Great Lakes Exposition, Official Souvenir Guide* (Cleveland: Great Lakes Exposition, 1937), 27.

Fig. 19. Interior view of the

Florida Manor House. From

Official Great Lakes Exposition

View Book (Cleveland, 1936).

The Mitchell Wolfson Jr.

Collection, The Wolfsonian,

Florida International University,

Miami Beach, Florida.

Manor House distinguished this exhibit from Chicago. According to one description of the proposed pavilion: "Visitors will be met at the door by a stooped, gray-haired colored butler. A staff of 45 servants, maids, houseboys, porters and gardeners will be in attendance during the Exposition." Outside in a small orange grove, "Negro entertainers will sing and dance for the visitors. Servants in colorful Colonial costumes will serve the spectators."[70]

In the context of an exposition dedicated to modern industry, the Florida Manor House seems patently out of place, an icon of outmoded social and agricultural practices. The pavilion itself would have fit nicely among the Neoclassical state buildings of the World's Columbian Exposition. But in the context of the Colonial Revival sweeping the nation, the Florida Pavilion does not seem so odd. In fact one of the Cleveland exposition's model houses, the American Home of Wood, demonstrated sympathy for the aesthetic ideals of the Florida structure. And as the Miami-designed exhibits of 1933 might have been seen as promoting South Florida, perhaps it was hoped that the plantation pavilion would shift some attention north. The return to plantation-era culture, with its legions of servants, is, however, more confounding. Ohio had associated strongly with the abolitionist cause, so there seems little reason to assume this nostalgic interpretation would be popular with locals. Perhaps the exhibition was meant to convince prospective vacationers of Florida's potential for gracious hospitality and attentive service.

Florida's earlier submissions pale in comparison to that created for the 1939–1940 New York World's Fair, FNE's *pièce de résistance*. This Florida pavilion is likely the best-documented piece of Florida's exposition history (figs. 20 and 21). The New York fair commemorated the 150th anniversary of George Washington's inauguration while looking towards "a better world of tomorrow with the tools of today."[71]

Although New York was clearly an important market, Florida's participation in the 1939 fair was not a certainty. As of January 1937 Earl Brown and Nathan Mayo

70. Herbert Frickes, unpublished manuscript, "General Story on Great Lakes Exposition," c. 1936, 16–16a. The Mitchell Wolfson Jr. Collection, The Wolfsonian, Florida International University.

71. "The Plan of the Fair," *New York Times*, 5 March 1939, sec. 8, 8.

Fig. 20. Paist and Steward, Florida Pavilion at the 1939–1940 New York World's Fair, inked photograph. Exhibit Builders, Inc. (EBI), DeLand, Florida.

Fig. 21. Paist and Steward, Florida Pavilion at the 1939–1940 New York World's Fair. EBI, DeLand, Florida.

were considering the alternate possibility of mounting another exhibit in Rockefeller Center, having found New York fair officials unresponsive to their needs.[72] The dialogue advanced but was not resolved immediately. In May 1937 Brown and Ed Ball asked for several concessions. New York representative A. E. MacKinnon claimed to have scoffed at their request. But in a memorandum to Dennis Nolan, the fair's director of government participation, MacKinnon acknowledged FNE's incredible reputation and the importance of ensuring that Florida not be lost to San Francisco's 1939 Golden Gate International Exposition. His comments merit quotation:

> San Francisco is offering them every inducement under heaven to come there and in this I have a feeling they are more actuated by a desire to prevent [Florida's] participation in New York than to make them a source of revenue....
>
> In like manner the Great Lakes Exposition has and is making a wonderful play to them. They have been the key feature at the show and in matters of attendance at exhibits they have smashed all records, as they did at Chicago, even beating out the Ford and General Motors presentations. I have gone over the signed letters from many of the outstanding men of this country and the Brown claims are amply substantiated.
>
> In my opinion we must, and will have Florida.[73]

And so they would. In June 1937 the bill requesting an appropriation of $200,000 from the Florida legislature failed to carry.[74] Plans proceeded nonetheless, and funds would be raised through subscription. In September Governor Fred Cone (1871–1948, served 1937–1941) notified Grover Whalen, president of the New York World's Fair, that Earl Brown was to be the state's official representative.[75] Paist and Steward, architects of the Florida Hall at A Century of Progress, were engaged to design the pavilion, and by December 1937 their preliminary scheme was approved.[76] In December Brown estimated the value of Florida's participation in excess of $900,000.[77]

Twenty-three states and Puerto Rico were represented in the Court of States, a group of predominantly Neoclassical buildings clustered around a pool (fig. 22). Terminating the grouping at one end rose the Virginia pavilion, with its conspicuous dome and portico. Perhaps illustrative of the fair's objective to build "A happier way of American living through a recognition of the interdependence of men,"[78] the buildings in the Court of States are compatible and cohesive, reminiscent of the University of Virginia's original campus. More interested in promotion than cooperation, Brown requested a plot comparable in size to the one he had taken in Cleveland. This would be too large for the Court of States, so the Florida Pavilion was relegated instead to the fair's Amusement Zone.[79] At 118,000 square feet, Florida's plot was the biggest

Fig. 22. Court of States at the 1939–1940 New York World's Fair. From *Seeing New York World's Fair in Colors* (New York: Manhattan Post Card Pub. Co., 1939). The Mitchell Wolfson Jr. Collection, The Wolfsonian, Florida International University, Miami Beach, Florida.

72. George Byrnes, memorandum to Dennis Nolan, 21 January 1937, NYPL 39–40, Box 92.

73. A. E. MacKinnon, memorandum to Dennis Nolan, "Report of Day's Work from Florida," 12 May 1937, NYPL 39–40, Box 92.

74. Dennis Nolan, memorandum to H. A. Flanigan, 8 June 1937, NYPL 39–40, Box 92.

75. Fred P. Cone, letter to Grover Whalen, 25 September 1937, NYPL 39–40, Box 92.

76. C. L. Lee, memorandum to Dennis Nolan, 21 May 1937, NYPL 39–40, Box 92.

77. Earl Brown, letter to Maurice Mermey, 13 December 1937, NYPL 39–40, Box 92.

78. "The Plan of the Fair," 8.

79. Minutes of conference between Florida National Exhibits and New York World's Fair, 1 October 1937, NYPL 39–40, Box 546.

Fig. 23. Earl Brown, *left*, Grover Whalen, *center*, at the Florida Pavilion, 1939–1940 New York World's Fair. Box 1441, Manuscripts and Archives Division, New York Public Library.

contracted by any single state. Also in this quarter of the fair were a Hawaiian Village, a Cuban Village, Old New York, and Merrie England, all suggestive — perhaps like Florida — of a themed attraction more than an actual place. Unlike the other amusement spectacles, the Florida Pavilion sat west of Fountain Lake.[80] To draw people in, FNE prevailed upon fair officials to name the street in front of their building Orange Blossom Lane. Brown also requested that signage and Greyhound shuttle-bus service be improved.[81] The lakefront site with its simulated beach did enhance the pavilion's Floridian ambiance and offered an alternative means of access, as evidenced by a photograph of the fair's president, Grover Whalen, visiting with Earl Brown at the Florida dock (fig. 23).

Organizers of the 1939 New York World's Fair had determined that imitations of historic architecture or of permanent materials would not be allowed, "with

80. Geographical information from Frank Monaghan, ed., *Official Guide Book New York World's Fair 1939* (New York: Exposition Publications, Inc., 1939), 32–33, 122.

81. Helen Pillsbury, letter to J. L. Hautman, 21 March 1939, NYPL 39–40, Box 92; and J. L. Hautman, memorandum to Director Foreign Participation, 10 May 1939, NYPL 39–40, Box 92.

Fig. 24. Interior of Florida
Building, 1939–1940 New York
World's Fair, rendering.
Myrna and Seth Bramson
Collection, Miami, Florida.

one exception only, namely in the sector devoted to exhibits of the States."[82] Clearly this exception also applied to the Amusement Zone, for the dignified Florida Pavilion, composed of materials native to the state, took the form of a Mission-style church. Its tower housed what was reputed to be the world's largest carillon.[83] Like the exhibits erected at Chicago in 1893 and 1933, the 1939 pavilion is again evocative of Florida's colonial past and the upscale developments of Palm Beach, Miami Beach, and Coral Gables. According to FNE, by this time the style was "the theme of Florida architecture, a blend of Moorish and Spanish," and the pavilion itself was "symbolic of the Spanish cathedral construction of early Florida."[84] More explicitly than Florida's unrealized proposal for the Sesquicentennial Exposition, this 1939 structure openly alludes to the Spanish missions, whose proselytizing program aimed to "enlighten" others and entice them into the Church. With a zeal reminiscent of the missionaries that preceded them, FNE promoted the state's appeal as a land of opportunity and redemption.

The exhibits within are well documented and provide insight into FNE's artistic and interpretive prowess. At the building's entrance, a large talking statue of Ponce de León invited passersby to visit the "land of flowers." Behind him a huge panorama with live birds and trees depicted the explorer's landing in Florida. Nearby was the Aqualux Fountain, "with liquid red, amber and green in different sprays rising as high as 35 feet" in a twenty-one-minute cycle touted as showing 126 different combinations of color and water.[85] In the "nave" of the building, which was reputedly permeated by the sweet scent of orange blossom, visitors could view exhibits from three graduated levels (fig. 24).

82. Monaghan, ed., *Official Guide Book*, 20.

83. The carillon was produced by J. C. Deagan, Inc. for the Florida Stephen Collins Foster Memorial, which lent it for the New York World's Fair. Brown, incidentally, was one of the Foster Memorial's original commissioners from 1939. "Stephen Foster Carillon Tower Opens Sunday," n.p., 9 January 1958, LCD.

84. F. X. A. Eble, "The Spirit of Florida," 3.

85. Ibid.

Overhead, a painted sky simulated the journey from Florida's rosy dawn to its starry night in twenty magical minutes.[86]

Forty-five exhibits were disposed primarily along the building's periphery, in the "aisles" and "chapels." FNE's craftsmen created a large array of dioramas and spectoramas on Florida's people, places, and things. All are instructive; many are amusing. Consider, for example, the Annual Gasparilla Celebration at Tampa display, playfully alluding to the swashbuckling carnival at the Florida State Fair and its increasingly cosmopolitan host city (fig. 25). There was also the Daytona Beach diorama complete with oceanfront hotels, bathing beauties, and rolling waves on electrically powered wooden rods (fig. 26). And, not unlike a "naughty-girl" drama with Joan Crawford and Betty Davis, there was the full-scale Tarpon Fishing Spectorama (fig. 27). Onlookers stood in the simulated cabin, while "outside" the faux fisherman set his hook and the tarpon flew through the air. In the "apse" of the pavilion were two crowning achievements: the Citrus Spectorama and transportation mural. The Citrus Spectorama was a complex undertaking involving the work of a team of artists and craftsmen (figs. 28 and 29). Using extensive animation, it depicted twenty-five square miles of Florida citrus country in perspective, with ten thousand handmade orange blossoms and handmade trees ranging from life-sized in the foreground to one-half inch in the rear. Above this rested the twenty-four-by-thirteen-foot mural by artist Byron Stephens, depicting a contemporary beach scene, a map of Florida, and the evolution of transportation (fig. 30). Emerging from the clouds and winding down across the mural were a caravel, a conquistador on horseback, an ox-drawn cart, a horse-drawn carriage, a steamboat, and trains, planes, buses, and automobiles of several varieties. The mural implicitly illustrated Florida's increasing accessibility to the rest of the country.

The side of the pavilion accommodated a patio, a tropical garden with some six thousand Florida plantings, and several pieces of sculpture, including that perennial favorite, Ganiere's *Spirit of Florida*. Along the shore of Fountain

86. Ibid; and *Florida's Pavilion at the New York World's Fair* (c. 1939), Myrna and Seth Bramson Collection.

Fig. 27. Tarpon Fishing Spectorama, 1939–1940 New York World's Fair. EBI, DeLand, Florida.

Fig. 28. Citrus Spectorama

under construction, c. 1939.

EBI, DeLand, Florida.

Fig. 29. Citrus Spectorama, 1939–1940 New York World's Fair. EBI, DeLand, Florida.

Fig. 30. Byron Stephens in front of his transportation mural, 24 x 13', 1939. EBI, DeLand, Florida.

Lake, at least in 1940, there were cabanas, yachts, and a nighttime film flashing colorful scenes of Florida.[87] Off-site the state also installed seven citrus-juice lounges at buildings throughout the fair.[88]

Again distinguishing himself as a leader, Brown created an excellent public relations opportunity by signing the contract for Florida's 1940 participation before any other state exhibitor. Why not? The fair's director of promotion had, after all, estimated that an impressive twenty percent of all visitors to the New York exposition, or almost five million people, sought out the Florida Pavilion in 1939.[89] Leaving further record of FNE's success, Grover Whalen wrote to Brown in a letter solicited by the latter: "Every time I went to the Florida Building, I had an urge to leave immediately and go to Florida. If that was so in my case, it must have been true of the millions of visitors who went to your pavilion."[90] The sun shone brightly on FNE, despite the fact that most of the 1940 citrus crop had been lost to freeze and Europe was deep in war.[91]

Following the success of the New York World's Fair, Brown assembled an exhibition called World's Fair Highlights, intended to tour Cleveland, Detroit, Milwaukee, and Cincinnati. He also engineered a motorized fleet of exhibit vehicles to carry Florida dioramas, fruit displays, and tropical scenes to state and regional fairs in the agricultural Midwest. And in 1941–1942 Brown took similar exhibits to the Steel and Heinz piers in Atlantic City.[92] Like the New York Pavilion, these were to "have a Spanish flavor appropriate to the colorful exhibits of the country's only sub-tropical state."[93] Among the opportunities

87. F. X. A. Eble, "The Spirit of Florida," 3.

88. This was discussed in much correspondence, for example, Earl Brown, letter to Dennis Nolan, 7 January 1938, NYPL 39–40, Box 92.

89. Florida National Exhibits, *Florida World's Fair-O-Gram* (newsletter), January 1940, 2, 4, NYPL 39–40, Box 92.

90. Grover Whalen, letter to Earl Brown, 10 February 1940, NYPL 39–40, Box 92.

91. Earl Brown, letter to Dennis Nolan, 16 March 1940, NYPL 39–40, Box 92.

92. "Brown Enters World Fair Show," *Florida State Fair News*, 4 February 1941, LCD.

93. Florida National Exhibits, "Fair News," *Forward Florida* (newsletter), April 1941, 3, LCD. Several numbers of this bulletin were published.

Fig. 31. "Mr. America" and friend pose with Ponce de León statue, Heinz and Steel Piers Exhibit, Atlantic City, 1941. Courtesy of James Burkhalter, DeLand, Florida.

created by the exhibition were celebrity photographs, including a playful portrait of "Mr. America" (Bert Goodrich) and a friend eating ice-cream cones with Ponce de León (fig. 31). Unlike the world's fair pavilions that preceded it, the Atlantic City exhibit was supported by a state appropriation of $43,000.[94]

After a wartime hiatus FNE reorganized as Exhibit Builders, Inc. (EBI), an entrepreneurial exhibition-design firm. Maintaining a strong interest in Florida promotion, in 1947 EBI built Florida State Fair exhibits for the Citrus Exchange and designed Florida Citrus Commission juice bars for installation at race tracks statewide. In 1952 the firm would also design dioramas for the State Citrus Museum in Winter Haven.[95] EBI contributed an exhibit to the Chicago Railroad Fair in 1948; it featured a twenty-six-foot-tall replica of Bok Tower and a colonial manor house reminiscent of that at the Great Lakes Exposition.[96] That same year B. Fred Grantham assumed the presidency of EBI, having worked as a designer with the firm since 1937.[97] In March 1950 a still very active Earl Brown directed the first Miami Manufacturers Exposition, a ten-day exhibit of Miami products on display in the Dinner Key auditorium.[98] And in the same year, EBI built dioramas for the Stephen Collins Foster Memorial in White Springs, Florida, for which Brown was chairman.

94. Florida National Exhibits, "Florida Exhibit Will Open May 24th in Atlantic City," *Forward Florida* (newsletter), May 1941, 1, LCD.

95. "Exchange Exhibit at Fair" (newspaper article), n.p., February 1947, LCD; *Citrus Magazine*, December 1947, LCD; and "Too Late to Classify," *Tampa Free Press*, 9 February 1952, LCD.

96. "Three Months in a City," *Hastings Journal*, 25 November 1949, LCD.

97. Grantham served as president of EBI until his death in 1965. He was succeeded by James C. Burkhalter, an artist who had been with the firm from 1957. In 1993 Penny Morford, who had trained with Burkhalter for ten years, assumed ownership of EBI. Information provided by EBI.

98. "Manufacturers Show Closes Tonight," *Miami Herald*, 12 March 1950, LCD.

Fig. 32. Exhibit Builders, Inc.,

Florida's float for the 1949

presidential inauguration.

EBI, DeLand, Florida.

The list goes on but three of EBI's projects from the 1950s and early 1960s demand special mention in the context of Floridian promotion. In 1949 and 1953 the firm designed and constructed Florida floats for Harry Truman's and Dwight D. Eisenhower's inaugural parades in Washington, D.C. The 1949 float carried four women in formal gowns, one of whom appeared to be towed by large blue sailfish, and the remainder of whom posed against palm trees at the rear of the float, tossing oranges to the crowd (fig. 32). This float brandished the pithy Florida phrase, "Where Summer Spends the Winter." EBI's 1953 inaugural float, which earned first prize in a competition, was described as a replica of Ponce de León's ship.[99]

Perhaps in an effort to re-create the excitement of their world's fair activities, EBI took the unusual step in August 1955 of opening a tourist attraction in DeLand. Called Florida Prevues, the site was analogous to FNE's exposition pavilions (fig. 33). Florida Prevues was Fred Grantham's brainchild. A DeLand city commissioner at the time, Grantham hoped that Florida's tourists would consider his novel attraction a "must see." Florida Prevues was intended as a public service, to provide information on the state's scenic, industrial, and agricultural highlights, and admission was free. Planned for the site were murals; displays of fish, birds, and shells; and EBI dioramas of the citrus and phosphate industries, fishing scenes, and the Ringling Art Museum.[100]

In an extraordinary project conducted on behalf of the Florida Development Commission in 1963, EBI designed and built two Florida buses to promote the state across the U.S. and Europe — a veritable world's fair on wheels. EBI's preliminary designs reflect the firm's vibrant creativity (fig. 34). Within the bus they envisioned potted palms, a cage with exotic birds, an orange-juice cooler beneath an aquarium, views of Florida, and motion pictures. In the luggage holds below, EBI proposed what appears to be a live alligator and some other type of creature. With an extensive array of pamphlets in place of these animals, and promotional panels and films within, two Florida Travelling Showcases

99. Unidentified newsclipping, 21 January 1949, EBI; and *Miami Herald*, 22 January 1953, EBI.

100. *DeLand Sun News*, 5 August 1955, EBI; and "Construction of Buildings Under Way" (newspaper article), n.p., 1955, EBI.

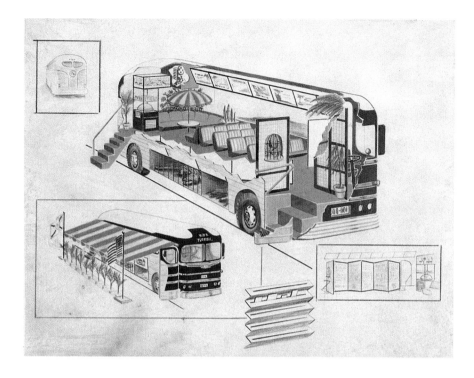

were deployed across North America and Western Europe (fig. 35). The former departed Tallahassee in March 1963 for a tour of sixty major cities in the United States and Canada. The latter, with documented stops in Rotterdam, The Hague, Brussels, and Copenhagen, was parked and open to the public at "high-density pedestrian locations" and used occasionally for travel-agent presentations. The Moroccan-born operator of the European bus, Fabienne Johnson, believed her primary mission was to dispel the image among Continental patrons "of Florida as a millionaires' playground that is much too expensive for anyone except the very rich."[101]

While other chapters in EBI's colorful history go beyond the scope of this essay, one final project returns us to our primary theme — the firm was called upon to provide preliminary designs for the New York World's Fair of 1964–1965. Following the state's successful showing at the previous New York World's Fair, and presumably convinced that New York was a market it needed to saturate, Florida representatives orchestrated their participation in the 1964 world's fair with confidence and conviction.

The New York World's Fair of 1964–1965 commemorated the three-hundredth anniversary of the founding of New York. Its theme was "Peace through Understanding," and its president was the autocratic Robert Moses.[102] In 1961 Dick Pope, proprietor of the tourist attraction Cypress Gardens, served as chairman of the Florida Council of 100's World's Fair Committee. The Council sought to develop industry and tourism in Florida, and the World's Fair Committee was charged with building support for the New York project. In May of that year Florida delegates selected a three-acre lakefront Amusement

---

101. "2 Buses Sell Florida in U.S., Europe," *Miami Herald*, 3 November 1963, EBI; and "DeLand Firms Play Important Roles in Designing State Promotional Buses" (newspaper article), n.p., c. 1963, EBI.

102. Daniel T. Lawrence, "New York World's Fair, 1964–1965," in *Historical Dictionary*, ed. John Findling, 322.

Fig. 37. Walter H. Knapp, Exhibit Builders, Inc., Florida Pavilion, 1964–1965 New York World's Fair (unrealized), Lake Shore Terrace, pastel, c. 1962. EBI, DeLand, Florida.

Fig. 38. Walter H. Knapp, Exhibit Builders, Inc., Agricultural Group, Florida Section, 1964–1965 New York World's Fair (unrealized), pastel, c. 1962. EBI, DeLand, Florida.

Area site in close proximity to that it had developed in 1939.[103] While size was again a factor, so too was the realization that Florida would erect an entertainment show requiring land and water.[104] The State of Florida appropriated $1,000,000 in support of the project, whose cost would later be estimated at $5,000,000.[105]

At this early stage EBI artist Walter H. Knapp prepared a spectacular set of pastel presentation drawings. These would grace the cover of the World's Fair Committee's marketing brochure (figs. 36 and 37). An A-frame fantasy with a rocket-launch sculpture at its front, Knapp's pavilion represented a dramatic departure from FNE's prewar perception of Florida. At the rear, on the lake facade, he placed an orange-juice bar, prospectively providing citrus sippers views of the beach and water shows. Knapp also executed an equally inspired drawing for Florida's agricultural buildings (fig. 38).

Following delay, in June 1962 Governor Farris Bryant (born 1914, served 1961–1965) finally appointed the official Florida World's Fair Authority (FWFA), its members drawn from the Council of 100, the Florida Development Commission, and the Florida Chamber of Commerce. The following month the FWFA convened to discuss the project. At this meeting there was passing reference to the A-frame plan, but William L. Stensgaard, who would later be named the organization's executive director, proposed an alternative design,

> which would generally follow the outline of the State of Florida. In the citrus belt we could have a sample orange grove, down in the Miami area we could have an actual simulated beach and palms, and we would have the other area on this 3 acres of ground properly identified with the actual section of the State.[106]

103. Wendell Jarrard, letter to New York World's Fair Management, 2 May 1961, Box 257, New York World's Fair 1964–1965 Records, Manuscripts and Archives Division, New York Public Library (hereafter cited as NYPL 64–65, Box 257).

104. J. Anthony Paunch, memorandum to Robert Moses, 20 June 1961, NYPL 64–65, Box 257.

105. "Florida Fair Tab $5 Million," *Long Island Star Journal*, 13 July 1963, NYPL 64–65, Box 257.

106. Minutes of meeting of the Florida World's Fair Authority, 20 July 1962, NYPL 64–65, Box 257.

Fig. 39. Aerial view of the Florida buildings, 1964–1965 New York World's Fair. Box 257, Manuscripts and Archives Division, New York Public Library.

In search of a theme the group considered focusing on Florida's opportunities, its reputation as a place for peaceful living, and its moon shot — though there was concern that the latter would seem "an accomplishment of by-gone days." At the same meeting the group agreed to enlist Earl Brown as a consultant.[107]

Neither the EBI nor the Stensgaard scheme was adopted. Instead the FWFA selected designs developed by Miami-based Pancoast, Ferendino, Skeels, and Burnham Architects, with Edward G. Grafton (1923–1990) as project manager (fig. 39). Like that of EBI, their project bore no similarity to the Florida pavilions that preceded it. The New York exhibitions were aimed at expressing Florida's history and its advantages for tourism, investment, and residence in a setting of "contemporary architecture." Despite the fact that the FWFA was headquartered in Palm Beach and the architects in Miami, the project was rich in citrus iconography. The scheme's centerpiece was a three-sided, one-hundred-foot citrus tower, with an illuminated orange at its crown and a Minute Maid stand at its base. Sponsored by the Citrus Commission, the tower was inaugurated several months in advance of the fair to promote Florida on the nearby expressways. During the fair it identified the state's location within the grounds.[108]

107. Ibid.

108. Hank Meyer Associates, Inc., press release, 18 October 1963, NYPL 64–65, Box 257.

Behind the tower on one side was the stadium and pool, which housed the first live-porpoise show in the history of world's fairs, with photo opportunities aplenty (fig. 40). One cannot help but notice that its sectioned roof more than slightly resembled a halved orange. Adjacent to this structure was the Florida Exhibition Hall, its alternating panels depicting the sun and a map of the state. Within were the primary exhibits, including those submitted by individual cities and counties, corporate exhibits by the likes of National Air Lines and Coppertone, a cultural-arts display with paintings from Florida's public and private collections, tourist information, and models and motion pictures from the Kennedy Space Center. Two pavilions that floated on Meadow Lake were devoted to exhibits of the Florida Development Commission and Minute Maid. And at the end of a boardwalk overlooking the lake, the Mackle Brothers, developers of Key Biscayne, erected a two-bedroom house, a response to the demands of Florida living far more modest than its forebear at A Century of Progress.

Fig. 40. Miss Florida and others watch Governor W. Haydon Burns (1912–1987, served 1965–1967) feed the porpoises, 1964–1965 New York World's Fair. Box 662, Manuscripts and Archives Division, New York Public Library.

In 1963 more than fourteen million tourists visited Florida, more than seven times as many as in 1927; yet "agribusiness" ranked as the state's largest source of revenue.[109] It is fitting then that Florida's exhibits at the 1964–1965 New York World's Fair depicted the state as a sun-filled, fun-filled, recreational playground — albeit one with a surfeit of orange juice. In 1965 this impression was redoubled when Florida occupied the building that had housed Billy Rose's Aquacade in the 1939 world's fair to mount the Florida Citrus Water Ski Show (fig. 41). Robert Moses had, to little avail, dreaded this condition. Back in 1962 he firmly rejected Dick Pope's proposal for water skiing on Meadow Lake, deeming the show noisy, dirty, dangerous, and trite, and he maintained that Florida's proclivity to become an amusement more than a state exhibit needed to be "watched and controlled."[110] As it turns out, the popularity of Florida has outlasted that of the grumpy New York executive.

Given their extreme enthusiasm for expositions outside of the state, it is not surprising that Florida's boosters have attempted to land the ultimate promotional prize, a Florida world's fair. Their unsuccessful efforts to do so provide final insight into this study of state identity. Following Florida's convincing demonstration of its Spanish heritage at the World's Columbian Exposition in 1893, the state offered excellent credentials to host the Columbian quincentennial fair ninety-nine years thereafter. It was hoped that the 1992 Florida Columbus Exposition, to be based on Miami's Virginia Key, would strengthen the bonds between the nations of South America, the Caribbean, and North America while recognizing the emerging destiny of southeastern Florida as a Pan-American meeting ground.[111] Had it occurred, the fair would have been welcomed by Hurricane Andrew.

Less predictable though more enduring was the plan for an Inter-American Trade and Cultural Center (Interama) in Miami, initiated in 1951 as a project of the State of Florida. Though Interama was intended to be a permanent Miami exposition, it was anticipated that the entire complex would open simultaneously in the manner of a fair. In 1965 the Community Facilities Administration approved a $22,000,000 loan to Interama, and in 1966 the U.S. Congress

109. Tebeau and Carson, *Florida*, 2:129.

110. Robert Moses, letter to W. E. Potter, 19 June 1962, NYPL 64–65, Box 257; and Robert Moses, letter to Bill Berns, 12 December 1962, NYPL 64–65, Box 257.

111. Report, "The 1992 World's Fair, Miami, Florida, U.S.A." (Miami: 1992 Florida Columbus Exposition, Inc., 1982), 1–1, University of Miami Archives and Special Collections.

Fig. 42. Minoru Yamasaki

with his model of the Tower

of Freedom. From *Interama*

News, February 1968. Myrna

and Seth Bramson Collection,

Miami, Florida.

Fig. 41. Promotional photo-

graph for Florida Citrus Water

Ski Show, 1964–1965

New York World's Fair.

Box 257, Manuscripts and

Archives Division, New York

Public Library.

passed a $5,870,000 appropriation for Interama's national exhibits.[112] By 1968 a group of internationally renowned Modern architects had planned the major buildings. Minoru Yamasaki (1912–1987), architect of New York's World Trade Center, designed the Tower of Freedom, a fair icon in the spirit of Seattle's Space Needle (fig. 42). The Latin American Communities division was likewise ready for bids (fig. 43). Here Paul Rudolph (1918–1997) designed the international bazaar with a sinuous roof; directly across the lagoon sat Harry Weese's (born 1915) Caribbean building; behind this (top of photograph) were Louis I. Kahn's (1901–1974) detached Central American pavilions; other structures were designed by José Luis Sert (1902–1983) and Marcel Breuer (1902–1981).[113] But Interama, like the Florida Columbus Exposition, was not to be.[114] Together, however, these two proposals, dedicated to Florida's relationship with Latin America, ironically suggest that the Sunshine State's Spanish-inspired self-identity of fairs gone by was more prophetic than it seemed. Yet Interama also demonstrated that Spanish identity could be expressed in Modern forms.

Florida's world's fair presence has been complex and curious. Statistics confirm that the state's lavish exhibits yielded economic rewards. From fair to fair, Floridians consistently exploited the central themes of agriculture and tourism. Likewise the aesthetic of Spanish Florida governed the fairs, despite the occasional incursion of other themes. Over the years, world's fairs provided carefully coordinated and abridged impressions of Florida, exposing the intersection of

112. Inter-American Center Authority, manuscript, "Interama: Chronological History," 3 August 1965. A group of Miamians had hoped to preempt Interama with a 1954–1955 Florida World Fair. See *Florida World Fair: World's First Atomic Fair* (Miami: Florida-World Fair, Inc., n.d.), both documents in the Myrna and Seth Bramson Collection.

113. Inter-American Center Authority, report, "Interama Today," April 1968, Myrna and Seth Bramson Collection.

114. However, one structure was erected on the site. That building is currently home to Florida International University's School of Hospitality Management.

Fig. 43. Model of Latin American Communities division at Interama. From "Interama Today," April 1968. Myrna and Seth Bramson Collection, Miami, Florida.

state perception and state ambition. Closer analysis of the murals and dioramas that Florida presented would, no doubt, provide considerable insight into prevailing views of race, religion, gender, and class. While the state's world's fair participation clearly expressed broad consensus, it also reflected the personal vision of a select few, eschewing uncomfortable topics such as the social and economic circumstances of Florida's African-American population. The traditional world's fair, with its place-bound exhibits and monolithic interpretations, might seem outmoded relative to the Internet's explosive emergence as the fairground of the future. Yet self-representation, self-promotion, and the processes that sustain them are very much with us today. □

Note

The author wishes to acknowledge the generous assistance of EBI's Penny Morford (who has donated the firm's archives to The Wolfsonian), Ann Aptaker, James Burkhalter, and Ruth Stanley; Linda Colvard Dorian; Seth and Myrna Bramson; Gail Farr of the Philadelphia City Archives; Carol Potter of the Queens Museum of Art; William Brown Jr. and his staff at the University of Miami's Archives and Special Collections; Pedro Figueredo of The Wolfsonian; and staff at Columbia University's Avery Library, the New York Public Library's Manuscripts and Archives Division, and the Historical Museum of Southern Florida.

William Henry Jackson and the Florida Landscape

By Michael L. Carlebach

Michael L. Carlebach, a photo-journalist and documentary photographer, teaches in the School of Communication at the University of Miami, Coral Gables, Florida. He is the author of several books, the most recent being *American Photojournalism Comes of Age* (Washington, D.C.: Smithsonian Institution Press, 1997).

Photographs by William Henry Jackson. From Archives and Special Collections, Otto G. Richter Library, University of Miami, Coral Gables, Florida, except where noted.

William Henry Jackson (1843–1942) came to Florida for the first time in 1887, lured in part by the state's comfortable climate. By then in middle age, the country's most famous frontier photographer welcomed the chance to spend the winter months in northern and central Florida. But Jackson was not on vacation. He came to Florida to photograph; that he could do so under a warm winter sun made the work much more pleasant, but it was still work. Nor was he in Florida simply to make fine-art pictures of the legendary Florida wilderness. Jackson's employers were railroad men and hoteliers, and they needed pictures to help sell the state as the country's premier tourist destination. He was the right man for the job (fig. 1).

Jackson was born in April 1843 in Keesville, New York, a tiny hamlet a few miles from Ausable Chasm, a tourist attraction bordering Lake Champlain in the northeastern corner of the state. He had some early training as a painter but drifted inexorably into photography, working first as an assistant in various photographic studios, then, after a brief stint in the Army during the Civil War, as a retoucher for the Vermont Gallery of Art. He left for the West in 1866 after a final, bitter argument with his fiancée.[1]

As Jackson was just beginning his great Western work from a small studio in Omaha, Nebraska, the Reverend Henry J. Morton, an Episcopal minister and a professor of chemistry and physics at the University of Pennsylvania, published a three-part series in *The Philadelphia Photographer*, a popular and influential monthly, extolling the opportunities awaiting serious photographers in Florida. Despite the state's well-known pictorial qualities, few professionals worked in Florida in that period immediately after the Civil War, preferring, at least in Jackson's case, the dramatic vistas of the mountain states. There was, as a result, a dearth of salable photographs of Florida, a fact that seemed to irritate Morton. "Florida, the land of flowers, ought also to be the land of photographers," he wrote. "The scenery is novel, varied, and beautiful, affording fine subjects for the artist…." He noted that Northern tourists flocked to campsites and hotels in Florida each winter but were usually disappointed with the selection of images available as souvenirs. "Few scenes in these

1. Jackson left for the West at 10:30 P.M. on Saturday, 14 April 1866. "I know because I wrote it down. I was methodical in my misery," he wrote in *Time Exposure. The Autobiography of William Henry Jackson* (New York: G. P. Putnam's Sons, 1940), 83.

Fig. 2. Stereograph of Mount of the Holy Cross, Colorado, 1873. This image, which seemed to many Americans to suggest a divine hand in the settlement of the West, was one of Jackson's most famous. Private collection.

regions have been photographed," he complained, "and these few, as far as we have been able to judge, are badly chosen and worse executed."[2] Morton was correct: there was a huge and mostly untapped market for photographs of Florida.

Despite the importuning of Morton and others, only a few professional photographers took advantage of Florida's burgeoning tourist industry in the two decades following the Civil War. During these years Jackson made his living trekking through the West, compiling thousands of views of the Rocky Mountains and the Yellowstone country as well as a stunning collection of portraits of Native Americans. In the process he became known as America's preeminent frontier photographer, and some of his images attained the status of icons (fig. 2).

Jackson was adept at capturing what many of his contemporaries perceived to be the very essence of Western settlement: the drama of building railways across a wild and seemingly savage land and the subsequent spread of Americans into that uncharted country. Although he assiduously cultivated an image of himself as a simple, if also courageous and gifted frontier photographer, he was, in fact, far more complex. As historian Peter Bacon Hales noted, Jackson "presided over the mapping, bounding, and settling of the American West and the larger American landscape." For more than half a century he meticulously documented the processes that fundamentally changed the American landscape. And the work he did in Florida mirrored his Western portfolio, offering compelling evidence of both an extraordinary technical mastery of the medium and an uncanny ability to make pictures encapsulating the dominant concerns of Gilded Age America (fig. 3).[3]

It was an age that endlessly extolled enterprise and industry, a time when the entrepreneur was king. Commercial values crept into all aspects of American society, affecting the arts and letters almost as much as politics and business affairs. After the Civil War, for instance, Horatio Alger Jr. philosophized to

2. Rev. H. J. Morton, "East Florida and Photography," *The Philadelphia Photographer* 4 (June 1867): 174.

3. Peter B. Hales, "A Visual Proponent of Myths About the American Landscape," *Chronicle of Higher Education* (26 October 1988): B64. See also Peter B. Hales, *William Henry Jackson and the Transformation of the American Landscape* (Philadelphia: Temple University Press, 1988).

Fig. 3. George Street, St. Augustine, c. 1880–1897.

generations of American children — especially boys — about the moral path to great wealth and happiness; in his 135 books for young readers, material success was always the paramount goal and prosperity the reward for hard work and clean living.

Jackson's work offered subtle corroboration and validation of that cultural stance. In his images the land is indeed beautiful, but so, too, are the uses made of it by men of vision and ambition. From 1871 to 1878 he worked for the United States Geological Survey of the Territories under Professor Ferdinand Vandiveer Hayden, providing the government with visual evidence of the shape and texture of the Western territories. The work done for the Hayden Survey conveyed to the world the wonders of the West. Some of the material, such as Jackson's views of the fabulous geysers and rock formations along the Yellowstone River in Wyoming Territory, so impressed members of Congress that they were moved to create the first national park. Preservation was never more than a secondary goal, however. Indeed, the Hayden Survey's detailed maps and geological studies were manna for a legion of businessmen, including the miners, railroad builders, ranchers, and farmers who were anxious to use and profit from the land.[4]

4. Richard A. Bartlett, *Great Surveys of the American West* (Norman: University of Oklahoma Press, 1962), xi–xii, 374–376.

Fig. 4. Coquina shoreline, Indian River (with lone man sitting amid the rocks), c. 1880–1897.

During his years with the Hayden Survey, both Jackson and his pictures became famous, and he began mass-producing photographic prints and selling them at his new studio in Denver, Colorado. In the days before the halftone transformed the printing industry, allowing photographs to be mechanically reproduced by magazines and newspapers, photographers often sold pictures to a public eager to own inexpensive views of celebrities, news events, and popular attractions. Jackson tapped into this market. He sold his photographs in a variety of formats, from cheap *cartes-de-viste* and stereographs to handsome display prints made from mammoth glass-plate negatives. The pictures helped publicize both the land itself and the work of railroaders and town-builders who were busily transforming it.

When Jackson left the Hayden Survey in 1879, commissions from a grateful railroad industry more than made up for the loss of his government salary and allowed him to combine his love for travel and the outdoors with commercial photography. "I wanted to get a line on my chances of doing some extensive work for the western railroads," he wrote in his autobiography. "It seemed to me they were missing a great opportunity to publicize and popularize their scenic routes."[5] Success was immediate, and he began referring to himself as a "commercial landscape photographer." It is a useful and entirely apt description and one that is helpful in interpreting the work he produced in Florida.

As railroads across the country contracted with Jackson to photograph their routes, he was able to take his pick of assignments. He noted that when "cold weather set in I found myself in Mexico or California or Louisiana or Florida." Hotels that catered to tourists arriving on trains also began using Jackson's services as their owners began "to understand the value of advertising their

5. Jackson, *Time Exposure*, 252.

scenic attractions...."[6] Being in the tropics during the winter months was far more enjoyable and productive than remaining hunkered down in Denver, and by his own accounts, Jackson relished the work (fig. 4). Nothing in his writing suggests dissatisfaction with either his clients or the assignments they threw his way. "I shall enjoy working here in the East," he told an interviewer late in the century, "for it is a little known country to me, compared at least, to the Rocky Mountain section." Using his many contacts in the railroad industry, Jackson planned "to roam at will over the North and South and East, arranging for series of pictures of the localities most visited by tourists both of our own and foreign countries."[7]

With other forms of transportation either scarce or hopelessly slow and uncomfortable, especially for one loaded down with hundreds of pounds of photographic paraphernalia, the railroads provided a neat and comfortable alternative, and usually did so for free. "I was moved from station to station and from point to point...," he wrote in 1875. "By making it a point to keep on the right side of all the various employees, I was enabled to go back and forth, and to be put off at any point I desired."[8] That is a bit of an understatement. Some of the lines for which he provided pictures went to great lengths to accommodate the famous photographer. The Denver and Rio Grande offered the use of the president's car, for instance, and others gave Jackson his own private car complete with darkroom and a servant.

Such cordial relations with the men who ran America's railroads made it possible for Jackson to go just about anywhere in the country and do so on short notice and in relative comfort. Provided with sturdy cases for cameras, lenses, and other equipment, "the travelling photographer may journey from one end of the continent to the other," Jackson wrote in 1888, "and be able to defy the...baggage smasher, the severest jolting and dust of the Concord coach, the more trying rattle of the lumber wagon and...the idiosyncracies of the festive pack mule...."[9]

Jackson's southern excursions in the 1880s and 1890s helped do for Florida what his work for the railroads and the government did for the West. A close examination of photographs of Florida credited specifically to Jackson indicates that he had commissions from Henry Morrison Flagler's (1830–1913) railroad and perhaps from several of Flagler's grand hotels. With such assignments Jackson was assured a tidy profit, and along the way he was able to add significantly to his collection of pictures that could be marketed to tourists, either as full-size display prints or postcards. After 1898, when he sold his archive of images to the Detroit Publishing Company, he increasingly turned his attention to the production of inexpensive views, many of them printed in color and sold to tourists eager to purchase some visual memento of their trip to Florida.[10]

Jackson's decision to enter the postcard business should come as no surprise, for he was always interested in making his pictures available to a mass audience.

6. Ibid., 259.

7. Cited in "Picturesque America in Colors," *Wilson's Photographic Magazine* 35 (April 1898): 179.

8. W. H. Jackson, "Field Work," *The Philadelphia Photographer* 12 (March 1875): 92.

9. W. H. Jackson, "Landscape Photography with Large Plates," in W. Jerome Harrison and A. H. Elliott, ed., *The International Annual of Anthony's Photographic Bulletin* (New York: E. and H. T. Anthony and Co. Publishers, 1888), 316.

10. Fritiof Fryxell, "William H. Jackson, Photographer, Artist, Explorer," in Frank R. Fraprie, ed., *The American Annual of Photography 1939* (Boston: American Photographic Publishing Co., 1938), 218.

Fig. 5. Green Street, St.

Augustine, c. 1880–1897.

Green Street, St. Augustine, Fla.

Fig. 6. Orange grove, Seville,

c. 1880–1897.

Fig. 7. Pelican Island on the Indian River, c. 1880–1897. The Detroit Publishing Company collection,

Fig. 9. Two women in bonnets, Silver Springs, c. 1902. The Detroit Publishing Company collection, U.S. Library of Congress, Washington, D.C.

Fig. 8. Three men in a boat, mangroves, Jupiter Narrows, c. 1880–1897.

Picture postcards had first appeared in the United States during the 1893 World's Columbian Exposition in Chicago. When Congress formally approved the new format five years later, the country was flooded with views almost overnight. Where others saw only a fatal decline in the intricate beauty of the handmade print, Jackson saw opportunity. The reproduction of his pictures in halftone, whether as postcards or periodical illustrations, made it possible to reach and affect more people, and that was always his primary objective. "As the process of halftone engraving improved," he wrote, "not only did magazine pictures cut into the old 'views' market, but cheap (and increasingly excellent) reproductions, in color as well as in black-and-white, further lowered the demand for photo prints. The latter had to be made one at a time, while photo-engravings could be turned out by the thousands."[11]

For Jackson, the association with Detroit Publishing led to a resurgence in his photographic output. Though undoubtedly interested in the manufacturing and marketing ends of the business, his first love was photography. "Now that I was assured that the pictures I took would be profitably reproduced," he wrote, "I went back to my outdoor career with a zest as great as I have ever known before."[12]

The Detroit Publishing Company collection, now housed in the Library of Congress, contains more than twenty-five thousand glass-plate negatives and transparencies, nine hundred forty-one of which were made in Florida. In addition, the collection contains more than nine hundred mammoth glass-plate negatives and prints made in Mexico and the United States during the last two decades of the nineteenth century with Jackson's eighteen-by-twenty-two-inch

11. Jackson, *Time Exposure*, 320.
12. Ibid., 324.

camera.[13] A small handmade book containing original prints of Florida by Jackson and a few others is now housed in the Archives and Special Collections of the Otto G. Richter Library, University of Miami, Coral Gables, Florida. On the surface, the photographs merely tell us what certain places in Florida looked like at the turn of the century. But there is considerably more to the story.

The choice of subject matter is significant. Hotels and other tourist facilities are lovingly presented; so, too, are well-known attractions such as the narrow streets and ancient buildings of historic St. Augustine (fig. 5). Fecundity and easy living are subtexts throughout, from Jackson's images of lush orange groves near Seville (fig. 6) to those of mud flats in the Indian River teeming with pelicans (fig. 7). The photographs Jackson produced in Florida were meant to promote tourism and development, and the message is decidedly beneficent and alluring. Absent from Jackson's Florida portfolio are any images that question or cast doubt on the rush to exploit either coastal hammock or riverside. We see instead a pretty state, one that offers visitors and residents alike effortless living amid natural beauty. Transportation, whether by rail or boat or horse and carriage, is readily available, and accommodations for visitors are plentiful and luxurious.

Jackson's photographs of rivers in Florida seem at first to offer a slightly less salubrious view, occasionally conveying a sense of mystery and awe. But that view is usually tempered by the presence of human figures. Jackson photographed a twisted and forbidding tangle of mangroves along Jupiter Inlet, for instance, but included in the scene three men relaxing in a rowboat (fig. 8). At Silver Springs on the Oklawaha River, Jackson made a number of pictures, and all of them included whimsical touches of humanity. In one, two women

13. Access to the Detroit Publishing Company collection is now available on the Internet at the American Memory collection. See www.loc.gov.

Fig. 12. Deep Creek, c. 1880–1897. This appears to be a cropped version of negative number 3586 in the Detroit Publishing Company catalogue.

in fancy bonnets pose in their canoe (fig. 9); in others, a jaunty excursion boat loads up with passengers and drifts in the current (figs. 10 and 11). On the narrow reaches of Deep Creek, he photographed a small steamer plowing through the mist toward a lone silhouetted figure in a skiff (fig. 12). Here was raw nature, slightly menacing perhaps, but made much less so by the presence of plucky human beings, as wilderness gave way, slowly, to the hand of man. For Jackson and many other Gilded Age Americans, this process of settlement and the development of natural resources was inevitable and ultimately beneficial, and his pictures reflected this philosophy. He was, after all, a *commercial* landscape photographer. □

Fig. 1. Hotel Ponce de León, front view, St. Augustine, Florida.

Henry M. Flagler's Hotel Ponce de León

By Thomas Graham

Thomas Graham is a professor of history at Flagler College, St. Augustine, Florida. A native of Miami, he claims early-seventeenth-century Spanish Florida ancestry. He is the author of *The Awakening of St. Augustine* (St. Augustine: St. Augustine Historical Society, 1978).

Photographs courtesy of Flagler College, St. Augustine, Florida. Unless otherwise noted, all color photographs are by Tommy L. Thompson, 1992.

n the winter of 1909–1910 Edwin Lefevre, a writer for *Everybody's Magazine*, interviewed Henry Morrison Flagler (1830–1913) in Palm Beach, the capital of Flagler's Florida empire. That realm stretched from Jacksonville to Miami and at the time was being extended to Key West via the steel bands of the Florida East Coast Railway. "How did you build your system?" Lefevre asked Flagler. He had already observed that Flagler was "distant" and reluctant to talk much about anything. Flagler's reply was: "Oh, it's one of those things that just happen. I happened to be in St. Augustine and had some spare money."[1]

Lefevre asked Flagler to recall his greatest challenge in Florida. "Building the Ponce de León," replied Flagler (fig. 1). "Here was St. Augustine, the oldest city in the United States. How to build a hotel to meet the requirements of nineteenth-century America and have it in keeping with the character of the place — that was my hardest problem."[2]

Flagler began pondering this problem in the winter of 1885 while staying at St. Augustine's recently built San Marco Hotel, which overlooked the gray stone Castillo de San Marcos and the city's narrow streets. Flagler had initially come to Florida in 1878 with his first wife, Mary Harkness Flagler, for the sake of her health. He stayed in Jacksonville, with only an overnight visit to St. Augustine, which he found depressingly full of consumptives and other invalids. After Mary's death in New York City in 1881, Flagler married Ida Alice Shourds and brought her to St. Augustine in December 1883 for their honeymoon. He found the old town remarkably rejuvenated by an influx of Northern visitors who enjoyed both good health and affluence. A third visit in February 1885 found him in the San Marco Hotel — and launched a new era of Florida history.

He walked the sandy streets of St. Augustine, strolled the plaza, and followed the seawall back to the hotel. There wasn't much else to do. "But I liked the place," recalled Flagler, "and the climate, and it occurred to me very strongly that someone with sufficient means ought to provide accommodations for that class of people who are not sick, but who come here to enjoy the climate, have plenty of money, but could find no satisfactory way of spending it."[3]

By 1885 Flagler was extraordinarily rich, having helped John D. Rockefeller build Standard Oil into the largest company in the world. At the time of his third St. Augustine visit, he was ready to embark on a venture wholly his own. The first element of his plan was the construction of a grand resort hotel.

1. Edwin Lefevre, "Flagler and Florida," *Everybody's Magazine* (February 1910): 168–186.
2. Ibid.
3. Ibid.

He hired the San Marco Hotel's builders James McGuire and James McDonald; however, Flagler had a less conventional idea of whom he wanted to design his hotel.[4]

He chose Thomas Hastings (1860–1929) and John Carrère (1858–1911), young men in their mid-twenties who recently had left the important firm of McKim, Mead and White to set up shop on their own in New York City.

Flagler was a close friend of Hastings' father, a Presbyterian minister, and had tested Thomas with a few small projects in New York. Flagler brought these young architects down to St. Augustine in his private railroad car in May 1885 to let them size up the problem. Hastings, already full of ideas, sketched an elevation and design while riding in Flagler's car. At this point Flagler was thinking that Carrère and Hastings would provide only a "picture" that McGuire and McDonald would turn into a building.

Hastings' introduction to the site of the proposed hotel was dismaying: "When Mr. Flagler led me to the spot where he wanted the Ponce de León to stand I was discouraged for it was low and marshy, in fact, a continuation of María Sanchez Creek."[5] Flagler assured him that plans were already well advanced to fill the site with sand hauled in by rail.

Hastings next turned his attention to the town itself. St. Augustine was then just a village of approximately three thousand inhabitants living in an odd assortment of crumbling Spanish stone houses, rotting frame houses built before the Civil War, and freshly painted cottages erected by newcomers from the North. Not a single avenue was paved, and pedestrians waded through deep white sand covering the streets. "I spent much time roaming around St. Augustine endeavoring to absorb as much of the local atmosphere as possible. I wanted to retain the Spanish character of St. Augustine and so designed the buildings with the architecture of the early houses here with their quaint over-hanging balconies," Hastings said.[6]

Born in 1860, Hastings left his New York home to study at the École des Beaux-Arts in Paris, where he met Carrère. After his studies Hastings took a trip to Spain to sample the architecture. He returned to New York to work for McKim, Mead and White briefly before going into partnership with Carrère.

Carrère was born in Rio de Janeiro, the son of an American coffee planter. Thus he grew up with Spanish and Portuguese architecture. "Yet," Hastings later said, "it was not so much our predilections for Spanish architecture as our conscientious scruples against destroying the characteristic atmosphere of St. Augustine that guided us."[7]

St. Augustine had been a very modest settlement on the edge of Spain's empire, and the only monumental structures in town were the *castillo* and the Catholic church. The rest of the buildings dating from Spanish times were relatively simple dwellings. Carrère and Hastings would build a regal castle that dwarfed the abodes of the commoners. In the design they incorporated three elements from the town: the overhanging balconies, the arch, and the coquina stone texture of the walls.

4. The history of Flagler's St. Augustine hotels can be found in two booklets written by the author and published by the St. Augustine Historical Society: *Flagler's Magnificent Hotel Ponce de León* (1975) and *Flagler's Grand Hotel Alcázar* (1989).

5. "A Letter from Thomas Hastings," *American Architect* (7 July 1909): 3–4.

6. Ibid.

7. Ibid.

While he was in St. Augustine in that summer of 1885 Hastings visited the coquina limestone quarries on Anastasia Island, across the bay from town. Flagler had decided to construct his hotel of concrete and intended to use local coquina shell as the aggregate. McGuire and McDonald conducted experiments with this innovative method of raising walls. They even considered using iron-reinforced concrete in the floors, and stacked barrels of cement on concrete slabs to determine the strength of test slabs. In the end, wood was used for the floors, but the walls were monoliths of poured concrete.[8]

Returning to their New York office, Carrère devoted himself primarily to the business side of the project, while Hastings handled the artistic side. "We made more elaborate perspective drawings and studies and plans, but gradually transferred these drawings into more practical working drawings, finally figuring the plans. These plans were intricate in outline, and for a building covering somewhat over six acres of ground," according to Hastings.[9]

Carrère and Hastings soon became full-fledged partners with McGuire and McDonald in the construction of the hotel, contracting for materials that would go into the hotel and checking that they were sent off to Florida.

As the concrete outlines of his mammoth hotel began to take shape in the sand, Flagler wrote McGuire and McDonald: "I think it more likely I am spending an unnecessary amount of money in the foundation walls, but I comfort myself with the reflection that a hundred years hence it will be all the same to me, and the building the better because of my extravagance."[10]

The hotel was under construction from December 1885 to May 1887 (fig. 2). Flagler's builders put down temporary railroad tracks on St. Augustine's

8. J. A. McGuire, letter to Carrère and Hastings, 25 June 1910. A copy of this letter appeared in the 1910 McGuire letterbook that was part of the collection at Flagler College. Unfortunately, the letterbook has been lost.

9. "A Letter from Thomas Hastings."

10. Henry Flagler, letter to Franklin W. Smith, 26 December 1885, quoted in Edward N. Akin, *Flagler: Rockefeller Partner and Florida Baron* (Ohio: Kent State University Press, 1988), 121.

Fig. 3. Hotel Ponce de León, 1888.

streets to haul in landfill and building materials. Although the work was essentially completed by May 1887, the winter tourist season was long over and the grand opening of the hotel was delayed until January 1888 (fig. 3).

Guests arriving for the inaugural season were transported from Flagler's newly constructed railroad depot to the hotel on freshly paved asphalt streets in colorfully painted carriages. Flagler had proposed changing the name of the avenue leading to the Ponce de León from King Street to "The Alameda" and envisioned it as the entrance to America's winter Newport. As it turned out the city council never made the name change, and later, over Flagler's objections, they permitted a prosaic trolley line to be run down the street.

On arrival guests followed a specific sequence. They were deposited at the front gate of the hotel, while the carriage continued around to the rear to unload the baggage into the basement. Then it was carried by freight elevator to the guests' rooms. No luggage ever marred the atmosphere of the lobby. Guests passed through the hotel's arched front gate with its medieval portcullis and embarked on a fantasy trip, which was the intention of the building's architects as well as the expectation of the guests. Like the eponymous explorer Juan Ponce de León, resort visitors desired an escape into an exotic realm.

Above, to the left and right on the building's facade, were overhanging balconies patterned after those Hastings had noted along St. Augustine's streets. Above these at the four corners of the hotel's front were "Mirador Rooms" that vaguely echoed the sentinel boxes at the corners of the Castillo de San Marcos. These lookout alcoves were intended to be sitting rooms where guests could enjoy the passing scene on the street below (fig. 4).

The overall impression was that a Spanish Renaissance palace had been magically transported across the Atlantic and deposited on Florida's shores. Carrère and Hastings' creation was clearly imitative of European and South American architectural antecedents, yet the style was new to the United States. The Hotel Ponce de León would itself become the inspiration for Spanish Renaissance buildings throughout Florida and the country.

Fig. 4. Overhanging balconies and the corner Mirador Rooms borrow familiar motifs from St. Augustine architecture but are blended into Carrère and Hastings' eclectic Spanish Renaissance palace. The banners hanging from the light-posts announce the visit of the *Santa Maria, Pinta*, and *Nina* to St. Augustine in 1992.

Fig. 5. Hotel Ponce de León, view of towers at sunset.

The general lines of the hotel's structure were horizontal, befitting the flat landscape of Florida — but rising above the hotel were a pair of square towers that became octagonal near their summits and then tapered into cones (fig. 5). Heavy terra-cotta balconies hung from the towers, firmly held in place by iron railroad tracks embedded in the concrete. Behind the arches of the towers stood large iron tanks holding the water used throughout the hotel. Thus, the towers were functional as well as decorative. Between the towers rose a central dome topped with a bronze lantern. In Flagler's day potted orange trees graced the hotel's two small rooftop gardens below the towers. Guests entered the gardens through the solarium under the dome.

Beyond the gate, guests passed into a courtyard enclosed by an arched loggia containing rows of green rocking chairs. The courtyard had a southern exposure, and on winter days the slanting rays of the sun would warm guests sitting on the loggias or in the grassy yard, while the mass of the hotel sheltered them from the north wind. A fountain occupied the center of the courtyard (fig. 6), and tropical plantings contributed to the foreign atmosphere. Looking down from overhead were tin gargoyles with light bulbs in their mouths. Such a mix of the old and the modern typified the eclecticism of Carrère and Hastings' creation.

The entranceway was marked by a pair of heavy oak doors. They were set in a brick and terra-cotta arch inlaid with a mosaic of tile fragments and studded with bronze scallop shells (figs. 7 and 8). The varnished wooden doors and bright mosaic were unique features in an exterior that otherwise consisted of cool gray concrete and warm salmon terra cotta. McKim, Mead and White had developed this muted orange-colored terra cotta, and its use by Carrère and Hastings was a natural choice. The salmon of the fired clay blended with the orange of the brick used around the windows and arches, as well as with the barrel tiles of the roof. The only other splashes of color on the exterior were the golden-painted wood of the balconies and window trim. This color would become known as "Flagler yellow," since it was used on all of Flagler's future hotels as well as on the passenger cars of his railroad.

Fig. 6. Terra-cotta frogs that encircle the ornamental fountain in the center of the courtyard.

below right,

Fig. 7. A mosaic and a monumental terra-cotta arch surround the front door of the Hotel Ponce de León. The plaques recognize the work of Carrère and Hastings, architects, and McGuire and McDonald, builders.

Fig. 8. Spanish proverbs appear in a number of locations throughout the building. Beside the front door, roughly trans-lated: "You can't make an omelet without breaking eggs."

Fig. 10. Hotel Ponce de
León, rotunda.

Fig. 9. Four-sided oak caryatids
serve as columns upholding the
rotunda's dome.

Stepping through the front doors, guests journeyed deeper into an enchanted realm. From the bright Florida sun, they came into a room where light entered only through stained glass or radiated from electric wall sconces. Here the visitors first experienced a device used by Carrère and Hastings in several other places in the building. Although the entrance foyer was part of the large rotunda, it was made to seem a smaller separate room, set apart by its low ceiling and a screen of wooden columns (fig. 9). A few more steps and the soaring space of the rotunda dome was revealed (fig. 10).[11]

The room was embellished richly with oak, oriental rugs, potted palms, and a golden ceiling covered with painted murals. Carrère and Hastings used electric light bulbs to illuminate the dome above the rotunda. It was a jewel of woodwork and plaster ornament. The murals were the work of George W. Maynard (1843–1923), the country's leading artist in that specialty. The motifs were allegorical female figures, augmented by images from Florida's Native American and Spanish history as well as from the heraldry of Spain. Two sets of figures alternated in the major coves of the dome. In the first, "Adventure" in the dark blue gown and silver breastplate was easiest to locate, "Civilization" wore white and held an open book, "Conquest" was dressed in red, and "Discovery" was wrapped in sea blue. Maynard worked his name and the date 1887 into the bodice of Discovery's gown. The other set of women represented earth, air, fire, and water. The painting was done on dry plaster and began to deteriorate almost immediately in the humid atmosphere. Restoration of the murals began in Flagler's day and has continued to the present.

Behind the painted plaster was wooden lath fixed to a complex system of wood trusses that formed the dome. Carrère and Hastings also employed this technique in the vaulted ceiling of the dining room. Buried inside the walls of the rotunda were great structural steel beams that supported the central dome. Concrete was not the only innovative building material employed in the Ponce de León.

11. Channing Blake, "The Early Interiors of Carrère and Hastings," *Antiques* (August 1976): 344–351.

Fig. 11. Venido Room ceiling.

Fig. 12. One of two huge panels of early Louis Comfort Tiffany glass that flank the stair landing outside the dining hall. Photograph by Ken Barrett Jr., 1993.

The central rotunda of the hotel was the point around which Carrère and Hastings had diagrammed the plans for their building. A north-south axis led from the front gate, through the rotunda, to the dining room. An east-west axis led to the two guest-room wings of the hotel. The symmetry was nearly perfect, an ideal of the École des Beaux-Arts.

From the rotunda guests ascended a flight of marble stairs to the dining room, again going through a low entry passage before entering the great vaulted hall. The height of the ceiling added to the perceived size of the hall proper, but two rows of columns divided the central hall from the semicircular Venido Rooms to the left and right. Maynard's paintings again covered the walls and ceilings (fig. 11).

The dining room, in contrast to the rotunda, was bright and airy, shining with gilt. Rows of clerestory windows pierced the vault, and the curved walls of the Venido Rooms were lined with huge windows. The stained-glass designs of all these windows were made by Louis Comfort Tiffany (1848–1933), who was just embarking on his labors in the art of glassmaking (fig. 12). Tiffany was described in Flagler's brochures as one of the interior decorators of the Ponce de León, but his specific contributions are not recorded.

Tiffany frequently said that the decorative arts employed in homes and public buildings played an essential role in educating public taste. His windows in the Hotel Ponce de León gave prominence to his artistry and certainly increased the popularity of Tiffany windows, but this very popularity also led to charges of commercialism. The windows embodied Classical themes befitting their setting, but soon Tiffany—perhaps stung by the criticism—ventured into fresh Art Nouveau compositions.

The vaulted ceiling of the dining hall carried two Maynard interpretations of the four seasons, Spanish galleons in full sail, the crests of Spanish kingdoms, and more proverbs (figs. 13 and 14).

The young architect Bernard Maybeck (1862–1957) was then an employee of Carrère and Hastings. Some historians claim to see his handiwork in the interiors, but there are no mentions of Maybeck in the scant existing documents

Fig. 13. Vaulted ceiling in the dining hall.

Fig. 14. George Maynard's mural and one of the dining hall's clerestory windows with the crest of Toledo.

relating to the hotel's construction. Hastings himself declared that he had attempted some of the interior decorating work "in the enthusiasm of youth." Consequently, separating the interior design work of Tiffany, Maybeck, and Hastings is an exercise in conjecture.[12]

Behind the dining hall stood the semi-detached utility wing of the hotel that housed the kitchen, servants' quarters, and workshops. To the rear of this was the boiler room with its Edison dynamos that generated electricity for the hotel.

Returning to the rotunda from the dining room, guests might turn left down one axis of the main hall to the writing room, billiard room, barber shop, or telegraph room. A turn to the right would lead to the grand parlor (fig. 15). This large, low-ceilinged, rectangular room was divided into three smaller spaces by two rows of arches.

The decor of the grand parlor was quite different from the rest of the building. The touch of the interior decorating company Pottier and Stymus seems evident. In contrast to the strong reds, golds, and browns of the rotunda and dining hall, the parlor radiated a more feminine ambiance: pastel carpets, cream-painted

12. Kenneth H. Cardwell, *Bernard Maybeck: Artisan, Architect, Artist* (Santa Barbara: Peregrine Smith, 1977), 21–25.

Fig. 17. New Hampshire painter Frank Shapleigh was among the artists at the Hotel Ponce de León. The concrete walls of the studios were covered with canvas.

Fig. 16. The cherubs painted by Virgillo Tojetti above one of the crystal chandeliers in the grand parlor.

walls, and crystal chandeliers.[13] The ceilings of the four corners of the parlor were covered with canvases painted by Virgillo Tojetti (1851–1901) in his New York studio, rolled up, shipped to St. Augustine, and pasted in place. The plump cherubs and doves portrayed in his paintings embodied a late-Victorian concept of youthfulness — a fitting theme in the land of the Fountain of Youth. Several optical illusions suggesting movement appeared to the observer intrigued enough to walk around the room with head uptilted (fig. 16).

An assortment of paintings by various artists hung on the walls of the parlor. Most notable was Joszi Arpád Koppay's series of eight portraits of Polish actress Helena Modjesha. In each one Modjesha was dressed for the role of a Shakespearean heroine.

The Hotel Ponce de León was host to the fine arts in one more way. At the very rear of the building, upstairs behind the boiler room, was a row of seven artists' studios occupied by painters who created souvenir paintings for guests of the hotel (fig. 17). Weekly receptions held by the artists provided a diversion for visitors.

Chief among this group of artists was Martin Johnson Heade (1819–1900), the New England landscape painter. In Florida Heade painted tropical flowers, hummingbirds, and glorious sunsets. Frank Shapleigh (1842–1906) stayed at the hotel in the winter and went north in the summer to paint landscapes in Crawford Notch, New Hampshire. Other artists in residence over the years included Felix de Crano, W. Staples Drown, George W. Seavey, and Robert S. German.

The Hotel Ponce de León's heyday and St. Augustine's moment of glory as the nation's leading winter resort were very brief because the Florida frontier was rapidly pushed south down the peninsula toward warmer latitudes. Flagler

13. For a discussion of the work of Pottier and Stymus, see David A. Hanks, "Pottier & Stymus Mfg. Co.: Artistic Furniture & Decorations," *Art & Antiques* (September–October 1982): 84–91.

Fig. 18. Hotel Alcázar, front view.

Fig. 19. Hotel Alcázar viewed

from the Hotel Ponce de León

loggia.

himself led the way, extending his Florida East Coast Railway to Palm Beach, Miami, and eventually Key West.

In the midst of his business triumphs, tragedy struck Flagler's personal life. During the 1890s Ida Alice Flagler went insane and, following prolonged medical treatments, Flagler had her committed to an asylum. In 1901 he divorced her and married Mary Lily Kenan, daughter of a prominent North Carolina family. Carrère and Hastings built Flagler's palatial Palm Beach home, Whitehall (1901), for the couple, where they spent the winters until 1913, when Flagler died there. His body was transported to St. Augustine and rested in state under the rotunda dome of the Hotel Ponce de León while last respects were paid. His remains were entombed in St. Augustine's Memorial Presbyterian Church (1890), another Carrère and Hastings creation standing near the hotel.

Meanwhile, the Hotel Ponce de León had become the dowager of the Flagler hotel chain. Although the Ponce was overshadowed by larger hotels in South Florida, Flagler never again constructed a hotel of its magnificent architectural standards.

As a support for the Hotel Ponce de León, Flagler built the Hotel Alcázar across the street (figs. 18 and 19). Carrère and Hastings designed the smaller Alcázar to complement its imposing neighbor. It opened in 1889, a year after the Ponce de León. The Alcázar would open each December and close in April, while the Ponce de León was open only from January through March. The Alcázar was lower priced and less formal than the Ponce de León (figs. 20 and 21).[14] Other Flagler hotels were richly ornamented, including the Breakers (1896)

14. Today it is the City Hall of St. Augustine and is home to the Lightner Museum, a collection of Victoriana.

Fig. 20. Hotel Ponce de León viewed from the Hotel Alcázar tower.

Fig. 21. The Hotel Ponce de León dominates the skyline of St. Augustine and serves as a beacon for visitors to America's oldest city.

Fig. 23. The Hotel Ponce de

León is now Flagler College.

Fig. 22. Grace Methodist

Church, 1888.

and Royal Poinciana (1894) in Palm Beach and the Royal Palm (1897) in Miami, but they were conventional wood-frame hotels.

The same work crews that built the Ponce de León and Alcázar also built Grace Methodist Church (1888), using the same materials. This compact structure is one of the most pleasing of Carrère and Hastings' conceptions (fig. 22).

Carrère and Hastings went on from their triumph in St. Augustine to design the Jefferson Hotel in Richmond, Virginia (1893–1895); the House and Senate Office Buildings in Washington, D.C. (1909); the New York Public Library (1902–1911); and many other public buildings and private homes.

Years later, in 1924, Hastings returned to St. Augustine for a visit. He told the local newspaper, "I feel like Rip Van Winkle." He was asked how the Hotel Ponce de León had stood the test of time and replied that if he had it to do over again, he would make few changes to the exterior but would like to alter some of the interior. "The dining room, however," he declared, "I think I would leave as it is."[15]

In April 1967 the Hotel Ponce de León closed its doors for the last time, and in September 1968 Flagler College began holding classes in the old artists' studios and housing students in the guest rooms. Since then Flagler College has completed a multimillion-dollar restoration of the hotel complex (fig. 23). Today students and tourists walk through the arched gate that once welcomed the Rockefellers and Vanderbilts (fig. 24). Already a decade into its second century, the building remains one of Florida's wonders. □

15. *St. Augustine Record*, 21 January 1924, 1.

Fig. 24. Statue of Henry M. Flagler in front of Flagler College, 1902.

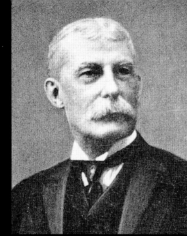

Fig. 1. Henry Bradley Plant. From

The Life of Henry Bradley Plant, by

G. Hutchinson Smyth, D. D. (New York: The

(nickerbocker Press, 1898), frontispiece

Fig. 2. Henry Morrison Flagler. From a post-

card, c. 1904.

Fig. 3. Henry Shelton Sanford, photograph,

1923. The Florida State Archives.

A Tale of Three Henrys

By Seth Bramson

Seth Bramson is the author of
Speedway to Sunshine:
The Story of the Florida East
Coast Railway (Erin, Ontario:
The Boston Mills Press, 1984).
He has significant collections
of Florida East Coast Railway
and Florida transportation
memorabilia and of Miami,
Miami Beach, Coral Gables,
and Dade County memorabilia.
He is a professor at Johnson
and Wales University, North
Miami, Florida.

The legendary head-to-head rivalries of the Morgans, the Goulds, and the Vanderbilts were great commercial competitions involving the building of railroads; they were not battles for supremacy in building cities and resorts, with accompanying transportation services to support those communities. While those rivalries have attained the status of folklore, the greatest rivalry in American railroad building and innkeeping occurred in Florida between two men who were cordial, if not friendly, and to a lesser extent, a third individual whose importance to Florida's commercial history has been generally overlooked. Each of these men would affect the area of the state that he was concerned with more than any other single individual and, by some quirk of fate, each of the three had the same first name — each was a "Henry."

Henry Bradley Plant (1819–1899) (fig. 1) and Henry Morrison Flagler (1830–1913) (fig. 2) were household names in their time — not to the extent of Fred Harvey (of the Harvey Houses) or George M. Pullman (the inventor of the sleeping car) — but certainly names of power and importance to the eastern half of the United States during the late nineteenth and early twentieth centuries. The least well known of the three men was Henry Shelton Sanford (1823–1891) (fig. 3).

The competition between Plant, the builder of Florida's west coast, and Flagler, the builder of the east coast, is an epic story of railroad building, hospitality operations, construction, public relations, tourism promotion, and development in a state that was little more than a place name on a map, inaccessible to the majority of Americans. However, it was unlike the rivalries in the Northeast and the West, which were battles for turf, right-of-way, mail contracts, and land grants — and which ultimately led to armed warfare between railroads and to large-scale financial frauds. The battle between Plant and Flagler was not one that required reaching a given locale first. Rather, it was a strong-spirited but good-natured competition, pitting the talents and the pocketbooks of the protagonists against each other. In this competition there was nary an unkind word, much less a threat, ever uttered, for neither the railroads nor the hotels nor the steamship companies competed in the same cities or served the same population.

Plant and Flagler shared the same goals — to open up Florida, get people to come, sell train tickets, book hotel rooms, and market land for living and for farming. Their competition was about prestige and about whether people would go to Plant's west coast and central Florida or to Flagler's east coast and the Florida Keys. It was about building more elaborate passenger cars, more elegant hotels, more powerful locomotives, more beautiful steamships (figs. 4, 5, and 6). From the establishment of Flagler's Hotel Ponce de León in

Images are from the Myrna and
Seth Bramson Collection, Miami,
Florida, except where noted.

Fig. 5. Florida East Coast Railway dining-car interior, c. 1928.

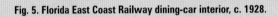

Fig. 4. Early Florida East Coast

Railway parlor car, c. 1898.

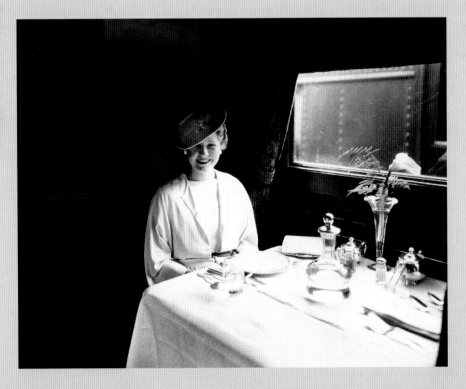

Fig. 6. Florida East Coast Railway dining-car interior, c. 1928.

Fig. 7. VirgilloTojetti's paintings, the Hotel Ponce de León's ballroom ceiling. From a postcard, c. 1904.

St. Augustine in early 1888 until Plant's death in mid-1899, the rivalry between these immensely wealthy gentlemen was unceasing.

Although neither G. Hutchinson Smyth's *The Life of Henry Bradley Plant* nor Sidney Walter Martin's *Florida's Flagler* pinpoints the beginnings of this competition, it is highly likely that its genesis was the opening of Flagler's Hotel Ponce de León (fig. 7).[1] On 10 January 1888, the first vestibuled, electrically lighted train ever to operate in the United States pulled into the St. Augustine depot.[2] Its passengers, invited guests of Flagler, were taken to the Hotel Ponce de León at dusk and saw, for the first time, the majestic hotel glimmering with electric lights. Those taking dinner with Mr. and Mrs. Flagler that evening were the hotel's architects, builders, artists, and several railroad executives, from Flagler's line and others.[3] Although the names of the railroad executives from the other roads are not available, it is likely that if Plant was not among them, then Plant's system passenger traffic manager, B. F. Wrenn, was.

Two days later, the hotel opened its doors to the public. The first grand ball was held in the large vaulted dining hall, with two orchestras playing in balconies at either end of the room. Among the hundreds of guests were Mrs. Ulysses S. Grant, widow of the former president, and Frederick Vanderbilt. Another ball held later in the season was attended by Standard Oil executive William R. Rockefeller.[4] As with the opening of any grand hotel, the initial seasons attracted higher levels of wealth and society, but at the Hotel Ponce de León, that attraction lasted for many years — during the hotel's first half-decade it was reputedly the most exclusive winter resort in the nation, and for well into the twentieth century it was considered a "must" stop on the winter social circuit. Then-future president Grover Cleveland paid a brief visit to the

1. G. Hutchinson Smyth, D. D., *The Life of Henry Bradley Plant* (New York: G. P. Putnam's Sons, 1898); Sidney Walter Martin, *Florida's Flagler* (Athens, Ga.: The University of Georgia Press, 1952).

2. Atlantic Coast Line Railroad brochure, "The New York and Florida Special/The First Electrically Lighted and Vestibuled Train in the World" (fall 1887), Myrna and Seth Bramson Collection.

3. Louise D. Castleden, ed., *The early years of the Ponce de Leon: Clippings from an old scrap book of those Days* (n.p., c. 1957), 30.

4. Ibid., 38–40; *St. Augustine News*, 4 March 1888.

THE PARLOR, TAMPA BAY HOTEL, TAMPA, FLA.

Fig. 8. The Tampa Bay Hotel

parlor. From a postcard,

c. 1910.

hotel only a month after its opening, and returned for four more visits, in 1893, 1899, 1903, and 1905.[5]

Plant, although busy building, buying, and consolidating his railroad interests while serving as president of the Southern Express Company, was observing the events on the east coast of Florida with great interest, if not a touch of envy. It became quite clear to Plant that having his own hotel—and eventually his own chain of hotels—would enable him to control the entire hospitality operation: to bring tourists to the west coast of Florida via the Plant System of Railways, transfer them to a Plant hotel, and arrange their tours to surrounding venues on boats owned and operated by the Plant Steamship Company.

Plant was determined that his hostelry be grander and more glamorous than Flagler's. The Tampa Bay Hotel, designed by New York City architect John Wood, opened on 6 February 1891 (fig. 8). The *New York Journal of Commerce* was effusive in its praise:

> It is not to be denied that this Tampa Bay Hotel is one of the modern wonders of the world. It is a product of the times. It illustrates the age, the demands of the people, what they enjoy, and what they are willing to pay for. Each work of art (of which there are hundreds and hundreds) is chosen by someone who has exercised taste of high order. The paintings are of extraordinary rank. The table porcelains are exquisite works of ceramic art. And just here, I may add, the cooking and the service are exceptionable. The table is of the very best class, and equal to that of any hotel in the world, including those of Mr. Flagler. This, too, is miraculous, in a new house at this remote point.[6]

An article in Boston's *Saturday Evening Gazette* was even more enthusiastic, calling it:

> the most original, most attractive, and most beautiful hotel in the south, if not in the whole country; and it is a hotel of which the whole world

5. Ibid., 59.

6. W. C. Prime, *New York Journal of Commerce*, 13 February 1891.

needs to be advised. It has one vase, which is the admiration and wonder of all who behold it, in the grand office rotunda, where ladies and gentlemen congregate at all hours of the day and evening. The entire estate, including land and building, cost two millions of dollars, and the furniture and fittings half a million more.

No one who does not see it and dwell in it for at least a day, can form the faintest idea of the comprehensiveness of its purpose, the breadth of its plan, the ideal refinement of its comforts, the noble scale of its luxuries. Nothing offends the eye or the taste at any point, and while the first view of the hotel exteriorly is impressive, the effect produced by a first glance on entering its broad and inviting portals is one of astonishment and delight.[7]

Flagler responded to the opening of the Tampa Bay Hotel by refurbishing the Hotel Ormond, in Ormond Beach, which he purchased in 1890, and by continuing to buy and build railroads along the east coast (fig. 9). But while the lengthening of the ribbons of steel down each coast was conducted in an almost tit-for-tat fashion, the most telling symbol in the years of one-upmanship was the most likely apocryphal story of two telegrams. For years, Plant aficionados bandied about the tale that Flagler, noting the growth of Tampa, sent a wire to Plant inquiring, "Where is Tampa?" Plant supposedly wired Flagler back the message, "Just follow the crowds." There are no such telegrams in the files of either the Henry B. Plant Library and Museum in Tampa or the Henry Morrison Flagler Museum in Palm Beach, but if such telegrams had been sent, most likely it would have been in the other direction, with Plant asking Flagler, following Miami's birth as a full-fledged city on 28 July 1896, "Where is Miami?"

While two of the three Henrys have survived in both fact and legend, and one of the two has become a prominent historic name, the third Henry, as important as his contributions were, has been given terribly short shrift. Henry S. Sanford deserves better.

An article about Sanford, Florida and the role of the Atlantic Coast Line Railroad in the city's development that appeared in the *Sanford Herald* on 28 October 1940, has the words "Forgotten History" as the first subhead. Considering the paucity of information available on Henry Sanford, that subhead has an eerie truthfulness.

According to the article, "The man to whom most thoughtful historians credit the discovery of Florida, in the modern sense, as a delightful place to live, especially in winter, and also its marvelous, untapped resources of soil and climate was General Henry S. Sanford."[8] Sanford, a Union Civil War general, served as President Grant's ambassador to Belgium. Sometime around 1870 he resigned as ambassador and moved to Lake Monroe, near present-day Sanford, and started growing oranges.[9] However, Sanford remained close to Grant. The *Sanford Herald* article also stated that "General Sanford's greatest service to Florida was getting President Grant to visit Sanford, during which visit trips were made to various points, including Silver Springs."[10]

Fig. 9. Menu from the Ormond Hotel, Ormond Beach, for 28 February 1892.

7. Henry Parker, *Boston Saturday Evening Gazette*, February 1891.

8. "Sanford, Florida and the Atlantic Coast Line Railroad," *Sanford Herald*, 28 October 1940, 8.

9. Sidney Lanier, *Florida: Its Scenery, Climate and History* (Philadelphia: J. B. Lippincott and Company, 1876), 130.

10. "Sanford, Florida and the Atlantic Coast Line Railroad," 8.

Fig. 10. South Florida Railroad Station, Sanford, Florida. Photograph by Stanley J. Morrow, 1883. Florida State Archives.

Fig. 11. Sanford House Hotel, Sanford, Florida. Photograph by Stanley J. Morrow, 1886. Florida State Archives.

In his 1873 book, *Florida, Its Scenery, Climate, and History*, the Georgia poet and writer Sidney Lanier noted that Henry Sanford, whose lands adjoined William Astor's, would eventually incorporate the then-thriving town of Mellonville into what was to become the town and then the city of Sanford. Once the amalgamation was complete, according to Lanier, it would be Sanford who would bring a flourishing Swedish colony to the area. Lanier further noted that "in Sanford there is a money-order post office, a sanitarium, and the Orona Hotel."[11]

Mellonville, on the site of the former army post known as Fort Mellon, had a landing for the St. Johns River steamboats only two miles south of Sanford's landing on Lake Monroe. Prior to Grant's visit, Sanford had apparently decided to merge the two locales into one entity to be known as Sanford. Knowing that Grant had a desire to visit Florida and the South, Sanford orchestrated a visit that would center on Sanford, the community. Though the trip was to originate in Savannah and proceed to Fernandina and then to Jacksonville, Palatka, and Enterprise, Sanford made sure that Grant's most important activity would take place in Sanford.

On 10 January 1880 the two generals attended the ground-breaking ceremony, at Sanford, for the South Florida Railroad, which was to run from the St. Johns River to Charlotte Harbor on the Gulf of Mexico (fig. 10). Grant turned over the first spadeful of earth.[12] Henry Sanford was joyful over the positive publicity the event engendered. Not only had the beloved former president visited Florida, but he had come to Sanford to perform an important commercial function, and that function was the central theme of the ensuing publicity. The reputation of the town was enhanced and growth began almost immediately.

Henry Sanford was both host and fervent promoter for the town. Through his efforts the facilities on Lake Monroe were improved so dramatically that, in time, three steamship companies—Baya's, Clyde, and the DeBary lines—all offered St. Johns River service to the town.

Henry Sanford was active in several spheres: he was a land developer and tireless booster of central Florida, particularly the Sanford area; he was a farmer and produce-shipper, and advertised the availability of farmland at modest cost to homeseekers and others interested in pursuing the production of citrus and truck in Florida; he invested in the railroads of central Florida; and, finally, he built and operated the Sanford House Hotel (fig.11), which was proclaimed to be "the most attractive tourist hotel in the state."[13]

While Henry Sanford was building a mini-empire in central Florida, Henry Plant was busy building an even larger empire that eventually consolidated a group of railroads into the Savannah, Florida and Western Railway, also known as the Plant System of Railways. In addition, he built and operated steamships in Florida and New England and became the largest hotelier on Florida's west coast. According to one early treatise, Plant's career "has known no failure, and his business sagacity has been crowned with success."[14]

11. Lanier, *Florida*, 130–131.

12. Edward Mueller, *Steamboating on the St. Johns* (Melbourne, Fla.: Kellersberger Fund, South Brevard Historical Society, 2nd ed., 1984), 78.

13. "Sanford, Florida and the Atlantic Coast Line Railroad," 8.

14. Judge Joseph Tillman, *Compendium of Reliable Facts of the Plant System of Railways and Steamship Lines* (Savannah: The Morning News Print, 1895), 4.

Born in Branford, Connecticut in 1819, Plant began his business life working on the steamboats that operated from New England into and through the Long Island Sound. The origins of his fortune, however, can be traced to his employment with several parcel express companies, which moved packages by either stage or rail, in either contract service or on their own buckboards, utilizing water transport when necessary.

In 1853 Plant was named superintendent of the southern division of the Harnden Express Company, which forwarded express mail and goods from New York to the South. It was about this time that the Adams Express Company was organized and acquired a number of express companies, including Harnden. Alvin Adams, of Boston, was the chief shareholder. In 1854, following the consolidation, Plant was named superintendent of Adams Express. He was placed in charge of the interests then controlled by Adams Express and all that might be acquired by the company in the South under his management or through his efforts.[15] During Plant's administration the lines were extended throughout the South so that many of the railroads of the region would be affiliated with Adams Express and would transport packages for that company.

By 1860 Plant was convinced that war between the states was inevitable. Adams Express, believing it would be hazardous for Northern citizens to hold property in the South, decided to dispose of its interests there. After unsuccessful negotiations with other parties, the company transferred their entire interest in the express operations throughout the South to Plant, for a series of long-term notes. Plant then formed a corporation under the laws of Georgia, called it the Southern Express Company, and served as president of that company from 1861 until his death. The offices were established in Augusta, Georgia, and it was there that Plant made his home.

Plant operated the Southern Express Company efficiently, and its profits enabled him to expand his horizons. In 1879, with partners, he purchased the Atlantic and Gulf Railroad of Georgia, reorganized it as the Savannah, Florida and Western Railway, and became president of the line (fig. 12). Obviously, express services on the Savannah, Florida and Western were operated solely by Southern Express Company.[16]

The Savannah, Florida and Western actually originated in Charleston, South Carolina. Much as Flagler was to do, Plant bought and built the lines of railroad as needed. In 1885 the southern terminus of the Plant System of Railways was established in Tampa when the city was barely more than a village, with a population of less than one thousand. The South Florida Railroad was one of the best-equipped railways in the South, extending 124 miles from Sanford to Port Tampa.[17] The Plant System of Railways would eventually stretch from Charleston and Savannah through Waycross, Georgia to Montgomery, Alabama, but the great majority of the system's mileage was in Florida.

The Florida lines reached as far west as Live Oak and High Springs but did not extend to Tallahassee or the Florida Panhandle. The lines did, however, blanket much of central and west-coast Florida, operating into or through Palatka, Sanford, Bartow, Lakeland, Tampa, and Punta Gorda. Eventually, the

15. Smyth, *The Life of Henry Bradley Plant*, 52.
16. Tillman, *Compendium of Facts of the Plant System*, 4.
17. Smyth, *The Life of Henry Bradley Plant*, 77.

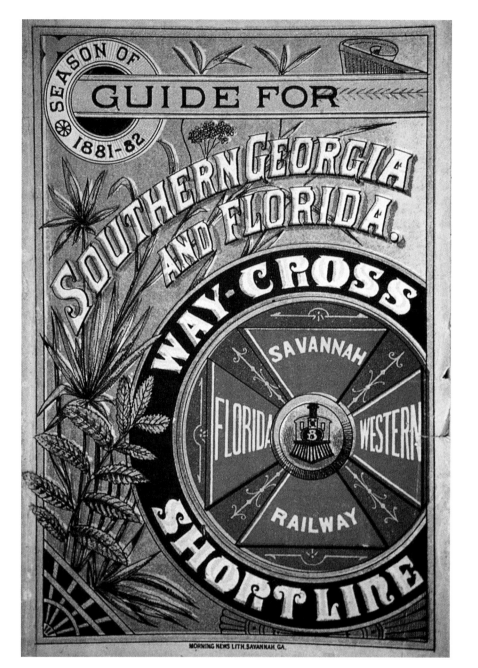

Fig. 12. An early Savannah, Florida and Western Railway (Plant System) brochure cover, 1881–1882.

Plant System would grow to twenty-two hundred miles of railroad. The primary Florida components of the company included the South Florida Railroad, the St. Cloud Sugar Belt Railway, the Silver Springs, Ocala and Gulf Railroad, the Tampa and Thonotasassa Railroad, the Florida Midland Railway, Barr's Tram (a twenty-seven-mile logging railroad), the Winston and Bone Valley Railroad, the Sanford and St. Petersburg Railroad, and part of the Jacksonville, Tampa and Key West System, among others.

Integrating the various railroads into a cohesive system was done with relative ease. The greatest difficulty was standardizing the track, stations, and equipment. Several of the railroads originally were built as narrow-gauge lines and had to be widened to the standard gauge of four feet, eight and one-half inches. The

Fig. 13. Port Tampa, showing the Port Tampa Inn and the Port Tampa depot. From a postcard, c. 1906.

freight and passenger equipment, made of wood, had to be brought up to an acceptable level of quality for a first-class system.

Passenger cars, some as short as thirty feet long, were either lengthened or scrapped. Sleeping-car and dining-car services were operated by the Pullman Company. To provide genuine first-class service, all car interiors were remodeled, and the coaches fitted with plush mohair seats and Pintsch gas lamps, replacing the old wood stoves. An 1889 Plant System brochure referred to the new cars as being as "beautiful as they are comfortable." Freight cars also were brought up to acceptable interchange standards. Underframes were strengthened and new refrigerator cars, with ice providing the cooling element, were built and placed in special fast freight-train service between Florida and the Northeast. Stations presented another set of issues. The railroad had inherited several types and styles of stations from many different lines, and it was necessary to modernize while being cost-effective. Although the architecture of many of the stations was unique, eventually most of them were demolished.

Recognizing that rail transport would be successful only if combined with steamship services, Plant began to plan a series of steamship operations. In 1886 the Plant Steamship Line was organized, and a vast deep-sea terminal was constructed at Port Tampa, which is still in use today (fig. 13).[18] With Port Tampa as the base of his steamship operations, Plant then connected the port to the city of Tampa by rail and inaugurated steamship service from Port Tampa to Key West, Florida; Havana, Cuba; Mobile, Alabama; and the West Indies, in addition to providing local service to coastal points south of Tampa.[19]

In starting his new steamship line, Plant decided that it would be best to build his own ships. The William Cramp and Sons Company of Philadelphia received a contract from Plant for a new vessel to be constructed for operation between Tampa, Key West, and Havana. Plant obtained the United States mail contract for the route and a new iron-screw steamer was ready for service for the 1886 winter season.

18. Richard Prince, *Atlantic Coast Line Railroad* (Green River, Wyo.: privately published, 1966), 21.
19. Ibid.

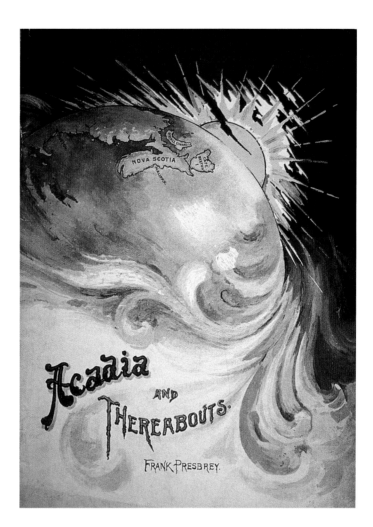

Fig. 14. Plant System booklet cover, 1896.

The new ship, *Mascotte*, was 215 feet long and thirty feet wide, with a twelve-foot depth of hold. Its one-thousand-horsepower engine was of the triple-expansion compound type, and it had a capability of steaming at not less than fifteen knots for twenty-four consecutive hours and carrying fifty first-class passengers. On 27 October 1885 the *Mascotte* was launched.[20]

The *Tampa Tribune* published a glowing report of the *Mascotte*, describing it as "one of the most handsome and complete steamships of the sea, its appointments being in every respect really luxurious while in point of seaworthiness it is everything that the most expert mechanism could make it. Its staterooms are as dainty as boudoirs while its saloon is exquisitely fitted up as any drawing room."[21] Public response to the Tampa-Key West service was so favorable that Plant ordered another vessel from the Cramp Company. At 291 feet the *Olivette* could carry 150 first-class and 125 second-class passengers.

The ships headed north in the spring to serve the Plant System on what was known as the Acadian routes, which shuttled between Boston, Massachusetts and Bar Harbor and Eastport, Maine, with additional service to Canada (fig. 14). By 1891 the service included seven ships, some owned and some leased.

20. Edward A. Mueller, *Steamships of the Two Henrys* (DeLeon Springs, Fla.: E. O. Painter Printing Company, 1996), 22–23.
21. Ibid., 23–24.

In 1893 Plant chartered the *Halifax* from the Canadian Atlantic Line for a few winter trips to Nassau and Jamaica. On one such ten-day excursion, beginning 16 February, guests included Mr. and Mrs. Henry Flagler. Just prior to that, the Plants had returned from a trip with the Flaglers to Rockledge, on Florida's east coast. Although at times they differed greatly, each man understood the business of making money and of respecting the other's territory. While no one knows the exact details of the business matters discussed or the agreements reached on these two trips, it seems likely that fundamental and far-reaching decisions regarding both hotel operations and steamship consolidations were made.

Shortly after the two Plant-Flagler sojourns, Plant began to focus on adding another hotel facility to the then-single property operation that consisted of the Tampa Bay Hotel. After well over a year of researching and site-seeking, he chose Belleair, Florida, in upper Pinellas County, as the next site. The Belleview was designed by Michael J. Miller and Francis J. Kennard, and construction began in 1895. With its opening on 15 January 1897, it became a millionaires' playground. Plant's nephew, C. E. Hoadley, oversaw the project and supervised considerable expansion over the years. Although Plant provided a six-hole golf course on the premises, it was his son, Morton, who expanded the facility after his father's death and brought the hotel to the status of a nationally renowned resort.[22]

Eventually, the Plant System of Hotels consisted of eight properties: The Tampa Bay Hotel in downtown Tampa; the Inn at Port Tampa; the Belleview at Belleair; the Punta Gorda Hotel; the Fort Myers Hotel; the Ocala House; the Seminole Hotel in Winter Park; and the Hotel Kissimmee.

With the exception of the Tampa Bay Hotel, all of the hotels primarily were of wooden construction, and most had verandahs either encircling the building or on the front and sides. They were massive in size — not necessarily in terms of capacity but in relation to their surroundings. In terms of capacity, the Tampa Bay Hotel could accommodate 700 guests; the Inn at Port Tampa, 130; the Belleview, 300; the Ocala House and the Punta Gorda Hotel, 250 each; the Seminole, 250; and the Hotel Kissimmee, 150. The only relatively small property was the Fort Myers Hotel, accommodating a mere 50 persons.[23]

Most of the hotels were to meet their fate at the hands of either fires or the wreckers, but two have survived, and the Belleview remains a resort hotel. The Tampa Bay Hotel, magnificent as it was, never achieved the potential Plant envisioned. In 1905 the city of Tampa, for the even-then modest sum of $125,000, acquired the hotel and its property and continued its operation. However, the city's interest waned when it lost money, and in 1920 the building was leased to W. F. Adams, who was successful with the hotel during the great Florida real estate boom of the 1920s. In 1933 the city of Tampa gave the hotel to the University of Tampa, which was then making the transition from a two-year to a four-year institution.

Much of the success of the Plant System was — as Flagler's would be — a result of unstinting advertising and promotional efforts. While the bulk of the Flagler System's printing was done in Florida by the Record Press in St. Augustine, the

---

22. Ibid., 28–29.

23. Plant System of Railways booklet, "Directory of Principal Hotels and Boarding Houses along the Plant System of Railways 1900–01," Myrna and Seth Bramson Collection.

left,

Fig. 15. Plant System map,

front cover, c. 1897.

right,

Fig. 16. Plant System map,

back cover, c. 1897.

bulk of Plant's was done in Buffalo, New York, by the Matthews-Northrup Company, which printed timetables and brochures for a number of railroads including the New York Central System. As with most promotional printing of the day, scrollwork and flourishes were plentiful, and fine-line etchings and engravings were consistent with verbiage that was elegant and descriptive. These characteristics were evident in all of Plant's public promotional material. Prominent on all passenger-directed material of the railroad system, the steamship company, and the guest-directed material of the hotel company were Plant's name, as president, and the words, "The Plant System," with one word above the other in a large iron cross (figs. 15 and 16).

Despite Plant's accomplishments, ultimately he was overshadowed by the third of the three Henrys. The story of Henry Flagler, the subject of three books and numerous articles, is comparatively well known. Born in Hopewell, New York, in 1830, he worked his way west, becoming involved in both whole-sale and retail businesses ranging from mercantile goods to salt to petroleum. Eventually he became the treasurer of the Cleveland-based petroleum firm Rockefeller, Andrews, and Flagler, which became The Standard Oil Company. In 1883 Flagler retired from Standard Oil. He was fifty-three years old and a man of immense wealth. He dedicated his remaining thirty years to the development of the east coast of Florida, and in so doing earned the sobriquet "Florida's Empire Builder."

How was it that Flagler became synonymous with Florida? How, when Plant built and bought far more railroad mileage than Flagler, did Flagler become one of the most important names in Florida's history? Much of the answer lies

left,

Fig. 17. Florida East Coast

brochure, front cover,

1912–1913, depicting

Henry M. Flagler and

Mary Lily Kenan Flagler.

right,

Fig. 18. Florida East Coast

brochure, back cover,

1912–1913.

in their ages: Flagler was, by eleven years, simply younger than Plant. Although Flagler was only three years older when he died than Plant was when he died, the years from Plant's death in 1899 to Flagler's death in 1913 were crucial to both the level of recognition Flagler was to receive and the completion of the tasks he undertook (figs. 17 and 18).

Had Plant lived, had his son, Morton, and his widow, Margaret, not broken up his system of railroads, steamships, express company, and hotels, it is conceivable that the Plant name would have been better known. But that is conjecture. The fact is, Flagler lived until 1913 and in so doing, completed the building of the greatest single railroad construction feat in United States (and, perhaps, world) history. Flagler, Florida, and the Key West Extension are linked inextricably.

When Flagler first visited St. Augustine, in 1878, he was smitten with the town's scenic beauty and climate. In terms of climate, north Florida is substantially different today than in Flagler's time. In the last two decades of the nineteenth century, the citrus belt began just south of Jacksonville, in the town now called Orange Park, in Clay County. St. Augustine's winter temperatures in those days were minimally lower than Dade County's average temperatures today.

But Flagler was dismayed to find a lack of decent lodging in St. Augustine, then a small sleepy town. He decided to create an atmosphere of elegance and comfort for himself and his friends and associates, who were people with such names as Rockefeller, Stuyvesant, Astor, Clinton, Morgan, and Gould. Neither they nor he would deign to stay in any hostelry that was short of palatial for anything other than a very brief visit.

Flagler decided to build the most glorious hotel that Florida — and possibly the nation — had ever seen. Basing his concept on a St. Augustine mansion known as Villa Zorayda, owned by Franklin W. Smith, Flagler commissioned the young architectural team of John M. Carrère (1858–1911) and Thomas Hastings (1860–1929) to prepare plans for the Hotel Ponce de León. In the summer of 1885 the site was prepared by dumping tons of sand and driving in hundreds of pine pilings into the marshes just outside of the early Spanish fortifications.[24] When it was completed, in 1887, the Hotel Ponce de León was the first major building in the United States constructed of poured concrete. Recent engineering studies have shown it to be in perfectly sound condition.[25]

While the Hotel Ponce de León was under construction, Flagler learned that his crews were having difficulty getting various building materials. He asked his contractors, John McDonald and James McGuire, to explain the reason for the delays. The answer was that the rickety, little, narrow-gauge railroad used to transport the construction material was in such poor condition that breakdowns were frequent and delays nearly interminable. Was it possible, they asked, for Flagler to intercede?

After repeated entreaties to the owners of the line proved useless, Flagler lost patience. On 31 December 1885 he purchased the tracks, ties, right-of-way, and all assets of the Jacksonville, St. Augustine, and Halifax River Railroad (JStA&HR). Flagler was in the railroad business, and upgrading the line was an immediate priority.

Meanwhile, Flagler realized that the Hotel Ponce de León, because of its sheer size and projected rate structure, might not appeal to those guests who, though they had the funds to travel, would not be able to afford to stay in so elegant a hotel. He again moved quickly, commissioning the construction of the Hotel Alcázar across the street, also designed by Carrère and Hastings. Both hotels opened in 1888, just a few months apart. Many people chose the Alcázar, and not necessarily because it was less expensive. Most of the guests of the Alcázar simply found it to be a warmer, less formal environment.

While the Alcázar and the Ponce de León were under construction, so too was the Casa Monica Hotel, a Spanish-Moorish-style property located immediately east of the Alcázar and diagonally southeast of the Ponce de León. Flagler purchased the Casa Monica Hotel in 1889 and changed its name to the Cordova.

Some miles down the coast from St. Augustine, two young men, John Anderson and Joseph Price, had grandiose plans for a clearing called Ormond Beach. They erected the wooden Ormond Hotel, which opened on 1 January 1888. Flagler, though noting the opening, was unconcerned. Although the railroad had reached Ormond Beach in 1886, the route, unlike that to St. Augustine, was circuitous, and the service undependable. Flagler had no plans to either go further south through railroad ownership or to build or buy additional hotels.

By the end of the 1889 season, Anderson and Price were on the verge of financial ruin. In a state of near-desperation, they knew that Flagler was their only hope. After considering their request, Flagler went to Ormond Beach for a personal look. He told Anderson and Price that not only would he purchase and upgrade the railroad to Ormond Beach, tying it into his own system, but he would buy the hotel from them, if — and only if — they would remain to manage it. Flagler also promised to build a spur from the main line of the

24. Thomas Graham, "Flagler's Magnificent Hotel Ponce de Leon," *Florida Historical Quarterly* 54 (July 1975): 8.
25. Ibid.

A 15363 Colonnade, Hotel Royal Poinciana, Palm Beach, Fla.

Fig. 19. The Royal Poinciana Hotel, Palm Beach, Florida. From a postcard, c. 1910–1912.

railroad directly to the hotel, and to operate trains and through cars to the hotel in the winter season. He offered Anderson and Price $112,000 for their interests in the Ormond Hotel, which they accepted, so by 1890 Flagler's "chain" was up to four hotels.

Under Flagler's ownership, wings were added to the Ormond Hotel, and a swimming pool, casino, dormitory, laundry, beach pavilion, and pier were built. The Otis Elevator Company installed three hydraulic elevators, one in each wing. The elevators were finished in dark wood with a large portion of the sides covered by mirror bordered with iron-grille work. Along the back walls of each elevator was a leather-covered bench. Passengers could arrive at the hotel either by train or by a mule-drawn tram car that operated on the same rails, similar to the car later used at Palm Beach between the Breakers and the Royal Poinciana hotels. The mule car ran on a regular schedule, connected with all trains, and transported passengers only; baggage was brought to the hotel on a two-mule dray operating on the adjacent road.[26]

By this time both railroads and hotels were in Flagler's blood, and he was hearing tales of a magnificent undeveloped spit of land, an island known as Palm Beach that was just off the southeast coast. A trip by boat brought Flagler to the island, and that visit convinced him that it was his destiny to develop Palm Beach. He extended the railroad south and bought the small, unpretentious inn on the island. In addition, he built a hotel, which was the largest wooden hotel in the world.

In May 1893 Flagler's forces broke ground for the Royal Poinciana, designed and built by his St. Augustine contractors, McDonald and McGuire (figs. 19 and 20). The railroad, renamed the Jacksonville, St. Augustine, and Indian River Railway (JStA&IR), reached West Palm Beach on 22 March 1894, with regular service beginning on 2 April. Construction of the bridge across Lake Worth, connecting the island to the mainland, began in June of 1895, and regular train service commenced on 12 November 1895. Two months and three days earlier, on 9 September 1895, the name of the JStA&IR was changed to Florida East Coast Railway (FEC), the name still retained by the company today.

26. Marian M. Hartshorn, *The Story of the Ormond Hotel* (Daytona Beach: Burgman and Son, 1962).

Fig. 20. The Garden Grill room of the Royal Poinciana Hotel, Palm Beach, Florida. From a postcard, c. 1910–1912.

Before Flagler's arrival, Palm Beach was little more than a tree- and shrub-covered island with dirt lanes and a handful of small houses. But when Flagler bought the McCormick property for $75,000 and announced that he intended to construct a great hotel, everything changed. Overnight, land values jumped from $150 to $1,000 an acre, people flocked in, and a land boom was soon in full swing. Work on the hotel began 1 May, and men and material arrived daily. Shacks and tents and boarding houses were erected and rents skyrocketed. Before long there were more than one thousand men and women in the camp.[27]

The Royal Poinciana Hotel opened on 11 February 1894. Constructing it had been a herculean task, since every piece of building material had to be transported by river from Eau Gallie, the then-terminus of the railroad, to Jupiter. Each item was then transferred to the Jupiter and Lake Worth Railway (called the Celestial Railroad because it stopped at Jupiter, Juno, Venus, and Mars) for transportation eight miles to Juno and then down the lake to the building site. The hotel contained 540 bedrooms and a one-thousand-seat dining room. As magnificent as the hotel was, Flagler was not yet satisfied—the Royal Poinciana was too far from the ocean. He decided to build another hotel directly on the ocean, immediately east of the Royal Poinciana. The Palm Beach Inn, also built by McDonald and McGuire, opened for guests late in 1895. It connected to the Royal Poinciana by railroad tracks that, in addition to through trains and private railroad cars, saw regular operation by another of the Flagler System's mule cars.[28] In 1903 the name of the Palm Beach Inn was changed to the Breakers. A disastrous fire later that year reduced the hotel to ashes. Upon learning of the disaster, Flagler advised McDonald and McGuire to put up a new hotel as quickly as possible.

In Palm Beach Flagler built a marble mansion, Whitehall, for his third wife, Mary Lily Kenan, also designed by Carrère and Hastings (fig. 21). When she expressed dismay over its proximity to the FEC Railway bridge across Lake Worth, Flagler demolished the old bridge and built a new bridge just north of

27. J. W. Travers, *History of Beautiful Palm Beach* (West Palm Beach: Palm Beach Press, 1928), 24–25.
28. Ibid., 25.

Palm Beach, Fla., H. M. Flagler's Residence

Fig. 21. Flagler's Palm Beach mansion, Whitehall. From a postcard, c. 1910.

the Royal Poinciana grounds, putting a new station and additional private railroad car parking tracks in place at both hotels. The old trackage on Palm Beach, however, was retained, and until the second Breakers fire, in 1925, the mule car continued to trundle its way across the island, delighting photographers and children (figs. 22 and 23).

In the early Flagler days Palm Beach was home to three major commercial buildings: the Royal Poinciana, expanded to 1,150 rooms; the Breakers; and Colonel E. R. Bradley's Beach Club, the most exclusive gambling establishment in the United States. The Royal Poinciana, and later the Breakers, established the basis for Palm Beach social life.

Many seasonal vacationers came to Palm Beach in their own private railroad cars. During a single season, as many as one hundred private cars would arrive in Palm Beach and be shunted about by the FEC's steam-switch engines to the proper tracks near either the Royal Poinciana or the Breakers. Sometimes, at the height of a winter season, as many as sixty cars would crowd the private car tracks. Owners had large suites in the hotels and their servants lived in the cars. Among the guests listed in a 1903 guest register of the Royal Poinciana were August Belmont, the Duke and Duchess of Manchester, Harold S. Vanderbilt, Mrs. Oliver H. P. Belmont, Countess Boni de Castellane, Colonel John Jacob Astor (he would perish in the Titanic disaster), Mrs. George Jay Gould, and Charles D. ("Bet-a-Million") Gates.

A typical Palm Beach day included breakfasting in the Royal Poinciana's dining room, then walking, taking the mule car, or riding an Afromobile to the Breakers' bathing casino, which was open to both Royal Poinciana and Breakers guests. The combined orchestras of the two hotels serenaded the guests until they went for lunch, followed by a visit with friends on the verandah and then, perhaps, nine holes on the Flagler System golf course, located between the two hotels. After golf, tea was served, followed later by dinner, accompanied by Signor Migionico's orchestra, which played discreetly in the background, hidden behind a palm facade.[29]

29. Theodore Pratt, *That was Palm Beach* (St. Petersburg: Great Outdoors Publishing, 1968), 32–33.

Fig. 22. The Breakers, Palm Beach, Florida, prior to the 1925 fire. From a postcard, c. 1919.

Photo. only, Copyright 1904 by the Rotograph Co.
G 15318 The Breakers, Palm Beach, Fla.

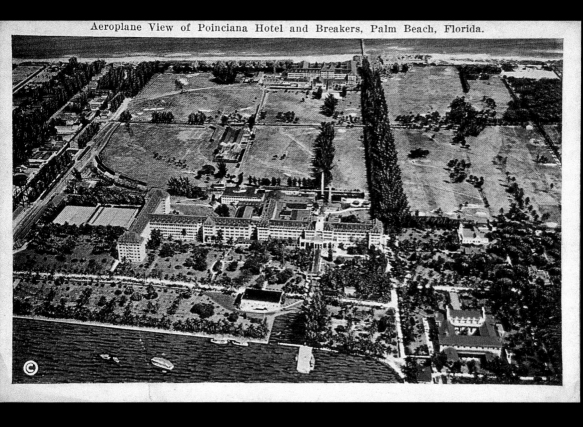

Aeroplane View of Poinciana Hotel and Breakers, Palm Beach, Florida.

Fig. 23. Aerial view of Palm Beach showing Whitehall at lower right, the Royal Poinciana hotel, lower center, and the Breakers in the distance. From a postcard, c. 1924.

Content with his accomplishments, Flagler's plan was to relax. Fate, however, had other ideas, which involved a tiny community on the shores of Biscayne Bay, sixty miles south of Palm Beach. Flagler's greatest challenges and triumphs were yet to come.

Julia Tuttle moved to Miami from Ohio in 1891. She had met Flagler on several occasions. Her father, a Sturdevant, previously had established a homestead on the Miami River. Tuttle had tremendous faith in the future of this minuscule settlement at the mouth of the Miami River, and she continually preached the virtues of its soil and weather. She repeatedly had beseeched both Plant and Flagler to extend their railroads to the shores of Biscayne Bay. Each time, however, her pleas were met with polite, but absolutely unqualified, refusals.

Then came the winter of 1894–1895, one of the most disastrous winters in recorded Florida history. The great freezes of December 1894 and January and February 1895 destroyed the entire citrus crop as far south as Palm Beach. But the region below the New River was virtually untouched by winter's scathing blasts. Tuttle rushed into action, writing and wiring Flagler, asking him to "come down and see that we are untouched by the recent hard freezes."[30] Because Flagler had reached West Palm Beach, Tuttle knew that the railroad would need to be extended only sixty miles to reach her settlement, whereas Plant would be faced with the daunting task of attempting to cross the Everglades, a route that would require at least 150 miles of track building from the southernmost point of Plant's rails. Tuttle sent Flagler several gifts, including fresh citrus flowers, citrus, and produce. Sending the agricultural products, she reasoned, would prove to Flagler that the region surrounding Biscayne Bay would be ideal for agricultural development, necessitating a railroad to haul out all that high-tariff tonnage.[31]

Flagler, though interested, was busy with other matters, and he assigned James E. Ingraham to evaluate the situation. Prior to joining Flagler, Ingraham was vice president of several of Plant's railroads, and apparently had met Tuttle previously. By boat to the New River, and by stage from there, Ingraham travelled from Palm Beach to investigate. He found the area was indeed untouched by the great freezes.

On 27 December 1895 Flagler wrote to the president of the Lehigh Valley Railroad. "I sincerely hope," the letter said, "that you will make us a visit during the winter." But it is the offhand manner in which he phrased the next three sentences that makes one truly cognizant of Flagler's magnitude. "I am extending the railroad to Biscayne Bay," he wrote. "It is under contract to be completed Feb. 1st, but like many such enterprises may be delayed ten to fifteen days. Fla. is very beautiful at this season of the year."[32]

On 15 April 1896, fulfilling an agreement Flagler made with Julia Tuttle and William Brickell involving donations of land to the railroad in exchange for the track being extended to the Miami River, the first train arrived at what eventually would become Florida's largest city. One week later passenger service began.

30. Ruby Leach Carson, "Miami 1896–1900," *Tequesta* 16 (1956): 5.

31. Seth H. Bramson, *Speedway to Sunshine: The Story of the Florida East Coast Railway* (Erin, Ontario: The Boston Mills Press, 1984), 27.

32. Henry Morrison Flagler, letter to E. P. Wilbur, 27 December 1895, Myrna and Seth Bramson Collection.

AEROPLANE VIEW, ROYAL PALM HOTEL AND MIAMI RIVER
MIAMI, FLA.

Even before the railroad arrived, the same air of excitement that affected Palm Beach took hold in Miami. People poured in, setting up homesteads in tents or throwing together flimsy dwellings from any type of wood or scrap lumber available. Three months after the arrival of the first train, on 28 July 1896, a large majority of Miami's 512 registered voters favorably approved the creation of the city of Miami. Without ever having been a village, a town, or an incorporated legal entity, Miami sprang into existence. As part of his promise to Tuttle and Brickell, Flagler constructed one of his great hotels. The Royal Palm Hotel held its grand opening ball on New Year's Eve 1896, and officially received guests in early 1897 (fig. 24). The hotel was the epicenter of Miami's social scene until it closed following the 1926 hurricane. The Royal Palm Hotel was so important to the community that the swimming pool was kept open all summer so that Miami's residents would have a place to bathe off-season.

Publicizing Miami was not difficult. Flagler's people already had coined the phrase, "The American Riviera," and Flagler System booklets and brochures bore the legend, "The East Coast of Florida is Paradise Regained," printed in a belt circling an aerial view of the state, with the sun shining out of the clouds on the east coast. It was not long before Miami became, according to the Flagler System, "The Magic City."

Growth was meteoric and eventually Miami became everyman's dream destination. Flagler's contractors, McDonald and McGuire, not only built the Royal Palm Hotel but oversaw construction of other Flagler buildings, including homes for those who took advantage of the opportunities afforded by the Flagler System's advertisements in innumerable publications, including its own, the *Florida East Coast Homeseeker*. Florida land—particularly South Florida land, and specifically Flagler properties—were not just homes or farm sites, but investments.

In conjunction with the Atlantic Coast Line, the FEC blanketed the Northeast and the Midwest with advertising for the hotels, railroad, and land companies (figs. 25 and 26). To encourage vacationers, the two railroads even opened the ACL-FEC Hunting and Fishing Bureau inside their New York City ticket office on West 45th Street.

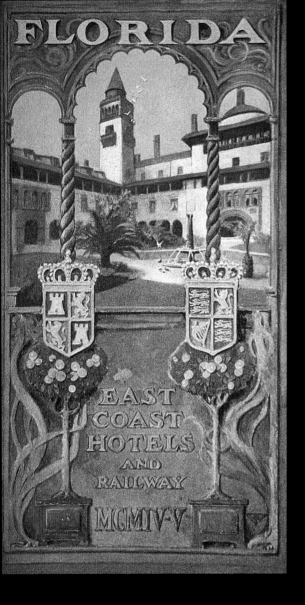

Fig. 25. Florida East Coast Hotels and Railway descriptive booklet, front cover, 1904–1905. Illustration depicts the courtyard of the Hotel Ponce de León.

Fig. 26. Florida East Coast Railway and Hotels descriptive booklet, front cover, 1905–1906.

Fig. 27. The Florida East Coast depot at Salerno was typical of the "flag-stop"-style stations erected at small locales, c. 1917.

Flagler's employees barely were able to keep up with him. He was intent on being apprised of each important detail in his various operations. Matters such as what passenger and freight equipment to purchase, which engines to buy, and where to locate stations were of interest to him. His vice presidents, particularly James E. Ingraham and J. R. Parrott, met with him regularly and corresponded with him voluminously. Under Flagler's domain everything was of the highest quality. Technological advances, such as vestibules, tight-lock couplers, air brakes, and improved telegraphy methods were incorporated. Passenger cars, service, and accommodations received his attention; he even reviewed excursion fares.

As soon as a town was large enough to warrant a station, one was built (fig. 27). Stations were of standard design and specifications, and it would only be years later that custom designs for stations were approved at places like Titusville, Boca Raton, and Daytona Beach. During Flagler's lifetime, all stations except the Union Depot in Jacksonville (fig. 28) were built of wood, with restrooms and waiting rooms for African-American and white passengers separated from each other, generally by the ticket office in the middle of the building (fig. 29).

Most of the stations were built pre-1920, before travel by road became popular. At that time, the depot was the center of town. The east coast of Florida has many prime examples—from Jacksonville to Daytona to West Palm Beach to Miami, the station was the point from which the town would grow. As the years passed some stations were expanded. Miami's station, originally at Sixth Street and Biscayne Boulevard (according to the pre-1921 street-numbering system) was moved in 1912 to Tenth Street and Avenue E, later 200 Northwest First Avenue. The original station site eventually became the location of the building now known as the Freedom Tower. The old Miami station became the "new" station's Railway Express annex, and the "new" station, over the years, was expanded through the addition of a second floor, an attached waiting room, a separate baggage room, and a dining-car commissary building almost a block south. In some places new stations were built (Daytona Beach; Titusville) or substantial additions made (New Smyrna; Ft. Pierce; Delray Beach; Boynton Beach; Miami; Key West).

Flagler, determined to develop the rich but unsettled lowlands south of Miami as viable farming acreage, tapped the region with a twelve-mile line in 1903.

Union Depot, Jacksonville, Fla.

Just arrived at Jacksonville, Fla.

Fig. 28. Jacksonville's Union Depot was shared by several railroads, many of which were part of the Plant or Flagler systems. From a postcard, c. 1907.

COCOA ROCKLEDGE

Fig. 29. The "Colored Waiting Room" at the Cocoa Rockledge Station. Photograph c. 1957.

That branch was used primarily for shipping fruits and vegetables and proved successful enough that the road was extended to what would become known as Homestead. Reaching there on 11 June 1904, the railroad, for the moment—but for only the moment—was complete.[33]

By then it was evident, without any diminution of Plant or his legacy, that Florida's future was inextricably tied to Henry Flagler. At its peak, the Plant System of Hotels numbered eight, the Flagler System, twelve. With Plant's death and the subsequent dissolution of his system, the Plant legend began to subside. However, by 1904 the Flagler legend was just beginning to build to the crescendo that it would reach when the first train arrived in Key West in 1912. Henry Plant, and, to a lesser extent, Henry Sanford, were identified with Florida. Henry Flagler *was* Florida.

Flagler, who had not set out to be a developer, nor envisioned himself as the proprietor of a railroad system or a chain of hotels or a steamship company or a series of land companies, was about to embark on his greatest venture. It was Flagler's belief that, with the new Panama Canal cutting thousands of miles off of the perilous ocean voyage between the two coasts of America, ships would head for the nearest deep-water port in order to unload. If that port were in Florida, so much the better. Miami's shallow harbor was unsuited to the task, and so Flagler sent William J. Krome, who eventually became chief engineer for the construction of the Key West Extension, to survey a route through the Everglades to a point in southwest Florida near today's town of Flamingo.

Emerging from the Everglades several months later, Krome told Flagler that there was not enough fill available in America to build a railroad across the Everglades. Flagler began to consider extending the railroad to Key West, then the largest city in Florida. As early as 1836, just six years after the first steam train ran in the United States, Key West newspapers had suggested that a railroad could and should be built to the island city. In 1866 a route survey was performed on behalf of the International Ocean Telegraph Company, and in 1894, Jefferson B. Browne, collector of customs for the Port of Key West, advocated for and laid out an almost complete route for the railroad to follow in an article in *National Geographic*.[34] Browne wrote, "A railroad to Key West will assuredly be built…The hopes of the people are…centered in Henry M. Flagler….The building of a railroad to Key West would be a fitting consummation of Mr. Flagler's remarkable career, and his name would be handed down to posterity linked to one of the greatest achievements of modern times."[35]

Flagler had Krome survey a route to Key West, and Krome advised Flagler that the task could be completed. Oblivious to obstacles, inured to criticism, and indifferent to the encroaching infirmities of age, Flagler took the Florida East Coast Railway to sea, funding the Key West Extension by himself, as he had the building of the entire railroad (fig. 30).[36] The extension became a reality, despite the hurricanes of 1906, 1909, and 1910, charges of labor abuse, which were dismissed by every court that heard them, and federal objections to filling in Trumbo Island at Key West to provide land for yards and a terminal.

33. Bramson, *Speedway to Sunshine*, 57.

34. Ibid., 67.

35. Ibid., 67–68.

36. Ibid., 67.

Fig. 30. View of a Florida East Coast passenger train on Long Key Viaduct. From a postcard, c. 1915.

On 22 January 1912, Flagler, almost blind, hard of hearing, and bent with the infirmities of age, stepped off the first train to Key West. The throng awaiting him, more than ten thousand strong, remains the largest gathering in Key West's history (fig. 31). Popular legend has it that Flagler, while being led to the reception area by the Navy's Admiral Young on one arm and Mayor Allen of Key West on the other, turned to them, while children were throwing rose petals at his feet, and said, "I cannot see the children, but I can hear them singing."

As noted, Henry Plant died in June 1899, at the age of seventy-nine. It was Plant's great desire that his empire not be broken up following his death, or, at the very least, that it be sold intact. His will stated that there should be no partition of his system until the majority of his great-grandson, who was then four years old.[37] Legal machinations involving state of residence were of no avail, and Plant's will, contested by his son and widow, was found to be without legality. Because Plant had been declared a resident of New York, and not Connecticut, there was no legal hindrance to splitting up his corporate empire.[38]

Plant's son and widow sold the railroad system to the Atlantic Coast Line, and in early 1902 the Plant System of Railways ceased to exist. The steamship company was sold to the Flagler interests and the Peninsular and Occidental Steamship Company was formed (fig. 32). Southern Express, along with all other express companies and the railroads, was taken over by the federal government during World War I, and after the war was consolidated with other companies to form American Railway Express. The hotels were liquidated.

Plant's memory lives on, of course. Plant City, east of Tampa, is Florida's strawberry capital. Many of the cities and towns on Florida's west coast have a street or school named for Plant, and one of Tampa's most revered buildings is the University of Tampa's administration building, the former Tampa Bay Hotel.

On 15 January 1913 at Whitehall, Flagler's leg gave way while descending a staircase. He was bruised and shaken, and his right hip broken. He was in

37. H. D. Dozier, *A History of the Atlantic Coast Line Railroad* (Boston and New York: Houghton Mifflin Company, 1920), 145.

38. Ibid., 146.

Fig. 31. Flagler being greeted after arriving on the first-ever train to Key West, 22 January 1912. From a postcard.

Fig. 32. Booklet cover depicting the *Mascotte* entering Havana harbor, issued by the Peninsular and Occidental Steamship Company, formed by the consolidation of the Plant and Flagler steamship companies, c. 1902.

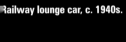

right,

Fig. 33. The Florida East Coast

Railway's freight house in

Jacksonville, Florida, c. 1921.

below,

Fig. 34. Florida East Coast

Railway lounge car, c. 1940s.

great pain, and although he rallied slightly after several days, he was too enfee-
bled to improve further. He died at 10:00 A.M. on 20 May 1913, at the age of
eighty-three.

Unlike Plant's passing, Flagler's death did not lead to the dissolution of his empire.
On the contrary, it continued to grow (figs. 33 and 34). A new line through the
Kissimmee Valley was opened by the railroad and a new Breakers, designed by
the architectural firm of Schultze and Weaver, was built in 1925 to replace the
second Breakers, which had burned. The beautiful Casa Marina, now a Marriott
resort, was built on the ocean in Key West in 1925, and continual improvements
were made to the Long Key Fishing Camp, where Zane Grey presided over the
Long Key Fishing Club. It was only with the Depression that the Flagler empire
began to splinter. The railroad, thrown into bankruptcy by Standard Oil in 1931,
emerged under new ownership in 1961. By the 1940s only the Ormond, the
Ponce de León, and the Breakers hotels were still under Flagler System ownership. Today, only the Breakers carries the Flagler banner. In the early 1960s the
Peninsular and Occidental Steamship Company was liquidated.

▲

Fig. 36. Florida East Coast
Railway steam engines
812 and 818 prepare to
leave Miami. Photograph
by Harry M. Wolfe, 1936.

right,

Fig. 37. Florida East
Coast Railway brochure,
front cover, 1921.

However, more than remnants live on. Whitehall, after a stint as a hotel, became the Henry Morrison Flagler Museum. Flagler Beach, the city, and Flagler County are named for him. Almost every town and city on Florida's east coast has a school, street, or park named for him. The former Hotel Ponce de León is now Flagler College, and Flagler Drive in Palm Beach and Flagler Street in Miami are nationally known thoroughfares. The Flagler Monument, erected on an island in Biscayne Bay between Miami and Miami Beach by Miami Beach developer, Carl Fisher, is seen daily by motorists and boaters (fig. 35). The Florida East Coast Railway, though no longer a Flagler property, celebrated its centennial in 1996.

Without Florida's two major rail systems in the late nineteenth and early twentieth centuries, clearly the face of the state would be much different than it is today (fig. 36). Without the trains, development would certainly have been slower, and without the advertising that convinced people to come to Florida via the trains, to stay in the hotels, and to buy land — all of which were managed by the Plant or Flagler organizations — the Florida we know today might not exist. Nowhere in the history of transportation or innkeeping have the two disciplines been so intertwined as in Florida.

Fig. 38. Florida East Coast Railway brochure, front cover, 1927–1928.

Although much has been lost in the form of steam locomotives, hotels, station buildings, shops, and other historic structures, much in the form of memorabilia remains. From the correspondence to the timetables to the booklets, brochures, and photographs, a superb record of the greatest days of Florida's transportation history remains (figs. 37 and 38). The legacy of art, architecture, advertising, and the immense contributions the three Henrys made to Florida will never go unremembered. □

Note

The author gratefully acknowledges the insights and encouragement given him in preparation for the writing of this article by Samuel Boldrick, director of the Florida Collection, Miami-Dade Public Library, Miami, Florida.

Fig. 1. Pan Am Annual Report, cover, 1943. The airline's annual reports were remarkable for their graphic design. The globe was often portrayed as a much smaller place, thanks to the services of Pan Am.

Pan Am: Miami's Wings to the World

By William E. Brown Jr.

William E. Brown Jr. is the director of Archives and Special Collections and an associate professor at the Otto G. Richter Library, University of Miami, Coral Gables, Florida. He has published in several fields and has received fellowships and grants from the Smithsonian Institution, Mellon Foundation, British Council, and National Endowment for the Humanities.

Images from Pan American World Airways, Inc. Records, Archives and Special Collections, Otto G. Richter Library, University of Miami, Coral Gables, Florida.

n 1925 the public heard Al Jolson croon the lyrics:

My Miami, you belong to me
My flowers, my land, my birdies, too;
Miami, take your sonny to your sunny clime!
Miami, tell me honey, I'll be there on time.

Only a few years later, Pan Am would help take the world to Miami, and would do so on time. People were to set their watches by Pan Am planes.[1] Indeed, Pan American World Airways, Inc.—"Pan Am" to generations of employees and travellers worldwide — helped change the nature of international air travel and commerce. Pan Am and Miami are bound in a historic, economic, and emotional relationship. To view Miami and South Florida through the words and images of Pan Am is to see a city and a region in a unique light. From its Florida base Pan Am introduced commercial aviation to virtually every corner of the globe, and in so doing, changed the way people viewed themselves and the world (figs. 1 and 2).

Pan Am inaugurated official mail service between Key West, Florida and Havana, Cuba, on 28 October 1927. Pan Am delivered mail, shipped agricultural products and manufactured goods, and transported business commuters, tourists, and other travellers. Pan Am did everything with enormous style, whether it was designing its memorable advertisements, creating its famed Clipper ships, or developing airport terminals. Its innovations in aircraft design and equipment revolutionized commercial air service. Pan Am's architectural commissions in Florida included its 36th Street Airport, which evolved into the vast Miami International Airport, and its seaplane terminal complex at Dinner Key in Coconut Grove. The Pan American Seaplane Base and Terminal Building is considered to be one of the finest buildings of its kind.

Florida is the birthplace not just of Pan Am but also of the nation's airline industry. The first scheduled domestic airline preceded Pan Am by more than ten years, as an aerial ferry service that began operating between St. Petersburg and Tampa in 1914. The St. Petersburg-Tampa Airboat Line shuttled passengers for three months.[2] The United States' most famous World War I flying ace, Eddie Rickenbacker (1890–1973), recognized that South Florida's ideal climate, potential as a winter resort, and strategic location between North and South America offered great promise for commercial aviation. In 1923 he and a group of investors

---

1. Lawrence Mahoney, *The Early Birds: A History of Pan Am's Clipper Ships* (Pickering Press, 1987), 8.

2. Pan Am press release, 1953, Box 406, Folder "PAA Florida," Pan American World Airways, Inc. Records, Archives and Special Collections, Otto G. Richter Library, University of Miami (hereafter cited as Pan Am Records).

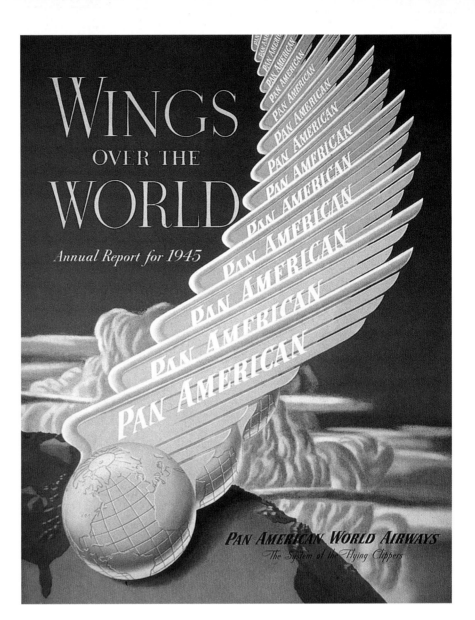

Fig. 2. Pan Am Annual Report, cover, 1945. The Pan Am logo dominates the page, dwarfing the earth below.

organized Florida Airways. However, in December 1926, despite a perfect safety record and almost three hundred thousand miles of air travel, Florida Airways closed its doors with debts of $250,000.[3] Another short-lived airline, the New York Rio and Buenos Aires Airline (NYRBA), led by Ralph O'Neill, pioneered air service to South America. O'Neill, also a World War I flying ace, personally delivered the first mail to Dinner Key Terminal from South America.[4] Competition for mail routes and foreign contracts was fierce, however, and the selection of Pan Am as the chosen airline for carrying United States mail to South America doomed the NYRBA, which merged with Pan Am in 1931.

Meacham Field in Key West was Pan Am's first home (figs. 3 and 4). Though born in Key West, Pan Am was not to stay there long. Late in 1928 the airline

---

3. Geoffrey Arend, *Great Airports: Miami International* (New York: Air Cargo News, Inc., 1986), 56, 62.

4. Ibid., 72–75.

Fig. 3. A Fokker F-7 waiting at Pan Am's first airport, Meacham Field in Key West, Florida, 1928.

Fig. 3. A Fokker F-7 waiting at Pan Am's first airport, Meacham Field in Key West, Florida, 1928.

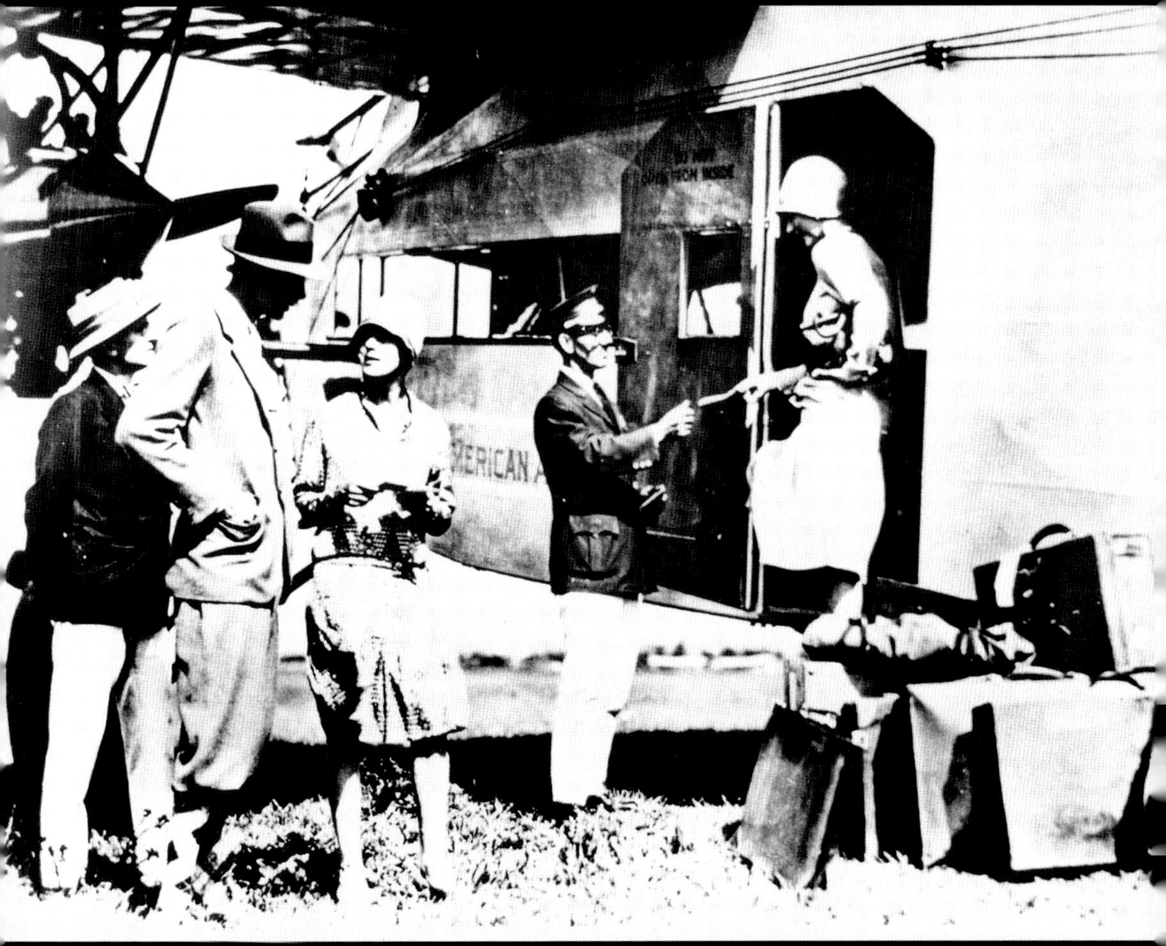

Fig. 4. Passengers and luggage preparing to depart Meacham Field in Key West for one of the first commercial flights in Pan Am history, 1928.

relocated to Miami (fig. 5). The move had significant financial implications, since Pan Am's contract for carrying mail to Cuba was a mileage contract, not a weight contract.

Juan Terry Trippe, Pan Am's twenty-eight-year-old founder, began operations with two airplanes, twenty-four employees, a monthly payroll of $4,800, and the goal "to provide mass air transportation for the average man at rates he can afford to pay" (fig. 6).[5] On 3 January 1929, Trippe addressed a national radio audience on station WABC, under the auspices of the Aviation Activities Hour. He spoke eloquently of the inauguration of air service from Miami to San Juan, Puerto Rico, via Havana and Camaguey, Cuba; Port au Prince, Haiti; and Santo Domingo, Dominican Republic. Trippe outlined a blueprint for international commercial aviation.[6] Many others also believed that Miami would have a significant role in the future of international aviation. Speaking on 22 July 1932, Minnesota Congressman M. J. Mass noted that "Miami's past will be forgotten in its new future…the development of aviation in all of its various fields, will bring a new social standard that will permit those in the most modest circumstances to live in luxury…."[7]

Miami's 36th Street Airport, which became Pan Am's base, was home to the first modern passenger terminal in the United States (figs. 7, 8, and 9). Designed by the New York architectural firm of Delano and Aldrich, the terminal was a two-story reinforced concrete and steel design built to handle twenty-five aircraft per day. The interior included a large waiting room divided for arriving and departing passengers. Customs, immigration, and public health officials were located near the arrival area. On the second floor was a balcony with Pan Am offices, pilot rooms, a restaurant, and viewing areas. The 36th

5. *The First Fifty Years of Pan Am: The Story of Pan American World Airways, Inc. from 1927 to 1977* (Pan American World Airways, Inc., 1977), 4.

6. Juan T. Trippe speech, 3 January 1929, Pan Am Records.

7. Press release, untitled, 7 July 1932, Pan Am Records.

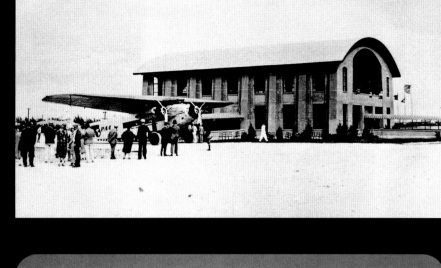

Fig. 7. The 36th Street Airport opened to great fanfare. Its architectural features included a distinctive cantilevered roof and numerous glass windows, 1929.

Fig. 8. Original terminal building at the 36th Street Airport with two long, low-level additions. From a postcard, c. 1940s.

Fig. 9. Jet aircraft from National Airlines are shown in the foreground of this round-cornered postcard, c. 1940s. Caption printed on postcard: "Miami's International Airport Gateway to Latin American Countries."

M27 Miami Terminal of Pan-American Airways

PHOTO BY PAN-AMERICAN PHOTO SERVICE   8A-H1074

Fig. 10. Aerial view of Dinner Key Terminal with two Clipper ships taxiing away from the building. The reverse side of this postcard has an inscription provided by the aircraft's captain: "In remembrance of your stay with us on the Flying Clipper NC-7521 on July 27, 1939, Capt. S. E. Robbins."

Fig. 11. An American Clipper (Sikorsky S-40 Flying Boat), arriving at Dinner Key Terminal. Passengers are welcomed by Seminole Indians in canoes, c. 1935.

Street Airport was a landmark building, and not just for Miami; it set the standard for commercial aviation structures for years. Other airlines soon joined Pan Am — by 1932 Eastern Airlines had moved its operations to the 36th Street Airport, and in 1937 National Airlines also began Miami-based operations.[8] The facility was expanded after World War II, and was later demolished. The site was eventually incorporated into Miami International Airport.[9]

The architects of the 36th Street Airport, William Adams Delano (1874–1960) and Chester Holmes Aldrich (1871–1940), were renowned society architects who designed clubs and residences for the Astors, Burdens, Havemeyers, Rockefellers, and Whitneys. The two architects began their careers with the New York firm of Carrère and Hastings but set off on their own in 1903. Like many architects of their time, Delano and Aldrich worked in a variety of styles; their range can be seen in New York City's Knickerbocker Club (1914), a Georgian building, and the Union Club (1932), a refined French Second Empire building. Later they turned to more functional buildings for such clients as Pan Am. Delano and Aldrich assumed a leading role in the design and development of Pan Am's international system of airports, terminals, hotels, and commercial facilities that grew from Florida to New York (where they designed the original La Guardia Air Terminal) and across the Pacific to Hawaii, Guam, Midway, Wake Island, and the Philippines.

The apogee of Delano and Aldrich's airline work in Florida was the Pan American Seaplane Base and Terminal Building at Dinner Key, which was constructed specifically to handle the airline's fleet of flying boats, dubbed the Clipper ships (figs. 10, 11, and 12). The Clipper ships were huge, luxurious passenger seaplanes that were dependent on waterways for their takeoffs and landings. In 1931 Pan Am began using Dinner Key, a small island that had been connected to the Coconut Grove mainland by the United States Navy during World War I. A houseboat from Havana served as the airline's first terminal

8. Arend, *Great Airports: Miami International*, 88–89.
9. Ibid., 89–103.

Fig. 12. Dinner Key Terminal, rear view, c. 1935.

there (fig. 13). Pan Am then erected three huge storage hangars and the terminal building itself. At the time of its construction, in 1933–1934, the Dinner Key Terminal was both the largest and most modern marine air terminal in the world. It opened the South Florida market to an expanded world of international business and tourists. In its day the terminal hosted as many as eighty thousand travellers per month as well as crowds that gathered regularly to watch the great flying boats.

The Dinner Key Terminal was designed in the Streamline Moderne style. The architecture of the building itself, a two-story central space flanked by symmetrical "wings," subtly reinforced the notion of air travel. The terminal was a steel-frame rectangular structure with a flat roof and exterior walls covered with smooth stucco. There were eleven bays across the front facade. The facade was highlighted by a frieze of winged globes—Pan Am's logo—and rising suns; the frieze was connected at the corners by sculpted eagles. The entrance doors were bronze, topped with bronze grilles.[10]

The terminal could accommodate multiple aircraft and move passengers from check-in service to food and beverage areas and observations decks (fig. 14). Perhaps the terminal's most innovative element was the layout for air-traffic control that allowed for the simultaneous handling of four aircraft. Dinner Key Terminal served as a model for seaplane bases in Rio de Janeiro, New York, and San Francisco. Its construction also marked the first time that the United

10. "Report of the City of Miami Planning Department to the Heritage Conservation Board on the Potential Designation of the Pan American Terminal Building 3500 Pan American Drive as a Heritage Conservation Zoning District," 1982, Pan Am Records.

Fig. 13. Prior to the construction of Dinner Key Terminal, a houseboat served as the passenger terminal. A Pan Am "aero-car" is parked in front, ready to transport passengers, c. 1930.

Fig. 14. The interior of the Dinner Key Terminal included a second-floor restaurant, c. 1935.

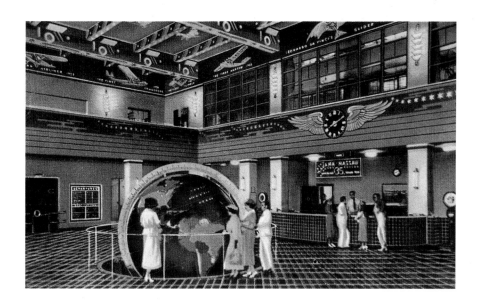

Fig. 15. Globe in the waiting area of the Dinner Key Terminal. From a postcard, c. 1935.

States government approved funds specifically for the dredging of a navigable channel for aircraft.[11] Additional innovations included solar-heated water and movable, telescoping walkways that protected passengers travelling between the planes and the terminal. These "jetways" are now a common feature at airports.[12] In the main lobby of the terminal, Pan Am installed a three-and-one-quarter-ton globe, ten feet in diameter. This rotating sphere, depicting the airlines of the world, became an international landmark as well as one of Pan Am's most famous icons (fig. 15).

In addition to its architects, Pan Am relied on other designers. Howard Ketchum, an interior designer, outfitted such planes as the Boeing 307 Stratoliner and the Boeing 314. The Boeing 314 offered the speed of air transport with the luxurious space of sea or rail travel. It was large enough to accommodate seventy-four passengers, or forty in sleeping configuration, and a crew of ten.[13] Ketchum wrote of his work: "It is difficult to provide proper credit to many interior aircraft designers, and it is equally difficult to trace the origins of the first 'planned interior' of a commercial aircraft. Many airliners of the late 1920s and 1930s have their interiors credited to the designer of the aircraft, usually the chief engineer."[14]

The noted theater and industrial designer Norman Bel Geddes (1893–1958) was one of the first in his profession to shape the interior space of a commercial airplane. He upholstered the spacious compartments with slipcovered seats and wall coverings that could be unzipped for cleaning and structural inspection.[15]

11. Ibid.

12. Arend, *Great Airports: Miami International,* 142–193.

13. John Zukowsky, ed., *Building for Air Travel: Architecture and Design for Commercial Aviation* (New York: Prestel-Verlag and The Art Institute of Chicago, 1996), 122.

14. Howard Ketchum, "Designing Interiors for Air Travel," *Interior Design and Decoration* (June 1940): 55–56.

15. Norman Bel Geddes' work was first described in print in 1935 by Linda Wellesley in "Flying Deluxe" in *The Airwoman* and by Shelden Cheney and Martha Candler Cheney in *Art and the Machine: An Account of Industrial Design in the Twentieth Century* (New York: McGraw-Hill Book Company, 1936).

Fig. 16. Charles A. Lindbergh in the cockpit of an airplane at Miami International Airport, c. 1929. The jagged line in the photograph is a crack in the original glass-plate negative.

Fig. 17. Charles A. Lindbergh prepares to dock his aircraft. The Dinner Key Terminal, visible in the background, still under construction, 1933.

Flush with its initial success, Pan Am expanded in the 1930s, acquiring new aircraft, employees, and routes. The airline ventured to the Caribbean, Mexico, and Central and South America. Trippe also engaged the services of aviator Charles A. Lindbergh (1902–1974), who would serve as a technical advisor to Pan Am for forty-five years (figs. 16 and 17). The 1930s were exciting years for Pan Am, with many notable accomplishments. On 22 November 1935 the China Clipper, a Martin flying boat built to Pan Am's specifications, departed from San Francisco and began a six-day journey to Manila, completing the first trans-Pacific flight. In May 1939 the Yankee Clipper, a Boeing B-314 also designed and built for Pan Am, completed a New York-Lisbon-Marseilles route that inaugurated transatlantic flights. In 1942 Pan Am completed the first successful around-the-world flight.

The creation of the China Clipper, or Martin M-130, revolutionized commercial air travel (fig. 18). These enormous twenty-six-ton seaplanes could travel thirty-two hundred miles non-stop at speeds of 130 miles per hour, which brought the Pacific and European nations within easy reach of Miami. A technological wonder with classic lines, the China Clipper introduced unheard-of comfort and luxury to air travel. It was perhaps the most popular of all flying boats, and was even featured in a 1936 film of the same name starring Pat O'Brien and Humphrey Bogart.[16] The China Clipper had eight compartments — the bridge, galley, crew's quarters, a sixteen-foot lounge, two sitting rooms, toilets, and the aft stairs (fig. 19). The passenger quarters were sound-proofed and had blue-green furnishings.[17]

Crossing the Atlantic Ocean on a China Clipper in 1939 was an unforgettable experience. The cabins were spacious, and the seats had plenty of leg room.

16. Zukowsky, *Building for Air Travel*, 110.
17. Robert L. Levering, *The Clipper Heritage* (Inter-Collegiate Press, 1984), 44–47.

PHOTO BY R. B. HOIT   OFF TO WEST INDIES AND SOUTH AMERICA FROM MIAMI

Fig. 18. The China Clipper revolutionized long-distance air-passenger service. From a postcard, c. 1935.

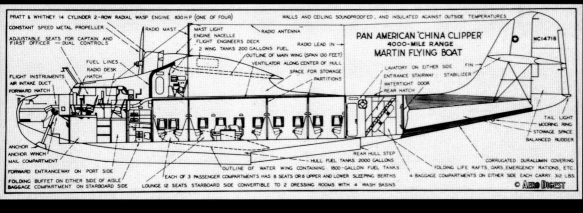

Fig. 19. Cross-section diagram of a China Clipper, c. 1935.

Fig. 20. Sleeping berth in a China Clipper, c. 1935.

Fig. 21. Dining table in a China Clipper, c. 1935.

The interiors included passenger lounges with Art Deco designs in "skyline green" and "Miami sand beige." Coordinated carpets added to the luxurious feel. The Pullman-like sleeping compartments were closed off by "Pan American blue" curtains. Each berth had a window, reading light, ventilator, steward call button, and clothes rack with hangers (fig. 20). The aft deluxe suite contained a love seat, coffee table, combination dressing table and writing desk, and davenport-style seat that converted to a bed. In the dining salon uniformed stewards served gourmet meals on polished black walnut tables covered with Irish linen, bone china, silverware, and European crystal (fig. 21). Such extravagance certainly made the $675 cost more tolerable, and helped pass time on the twenty-five-hour journey.

For a world full of adventurous travellers, the romance of commercial air travel was compelling. One regular passenger recalled, "You didn't just go to the waiting plane, you were always ushered into it. Really, looking back, it was like a movie."[18] Playwright and editor Clare Booth Luce wrote after one of her trips, "Fifty years from now, people will look back on a Clipper flight as the most romantic voyage in history."[19]

Pan Am cherished its choice of the name "Clipper" to describe its overseas aircraft. The term, borrowed from the great nineteenth-century sailing ships, was most appropriate for these flying boats. Pan Am's international advertising campaigns regularly depicted Clipper ships arriving in exotic locations. As a result, Pan Am became synonymous with the term, and promotional material for the airline noted, "If it isn't operated by Pan American, it isn't a Clipper." The word "clipper" entered the lexicon of American English in a variety of ways. Entire clothing lines appeared, including "clipper" dresses modeled after native fashions "discovered" in Central and South America. "Clipper" transoceanic portable radios manufactured by the Zenith Radio Corporation were one of the great early achievements in that company's history. Hollywood drew upon the name for feature film titles, including *Bombay Clipper*, a forgettable Universal Pictures story starring William Gargan and Irene Hervey. In 1942 the *Saturday Evening Post* ran a cartoon depicting three children, with the oldest child saying, "Mayflower—phooey…our uncle came over on the Clipper!"[20]

In its advertisements Pam Am lured passengers, told the world of its achievements, and lauded the flawless efficiency of both aircraft and crews, despite the fact that the logistics of handling huge amphibious aircraft often contradicted these promotional claims (figs. 22 and 23). As one employee recalled:

> We would move the big Clipper out of the hangar on its land wheels and shove it into the water like you would launch a giant boat. Then people we called the "beach crew" would go in the water in bathing suits to undo and remove the wheels from the plane…The passengers would sit, sipping coffee, watching all this. Then they would go out onto a dock, get on the Clipper, and prepare for the noisy, bumpy takeoff.[21]

Pan Am's advertisements depicted and described the wonders of air travel in romantic and effusive terms. The advertisements were colorful in both images and prose, as is evidenced by the text on a poster promoting Pan Am flights to Rio de Janeiro:

18. Mahoney, *The Early Birds*, 54.
19. "50 Years Ago: Bridging the Atlantic," *American History Illustrated* 24 (May 1989): 34–45.
20. *New Horizons* (Miami: Pan American World Airways, Inc., 1942).
21. Mahoney, *The Early Birds*, 44.

Fig. 22. Advertising poster. The female figure stands with one foot on Jamaica and the other on Puerto Rico. Her red- and white-striped dress and the blue water symbolize the United States flag. Careful shading of the woman's body reflects the multiracial Caribbean population.

Cutting their creamy wakes through the blue waters of the bay the flying boat Clippers go flying down to Rio…a long, slender thread is spun all the way from Miami's Dinner Key to Africa. When winter's ice chokes the harbors in Baltimore and New York, Dinner Key's warm tropical bosom provides a safe haven for the transatlantic clippers.[22]

Ultimately, the Clipper ships fell victim to further advances in technology. Seaplanes offered great savings to airlines and to cities located near large bodies of water, as they required no expensive runways and taxiways. However,

22. Arend, *Great Airports: Miami International,* 142.

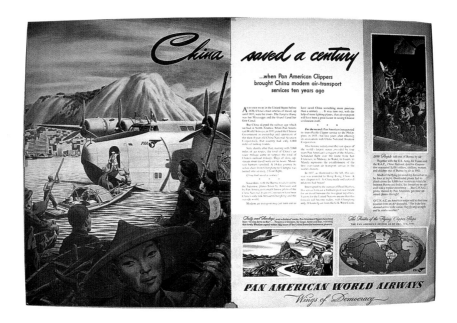

calm water was a requirement, and the conversion of aircraft from water to land was awkward and time consuming.[23] In 1939, only four years after the first China Clipper rolled off the assembly line, Pan Am received bids on its successor, the Boeing 314. Nevertheless, airline personnel and travellers the world over can still recall their emotional reactions to their first glimpse of one of the great flying boats such as the China Clipper, the Hawaii Clipper, the Dixie Clipper (fig. 24), or the Yankee Clipper.

The final Clipper ship to land at Dinner Key did so on 9 August 1945.[24] During World War II the United States Navy used Dinner Key for military purposes. Pan Am allocated extensive resources and personnel to support the war effort. The airline flew more than ninety million miles for the United States government, carried military personnel and cargo, ferried bombers and aircraft, and built fifty airports in fifteen countries. The airline also trained thousands of military pilots, navigators, and mechanics. Scores of American and British pilots, flight engineers, navigators, and crew members received classroom education at the University of Miami and practical flight and equipment training at the 36th Street Airport or Pan American Field, as it was known in 1941, which included a hangar on the west end for use by the United States Army.[25] Perhaps Pan Am's single most memorable wartime activity involved the 1943 Dinner Key flight that took President Franklin Delano Roosevelt on his top-secret meeting with Winston Churchill and Joseph Stalin in Casablanca. This flight required 10,964 miles and marked the first time that a president flew while in office.[26]

By 1946 Pan Am could proudly boast of its role in Miami's growth. No longer was the "Sunshine Capital" of the South merely a tourist town — it had become a leading seaport and the primary port of entry to the United States. In addition, the postwar boom had a large impact on air travel. Pan Am flew 13,341

23. Ibid.
24. Dinner Key Terminal now serves as Miami City Hall, and the globe is located at the Museum of Science in Miami.
25. Press release, untitled, 28 June 1943, Pan Am Records.
26. Arend, *Great Airports: Miami International*, 188.

flights in and out of Miami during the first six months of 1946, compared with only 2,555 for the same time period in 1941. Mail service also underwent dramatic growth from approximately 250,000 airmail letters flown to Latin America in 1930 to almost one hundred million in 1946.[27]

The postwar period saw many technical improvements in aviation, and Florida became an easy destination for both tourists and business travellers. Pan Am embarked on an ambitious expansion program that sought to "pioneer a system of mass air transportation throughout the Western Hemisphere, with Florida (Miami) as the aerial gateway between the Americas."[28] In promotional material, Pan Am contended that current flight times and costs would dwindle. The fifty-seven hour, $425 trip from Miami to Rio de Janeiro would be reduced to eighteen hours and $167.[29] "Those wings over Florida are wings of gold," a newspaper columnist wrote in 1950, summarizing an aviation industry that provided employment for some 150,000 Floridians at 210 airports, forty seaplane bases, and thirty-three personal-use airports.[30]

United States air-passenger service entered the jet age on 26 October 1958. Overnight, flying times were reduced by one-half, and the world became a much smaller place. On 1 May 1976, Pan Am's Liberty Clipper, one of the new 747 SPs, left New York and travelled east on a record-breaking around-the-world trip. With ninety-six passengers and only two refueling stops—in Delhi and Tokyo—the flight arrived back in New York forty-six hours from departure, breaking the previous mark by some fifteen hours. Pan Am celebrated its fiftieth anniversary in 1977 with another first, this time around-the-world service over the North and South poles, a flight that covered 26,300 miles in a little more than fifty-four hours. In January 1980 Pan Am merged with National Airlines, but economic difficulties during the 1980s caused Pan Am to cease operations in 1991.[31]

Pan Am's history is recorded in an enormous body of corporate records that includes memoranda, letters, photographs, technical reports, manuals, magazines, newspapers, advertising materials, scrapbooks, flight records, clippings, press releases, speeches, and related documents. These files are housed at the Archives and Special Collections of the Otto G. Richter Library, University of Miami, Coral Gables, Florida.

In its decades of operation Pan Am captured the imaginations of tens of thousands of world travellers. The airline embodied the thrill and romance of air travel with its architecture, advertising, and aircraft design. The surviving words and images of Pan Am are testimony to one of the most exciting chapters of aviation history in the United States, and they will continue to inspire and inform us as long as great aircraft serve as man's wings to the world. □

27. Press release, "Pan Am Has Helped Bring Economic Stability to Florida," n.d., Pan Am Records.

28. Press release, "Pan American's Growth and its Investment in the State of Florida," n.d., Pan Am Records.

29. Ibid; Currently the trip from Miami to Rio takes eight hours and thirty-seven minutes and costs $717.95 for the coach fare, according to American Airlines.

30. *Miami Herald*, 12 March 1950, sec. F, p. 5.

31. In 1996 the Pan Am name and logo were reintroduced by a new airline that purchased the rights.

Fig. 24. Dixie Clipper. From an advertisement, 1940. This image illustrates the enormous size of these aircraft.

Fig. 1. Bernhardt E. Muller, Administration Building, 1926. Photograph of opening event staged by Glenn Curtiss. Private collection.

(Address: 777 Sharazad Boulevard.)

Dream and Substance: Araby and the Planning of Opa-locka

By Catherine Lynn

Catherine Lynn teaches courses on American architectural history, ornament, and preservation at the University of Miami School of Architecture, Coral Gables, Florida. Her publications include *Wallpaper in America* (New York: Norton, 1980).

Fig. 2. Bernhardt E. Muller, Administration Building. Photograph by Catherine Lynn, 1992.

Opa-locka is a small city that attracts few of the tourists who speed past it on Interstate 95 just north of Miami. The signs point the way clearly enough to its center, inland a little west of the highway, where City Hall on Sharazad Boulevard is a fantastic concoction of a building that might have appeared on the pages of an *Arabian Nights* storybook (figs. 1 and 2). Part palace, part mosque, City Hall alone is well worth the visit. Its domes and towers terminate the busiest street in town, but business on Opa-locka Boulevard, even at the biggest store — the grocery — appears pretty slow, especially compared to the activity at South Florida's malls and beaches. Most people on the streets of Opa-locka are African-American, as is their mayor.

The citizens are justly proud of their bizarre City Hall and of about one hundred other exotic structures built to fulfill a developer's dream of Araby. The most impressive and curious buildings went up in a few months, beginning in 1925 amid frenzied boosterism for this planned new town. Then the hurricane of 17 September 1926 struck. It was but the first of a series of misfortunes that were to distort the original plans for Opa-locka. Despite it all, domed, crenelated, and turreted houses of the 1920s are suprisingly numerous, and the layout and the names of the streets themselves recall Opa-locka's never-quite-realized glories (figs. 3 and 4). Still, only dedicated architecture buffs count the town among South Florida's tourist meccas.

From *The Arabian Nights Entertainments; or the book of the thousand nights and a night*,[1] Opa-locka's developer, the pioneer aviator Glenn Curtiss (1878–1930), plucked the theme for his real estate venture (fig. 5). For those who have read even the introductory chapters of that classic work of literature in its fullest and most authentic translations, a visit to Opa-locka can set off a string of meditations on irony, for the power of African-Americans at city hall and their ownership of the little domed houses where tiny minarets hoist crescent moons above the telephone wires are unlikely elements in an epilogue to *The Arabian Nights*.

In the uncensored translations of "the great Arabic compendium of romantic fiction,"[2] fear of black power—especially of the sexual potency of male African

1. The title given here is as rendered by Richard F. Burton in his edition published in London in 1885. Burton's translation seems to have been the one most widely used by subsequent generations of popularizers who wrote in English. There are many alternate versions of the title.

2. This is the description offered in 1882 by John Payne, in his preface: "The present [which] is, I believe, the first complete translation of the great Arabic compendium of romantic fiction that has been attempted in any European language." John Payne, *The Book of the Thousand Nights and one night* (London: printed for the Villon Society by Private Subscription, 1882), 1:vii.

slaves and its allure for the cloistered princesses of Araby—dominates much of the text's opening pages. That fear underlies the framing tale that ties together all the thousand and one, and figures repeatedly in those wondrous stories Sharazad began night after night, talking for her very life. Linking all the others, hers is the familiar story of how, through a thousand nights, she intrigued the misogynous King Shahryar, who had been so enraged by the multiple adulteries of his first wife with African slaves that for three years he had put to death each day his bride of the previous night. Every night Sharazad captivated him with a new tale, leaving it unfinished at dawn so that he would spare her to continue the following night. In Opa-locka, a thing unthinkable to King Shahryar has come to pass: the blacks have taken over the world of Araby—or at least this fanciful image of it. It would surprise Opa-locka's early residents as well. On 15 December 1926, special census takers reported a population of 251, but they failed to count twenty-nine black residents.[3] Few then could have foreseen an economically depressed Opa-locka enmeshed in the urban sprawl of Fort Lauderdale-Miami with a population that has held steady at just above eighteen thousand for the past decade.

Who first had the vision of a new town in Florida where every building would call up a particular scene from *The Arabian Nights* is a question that is itself enmeshed in a web of fanciful tales, varied by their tellers to suit the occasion. In publicity pieces of the 1920s the story goes this way: Soon after the New York architect Bernhardt Emil Muller (1878–1964) was hired to work on the project, he happened to read a new edition of the tales. That night, he literally dreamed up the scheme and early the next morning wired his client, Glenn Curtiss, proposing it. Curtiss promptly brought Muller to Florida, where the designer painted an enthralling word-picture of his dream of Araby on the verge of the Everglades:

> I described to him how we would lay the city out on the basis of the stories, using a story for each of the most important buildings, naming the streets accordingly. In each building we would tell the story by means of mural decorations and wrought iron work carrying out the various features of the story. The style of the architecture would be governed by the country in which the story was supposed to have taken place. Mr. Curtiss was fascinated with my ideas and I made plans to actually create the phantom city of my mind.[4]

But there is another persistent account that credits the whole idea to Curtiss himself. In this version it was Curtiss who read a new edition of the tales, was inspired, and directed his architect to adopt the theme for Opa-locka. This story became part of the Curtiss biography retold in Miami newspapers on anniversaries of his daring flight of 1910 from Albany to New York City.[5]

Glenn Curtiss came to the Opa-locka project with previous experience in developing two other Miami suburbs. His first venture, launched early in the 1920s with a partner, James Bright, had been the city of Hialeah. There,

3. Esperanza B. Varona, *The Bernhardt E. Muller Collection: 1923–1960, Register*. A typescript document in the Archives and Special Collections of the Otto G. Richter Library, University of Miami, dated 30 December 1986, revised 21 January 1987, accession number 65–2, 11.

4. Bernhardt E. Muller, "Bernhardt Muller's Dream of Arabian City in Florida is Reality," *Opa-locka Times*, 23 February 1927, 1.

5. Several Miami newspaper articles celebrating Curtiss' flight are preserved as clippings in the Bernhardt E. Muller Collection of the Archives and Special Collections of the Otto G. Richter Library at the University of Miami (hereafter referred to as the Muller Collection).

Fig. 3. Bernhardt E. Muller, residence, c.1926. Photograph by Catherine Lynn, 1992.

Fig. 4. Bernhardt E. Muller, residence, c.1926. Photograph by Catherine Lynn, 1992.

unanticipated growth during the building boom had yielded chaotic sprawl, a disappointment to Curtiss. In their next venture, Country Club Estates, now Miami Springs, begun in 1924, Curtiss-Bright had tried to improve on that experience with careful initial planning that incorporated more rigid zoning controls and an architectural theme, the Spanish pueblo. A year later, Curtiss formed the Opa-locka Company to develop a whole new town bearing a name that was his shortened version of the Seminole name for the place, Opatishawockalocka (hammock).[6] He was clearly in the market for an inspiring theme. But it is equally clear that he was not bothered by questions of logical consistency between the place name and the theme itself.

And there is yet a third account of how Curtiss came up with his theme. In 1976 Frank S. FitzGerald-Bush, author of the only history of Opa-locka, credited his mother with giving Curtiss the *Arabian Nights* idea. Mrs. Bush was the wife of one of Opa-locka's first home-builders, the electrical contractor for its development company. When Curtiss showed Mrs. Bush the town site with its unspoiled native hammock and talked of plans for building there she is supposed to have exclaimed: "Oh, Glenn, it's like a dream from the Arabian Nights!"[7] Fitzgerald-Bush also wrote that an English Tudor scheme had been Muller's first proposal for the new town in Florida, a proposal Curtiss dismissed in favor of the idea that Mrs. Bush inspired.

It seems most likely that the choice of the *Arabian Nights* theme for Opa-locka was in fact made in more mundane circumstances, in meetings and discussions among developers, architects, and planners who were competing with others of their kind during Florida's real estate boom. Curtiss seems to have known the work of his competition well and to have borrowed freely from it. Among the borrowings was the practice, already well established, of basing the architecture of a Florida real estate development on a theme. The advantages soon became obvious to everyone involved. Themes served to distinguish one flat tract of newly drained land from another. They were useful to writers of advertising copy. Festivals and other events could be keyed to them, attracting people — and free press coverage — to a site. But even more important, themes imposed architectural coherence when different designers and contractors were putting up large numbers of buildings all at once.

The dominant theme of the 1920s was Mediterranean, grandly exploited by the architect Addison Mizner (1872–1933) for Palm Beach and adapted by the developer George Merrick (1886–1942) for Coral Gables. Coral Gables had been under construction for four years when Curtiss, Muller, and the town planner Clinton Mackenzie (1872–1940)—another New Yorker—began work on Opa-locka in the fall of 1925, and Coral Gables was clearly their most important model. In Merrick's work Curtiss found the seeds of ideas with which he was to experiment at Opa-locka: a theme linked to a specific work of literature with its own special architectural character, combined with careful town planning and elaborate landscaping.

The vernacular and classical traditions of southern Europe dominated the architecture of Coral Gables, but George Merrick also permitted a few more exotic details among the buildings he called Mediterranean. Under this rubric there was of course a perfectly logical basis for permitting Arabic architectural variations: they were appropriate to the Mediterranean Sea's African and Near

Fig. 5. Glenn Curtiss, 1910. This photograph was taken at the end of Curtiss' historic flight from Albany to New York City, considered the first long-distance airplane flight. Glenn H. Curtiss Museum, Hammondsport, New York.

6. Frank S. FitzGerald-Bush, *A Dream of Araby: Glenn H. Curtiss and the Founding of Opa-locka* (Opa-locka, Fla.: South Florida Archaeological Museum, 1976); and Muller Collection, clippings.

7. Ibid., 4.

Eastern shores, and to Spain. But Merrick chose to identify his exotic Eastern motifs exclusively with their Moorish incarnations in Spain itself, and quite emphatically with a particular literary work that enjoyed great popularity during the nineteenth and early twentieth centuries. This was Washington Irving's *Legends of the Alhambra*, first published in 1832. The numerous illustrations in its various editions inspired Moorish architectural embellishment such as crenelation, pointed arches, battered Egyptoid entrance pieces, and crescent motifs on little streets in Coral Gables like Obispo Avenue. Irving's work also furnished the names for the town's major thoroughfares—Alhambra and Granada—and for many of the smaller streets.

Like Irving's volumes, tales derived from *The Arabian Nights* enjoyed great popularity during the early twentieth century. That popularity was enhanced by musical works and ballets based on the tales, and it was extraordinarily broadened by the early movies they inspired. In hitting upon this particular motif, one so much more specific and fantastic than merely Mediterranean, Curtiss took the technique of theming much further than his real estate competitors yet had done. Indeed, he pre-Disneyed Disney by more than a quarter century. In building Arabian architectural forms he also placed himself squarely in the tradition of the nineteenth century's greatest showman and self-advertiser, P. T. Barnum. In 1848 Barnum moved into Iranistan, a minaretted pleasure dome he built as his home in Bridgeport, Connecticut. It quickly became a wonder of New England, though a short-lived one, for it burned to the ground in 1857. Like Barnum, Curtiss needed publicity to sell his product, and he gave his own publicists good material to work with in *The Arabian Nights*. He also attracted free editorial coverage by turning out buildings that photographed sensationally, looked spectacularly unlike the competition, and came with ready-made stories that everybody loved.

Curtiss was drawing on tales with origins that have been traced to seventh-century Persia. Around the year eight hundred, in Baghdad, at the court of Haroun er Reshid, "Aaron the Orthodox" (786–809), the seamless whole of stories within stories that was to become *The Arabian Nights* probably began to coalesce. By the thirteenth century, with additions from Egypt, India, and Arabia, it was assuming the form that was to take an important place in world literature. The tale used to link all the others was by now Sharazad's.

By the seventeenth century a great compilation of the tales, including 264 romances, anecdotes, supernatural fictions, historical fictions, poems, inventions, fables—every kind of story gathered from the far ends of the Mohammedan empires—had taken its classic shape. Fragments of the work first reached Europe in French translations by Antoine Galland, published between 1704 and 1717. Between 1839 and 1841, E. W. Lane produced a multi-volume edition of English translations "for the drawing-room table" expurgated of the eroticism that he thought too lurid for English readers. Not until 1881, when John Payne published his English translations in nine volumes from the Arabic, Persian, and Indian sources, was there any comprehensive edition of the work in a European language. In 1885 his friend Sir Richard Burton brought out another version in seventeen volumes that relied precisely on Payne's work, but added copious notes on Arab customs, especially the erotic.[8]

8. This summary of the history of the tales is based on Bennett A. Cerf's introduction to *The Arabian Nights' Entertainments or the Book of a Thousand Nights and a Night* (New York: Modern Library/Random House, 1932), vii–xiv, 1, and on Joseph Campbell's introduction to *The Portable Arabian Nights* (New York: Viking, 1952), 1–35. Cerf's edition is based on Burton's translation; Campbell's on Payne's.

Fig. 6. Title page of
Lady Burton's Edition of
her Husband's Arabian
Nights…prepared for
Household Reading **(London:**
Waterlow and Sons Limited,
London Wall, 1886).

Victorian intellectuals deciphered the full texts replete with their dream-like, sometimes nightmarish, sequences of fantastic events; their representations of human sensuality, treachery, and violent dismemberments; their portrayals of greed, adultery, jealousy, trickery, and clever dodges of all kinds. In recurring accounts of the passion of faithless wives for black lovers, a modern reader may sense thinly veiled explorations of obsessions and fears born of sexual and racial slavery. But such deep, dark, erotic, and exotic preoccupations were in large part left to scholarly contemplation when the great work was mined for wondrous fairy stories to be consumed by Anglo-American families.

Lady Burton's Edition of her Husband's Arabian Nights…prepared for Household Reading, which appeared in 1886, was but one among dozens of retellings of selected favorites in terms deemed appropriate for innocent Western sensibilities (fig. 6). In America as in Europe, Arabian tales were "arranged for family reading," to quote from the title page of a Philadelphia edition of 1860. Harriet Beecher Stowe (1811–1896), who was much concerned with the propriety of wholesome literature for the Christian home, included selections from the tales among "nine standard masterpieces" when she edited *A Library of Famous Fiction*, published in 1873. Carrying this nineteenth-century tradition well past World War I, publishers filled American homes with nursery-tale versions of "Aladdin and his Magical Lamp" and "Ali Baba and the Forty Thieves." Any child who had not read the tales at home was sure to encounter them at school, in the primers where they had become standard fare.

Frank Lloyd Wright's (1867–1956) six children had an image of what he called the "allegory" of "The Fisherman and the Genii from the Arabian Nights" as a mural over the fireplace in the playroom he added to his home in Oak Park, Illinois, during the 1890s.[9] The great architect mentioned the painting only

9. Neil Levine, *The Architecture of Frank Lloyd Wright* (Princeton: Princeton University Press, 1996), 25. According to Levine, the mural was designed by Wright and painted by Orlando Giannini, an attribution he based on Ann Abernathy with John G. Thorpe, ed., *The Oak Park Home and Studio of Frank Lloyd Wright* (Oak Park, Ill.: Frank Lloyd Wright Home and Studio Foundation, 1988), 26.

cursorily in his autobiography, commenting that a "lesson was to be drawn from the subject matter by the children. I forget what it was. Perhaps never to be too sentimental, or curious, or meddlesome, or there would be consequences."[10] No wonder Wright had lost track of the point, so convoluted is the fisherman's tale, or rather the series of tales that begins with a fisherman netting a brazen vessel with a leaden seal that, when removed, releases a genie or Afrit who promptly vows to kill the fisherman. Their duel of wit and power takes the form of swapping stories about kindness repaid by treachery—or alternatively by great reward—and in the end leaves the fisherman the richest man of his day—a status to which he has been led by the genie. In the surviving Oak Park mural the fisherman is realistically rendered sitting to one side of the great half-round scene dominated by the central figure of the enormous, abstractly rendered figure of "the Genii…done in straight line pattern," as Wright described it.

During these years, while school children and their parents everywhere were reading the tales, *The Arabian Nights* was also inspiring major works of performance art elaborately produced in the cultural capitals of Europe and the United States. Nikolai Rimsky-Korsakov based his symphonic suite, *Scheherazade*, on the theme and in 1910 his music inspired Sergei Diaghilev, the great Russian shaper of the modern ballet, to mount his production of the same name.

But without doubt it was in the movies that tales from *The Arabian Nights* made their most vivid impression on the generation to whom Curtiss hoped to sell lots in Opa-locka. The magical new medium itself seemed to rival a flying carpet in its ability to take moviegoers anywhere on earth. Genie-like, it conjured up every conceivable image and showered sudden riches on moviemakers and fame on actors. Listings of the earliest known movies reveal titles that include *Allabad, The Arabian Wizard* in 1901. *A Princess of Bagdad* was a silent film of 1916 advertised as "an original Arabian Night's story." It was followed in 1917 by *Aladdin and the Wonderful Lamp*, and in 1918 by *Ali Baba and the Forty Thieves*. Even more numerous were silent movies that put magical objects, familiar from the stories, into modern hands. Among the first of this type were *The Carpet from Bagdad*, a film of 1915 with a New York setting, and *Aladdin's Other Lamp*, which brought a genie to the America of 1917. When Terry Ramsaye wrote one of the earliest histories of the movies in 1926, the title, *A Million and One Nights: A History of the Motion Picture*, further suggested the new industry's fix on the theme.

In the movies the aura of eroticism that had been all but deleted from the storybook versions of *The Arabian Nights* was spectacularly rehabilitated. Though the plot was not based on one of the tales, Rudolph Valentino, in *The Sheik* (1921), made it practically impossible for his swooning fans to separate their notions of Araby from the very image of the romantic sex idol.

In 1924 when Douglas Fairbanks produced and starred in *The Thief of Bagdad: An Arabian Nights Fantasy*, he definitively glamorized the theme for a whole generation.[11] *The Thief of Bagdad* set new Hollywood standards. Technically, the magic and the flying-carpet special effects surpassed anything the industry had produced to date.

---

10. Frank Lloyd Wright, *An Autobiography* (New York: Duell, Sloan and Pearce, 1943), 112.

11. *The Thief of Bagdad* is available on video. My descriptions of the sets are based on viewings of the film itself.

The magnificence and splendor of the movie's costumes and sets, created by the art director William Cameron Menzies, also established a new standard. To make the movie, Fairbanks built a city that covered six acres of movie lots. Its palaces, gates, and public squares were architectural hybrids, dream images of Baghdad, stylized—sometimes blank and abstract, sometimes dense with geometric patterns. Often, great expanses of plain walls fill most of the screen, focusing attention on a few rickety balconies, on pointed and horseshoe-shaped arches, and most of all leaving the eye to seek gleaming domes of many shapes atop nearly every structure. Mammoth jars are always in sight; Fairbanks seemed to find constant cause to leap in and out of them, or to hide evil-doers within them. Menzies interjected touches of Art Deco, especially in interiors with pierced and filigreed screens. And he created visions of China as well, of the Mongol empire and its swarming armies. It was dazzling.

A full-page advertisement for Opa-locka that appeared in Miami newspapers during May 1926 suggests that Glenn Curtiss counted on those movie sets to have impressed just about everybody in the United States. In presenting Opa-locka as a "City of Parts"—the parts included plan, landscaping, public utilities, recreation, and transportation—the architecture part needed little description. The advertising copy ran: "Of course you have seen Douglas Fairbanks' 'Thief of Bagdad,' with its wealth of Oriental picturesqueness reminding one, indeed, of the famous illustrations to the Arabian Nights."

At Opa-locka, the architecture "part," or the Arabic part of that architecture, was much like a movie set: all facade, all for the camera, which here was a still camera for publicity shots. While Opa-locka's publicists were reaping the benefits of associating their project with the famous movie, they clearly sensed a danger in identifying it too closely with Hollywood. "No 'flats' of Arabian scenes built for moving picture 'sets,' but solid, massive structures designed to live for generations to come," they stressed in an advertisement of 5 February 1926, published in the *Miami Daily News and Metropolis*. Beneath the exotic trappings, Opa-locka's houses were as solidly built as most of the others springing up across Florida during the 1920s. These *Arabian Night*s structures were in fact much like the others except for their novel system of exterior decoration.

Bernhardt Muller was not perhaps so "famous" as the Opa-locka Company was to bill him. He was forty-seven when Curtiss hired him in 1925, and had covered a lot of territory since 1878, the year of his birth in Fremont, Nebraska. He based his architectural career on studies in Paris at the École des Beaux-Arts between 1903 and 1905, and in Italy, France, Austria, and Germany during an additional year. He settled in New York in 1906 and worked for a succession of firms, including Trowbridge and Livingston, Robert J. Reiley, and D. Everett Waid, until 1914, when he opened his own office. In the two years before coming to the Opa-locka job, he had designed several Mediterranean and Spanish-style houses in and near Miami.[12]

Like the moviemakers, Muller dealt in pictorial, painterly, and narrative terms with buildings appropriate to the *Arabian Nights* theme. He wanted his buildings to call up the narratives visually, an intention expressed in the statement, quoted above, that he "would tell the story by means of mural decorations and wrought iron work carrying out the various features of the story."

Muller's drawings for Opa-locka have been well preserved. In the 1960s the Archives and Special Collections of the Otto G. Richter Library at the University

12. The Muller Collection includes clippings, obituary, and typescript biographical information on Muller.

of Miami acquired a large number of Muller's drawings for Opa-locka as part of a collection of more than nine hundred architectural drawings and related materials. The materials have provided documentation for subsequent preservation efforts in the town.

Ephemera in the library's Bernhardt E. Muller Collection includes a publicity piece of February 1926 that described the "famous New York architect" as having "extensive experience with the technique of the ancient architects of Persia, Arabia, and South Central Europe." But in 1959 Bernhardt Muller himself told Janet Bolender, an interviewer whose article about Muller was published in the *North Dade Hub*, that his wife had become his instant expert on exotic styles once the theme was set: "Muller proclaimed that his wife deserves much of the credit for the Arabian-Persian architecture. His wife fell heir to the huge job of delving into books, doing research, categorizing, providing her husband with all the background material he needed as a prelude and guide to designing the buildings."[13]

What Muller pulled from these sources were the facades, the outside effects. He and the developers required only exterior conformity to a look deemed appropriate to the geographical setting of a story selected from *The Arabian Nights*. To ensure that they would get a degree of stylistic conformity throughout the town, Muller was to review and approve drawings for any proposed building that he himself did not design. His basis for judgment was a very generalized and eclectic understanding of the styles appropriate to the settings of the far-flung tales of Arabia, Egypt, Persia, China, India, and their neighbors.

The most ambitious example of the image that Muller and the developers were after is the Opa-locka Company's Administration Building, now City Hall (fig. 7). It was the first major structure they built and it remains the grandest emblem of their *Arabian Nights* theme. By August of 1926, less than a year after initial plans for the town were seriously discussed, the building was ready for occupancy. That striking exterior served its owners far better than a billboard could have done to announce that a grandiose — to many a ridiculously fantastic — real estate scheme was becoming actuality.

13. Janet Bolender, "Architect Believes in City: 'It Can Still Be Done' Muller Tells Opa-locka," *North Dade Hub*, 9 July 1959, 3.

It looks enormous in all the photographs and drawings, and the Opa-locka Company published pictures of it right through its hasty construction process and afterward at every possible opportunity (fig. 8). A gorgeous, five-domed, many-colored, and multibalconied structure, crowned by crenelations, and surrounded by minarets and walled courtyard-gardens, it is impressive as it rises today in restored splendor above Opa-locka's low-lying buildings. But in fact it is not a large public building. Its interior scale seems nearly domestic, a surprise considering the impact of its silhouette seen from afar.

About fifty of Muller's drawings for the Administration Building survive in the collection at the University of Miami, more than for any other single building in the town. The design was his most elaborately detailed effort for Opa-locka.

The presentation rendering of 1925 would have made a fine illustration for yet another edition of *The Arabian Nights*, as the watercolor drawing has that storybook quality (fig. 9). In it the building looks vaguely like a mosque but was entitled the Palace of King Kosroushah (or Khusrau Shah), from the tale of "The Two Sisters Who Envied Their Cadette." *Cadette* is a Persian word meaning "City-queen," according to Sir Richard Burton. The story is a long and convoluted account of how the Persian king was united with his two sons and daughter, Princess Periezade, whose births had been kept secret from him by his queen's wicked sisters. In large part the tale recounts successive quests for the Singing Tree, the Golden Water, and the Speaking Bird. The young men fail arduous tests en route to these peculiar prizes, and it is their sister who finally faces down the perils, stopping her ears against the frightful sounds along the way.

Opa-locka's publicists pointed out that Muller had used Moorish and Arabian architecture to concoct a palace associated with a Persian king. From the beginning, then, it would seem that the reviewers were pretty lax about deciding which architectural style was appropriate to the geography of a given tale. As architectural specificity faded, a generally Eastern air could be suggested by propping large terra-cotta jars against a wall, and the jars were always handy for leaning on when celebrants of early Arabian Nights Festivals posed for photographs.

Muller, however, stayed close to the specifics of the story in designing and naming details within the Administration Building. Drawings for the Fountain of the Princess Periezade (figs. 10 and 11) are signed "E. S." and bear the most distinctive stamp of Art Deco stylization of any illustrated here. Publicity pieces of the 1920s enumerate other features of the courtyard-garden, such as the Singing Tree, the Golden Water, the Talking Bird, and a man-shaped black rock like those into which the brothers were transformed when they failed in their quests for the three rare objects. "Mural decorations giving the splendid banquet scene where the identity of his children was revealed to the king by the dish of green cucumbers stuffed with pearls," are recorded in a feature article on Opa-locka in the English magazine, *Country Life*, of November 1928. Muller was at pains to design and to have designed other elaborate, if nonnarrative, details for this building, such as the banding of colorful tiles gleaming around the base of the principal dome. The tiles were made by the Batchelder-Wilson Company of New York. The domes were "blue or soft browns, the colors graduating upward to white or cream," according to an article in the *American Institute of Architects Journal* published in April of 1928 and signed by Opa-locka's mayor, H. Sayre Wheeler.[14]

The domes of the Administration Building cast a large shadow over the foreground of Muller's sketch for Opa-locka's marketplace (fig. 12). In fact, Muller was cheating, as the shadow would not have been so grand, nor fallen just that way, but with this device he pictorially interlocked the dominating structure with the commercial center. In a series of drawings of 1926, Muller gives us closer looks at simple little stands, like stalls in an Eastern bazaar, that would have brought bustle to the marketplace. One group of them is captioned "Stone City Shops," an ironic name for the proposed site of lively commerce (fig. 13). The Stone City is described in the "Tale of the Ensorcelled Prince," a tale within the "Tale of the Fisherman and the Jinn." Here, a truth-searching king found that every inhabitant had been turned to stone by the enraged and faithless wife of the prince, and that she had conceived even more excruciating

14. H. Sayre Wheeler, "Opa-locka, Created from the Arabian Nights," *American Institute of Architects Journal* (April 1928): 157–8.

Fig. 10. Scale details of fountain in Garden of Princess Periezade, Administration Building, drawing of plan, section, and elevation, pencil on tracing paper. Signed "By E. S. for Bernhardt E. Muller, architect, N.Y.C" and dated 21 April 1926. The fountain's niche, tiles, and metal head survive on an interior courtyard wall of Opa-locka City Hall.

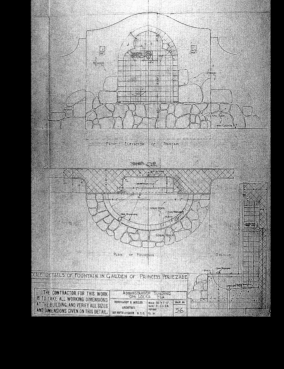

Fig. 11. Princess Periezade waterspout in fountain, full-scale detail drawing, pencil on tracing paper, showing front and side of the metal head for the fountain and detailing placement of a waterspout in the mouth. Signed "E. S. for Bernhardt E. Muller, architect, N.Y.C." and dated 21 April

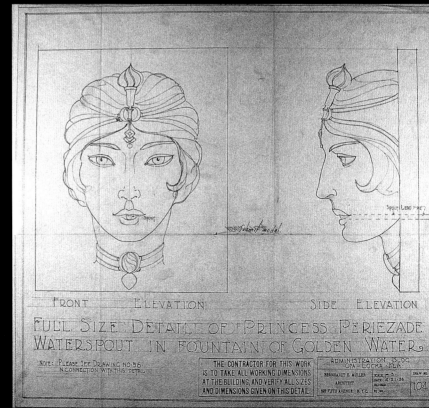

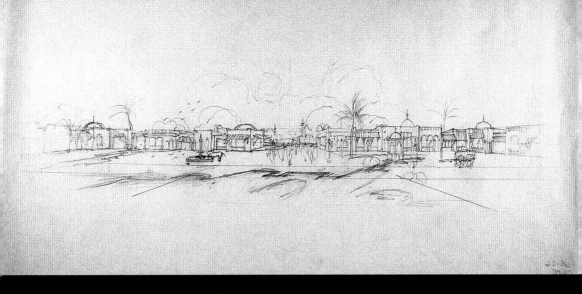

Fig. 12. Marketplace, perspective sketch, pencil on tracing paper, unsigned, undated.

"THE STONE CITY"
Shops.

Bernhardt E. Müller Arch't.
527 · 5th Au. N.Y.C.

Fig. 13. The Stone City Shops, colored and rendered perspective drawing, pencil, watercolor, and colored pencil on tissue paper.

"Administration Building, Opa-locka" erased from caption. Signed "Bernhardt E. Muller, arch't, N.Y.C. 1926."

Fig. 14. Gas station, negative photographic print, white on black, of a rendered perspective drawing. Signed and dated "Muller '27" lower left and "Bernhardt E. Muller Architect / Alfred O. Bleekman Con. Eng. / 527 5th Ave. N.Y.C.," lower right.

tortures for her husband. She had turned him to stone too, at least from the waist down, after he had mortally wounded her black lover, whom she then nursed and comforted within her husband's hearing. But the visiting king punished her and her lover with death and restored all the good people and the prince to life and health once more.

Among the commercial necessities of a new town of the 1920s was, of course, the gas station, and Muller seems to have enjoyed designing one as an Arabian whimsy. He gave it a dome, placed tiny minarets where they seem to dignify and protect the pumps, which he drew rather like little sentinels. A negative print, white on black, makes it all look like a night scene, glowing in the dark. His perspective drawing is dated 1927 and captioned "Super Gas Station, Opa-locka, Florida" (fig. 14). This gas station, however, was probably never built.

In one of the most romantic of his renderings, Muller envisioned a ruinous Egyptian temple to serve as Opa-locka's bank (fig. 15). Here he seems to have conflated images of two of the most familiar temples that still have their double pylons — the temple of Horus at Edfu and that of Amon at Luxor. Muller's central portal is like the one at Edfu, topped by a cavetto cornice ornamented with the royal symbol of the winged sun. He placed an obelisk in front, just to the left of the portal, where an obelisk stands at Luxor. This essay in Egyptian architecture was sanctioned by identifying it with the "Tale of Zayn al Asnam," which relates the adventures of the young inheritor of the Sultanate of Bassorah, who lost his father's riches in profligate living during the first years of his rule, and regained them only after two dream-directed journeys to Cairo.

The drawing shown here is dated 1928, a date of some significance because construction had begun two years earlier on the "Egyptian Bank." Opa-locka's developers rushed to begin it, but despite reports in the *Hialeah Press* of 6 August 1926 that the "Bank building also is nearing completion," it never was finished, and never opened as a bank. At some point, Muller drew another version of it, more lavishly detailed with a cavetto cornice crowning every wall. Perhaps that was the design on which construction was originally based. The drawing eliminates the cornice detail, which would have reduced building costs, and presents a dreamier and a more abstract image, in which the temple looks decayed. Could this rendering have been part of a proposal for a less expensive revision, a pretty picture painted to induce a banker to complete the standing shell? If so, it failed. The shell was soon adapted to serve as the First Baptist Church. Today it is home to another congregation, and the imprint of Muller's intention can still be seen in its battered walls and its massing (fig. 16).

Fig. 15. Bank building in the form of an Egyptian temple, colored and rendered perspective drawing, watercolor, pencil, and colored pencil on illustration board, of what appears to be a ruinous temple of double-pylon form. Signed and dated "Muller '28" lower left. The unfinished shell at the corner of Caliph Street and Bahman Avenue was incorporated in a church and survives.

Fig. 16. Bernhardt E. Muller, Egyptian bank, now a church, c. 1928. Photograph by Thorn Grafton, 1992.

Fig. 17. Observation tower, front elevation, pencil on tracing paper, for a domed tower with exterior stairs and balconies. Signed "By S. M. and C. J. for Bernhardt E. Muller, Architect, N.Y.C." and dated 29 December 1925. Built in 1926, it was demolished by the Navy during World War II.

Muller's scheme of December 1925 for an observation tower more than fifty feet high was fully and promptly realized, for it had an important role in the chief activity of the Opa-locka Company, which was selling lots (fig. 17). It provided a platform high above the native trees of the hammock from which prospective buyers, brought out from Miami in busloads, could get the best view of the town-in-the-making. Given his theme, when the chief requirement was height, it is surprising that Muller did not create an overgrown minaret or a crenelated watchtower. He may have been recalling and heightening the low, rounded forms of North African villages built of mud, or perhaps images from Fairbanks' *The Thief of Bagdad* took over here: Menzies' dream visions of the towering, domed "abode of the flying steed" in the film may have lodged in Muller's mind. Like many of the sets in the movie, the observation tower was all balconies and exterior stairs. Whatever Muller was after, he surely achieved an exotic effect in the building. It was demolished during World War II when a nearby Navy base, for which Glenn Curtiss had given the original land, ruthlessly expanded, destroying everything of Opa-locka in its path. It wreaked havoc on Muller's buildings, about a hundred of which had been built during the 1920s. In 1943 five domes were removed from the Administration Building.[15] Indeed, the Navy did Opa-locka far greater damage than any it had suffered in the hurricane of 1926. It was neither the forces of nature, nor neglect when money ran out, that ruined Opa-locka's beautiful natural setting. The Navy bulldozed the hammock that Curtiss had preserved as a park.

In a few cases the Navy kept Muller's buildings at the core of the structures it altered and enlarged beyond recognition. The old archery club was the most important of these. In 1941 the Navy expanded it for use as an officers' club, engulfing Muller's crenelations and arched openings. The archery club had been completed late in 1926, one of the major amenities that Curtiss continued to build after the hurricane in September of that year. Among the others was a large bathing casino including a dance floor, volleyball courts, and a pool with grandstand seating for much-advertised performances by Johnny Weismuller and Jackie Ott, "The World's Perfect Boy." Muller's office also produced specifications and forty-five working drawings for the golf club of "Ali Baba and the Forty Thieves." Although they continued to work on the design, which began in June of 1926, it never was built.

A design that was executed was the tiny archery pro shop built north of town, beyond the hammock (fig. 18). In his drawing for it Muller carefully detailed simple adornment—crenelation and a little turret holding a crescent aloft— that stamped this utilitarian structure "Arabic." Today there is a nondescript hot-dog stand in the middle of Opa-locka, very near City Hall, that looks suspiciously like the old archery pro shop. Perhaps it is, moved and shorn of decoration.

When Muller designed a hot-dog stand for Opa-locka, he crowned a small stucco-covered structure with a dome and gave it exterior stairs to a roof enclosed by a parapet whose edges are rounded and irregular (fig. 19). It looks like something shaped by long use in a dusty North African town, though the front of the parapet is inscribed "DOGS." The drawing is dated 1929. During the previous year, Curtiss admitted the impossibility of continuing to build his dream for Opa-locka. However, it would seem that even with the Great Depression closing in, Muller was still designing buildings.

15. In addition to clippings in the Muller Collection, FitzGerald-Bush's *A Dream of Araby* is the source for some of this later history of Opa-locka, as are the National Register Nomination for Opa-locka, Esperanza B. Varona's Register of the Muller Collection (cf. note 3), and Clarke Ash, "Opa-locka: A Page from Arabian Nights," *Florida Living Magazine of the Miami News*, 5 April 1959, 6–7.

Fig. 18. Archery pro shop, rendered and colored perspective drawing, pencil and colored pencil on tracing paper. Signed, lower right "Bernhardt E. Muller Arch't / Opa-locka, Fla." Undated, but probably January 1927, the date on an elevation for the building. A building located at 103 Perviz Avenue is thought to be the archery pro shop, now relocated and stripped of its Arabic embellishment.

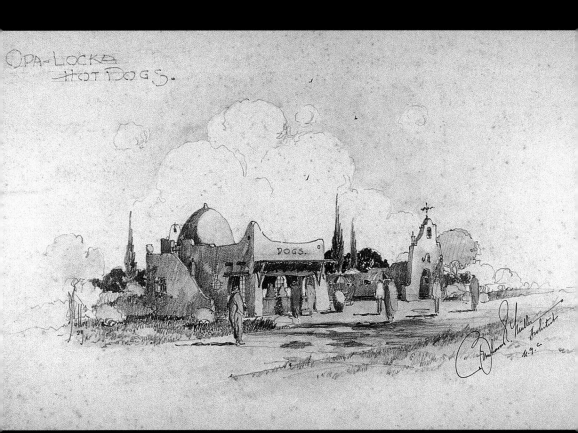

Fig. 19. Hot-dog stand, rendered and colored perspective drawing, pencil and watercolor on tracing paper on illustration board. Front para-

HOTEL for OPA-LOCKA

One of the grandest of his post-hurricane designs is for a "Hotel for Opa-locka" dominated by a tower that would have looked like an enormous Chinese pagoda (fig. 20). A sketchier rendering of the same design is inscribed "The Tale of Aladdin and His Lamp," one of the most familiar of the tales that few would have failed to know was set in "a city of the Cities of China." (The South Dade town of Aladdin was also inspired by this tale, but it was a very different project from Opa-locka [fig. 21]. The Aladdin Company of Bay City, Michigan manufactured and shipped "redi-cut" houses to factory towns. "A New City" in South Dade was to bear the company name that played on the wonder, worthy of Aladdin's own genie and his lamp, of the nearly instantaneous erection of houses that arrived as kits-of-parts on railway cars. The South Dade project had just started when the hurricane of 1926 was followed by Florida's real estate crash. The place name Aladdin survives just east of the intersection of Southwest 216th Street and Southwest 167th Avenue.) Dates in 1927 and 1928 appear on several of the twelve unrealized plans, elevations, and perspectives for this building. They give evidence that long after the hurricane had precipitated an early depression in Florida, Curtiss continued to support Muller's work on extravagant attractions that he still hoped to build in Opa-locka.

As late as 10 April 1930, just a few months before Glenn Curtiss died, one of Muller's drawings for this "Hotel Aladdin" was published in Boston's *Christian Science Monitor*. It appeared in an article inflated with the expectation of future construction in Opa-locka and with the boosterism so typical of earlier publicity.

One remarkably late drawing for a public building for Opa-locka is that for the First Church of Christ, Scientist, dated 1930 (fig. 22). A Christian Science connection is supposed to have won the Opa-locka job for Muller in the first place. According to Frank S. FitzGerald-Bush, an aunt of Glenn Curtiss belonged to a Christian Science Church in New Jersey that Muller designed, and she recommended him.

Among Muller's proposals for Opa-locka, this drawing seems unusually sober and blank. The simple frontal-gabled facade is distinguished only by a stark arched central opening under a relatively small window and by corner piers topped by finials made up of two little globes. At the time it was designed, there had been no funding of design or construction work in Opa-locka for about two years. With this drawing of 1930 could Muller have been proposing

Fig. 21. Full-page advertisement for a new town in South Dade called Aladdin, from the *Miami Daily News and Metropolis* of 3 January 1926.

a memorial to Curtiss, who died in July of that year? Whatever the case, it was not built.

Even though Muller and the publicists for Opa-locka lavished a great deal of attention on the town's institutional and commercial buildings, it was the residential buildings that were at the core of the real estate venture. Success depended upon their sales and Muller's designs for them were key sales tools. By providing many kinds of housing—among them single-family and multi-family houses, mixed commercial and residential buildings, and apartment buildings—Opa-locka's planners hoped to attract many kinds of people to their new town.

Drawings for more than sixty houses survive. Sixteen bear no dates, but the vast majority, forty-seven, were designed in 1926. During August and early September, just before the hurricane hit on 17 September, Muller's office seems to have been especially busy with them. Drawings for fifteen clients who are named bear dates for the remaining days of 1926, and three more houses were drawn up for other clients in 1927. No later dates appear on residential designs in the collection. During the post-hurricane period, Muller's

FIRST CHURCH OF CHRIST, SCIENTIST
OPALOKA,   FLORIDA.

Fig. 22. First Church of Christ

Scientist, rendered and colored

perspective drawing,

pencil and watercolor on illus-

tration board. Signed and

dated, lower left "Muller '30"

and again "Bernhardt E. Muller

/ Architect / New York City, N.Y."

lower right.

office also produced drawings for one four-family building, three duplexes, and one residence with a shop.

Most of the house designs are labeled as Muller's, though a few are clearly credited to his assistant, Carl Jensen, who, with Paul Lieske, also executed many of the plans and elevations in the collection. The assistants almost certainly contributed to house designs that became fairly formulaic. Some houses were commissioned by the Opa-locka Company, some by investors who bought lots and put up several houses for resale, but most by individuals. Surprisingly, fewer than five sets of drawings seem to have been dreamed up simply as models when no client was at hand. One of these was the undated "Residence of Ali-Baba on Sharazad Boulevard, Opa-locka."

Drawings for the diminutive "Thatched Roof Residence" (fig. 23) and for the "Oriental House" (fig. 24) suggest a wide variety of architectural styles in Opa-locka houses, which is perhaps misleading. Although there were still other variations, including Egyptian designs with lotus capitals, battered walls, and cavetto cornices, Muller's brand of "Arabic" is more representative of the houses that were built. To create it, he shuffled a repertoire of forms and ornaments around the elevations, including crenelation, balconies, pointed and horseshoe arches, and awnings supported by spears (a feature in Coral Gables houses as well). Domes crown houses of every estate, and roofs sport diminutive turrets with crescents for finials. The "Proposed Residence for Opa-locka, Suitable for 50'-0" Lot" may stand for a great many of the smaller essays in this genre (fig. 25). Carl Jensen executed the rendering two months after the hurricane, and it virtually sums up much of the firm's residential design for Opa-locka during the previous year. Even the inevitable terra-cotta jar is in view beside the entrance arch.

The elevation and plan for "The Hurricane-Proof House" (fig. 26) is a more modest presentation of many of the same elements, with a jazzier checkerboard paint scheme, and a heavier grille barring the windows. The drawings

Fig. 23. Cottage with thatched roof, rendered and colored elevation, pencil with colored pencil applied verso on tracing paper. Signed and dated "Muller 26." No existing house based on this particular design has been identified.

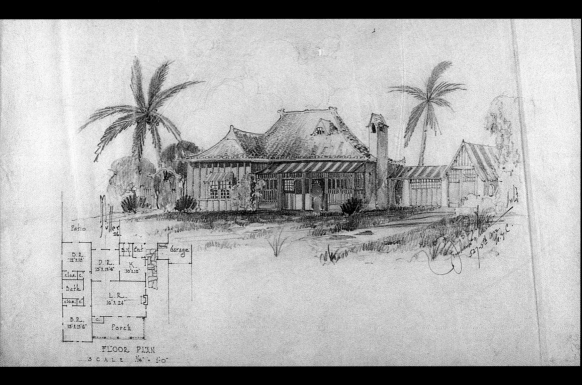

Fig. 24. Small oriental-style house, rendered and colored perspective drawing, pencil, colored pencil, and watercolor on tracing paper. Signed "Muller 26" lower left and again "Bernhardt E. Muller Archt. 527 5th Ave. N.Y.C." lower right. No existing house based on this design has been identified.

Fig. 25. "Proposed Residence for Opa-locka, Suitable for 50'-0" Lot," rendered and colored perspective drawing, pencil on tracing paper, with colored pencil on a second sheet below. Signed and dated "Bernhardt E. Muller Architect By Carl Jensen Nov. 16 '26." No existing house based on this design has been identified.

Fig. 26. "The Miami Daily News 'Hurricane Proof' House," rendered front elevation, ink with pencil border on tracing paper. Signed "Bernhardt E. Muller Architect / New York Opa-locka" lower right and "Carl Jensen" lower left, undated. No existing house based on this design has been identified.

were executed in November and December of 1926 specifically for publication in the *Miami Daily News and Metropolis*. While Muller's name is the one that appears prominently on the elevation, Jensen's signature is hidden in the grass of the lower left.

Among more substantial designs for larger houses, the Muller Collection includes a perspective dated 1926 for the residence of Opa-locka's mayor, H. Sayre Wheeler, a house that survives in a fine state of repair (fig. 27). Its construction between March and July of 1926 is amply documented in photographs.

Neither in plan, nor volume, nor material were Muller's buildings true to their various Eastern sources, as his drawings for Opa-locka make clear. Scrutinizing the plans, one might stretch a point and cite his use of enclosed gardens — especially the walled courtyards of the Administration Building — as a planning element taken from Eastern models. But Muller's plans overwhelmingly conformed to American standards of his day. His house plans were much like those in other Curtiss-Bright developments and like the smaller houses of Coral Gables. Many were modest arrangements of rectangular rooms on a single floor — two bedrooms, one bath, kitchen, living room, dining room, perhaps an entrance hall, and often a porte-cochere to shelter a car.

In section as well, the houses were a great deal more ordinary than their elevations might lead one to expect. Although domes topped many of them, they were merely exterior decorations that were not expressed in interior volume. No great vaulted rooms greeted visitors, whether they entered a private residence with a single small dome, a commercial building like the Hurt Building where a larger central dome was flanked by two others, or the architect's most ambitious essay in domes — the Administration Building, which was originally topped by six of them. To get the exterior effect he wanted, Muller simply set hollow half-spheres on the flat roofs of his buildings. Their placement bore no relationship to the interior plans, nor was their presence visible from rooms immediately under the domes. In fact, domes often spanned the partitions between two rooms on an upper floor.

Muller's drawings reveal no concern for using authentic materials appropriate to his Eastern models. He used reinforced masonry block finished with stucco for the major public and commercial buildings. For the Administration Building he specified hollow tile blocks, brand-named "Natco," manufactured by the National Fireproofing Company, steel reinforcement, and brick spanning for arches, as well as a stucco finish with pseudo-aging. In drawings for his show-place, the Administration Building, Muller carefully detailed just where the stucco was to be interrupted so it would look as if it were cracked, revealing a fake structure of "ancient" bricks that had to be inserted into the real structure at the proper places.

Opa-locka's publicists boasted that all the houses were made of reinforced concrete block. However, details for wood-frame structures supporting a stucco finish show up in some of Muller's working drawings, including those for Mayor Wheeler's house. The construction photographs clearly confirm that the structure was built as Muller drew it, with broad horizontal boards filling a wooden frame and supporting veneers of stucco and native coral rock.

Whatever they were made of, Opa-locka's buildings survived the infamous hurricane of 1926 better than did construction in other Miami suburbs. Mayor Wheeler assured readers of the *American Institute of Architects Journal* in April 1928 that "the domes obviously caused less wind resistance than the flat surfaces while the thin minarets and towers successfully withstood the blow." Opa-locka's publicists failed to mention that the eye of the storm avoided the city. But after that date there was a shift in their emphasis. They wrote a great deal about substantial construction, as their promotion of the hurricane-proof house directly after the hurricane attests.

"Substantial" is a word that had figured prominently in the advertisements for Opa-locka from the first, and the copywriters seem to have delighted in the shock value of juxtaposing it with pictures of the most improbable fantasy architecture. But they nearly always associated the word with the town plan as a whole. "The City Substantial" headlined full-page newspaper advertisements that carried long columns detailing the superiority of Opa-locka's planning and singing the praises of its planner, Clinton Mackenzie (fig. 28).

Glenn Curtiss put his faith in planning after he saw what a lack of preplanned, regulated growth had yielded in his earlier venture at Hialeah. In his advertisements for Opa-locka he emphasized the plan as the special feature from which a homebuyer would benefit: "Beauty in Building—Permanence in Plan" began an advertisement in the *Miami Daily News and Metropolis* of 5 February 1926.

On these subjects, one of the most explicit advertisements appeared in the same newspaper on 3 May 1926, which read in part:

> Nothing is haphazard—nothing guessed at—nothing left to chance…First of all, Opa-locka was born…in the trained mind of Mr. Clinton Mackenzie. In his New York Studio he made "study" after "study" of the city that was to be. In his vision—at once artistic and practical—he "saw" Opa-locka… and it was only when he had thus "seen" that pencil was put to paper… Everything was thought out in advance…the locating of Civic Centers, Parks, Public Buildings, Golf Course, Residences, Commercial and Industrial Sections, Seaboard Air Line Passenger Station was completely and fully planned…

When Mackenzie got the Opa-locka job in 1925, he was in his mid-fifties and in his stride as a planner whose practice, based in New York, was beginning to have a national impact. He was a director of the National Planning Association and Tenement House Commissioner for the State of New Jersey. During World

Fig. 28. Full-page advertisement for Opa-locka from the *Miami Herald* of 10 January 1926 evokes the *Arabian Nights* theme in image and word.

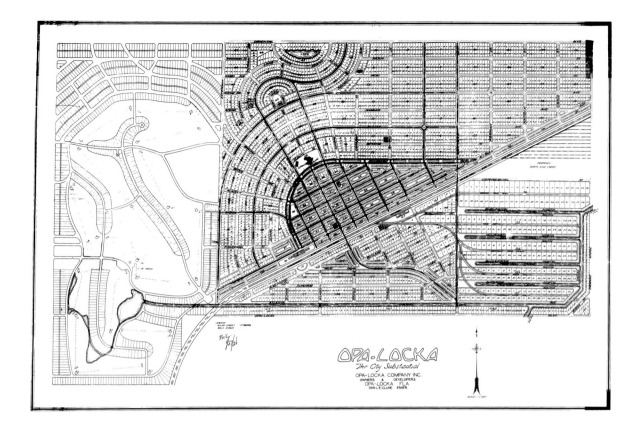

Fig. 29. Clinton Mackenzie's

town plan for Opa-locka,

c. 1926.

War I, he planned Amatol, New Jersey, for the United States Ordinance Department, and designed the massive office, dormitory, and munitions factories there. He also provided planning and architectural services for the U.S. Housing Corporation at Milton, Pennsylvania; for the National Cash Register Company in Dayton, Ohio; and for the International Coal Products Corporation at South Clinchfield, Virginia.

Mackenzie's most important work—a railroad station, hotel, apartment buildings, streets full of houses — had been executed in Kingsport, Tennessee, a planned industrial town, and the largest project of John Nolen (1869–1937), dean of U.S. planners. Just before the war, Kingsport was launched as a business venture and by 1920 it was being hailed as a model of profitable, rather than charitable or social, planning and housing.

In 1920 Mackenzie published a small volume called *Industrial Housing*. The town plan for Kingsport appears in that book, bearing the names of "Clinton Mackenzie, Architect, N Y City," and "John Nolen, Town Planner, Cambridge, Mass." The geometry of that plan for a town in the mountains is clearly the model for the layout of the streets of Opa-locka on the flat lands abutting the Everglades (fig. 29). As at Opa-locka, railroad tracks form the base of a rectangular grid that is confined to an asymmetrical triangular area. Above and around it curves an arc of parallel streets connected by cross streets that fan out like spokes.

Mackenzie's planning was impressive, so impressive that Opa-locka, like Coral Gables from which Curtiss borrowed so heavily, might even have pulled out of the Great Depression and resumed development along the lines he laid down in the 1920s. But everything in Opa-locka was haphazard from the Depression on. The Navy's expansion decimated the land and the landmarks, and swarms of naval personnel and their families swamped and then deserted the area. The Navy agreed to lease vacant facilities for private, industrial, and commercial development, reneged on the deal, and later decided it would lease some buildings. But by then tenants had lost confidence in ventures subject to the Navy's whim. The local economy has yet to recover fully from the dizzying pendulum swings.

"Streets will be always wide and wherever possible gently winding; every section of the city will be readily accessible by direct highways," promised an early brochure for Opa-locka. That promise, if few others of the mid-1920s, has been kept. From the heart of Miami, you can zoom very quickly up Interstate 95 to the economically depressed community that is Opa-locka today. Its native oak hammock is long gone. Donald Lawrence, "one of the most experienced landscape gardeners in south Florida," was never able to plant all the royal poinciana, bamboo, pithicolobium, eucalyptus, and some twenty-five hundred coconut palms that, he believed in 1926, "would make Opa-locka without question the most beautiful city on the East Coast."[16] But street signs still mark Sharazad Boulevard, Ali Baba Avenue, Aladdin Street, and dozens of others that have Arabic names and follow the geometry Mackenzie laid down on the land.

The Administration Building was restored in 1987 and, as City Hall, it is the pride of the community. Muller's drawings were vital to that restoration and to the more recent work of rehabilitating the Hurt Building, completed in 1991 by Grafton Architects, Inc. (figs. 30 and 31). For the burned-out train station — the only major Arabic landmark that Muller did not design — the future is still in doubt.

Since preservationists have identified over one hundred of the original buildings, more people are taking an interest in them. A well-stocked shelf of *Arabian Nights* storybooks at the public library makes it easy for children who live on Sesame Street to learn that it got its name not from a program on television but from Ali Baba saying "Open Sesame" to the magic door that guarded the treasure of the forty thieves. Aladdin has become a household word to them, as to most American children, since Disney brought out its film that takes the mischievous boy a long way from his fabled origins. But few of the African-American children who constitute the majority in the local classrooms of the town will ever encounter the erotic tales that reveal the ancient Arabian world's obsessive fear and hatred of the sexual power and allure of black slaves. Nor will their parents, who annually celebrate at the Arabian Nights Festival, donning costumes just as outlandish as those in which Opa-locka's residents of the 1920s posed for the sepia-toned photographs, smiling as broadly as their successors of the 1990s, who still lean, Fairbanks-like, on jars ever-handy for these now traditional occasions. □

Note

The author would like to acknowledge the help of the following people: William E. Brown Jr., head, Archives and Special Collections, Otto G. Richter Library, University of Miami; Patrick Campbell; Christopher Ondrick; Jorge García, curator, Slide Library and Visual Media Resources, University of Miami School of Architecture; Joseph Senker; and Thorn Grafton.

16. "Beautification Work is Progressing Nicely at Opa-locka," *Hialeah Press*, 13 August 1926, 1.

Fig. 1. Maurice Fatio, First National Bank of Palm Beach, 1927. Historical Society of Palm Beach County.

Inventing Antiquity: The Art and Craft of Mediterranean Revival Architecture

By Beth Dunlop

Beth Dunlop, for thirteen years the award-winning architecture critic of the *Miami Herald*, is the author of five books including *Building a Dream: The Art of Disney Architecture* (New York: Harry N. Abrams, 1996) and *Florida's Vanishing Architecture* (Sarasota: Pineapple Press, 1987). She writes regularly for *Architectural Digest* and *Architectural Record*.

The president of the First National Bank of Palm Beach commissioned the architect Maurice Fatio (1847–1943) to design a building for him in 1927. When it was finished, the new building on South County Road was redolent with atmosphere (fig. 1). Frank Shaugnessy, the bank's president, was so moved by the work of architectural art that he wrote to Fatio, effusively praising the new structure:

> The heavily paneled and richly stenciled cypress ceiling, showing multi-colored Moorish shields, is particularly beautiful. It looks hundreds of years old, and might easily have been an antique at the time Queen Isabella pawned her jewels to send Columbus on his memorable trip....Everything about the building breathes an old world atmosphere; yet it has all the modern accessories so necessary to the conduct of present day business....[1]

Elsewhere in the United States architects were working in the pure American style, which had evolved out of the Midwest's Prairie School of architecture, or were directly copying English or European models. But Florida itself was an invention, a tropical wonderland built on swamp and muck by canny and imaginative entrepreneurs, and it stands to reason that the Mediterranean Revival architecture that would come to symbolize this made-up place would be made-up as well, an architecture of fabrication more than scholarship, of improvisation more than precision.

Mediterranean Revival architecture was a picture-book pastiche offering instant history, imbuing a brand-new place with Old World charm. It came into being as an architecture for an elite — providing immediate ancient European pedigrees to the landed gentry of both Miami and Palm Beach. Quickly, however, the style found its fullest embodiment as an expression of a kind of democratic ideal in Coral Gables, where the city's founder, George Merrick (1886–1942), wished to build a near-utopian society. And across Florida came other Mediterranean Revival communities — Miami Shores, Fort Lauderdale's Progresso, Snell Island in St. Petersburg, Davis Island in Tampa.

In a place that was ripe for its own identity, Mediterranean Revival architecture had enormous image-making value, offering the words and pictures that would depict alluring, fanciful towns and cities and sell them at a distance. More than most others, the Mediterranean Revival style was a picturesque and narrative style, one dependent on art to guide it into being and elaborate

1. Frank A. Shaugnessy, letter to Maurice Fatio, 3 December 1927, *Maurice Fatio, Architect* (privately published, 1996).

phrase-making to tell its story, to sell it. It was intended, largely, to look Spanish, but it wasn't Spanish; it was a composite of Spanish Renaissance, Andalusian Moorish, Tuscan, Venetian, and Roman architectural elements, with allusions to classical Greece, Baroque France, and virtually any other place or era that seemed to fit.

The economist and author Ida Tarbell came to Florida for a whirlwind tour of its architecture in February 1926. Later she wrote that she had not expected to see anything revolutionary or even particularly interesting based on the images of Florida's architecture from early in the century: "The succession of builders who have in the past undertaken developments in Florida have thought architecturally in terms of Saratoga frame hotels, Middle West Queen Anne cottages or bleak New England farm houses, is the more puzzling."[2] And indeed, before the end of World War I, Florida did not have an architectural style to call its own.

Fatio expressed that idea in a letter he wrote to his parents, who lived in Switzerland: "There are no traditions to follow here if one wants to get away from the Colonial-style wooden house, and one is forced, for the Americans who don't want Modern art, to become eclectic, and to take one's inspiration from the best examples of the best periods of each European country."[3]

To make one's own way, however, required a comprehensive understanding of both the art and craft of building. Enormous attention was paid to every detail, from the coloration of thickly layered swirls of stucco to the artificial aging of wood ceiling beams. And architecture begat more than just buildings; a range of craft industries producing roof and floor tiles, furniture, and decorative accessories such as pottery grew along with it, providing the thousands of items needed both to create "Old World" houses and furnish them with what one advertisement termed "authentic furniture reproductions" of Spanish, Italian, and French designs (fig. 2).[4] Mediterranean Revival architecture was

2. Ida Tarbell, "Addison Mizner: Appreciation of a Layman," *The Florida Architecture of Addison Mizner*, ed. Ida Tarbell (New York: William Heilburn, 1928), xxxiii.

3. Maurice Fatio, letter to his parents, 13 December 1921, *Maurice Fatio, Architect.*

4. Advertisement for The Granada Shops, n.d., Florida Collection, Miami-Dade Public Library.

Fig. 3. A prototype Coral Gables residence constructed as an "everyman's Spanish castle," c. 1924. Fishbaugh Collection, City of Coral Gables Historic Preservation Department.

a descriptive, evocative architectural style that conjured up all the sensations of another time and place — a fictional and fabulous one at that — without specifically recreating anything in particular (fig. 3). And despite all the allusions to other places and other times, the Mediterranean Revival style is the only architectural style that can be said to have originated in Florida.

Most Mediterranean buildings were conceived first with pictures — elaborately detailed drawings in pen-and-ink or delicately washed with watercolor — which then were converted into prose poems for advertisements and articles that lyrically described their Old World attributes. The ultimate intention was effect: the pictures and words next were transformed into three dimensions, persuasive and atmospheric, and in the hands of the earliest and worthiest of practitioners the result was sophisticated and worldly.

Architecture was a sensory experience in Florida, and one that gave license to lush, untempered prose. In the late nineteenth and early twentieth centuries, travel writing, architecture writing, and promotional writing all focused on the quality of experience — sights, smells, sounds, textures, touches. For example, the pioneering journalist Marjory Stoneman Douglas described the houses in the emerging city of Coral Gables this way:

> Their doorways are thresholds of delight, leading by columns and arches through which sunlight and moonlight fall meltingly, into deep verandas and tiled patios where life in South Florida flows scented and leisurely and infinitely varied. Their great rooms are fit backgrounds for furniture and hangings redolent of conquistadores and armadas, but by reason of their great windows, are antechambers to the sky and air.[5]

5. Marjory Stoneman Douglas, *Coral Gables: Miami Riviera, An Interpretation* (Parker Publishing, 1927), 24.

A building that gave full expression to the ideas behind the Mediterranean Revival style was the Venetian Pool, built in Coral Gables in 1924. It is not truly a "Venetian" building, but its pictorial image is of a centuries-old lagoon-side building (fig. 4). "Nowhere has a swimming place been built which is so undoubtedly a work of great art," proclaimed a small book published in 1925 by the Coral Gables Corporation extolling the beauties of what was then called the Venetian Casino. The praise continued:

> The Venetian pool of Coral Gables not only focuses, with its broad green lagoons, its shady porticos and vine-covered loggias, its great Spanish towers, its tea rooms and dance floor and dressing rooms, the leisured life of

Fig. 5. Richard Kiehnel,

El Jardin, 1917, is generally

considered the first true

Mediterranean Revival

building. Photograph by

Ellen Uguccione.

a whole region, but it provides all America with a unique new architectural development of the highest artistic value, which will certainly set a new example for future builders….The artist wanted to create a structure as mellow in atmosphere as one of those old Venetian palazzos, worn old stones dreaming for centuries between the brilliancies of sun and sea and yet not at all in any slavish imitative way exactly Venetian.[6]

That text offers an enormous amount of information—the Venetian Pool is a "Spanish" building that is actually more Italian than Spanish. It was designed as a work of art as much as a work of architecture, and one intended to set a precedent. The purpose of melding so many architectural styles into a collage of architectural references and ornamental elements was to evoke antiquity, generally of a romantic Spanish nature. Mediterranean Revival architecture is often thought of as Spanish, and the two terms were (and still are) routinely used in an interchangeable fashion. Spanish was in vogue at the time; Spanish sold. In fact, Americans had begun their love affair with things Spanish in the late nineteenth century. In other parts of the country the Spanish style was an evolutionary style that grew out of continuous building traditions from the years of Spanish settlement. By contrast, in Florida, where despite a fort in St. Augustine and a handful of houses, there was no authentic Spanish architectural tradition, the style came in response to a need to express ideas about a place with no long history to draw on, no common culture, no unique aesthetic.

Mediterranean Revival architecture flourished in Florida in a compressed time period, starting in 1917, when Pittsburgh architect Richard Kiehnel (1870–1944) began designing a house on Biscayne Bay called El Jardin for Pittsburgh steel tycoon John Bindley (fig. 5). As Kiehnel was working on El Jardin in Miami, the architect Addison Mizner (1872–1933) was designing the Everglades Club in Palm Beach for sewing machine heir Paris Singer. A decade and a half later, most architects had turned their eyes to what we now call Art Deco or Moderne. The Mediterranean style dwindled away almost completely by the end of the

6. "Coral Gables Venetian Casino," promotional brochure, 1924, 7, Historical Museum of Southern Florida archives.

Depression as Moderne turned into Modern and the world went to war. By the end of World War II, sentiment was seldom a piece of the architectural parti.

So much happened so quickly during those few years that it sometimes seems to have happened all at once; architectural historians tend to be divided on the question of who really created the Mediterranean Revival style. Kiehnel's work has generally eluded scholarship, and he is little-credited with his prodigious contributions to the body of Florida architecture.[7] El Jardin is certainly the first building to explore the picturesque and romantic possibilities of the mixed-metaphor architecture of Mediterranean inspiration and the first in Florida to consciously employ creative crafting and coloration to make the new look old. However, Kiehnel went on to design buildings in a number of styles in addition to Mediterranean Revival, producing superlative work in every case, so it is difficult to give him credit for just one. Kiehnel's Coral Gables Congregational Church (1925), his Rolyat Hotel (1925), now Stetson Law School, in St. Petersburg, or his Rollins College buildings in Winter Park (spanning several years in the 1920s and 1930s) are much purer Spanish. His Scottish Rite Temple (1922) in downtown Miami was Egyptian Revival and it foreshadowed Art Deco by several years. His Carlyle Hotel (1941) on Ocean Drive in Miami Beach is a fine — and pure — "stucco deco" building.

Fig. 6. Addison Mizner,

center, shown here with

friends Marie Dressler and

Richard Barthelmmes, c. 1926.

Historical Society of Palm

Beach County.

Mizner, on the other hand, is virtually synonymous with the style; his last name is routinely used as an adjective, as in "a Mizner Mediterranean mansion," and most grand Palm Beach houses and commercial buildings have, at one time or another, been attributed to him rightly or wrongly. Mizner's first biographer called it the "Bastard-Spanish-Moorish-Romanesque-Gothic-Renaissance-Bull-Market-Damn-the-Expense Style," and he wasn't far from wrong.[8] As Mizner completed the Everglades Club, he became Palm Beach's most sought-after architect (fig. 6). In 1917 Palm Beach was a sleepy enclave of wooden "cottages" favored by just a few wealthy Americans; within a decade it had become the fabled winter resort for American society. Essentially, Mizner invented the town.

Mizner's work was daring, imaginative, romantic, and alluring. He was also prolific — his legacy in Florida alone was 160 buildings and ultimately much more. While working on the Everglades Club, it became clear that the accouterments he needed for his work — from carved doorframes to antiqued roof tiles — were not available in the quantities he would need. Consequently, he persuaded Paris Singer to open a factory to make these ornamental necessities. Eventually, Mizner Industries, as it grew to be called, supplied the decorative elements for most "Spanish-styled" houses throughout South Florida.[9]

Yet it is important to note that Kiehnel and Mizner were not the sole possessors or practitioners of the Mediterranean Revival style. The Swiss-born Fatio was in many ways the finest exponent of Mediterranean Revival (so much so that his houses and commercial buildings are often considered to be among Mizner's best designs); his work leaned more toward the Italian than the Spanish (fig. 7). Denman Fink (1881–1956), the artist and architect who was George Merrick's uncle, gave Coral Gables its otherworldly imprint in the earliest of

7. Kiehnel's architectural firm was Kiehnel and Elliott, but his partner John Elliott (whose name is sometimes seen without the second T on the end) "remains a mystery." Kiehnel came to Miami without Elliott. Albert M. Tannler, historical collections director of the Pittsburgh History and Landmarks Foundation, telephone interview by the author, November 1996.

8. Alvah Johnston, *The Legendary Mizner* (New York: Farrar, Straus and Young, 1953), 25.

9. Clemmer Mayhew III, untitled, unpublished biography of Addison Mizner, author's collection.

Fig. 7. Maurice Fatio. Historical
Society of Palm Beach County.

Fig. 8. Phineas Paist.
Photograph by Gleason W.
Romer. Romer Collection,
Miami-Dade Public Library.

buildings, including the Venetian Pool and the city's many gates, plazas, and fountains. The Philadelphia-born Phineas Paist (1875–1937) was the consummate colorist, taking what Kiehnel started in El Jardin and turning it into both science and art (fig. 8). Martin Luther Hampton, a Miami architect who worked with Mizner in the first few years of Palm Beach's emergence, spread the style in almost missionary fashion. Others — including Marion Syms Wyeth in Palm Beach, Francis Abreu in Fort Lauderdale, Dwight James Baum in Sarasota, Leo K. Elliott in St. Petersburg, and Walter deGarmo (1876–1964) and H. George Fink (1890–1975) in Coral Gables — also designed exemplary buildings in the Mediterranean Revival style.

Kiehnel was born in Germany in 1870 and educated there. He immigrated to the United States in 1898, living first in Chicago, then Cleveland (where the firm he was working for, Martin Dwyer and Associates, designed an addition to the great American architect Philip Johnson's [born 1906] boyhood home), and then Pittsburgh. In Pittsburgh he became a sought-after designer and a driving force in the intellectual community; he mounted exhibitions and introduced the city to the works of European architects. Ironically, he also came to be noted as one of Pittsburgh's foremost practitioners of the Prairie style. In 1917 after Bindley asked him to design a house on the edge of Biscayne Bay in Coconut Grove, Kiehnel moved to Miami. Though he kept his partnership and practice in Pittsburgh, he never really looked back and scarcely ever designed a Prairie-style building again.[10]

Only scant records exist from Kiehnel's prodigious, important, and prolific career in Florida, so his ideas and motivations largely have been lost to history. This much is known about El Jardin, however: researchers preparing the house's nomination to the National Register of Historic Places turned up evidence that Kiehnel carefully wrought the house's antiquity, using techniques he invented on the spot, such as layering paint to get an aged patina. Significantly, El Jardin drew its architectural inspiration from both Italy and Spain; it was at once Venetian and Andalusian. It sits tightly against its beautiful swimming pool as if it were built right up to a canal, but it also has the swirled decorative columns and the massing of a Moorish garden house. It combines rigorous knowledge of and reference to architectural history in a design that is ultimately impressionistic rather than accurate, thus the mixed architectural metaphor we now call Mediterranean Revival.

Mizner had enough personal imagery to mix metaphors all on his own. Born in Benicia, California, in 1872, he studied in Guatemala and Spain and then apprenticed with and later became a partner of the San Francisco architect Willis Polk (1867–1924). Always an adventurer, Mizner garnered a sizeable fortune in the Alaskan gold fields, then went to live in Hawaii, Samoa, and Guatemala before moving to New York. Mizner was coming into full favor as a society architect in New York when Paris Singer lured him to Palm Beach in 1918 to design the Everglades Club.

The Everglades Club was constructed at its now-prime location at the foot of what was to become the illustrious Worth Avenue. With its courtyards and cloistered walkways, the Everglades Club looked as if it had stood there for years, an evocation of eras past (fig. 9). Mizner biographer Donald W. Curl points out that during construction the reaction to the architecture was

10. One of Kiehnel's Florida buildings, Miami High School (1925), though considered to be Mediterranean Revival actually does share numerous characteristics with Prairie School buildings.

Fig. 9. A loggia at the Everglades Club, c. 1920. Historical Society of Palm Beach County.

lukewarm; by the time it was finished, the Everglades was garnering the typically overwrought adulation of the times and yielding new design commissions.[11]

Indeed, Mediterranean-inspired architecture was not prevalent in Florida at the time, despite St. Augustine's Spanish Ponce de León and Alcázar hotels and Tampa's Moorish Plant Hotel, and despite the fact that both cities were popular tourist destination. However, Mizner—with his Central American and Spanish education and his innate sense of the romantic—simply forged ahead, ultimately changing the face of Florida (fig. 10).

A 1918 article in the *Palm Beach Post* proclaimed that: "His artistic insight showed him that he had here an unique opportunity to adapt his architecture to his surroundings and not to force his environment into unwilling agreement with a style where there was no natural harmony between them." The article continued:

11. Donald Curl, *Mizner's Florida* (New York: The Architectural History Foundation and MIT Press, 1984), 41–52.

Instead of repeating the common and hideous mistake that has been perpetrated all through Florida of using a style of architecture adapted to northern surroundings and bleak and repellent climate, he has searched Italy, Spain and Northern Africa for a model, and has used a blended, softened type of color and line that will prove a revelation....it may be said that there is probably not another example of the feudal, medieval, Italian, Spanish style so blended in delicious harmony to be found in the United States.[12]

Some years later, Mizner wrote about his own design process, and what he had to say explains a great deal about the architectural style he was inventing. Basically, he created an imaginary history for his buildings: "I sometimes start a house with a Romanesque corner, pretend that it has fallen into disrepair and been added to in the Gothic spirit, when suddenly the great wealth of the New World has poured in and the owner had added a very rich Renaissance addition."[13]

The Everglades Club — designed in 1917 and 1918, remodeled in 1919 and then almost every year after that — gave Mizner ample opportunity to put this storytelling technique to practice. The *Palm Beach Post*, at the time of the club's opening, reported that Mizner had envisioned an ancient castle that became a monastery, an "ancient pile" that

Fig. 10. Addison Mizner, Playa Riente, 1923, designed for Joshua Cosden. Historical Society of Palm Beach County.

looms large and high and venerable....The living room is magnificent, being eighty-five [feet] long by forty-four feet wide and containing a fireplace six and a half feet high, and big enough to roast the proverbial ox. In fact the whole structure carries suggestions of barons of beef, flagons of wine, and of monks who may have figured in one of Boccacio's deathless tales.[14]

What is extraordinary about this effusive prose is that it was, in fact, selling nothing; the Everglades Club was conceived and opened as a home for convalescent soldiers returning from World War I. As such, it was a flop; despite the alluring descriptions, soldiers did not flock there, thus the first remodeling from convalescent center into private club.

Much of what went into the evocative Everglades Club had to be manufactured locally. As it became clear that Mizner was going to be much in demand by other clients, Singer threatened to close the plant Mizner had convinced him to open, so Mizner bought it. Begun as The Novelty Works, the plant became Los Manos, then Addison Mizner Industries and Antigua Shops, Inc., advertising the manufacture of "pottery, roof and floor tile, period furniture, wicker, upholstering, repairing, antique millwork and hardware, bronze sash, wrought iron, stained and leaded glass windows, reconstructed and ornamental stone and imitation marble." Mizner Industries produced almost anything that could have been found on or in a house in Spain or Italy or Morocco. Sales brochures show thousands of items — from roof and floor tiles, to ornamental iron and cast-stone work, to decorative pots and planters, to furniture for virtually every room in a many-roomed mansion (figs. 11 and 12). Furniture and ornament alike were copies of antiques or intended to look as if they had been rescued from a Central American church or a medieval Spanish convent. The techniques, however, were enterprising — the aging of wood, the battering

---

12. "Wonderful Artistic Effects Achieved in Architecture of Paris Singer's Homes for Convalescent Soldiers," *Palm Beach Post*, 27 October 1918.

13. "Addison Mizner: Appreciation of a Layman," xxxix.

14. "Wonderful Artistic Effects Achieved."

Fig. 11. Mizner Industries pottery sales brochure, c. 1923. Historical Society of Palm Beach County.

Fig. 12. Mizner Industries brochure showing a range of products, c. 1923. Historical Society of Palm Beach County.

Fig. 13. A mantlepiece crafted by Mizner Industries. Photograph by Ray B. Dame, 1926. Historical Society of Palm Beach County.

Fig. 14. Mizner Industries craftsmen at work. Photograph by Ray B. Dame, 1926. Historical Society of Palm Beach County.

Fig. 15. Mizner Industries craftsmen at work. Photograph by Ray B. Dame, 1926. Historical Society of Palm Beach County.

▶

Fig. 16. A promotional photograph for Mizner Industries, c. 1923. Historical Society of Palm Beach County.

of metal, the glazing of clay. Stories abound of the "aging" of furniture and building materials by pounding them with hammers, hatchets, ice picks, or even iron rods, of submerging wood or iron in salt water or an acidic compound, of using bicarbonate of soda to make aged cast stone (figs. 13 to 16). Simple but effective formulas ruled everything from the mixing of glazes to the making of mantlepieces.[15]

Many of those formulas survive today, preserved for perpetuity straight from the typewriter of C. R. Crandall, the general manager and Mizner Industries' longtime foreman. A transparent glaze, for example, was four parts ground

15. Christina Orr, "Addison Mizner, Architect of Dreams and Realities (1872–1933)," exhibition catalogue, Norton Museum of Art (West Palm Beach, Fla.: 1977), 52–59; and Curl, *Mizner's Florida.*

Fig. 17. The Granada Shops furniture showroom, c. 1925. Fishbaugh Collection, City of Coral Gables Historic Preservation Department.

flint glass, four parts ground white lead and one-fourth part oxide of zinc. One such recipe read:

> To make large Cast Stone Pots establish a pipe in the ground on a flat surface — make a sweep or template the shape of the inside mould or form for the pot, place a quantity of wet sand around the pipe and make a sand form, using the sweep to shape it — the sweep being made to form this mould; then apply neet [*sic*] cement to the outside of the form to harden it.[16]

Mizner Industries was a going concern by the time Merrick began planning his dream city of Coral Gables. Merrick — a poet and visionary as much as a businessman — fantasized a near-utopian planned city that would be virtually self-sufficient; his plans called for everything from agriculture to industry. The prospectus for the Crafts Section reflected his notion that artisans of all kinds would gather to create or manufacture almost anything that would be required by a self-sufficient society. Merrick's vision was different from Mizner's in that he was intent on building a community where people of greater and lesser means could raise crops, produce both necessities and baubles, be educated, and be entertained. The newspaper announcement of the Crafts Section pointed out that the work done there would include, among other things, fine printing and engraving, willow and rattan furniture, ornamental stones and jewelry, tapestries and rug weaving. The Crafts Section

16. C. R. Crandall, papers from Mizner Industries, Palm Beach County Historical Society archives.

also was to have an exposition center and "hundreds of charming homes which will house the artisans employed in the various industries, and these homes will be just as distinctive in architecture as will the craft shops."[17]

The Crafts Section remained a dream, for the most part, lost to the devastating hurricane of September 1926 and the subsequent bottoming out of the economy. One element of it that did get built was The Granada Shops, on Ponce de León Boulevard in Coral Gables (figs. 17 and 18). The Granada Shops — specialty "authentic reproductions"— produced a great deal of the heavy brocade and tapestry-clad carved-wood furniture that filled the sales centers, offices, and new homes of Coral Gables. Newspaper advertisements of the period show that a competing furniture producer, Imperial Furniture Shops, offered "Spanish, Italian and period furniture designed and executed by skilled craftsmen…original designs as well as reproductions."[18] Such furniture was used in the elaborately and carefully decorated offices and promotional sales centers in Coral Gables, and did indeed fill many houses.

The April 1924 issue of *National Home Builder* offered a typically effusive and promotional discussion of the design and development of Coral Gables, filled

17. Flyer announcing Coral Gables Crafts Section, n.d., Florida Collection, Miami-Dade Public Library.

18. Advertisement, Imperial Furniture Shops, *Pictorial Guide to Coral Gables*, A. B. Willis and Co., n.d.

with glorious descriptions. But it also contained a detailed discussion of architecture, explaining why and how the Mediterranean Revival style was then and remains so distinctive, and such a particular expression of Florida. House by house, the editors dissected both pragmatic and poetic secrets of the style, noting the "freehand" character of the detailing where nothing seems to have been copied from any precedent. "Here will be found no dry as dust copying but rather a type of architecture that is in keeping with its setting and its time," they wrote.[19]

Instant antiquity was the goal, and it was achieved (fig. 19). In 1924 Denman Fink wrote a treatise entitled *Castles in Spain Made Real*; part of it was devoted to a discussion of the "rawness" and "garishness" of most new houses being built elsewhere in the United States. In Coral Gables, however, Fink said:

> you are not going to sense this blatant newness, even from the start, for in very truth it will not be new. It will simply be ages-old material taking on new forms. What you see as a house today was the same time-mellowed rock a score of centuries ago. The rock that yesterday slept in the shade of the lovely lantana today is but a restful structural foreground to the grey-green of the spreading live oak.[20]

Likewise, Phineas Paist, who was the consulting architect for Coral Gables for many years, wrote about the painting and tinting of stucco, saying: "the effect tried for is that of an old building that has been colored many times and through time, or weathering, retains fragments of all its old age colorings."[21] There were no closely kept secrets. Although the architects were creating fantasy worlds, they also let it be known, proudly, just how they went about making the mystique.

In those expansive, ebullient years after World War I, architecture was part of the public discourse, and a good fake ancient Spanish castle or Italian palazzo was a triumph. No era before or since offered up so many romantic possibilities for Florida. Though the finished products often reflected the spontaneous whims of the architects and the improvisational impulses of the craftsmen, they were persuasively old and excessively elegant. The notion that a building or landscape could create an emotional response was generally accepted then, only to be lost in the era after World War II as Modernism took hold and the United States looked only to an efficient, unsentimental future rather than a romantic, imaginary past. □

19. "The Story of Coral Gables," *National Home Builder* (April 1924).

20. Denman Fink, "Castles in Spain Made Real," *Coral Gables—Miami's Master Suburb* (Coral Gables: privately published, 1924), 10.

21. Phineas Paist, "Stucco—Color," *National Home Builder* (April 1924).

Fig. 19. The George Merrick house appears almost as if it had risen from the ruins, imparting the idea that it was ancient, not modern,

c. 1926. Fishbaugh Collection, City of Coral Gables Historic Preservation Department.

Fig. 1. John Eberson, Tampa Theatre, stage and right sidewall, 1926. From a postcard, Bernard Zyscovich collection.

Dream Palaces: The Motion Picture Playhouse in the Sunshine State

By Michael D. Kinerk and Dennis W. Wilhelm

Michael D. Kinerk and Dennis W. Wilhelm are the authors, with Barbara Capitman, of *Rediscovering Art Deco U.S.A.* (New York: Viking, 1994) and are founding members of the Miami Design Preservation League. Michael Kinerk is also a founding member of the Theatre Historical Society and for ten years chaired the Art Deco Weekend festival in Miami Beach, Florida. Dennis Wilhelm is the chair of the Barbara Baer Capitman Archives and serves as archivist for Arquitectonica International.

It was a brief era, as golden eras go. It had swept in on a floodtide of splendor, of million-dollar real estate deals, of fantastic architecture, of music, laughter, and dreams, less than a decade before. And it was to end....The whole dizzy, prodigal, enchanted business came to gaudy full bloom, filled the night with its scent, wilted, and drooped in the short span of years that lay between the coming of Prohibition and the onset of the Depression. [1]

With their epic scale, tropical courtyards, dimly lit corridors, and opulent public salons, the motion picture dream palaces built early in our century paid tribute to architectural wonders of the past. The pyramids of Egypt, the Alhambra, and Versailles offered inspiration for movie theatres erected throughout the United States (figs. 1 and 2). However, there was a modern aspect that superseded the links to the past — all of the picture palaces had thoroughly new technology to project flickering images of romance or tragedy. After 1930 all of them were wired for sound. They had climate control to chill hot sultry nights and to warm the coldest winter freeze, in rooms so vast that the sultans who built the original palaces would have torn their turbans in envy.

From 1908 to 1917 Thomas A. Edison's (1847–1931) film patents were controlled by the Motion Picture Patents company, binding the earliest studios in a cartel finally broken by court order. [2] After this, the motion picture studio system grew rapidly. Each major production studio bought, merged with, or created a distribution arm, a publicity machine, and most importantly, bought or built increasingly spectacular chains of exhibition outlets. Fierce competition and the vast potential for profits dictated that by 1920 these theatres — flagships of the studio in each city — be the best. Each studio was forced, literally, to build dream palaces (figs. 3 and 4).

Though the balance shifted several times through the years, there was always a hierarchy in terms of the major studios. In 1931 it was, in order, Paramount, Warner, Fox, Loew's, and RKO. These firms were responsible for building the nation's most lavish showplaces. By 1931 Paramount Publix, the operating exhibition subsidiary of Paramount Studios, had 971 theatres; Warner had 529; Fox had 521; Loew's had 189; and RKO had 161. [3]

In 1927, the zenith of the silent-picture era, Florida had three exceptional dream palaces with more than two thousand seats, and twenty-one with more than

1. Ben M. Hall, *The Best Remaining Seats* (New York: Bramhall House, 1961), 12.
2. Richard Dyer MacCann, *The First Tycoons* (Iowa City: Image and Idea Inc., with Scarecrow Press of Metuchen, N.J. and London, 1987), 247.
3. Ibid., 181.

left,

Fig. 2. John Eberson, rendering of exterior facade of Tampa Theatre, 1926. From a printed color cover of a prospectus for building bonds, 11 x 14". Eberson Archive, Mitchell Wolfson Jr. Collection, The Wolfsonian, Florida International University, Miami Beach, Florida.

above,

Fig. 3. John Eberson, Tampa Theatre, exterior facade with upright sign, 1926. Eberson Archive, Mitchell Wolfson Jr. Collection, The Wolfsonian, Florida International University, Miami Beach, Florida.

Fig. 4. John Eberson, Tampa Theatre, box office and entry, 1926. Eberson Archive, Mitchell Wolfson Jr. Collection, The Wolfsonian, Florida International University, Miami Beach, Florida.

one thousand seats. In addition to the largest theatres, Florida had nearly one hundred smaller, more conventional cinemas, each less than one thousand seats, sprinkled across the state by the dozens in bigger counties, with at least one or two in practically every county. Between 1900 and 1950 more than five hundred movie houses were built in Florida. Population was the prime determinant in the construction of the theatres. Dade County (with both Miami and Miami Beach) had the most theatres operating in this period, followed by Hillsborough (Tampa), Pinellas (St. Petersburg), Duval (Jacksonville), Polk (Lakeland), and Broward (Fort Lauderdale) counties.[4]

The studios employed a select group of architects, primarily using the services of John Eberson (1875–1954), Thomas W. Lamb (1871–1942), and the brothers

4. Florida theatre operating data compiled from Motion Picture Association of America (MPAA) research department, *Theatre Directory, Atlanta Exchange Territory* (New York: February, 1948); and *Film Daily Yearbook* (Florida chapters) 1930, 1945, 1955.

Cornelius W. (1861–1927) and George Rapp (1878–1942), whose firm was known as Rapp and Rapp. Just as there was a second tier of theatre chains (Universal, Columbia, United Artists), there was a second tier of architectural firms working nationwide, including S. Charles Lee (1899–1990) and C. Howard Crane. These architects were also first-rate movie theatre architects; they merely designed fewer theatres than Eberson, Lamb, and Rapp and Rapp.

Florida's dream palaces were smaller than those in Northern states, where Paramount Publix's flagships were three-thousand-plus-seat titans, with as many square feet in the lobbies and corridors as in the auditoriums. Loew's "Wonder Theatres" were just as large. Fox built five spectacular five-thousand-seat houses in Atlanta, Brooklyn, Detroit, Saint Louis, and San Francisco. The strategy was to maximize revenues by holding enough people waiting in the massive lobbies to fill the auditorium quickly for the next show. People were lured in both by the extravagantly decorated lobbies and the entertainment provided within. The lobbies were, if anything, more sumptuous than the auditoriums, with huge chandeliers, towering marble columns, fine oil paintings, antiques, luxurious furniture (often imported from Europe), and other accoutrements appropriate for a true palace (figs. 5 and 6).

The lobbies often featured musicians, usually pianists, performing in the hours before the next show. Some of the largest theatres had a separate pipe organ in the lobby, and all true movie palaces had a mighty Wurlitzer, Kimball, or Robert Morton pipe organ within the auditorium. Nothing that could amuse the patrons was considered excessive, as Harold W. Rambusch, a renowned theatre decorator, explained in a 1927 article:

> The vast majority of those attending our theatres are of very limited means. Their homes are not luxurious and the theatre affords them an opportunity to imagine themselves as wealthy people in luxurious surroundings. They may come here as often as they please by paying a small fee within their means and feel themselves to be the lords of all they survey. In our

Fig. 6. John Eberson, Tampa

Theatre, main lobby, pent

eaves, staircase, floor lamps,

urns, stanchions, 1926.

Eberson Archive, Mitchell

Wolfson Jr. Collection, The

Wolfsonian, Florida

International University, Miami

Beach, Florida.

big modern movie palaces there are collected the most gorgeous rugs, furniture and fixtures that money can produce. No kings or emperors have wandered through more luxurious surroundings.[5]

In Florida no city was large enough to warrant such massive theatres.[6] However, in 1926–1927, Paramount Publix, as it was then known, opened four of the most spectacular of the hundreds of theatres built or yet-to-be built in Florida: the Tampa, Jacksonville's Florida, Miami's Olympia, and St. Petersburg's Florida.

Of Florida's dream palaces, none was finer than the opulent but compact Tampa Theatre, built in 1926, and designed by architect John Eberson (1875–1954). Roy A. Benjamin (1888–1963) and Robert E. Hall (1888–1963) also were affiliated with the project (figs. 1–10). The Tampa Theatre closely approached the standard set by its big-city counterparts, although it had neither a hospital, children's playroom, nor third- and fourth-floor foyers.[7] In keeping with Florida's three hundred years of Spanish history, the most stunning picture palaces were of Moorish-Iberian derivation. The Tampa Theatre was no exception and has been described by one historian as one of Eberson's finest "Andalusian bonbons."[8]

5. Harold W. Rambusch, "The Decorations of the Theatre," ed. R. W. Sexton, *American Theatres of Today* (New York: Architectural Book Publishing Company, 1930), 2:24.

6. U.S. 1920 Census figures: Jacksonville, 91,558; Tampa, 51,608; Pensacola, 31,035; Miami, 29,571; Key West, 18,749; St. Petersburg, 14,327; Orlando, 9,282; West Palm Beach, 8,659; Lakeland, 7,062; Gainesville, 6,860.

7. Restored in 1977 and placed on the National Register the following year, the Tampa Theatre is now a city-owned performing arts center offering film screenings. It is the only Florida movie palace used for its originally intended purpose. It had a Wurlitzer theatre pipe organ recently reinstalled to provide authentic accompaniment for silent film classics; Eberson job #571, Eberson Archive, Mitchell Wolfson Jr. Collection, The Wolfsonian, Florida International University. Data also from KBJ Architects' Roy A. Benjamin project list.

8. Hall, *The Best Remaining Seats*, 97.

Fig. 7. John Eberson, Tampa Theatre, upper mezzanine with antique fourteenth-century Spanish decorative cabinet, pitchers, vases, wrought-iron torchieres, large medieval tapestry, 1926. Eberson Archive, Mitchell Wolfson Jr. Collection, The Wolfsonian, Florida International University, Miami Beach, Florida.

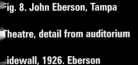

Fig. 8. John Eberson, Tampa Theatre, detail from auditorium sidewall, 1926. Eberson Archive, Mitchell Wolfson Jr. Collection, The Wolfsonian, Florida International University, Miami Beach, Florida.

Fig. 9. John Eberson, Tampa Theatre, stage and sidewalls, 1926. Eberson Archive, Mitchell Wolfson Jr. Collection, The Wolfsonian, Florida International University, Miami Beach, Florida.

The Tampa Theatre sat behind a ten-story brick office tower. Its design, in the words of a 1926 article from Tampa's *Daily Times*, was "of the true Hispano-Italian style — that which came into vogue during the reign of Ferdinand and Isabella, lovers of art, who invited Italian architects, sculptors and painters to participate in some of the architectural wonders built during this period."[9]

By 1926, the year the Tampa Theatre opened, there were more than eighty cinemas in Florida. Many were designed with tropical elements, in keeping with the state's climate. It is not surprising that Eberson, architect of the "atmospheric" style, cited Florida as his inspiration:

> I have been wintering in Florida for the past several years, and it is from this state that I got the atmospheric idea. I was impressed with the colorful scenes which greeted me at Miami, Palm Beach, and Tampa, where I saw happy, gaily-dressed people living constantly under azure skies, and amongst tropical splendor. Visions of Italian gardens, Spanish patios, Persian shrines and French formal garden lawns flashed through my mind, and at once I directed my energies to carrying out these ideas.[10]

The atmospheric style that Eberson popularized consisted not of domes, marble columns, or crystal chandeliers; rather, the effect was of romantic "outdoor" courtyards, surrounded by villas and tropical foliage, and topped by twilight blue skies with twinkling stars and slowly drifting clouds. Although this effect was created with plaster, electric lights, and projection machines, it was nonetheless galvanizing, and its popularity catapulted the architect to the forefront of his profession. Eberson designed hundreds of theatres during his career, but very few examples survive.[11]

Eberson described the atmospheric style in a 1927 article in *Motion Picture News*:

> Ambition and competition among owners and architects in these enterprises had resulted in the elaboration of ornamentation and architectural effort, until I felt the saturation point — if I may use the term in this connection — had been reached, and that an appreciative amusement-loving public could expect no more development in this direction. Under such conditions it was not unnatural that the elaboration of ornament should go to extremes and in some outbursts of the competitive spirit result in many cases where the ornament became oppressive and overshadowed the stage and screen presentations....
>
> Our first "atmospheric" design, the Majestic Theatre in Houston, Texas, has been the forerunner of over a hundred playhouses of this type in a comparatively short period of time. This rather quickly-won popularity may be attributed to the fact that these auditoriums are successfully different and are merely dignified imitations of nature glorifying classic architecture. Few innovations in the theatrical business have taken root as quickly as the Atmospheric Theatre...[12]

9. John Eberson interview, *Daily Times* (Tampa), 15 October 1926, sec. C, p. 10.

10. Ibid.

11. Eberson's greatest creation was the now-demolished 3,612-seat Paradise Theatre (1927), in Chicago. The 3,842-seat Loew's Paradise (1928), in the Bronx, New York, survives but its future is questionable. The Avalon (1927), a 2,387-seat Persian fantasy, survives in good condition on the south side of Chicago. Jane Preddy, "Palaces of Dreams, The Movie Theatres of John Eberson, Architect," catalogue for exhibition (San Antonio: McNay Art Museum, 1989).

12. John Eberson, "New Theatres for Old, Originator of the Atmospheric Style Discussed the Formula in Which Art and Showmanship Meet," *Motion Picture News* 1 (30 December 1927).

Plaza Theatre, St. Petersburg, Fla.

Fig. 11. Boniwell and Son, La

Plaza Theatre, St. Petersburg,

plaza entryway, auditorium in

rear, 1912. From a postcard.

Florida State Archives.

While Eberson is associated with the development of the atmospheric style, the Cort Theatre (1909) in Chicago, designed by J. E. O. Pridmore, often is cited as the first such theatre in the United States. In analyzing Eberson's design of the Olympia Theatre in Miami, architect Stuart Grant concluded:

> In a sense, it is unfair to Eberson to look for precedents. One can almost always find some similarities between different buildings of the same type. Eberson is to be credited with developing, perfecting, and marketing the Atmospheric concept. His theatres were more than just a painted sky. The illusion reached into every nook and cranny of his theatres—and it was convincing.[13]

After 1930, when the atmospheric style fell out of fashion and Art Deco came into vogue, Eberson and his son Drew designed many Art Deco theatres across the country. The style shift was due to a combination of factors — acoustical considerations for sound pictures along with the Great Depression rendered the large, opulently decorated atmospheric palaces obsolete. The Art Deco theatres were smaller, though still luxurious, and this streamlined style still is much identified with South Florida.

Despite the differences in style, both the extravagant 1920s' versions and the sleek 1930s' varieties of Florida's theatres trace their origins to 1897, when Jacksonville's Park Opera House was converted to allow the first commercial exhibition of a motion picture in Florida.[14] Within a decade there were about a dozen nickelodeons in the more populous regions of the state.

In 1904 Jacksonville's Duval Theatre became the first theatre converted exclusively to the showing of photoplays. The Empire opened on East Jefferson Street in the Panhandle town of Quincy shortly thereafter. In 1905 the Royal Palm Theatre opened on Central Avenue in St. Petersburg, becoming the first cinema in that city. Miami got its first motion picture venue when Kelly's Theatre opened on Flagler Street in 1906. Many early movie theatres were buildings converted from other purposes. One of the most notable of these

13. Stuart Matthew Grant, "Miami's Olympia Theatre" (master's thesis, University of Florida, 1987): 9.

14. Richard Alan Nelson, *Lights! Camera! Florida! Ninety Years of Moviemaking and Television in the Sunshine State* (Tampa: Florida Endowment for the Humanities, 1987), 108.

Fig. 12. Architect unknown, Community Theatre, Miami Beach, exterior marquee and courtyard entrance at night, 1921. Arva Parks collection.

was St. Petersburg's La Plaza (1912), which was renovated several times, and eventually got a dramatic entrance that went through a courtyard, then into the auditorium via bridge over the alley (fig. 11).[15]

By 1920 most of Florida's larger cities had a motion picture venue, with a statewide total of some forty theatres. By then a standard had emerged for movie theatres in small- or medium-size towns. They had to be decorative, inviting, and typically they had to have between six hundred and twelve hundred seats. Movies were shown under the stars in Miami Beach at a place called the Strand, but the first real motion picture theatre there was the seven-hundred-seat Community (1921) on Lincoln Road (fig. 12). Another typical theatre of this period was Fort Lauderdale's Sunset Theatre (1923), which opened with 757 seats; in 1934 it was remodeled by Roy A. Benjamin, and probably enlarged to 989 seats (fig. 13).[16]

15. Ibid.; Florida site file #GD00282, Tallahassee: Division of Historic Preservation, Secretary of State's Office, State of Florida; Ted White, "The Theatres of St. Petersburg, Florida," *Marquee, Journal of the Theatre Historical Society of America* 14 (fourth quarter 1982): 7, 14; Grant, "Miami's Olympia Theatre," 18.

16. MPAA, 1948; *Film Daily Yearbook*, 1930, 1945, 1955; the Sunset Theatre was demolished around 1970.

Fig. 13. Architect unknown, 1923, Sunset Theatre, Fort Lauderdale; Roy A. Benjamin remodeling, 1934, Art Deco sunset-motif marquee from remodeling. Romer Collection, Miami-Dade Public Library.

Florida's history with motion pictures extends beyond exhibition to film production. From 1908 to 1917 Florida emerged as the major winter film production center. Hollywood, California was known, but not preeminent until after 1915. In 1908 New York City reigned as the United States' film capital, while Jacksonville vied with Chicago and Hollywood for the number-two spot.

In fact, Jacksonville, with approximately thirty motion picture studios, was touted as the "winter film capital of the world" until an election in 1917 drove out of town the rowdy, vulgar, and often unscrupulous film producers. Jacksonville's Mayor "Jet" Bowden was a film booster, but after the conservative citizenry voted him out, the city's movie industry began its immediate decline. Sunshine and palm trees were not a Florida monopoly, and California soon became the center of the film universe.[17]

Until the Jacksonville election, studios such as Biograph, Edison, Gaumont, Kalem, Keystone, Klutho, Luben, and Selig regularly made feature photoplays

17. Nelson, *Lights! Camera! Florida!*, 26, 108.

in the state, using or leasing studios in Jacksonville. Among notable Florida productions were Edison Studios' 1898 newsreel scenes of American troops departing from Port Tampa for action in the Spanish-American War. That production came only four years after Thomas Edison founded the first motion picture studio in the United States. Later, many of director Mack Sennett's *Keystone Cops* comedies were filmed in Florida. Both Lionel Barrymore and Oliver Hardy began their film careers in Jacksonville. The legendary D. W. Griffith, who began in New York City as an actor for Biograph, directed several features in Florida, which included scenes on the beaches of Fort Lauderdale and Miami Beach.[18]

Jacksonville, in addition to being a production center, was also Florida's largest city during the boom-time era of the silent picture (1905–1927). As such, it was home to the state's largest dream palace: the 2,211-seat Florida Theatre (1927) designed by Robert E. Hall and Roy A. Benjamin (figs. 14, 15, and 16).[19] This theatre was in the heart of the city on East Forsyth Street, and featured a popular open-air roof garden above the auditorium. Although it had a rugged Spanish or Mediterranean fortress-like exterior, the Florida Theatre interior had romantic atmospheric lobbies with Spanish-tiled pent eaves overhung with flowering vines, framing an open blue sky on the domed plaster above them. Theatre historian David Naylor points out a striking resemblance between the Florida and the Tampa theatres' atmospheric lobbies, noting that Michael Angelo Studios of Chicago was used to furnish the Florida Theatre and was "often used by Eberson," architect of the Tampa Theatre.[20]

In fact, the Michael Angelo Studios was a wholly owned subsidiary of John Eberson's architecture practice. According to Eberson's son Drew, the staff of Michael Angelo Studios were his father, himself, and his mother, along with others. The historian Jane Preddy interviewed Drew Eberson in 1989:

> Michael Angelo Studios was the name of our design team….About 30 people…They moved from theatre to theatre installing the plaster ornamentation, the statuary, trees and birds, painting the walls. They hung the banners my mother and sisters made. My job was ordering and placing the statuary, mapping out the stars, and generally seeing to it that things went well….The ornamentation for the walls and ceiling was cast plaster produced from clay molds. The fellow responsible was Rudy Schmidt, owner of the Schmidt firm in Chicago. The free-standing sculpture we ordered from Caproni Studios…. As for the lighting fixtures, we designed them ourselves…then had them made in Chicago by Pearlman. Father used a lot of pink lightbulbs and since they were impossible to buy, he dipped them in pink paint….The tapestries?…Many of them were from a theatre supply company in New York….the furniture also…there, and from antique shops in New Orleans.[21]

The design team would work for weeks, painting every surface in appropriate polychrome. They would reenter the theatre shortly before the opening and "blitz" it with decorations. These always consisted of large wooden throne-like

18. Ibid., 14–15, 20–21, 28, 31, 108, 18, 43.

19. The Florida Theatre of Jacksonville was placed on the National Register in 1982.

20. Architect Robert E. Hall was supervisor of construction for Paramount Publix in Florida; see also Grant, "Miami's Olympia Theatre," 23; data from "Florida Theatre floor plans," R.W. Sexton and B. F. Betts, ed., *American Theatres of Today* (New York: Architectural Book Publishing, 1927), 1:78–79; David Naylor, *Great American Movie Theatres* (Washington, D.C.: Preservation Press, 1987), 97.

21. Preddy, "Movie Theatres of Eberson," 5, 15–16, 18.

Fig. 14. Robert E. Hall with Roy A. Benjamin, Florida Theatre, Jacksonville, view from mezzanine lounge looking down to atmospheric promenade, 1926. Photograph © Steven Brooke.

Fig. 15. Robert E. Hall with Roy A. Benjamin, Florida Theatre, Jacksonville, atmospheric promenade, 1926. Photograph © Steven Brooke.

Spanish chairs, halberds and halyards hung with heraldic banners, sideboards, torchieres, wrought-iron gates, and parchment-shaded Spanish and Italian floor and table lamps. Near every horizon along the sky would be dozens of stuffed birds, more hanging velvet banners, and tropical flowers in pots and on hanging vines. On projects for which John Eberson himself was chief architect, there would be a stuffed peacock, tail feathers folded down, perched on one of the many overhanging false balconies along the facades of the fantasy villa.[22]

Eberson also designed, with Hall, Miami's 2,147-seat Olympia (1926), Florida's second-largest theatre until 1950 (figs. 17–21).[23] Located on Flagler Street in downtown Miami, the theatre was situated behind the ten-story office tower in which Eberson maintained a branch office for several years.[24] On opening night, 18 February 1926, Paul Whiteman and his twenty-eight-piece jazz orchestra performed the grand finale, courtesy of George Merrick (1846–1942),

22. Surviving relics from the Michael Angelo Studios are exceedingly rare. Co-author Kinerk's personal study and site survey of six Eberson theatres, conducted from 1967–1994.

23. Eberson job #558, Eberson Archive, The Wolfsonian, Florida International University. The relatively short-lived twenty-two-hundred-seat Wometco Carib Theatre in Miami Beach superseded the Olympia as second largest in Florida when it opened in 1950. Data: City of Miami Beach building department.

24. Eberson letter, 17 April 1928, reproduced in "New Theatres for Old," *Motion Picture News* 1 (30 December 1927): advertising reprint.

Fig. 17. John Eberson, Olympia Theatre, Miami, northeast corner of office tower with upright sign and east theatre facade, 1926. Romer Collection, Miami-Dade Public Library.

Fig. 18. John Eberson, Olympia Theatre, Miami, stage and left sidewall with organ grille, 1926. Photograph © Dan Forer.

Fig. 19. John Eberson, Olympia Theatre, Miami, stage as seen from balcony, 1926. George Gerhart collection.

Fig. 20. John Eberson, Olympia Theatre, Miami, view across auditorium to sidewall and boxes, 1926. George Gerhart collection.

Fig. 21. John Eberson, Olympia Theatre, Miami, view from right box across auditorium to organ grille, 1926. George Gerhart collection.

Fig. 22. Roy A. Benjamin, Florida Theatre, St. Petersburg, marquee on Famous Players Theatre Building, 1926. From a postcard. Theatre Historical Society Archives, Elmhurst, Illinois.

the developer of Coral Gables. The theatre had an original 15-rank, 3-manual Style 260-special Wurlitzer pipe organ.[25]

When it opened, the *Miami Herald* described the Olympia as one of the "architectural and decorative masterpieces of the playhouse kingdom." Its highly embellished interior was designed to be an Andalusian garden, but the architectural references were both Spanish and Italian. Its walls were filled with applied ornaments such as shells, urns, and flowers, which were painted aqua, turquoise, coral, pink, and tan. Wall niches held Classical statuary. In front of the theatre a marquee sign spelled out "Olympia" in fifteen hundred electric lights.[26]

The third largest of Florida's dream palaces was St. Petersburg's twenty-one-hundred-seat Florida Theatre (1926), designed by Benjamin (fig. 22). It was on the northwest corner of South Fifth Street and First Avenue, behind the eight-story Famous Players Theatre Building, and it had a roof garden. Its opening program boasted:

> Paramount Publix's new theatre has Exotic Occidental Architecture, Decorations and Furnishings, Symphonic Orchestra. Giant Concert Wurlitzer Organ. Carrier Scientific Cooling and Ventilating. Model of Modern Safety Construction. Built to Present Every Character of Theatricals.

25. There are several pipe organs in Florida theatres, but all original installations except the Olympia's were at some point removed. The pipe organs now in the Tampa, Saenger, and Polk theatres are replacements of similar types to those used in the silent era. In the time of silent films, every major theatre had a pipe organ for accompaniment of the film presentations. Only the largest theatres employed full orchestras. The smallest theatres used pianos. The authors have documented twenty-three original pipe organ installations in Florida theatres. There were undoubtedly more.

26. In ensuing years, the Olympia became a vaudeville house, then a first-run movie theatre again. It was saved from proposed demolition by philanthropist Maurice Gusman, who renamed it after himself and renovated it as a philharmonic hall. In the course of that renovation, much of the Eberson signature ornament was removed or covered over. A recent renovation has brought the theatre closer to its origins. The Olympia/Gusman was listed on the National Register in 1984. Beth Dunlop, "Happy Birthday Gusman," *Miami Herald*, 16 February 1986, sec. K, p. 1.

Capacity: Two Thousand Five Hundred Persons. Cost: One Million Dollars. House Personnel: Sixty.[27]

It is the only one of the major Publix palaces that was not saved as a performing arts center by its community.[28]

Paramount was the industry giant—a ruthless and voracious enterprise. In the 1920s the company not only recruited actors and created stars, but it bought into hundreds of land deals, hired or brought in as consultants its own architects, and ensured the creation of the dream palaces necessary to offer its products to the public.

Paramount typically used its financial clout to build its own theatres in the larger cities, but in smaller cities, it often induced local financiers and property owners to build the theatres, then leased them back to operate under the Publix banner. This happened many times in Florida, which eventually had approximately one hundred Publix theatres. Its successor, Florida State Theatres, would operate about 130 theatres.[29]

Fig. 23. James E. Casale, Polk Theatre, Lakeland, right sidewall of auditorium from unfinished balcony, 1928. Original construction photograph. Polk Theatre, Inc. collection.

What happened with the eighteen-hundred-seat Polk Theatre in Lakeland is a telling example of Paramount's business practices (fig. 23). In 1925 John E. Melton, a Lakeland real estate developer, assembled land and financing to build a multipurpose office building, "anchored by a grand movie palace." He hired Italian-born architect James E. Casale (1890–1958) from Tampa, who specified and designed an atmospheric auditorium. In press reports, Casale credited his inspiration to Andrea Palladio's famed atmospheric Teatro Olympico (1580) in Vicenza, Italy. It is more probable that Casale, who had set up his architecture office in Eberson's Tampa Theatre building, received his inspiration to build an atmospheric movie palace complete with a plaster ceiling and electric stars, not from Palladio, but from Eberson.[30] Casale designed the theatre in the Italian Renaissance style, though it was less exotic and opulent than Eberson's work. Perhaps the austerity was due to the fact that Melton ran short of money. The theatre sat unfinished for a time, while the builder entered into a Faustian agreement with Paramount Publix to obtain funding. Publix took a lease on the uncompleted theatre, apparently with no intention of opening it; Publix had other operations in Lakeland and was in no hurry to increase its operating costs by staffing the Polk.

When the theatre was completed in the spring of 1927, Publix refused to open the Polk and would not advance further funds. The Polk finally opened 22 December 1928—*after* Melton sold his interest in the theatre to Publix. Publix then came up with $65,000 to upgrade the house to sound for talkies.[31]

27. Research indicates twenty-one hundred seats. Data: MPAA, 1948; *Film Daily Yearbook*, 1930, 1945, 1955. Many press accounts overstate seating capacity. Opening Program, 10 September 1926, Theatre Historical Society Archives, Florida Theatre (St. Petersburg) file, Elmhurst, Ill.

28. The Florida Theatre was demolished in 1967. The other major Paramount Publix palaces that have been preserved are described herein. They are: Jacksonville's Florida, Miami's Olympia, Lakeland's Polk, Pensacola's Saenger, and the Tampa.

29. Douglas Gomery, "The Paramount Theatre, Palm Beach, Florida," *Marquee* 14 (fourth quarter 1982): 6; MPAA, 1948; *Film Daily Yearbook*, 1930, 1945, 1955.

30. Stephen E. Branch, "Mass Culture Meets Main Street—the Early Years of Lakeland's Polk Theatre" (master's thesis, University of South Florida, 1994): 39, 35, 44.

31. Ibid., 39; a community-based non-profit corporation was formed in 1982 to save and restore the theatre. The Polk was listed on the National Register in 1993. Today it is a performing arts center, undergoing restoration in phases as funds are raised by the group, Polk Theatre Incorporated; it is said that Lakeland tycoon George Jenkins named his grocery store chain Publix in response to fond memories of Publix Theatre Corporation's Lakeland flagship, the Polk.

Paramount's driving force was its creator, Adolph Zukor, a Hungarian immigrant. Before becoming involved in movie theatres, he had a fur business in Chicago. On business trips to New York City, he noticed people flocking to novelty arcades showing short photoplays using handcranked viewing devices. These attracted a varied crowd of patrons who for a few minutes or an hour fed the machines with coins (thus the names penny arcade and nickelodeon).

Zukor entered the penny-arcade business in New York City in about 1902, with Marcus Loew as his partner. Ultimately Zukor presided over Paramount, and Loew over MGM. By 1910 the two had a chain of penny arcades all over the east.[32] Zealous in his desire to improve the product, Zukor split with Loew and started his own company. In 1912, with additional partners, he created Famous Players Film Company.[33] Stars such as Sarah Bernhardt, Mary Pickford, and Ethel Barrymore came on board. In order to book these early serious films into theatres, an independent distribution company called Paramount Pictures Corporation was formed.[34]

On 29 June 1916 Zukor's Famous Players Studio merged with the Jesse Lasky Feature Play Company to form Famous Players-Lasky Corporation. The studio lists this event as the beginning of Paramount Pictures. In September of that year the principals assembled for a photograph to mark the event (fig. 24). Zukor and Lasky were there, with partners, two of them legends of greater luminance than Zukor himself: Samuel Goldfish (who later changed his name to Samuel Goldwyn) and Cecil B. DeMille. Famous Players-Lasky soon absorbed other studios, and on 1 January 1917, acquired Paramount Pictures distribution company, but continued to operate as Famous Players-Lasky. In 1919 to combat the then-dominant First National Pictures, Famous Players-Lasky entered the theatre-owning business. Zukor took the company public, floating $10,000,000 in securities. In 1925 Zukor merged with the Midwest exhibition giant, Balaban and Katz (B and K), at which time Paramount Publix Theatre Corporation was created to operate all the company-owned theatres.[35] B and K partner Sam Katz was brought to New York to lead Publix Theatres. Eventually Zukor changed the name of the entire enterprise to Paramount Pictures. For years thereafter the B and K influence endured, as Sam Katz's partner Barney Balaban eventually succeeded Zukor to run Paramount.[36] However, when Zukor died in 1976 at the age of 103, he still reigned as chairman emeritus of Paramount Pictures.[37]

Florida's first major motion picture palaces went on the drawing board shortly after the creation of Famous Players-Lasky. Edward Sparks was general manager for Publix in Florida. From his office in the Palmer Building in Jacksonville, he oversaw the steadily growing chain, and under his leadership Publix gained total domination of the Florida market. Sparks retired in 1941, after Publix was declared a monopoly and broken up by court order in 1940.[38]

Publix tended to create local partnerships in each city or region, buying into existing operations or forcing competitors to sell out, as in the case of Lakeland's

32. MacCann, *The First Tycoons*, 245.

33. *Tampa Morning Tribune*, 15 October 1926, sec. C, p. 7.

34. MacCann, *The First Tycoons*, 243–246.

35. Ibid.

36. Carrie Balaban, *Continuous Performance, Biography of A. J. Balaban* (New York: A. J. Balaban Foundation, 1964), 107.

37. MacCann, *The First Tycoons*, 251.

38. Gomery, "Paramount Palm Beach," 6.

Fig. 24. Paramount founding partners, executives of Famous Players Film Company, and Jesse Lasky Feature Play Company, on occasion of their merger, September 1916. *Left to right*, Jesse Lasky, Adolph Zukor, Samuel Goldfish (Goldwyn), Cecil B. DeMille, Albert Kaufman. Photograph © Paramount Pictures, used by permission.

Polk Theatre. The story of the Leach family interests in Miami is another example of Publix operations from 1917 through 1933.

In 1922 the Leach family joined forces with Famous Players-Lasky to form Paramount Enterprises of Miami, with the Leachs initially enjoying controlling interest. Prior to this partnership, the family controlled many of Miami's early theatres.[39] They had an interest in the Airdome Theatre (1914) and a half-interest in the Fotosho Theatre (1915) on Flagler Street. There were two successive Airdomes and two Hippodromes in the period 1914–1925. Each was torn down, a new one built nearby, and the name perpetuated.[40] By 1925 the new Airdome already had closed to make way for Publix's Miami flagship, the Olympia.

The same thing happened with the venerable Paramount name. The Leach family apparently began booking Paramount films the same year the company was formed. The profits pouring into Paramount Enterprises (the Leach family concern) fueled the construction of ever-larger and more elaborate dream palaces. Their first Paramount theatre opened in 1916 on Flagler Street at Southeast First Avenue. The second Paramount was created in 1927, when they converted and renamed the 1922 Fairfax Theatre, also on Flagler Street. At that time they closed the original Paramount. The second Paramount was

---

39. George W. Gerhart, "A Moon Over Miami," *Theatre Organ-Bombarde*: *Journal of the American Theatre Organ Society* (April 1967): 11.

40. Grant, "Miami's Olympia Theatre," 19.

Fig. 25. Architect unknown,

Paramount Theatre, Miami,

1927; Robert Law Weed,

remodeling, 1938, exterior,

marquee (c. 1955), and upright.

Photograph © Miami Herald,

1972, used by permission.

Fig. 26. E. T. Wells, architect,

with Adolph Vollmer, decorator,

Capitol Theatre, Miami, exteri-

or, marquee and upright, 1926.

Photograph © Miami Herald,

used by permission.

updated to an Art Deco appearance in 1938 by Miami architect Robert Law Weed (1897–1961) and lighting engineer C. Burton of Rambusch, of New York (fig. 25).[41]

Though Miami was still a small city, it enjoyed a booming economy through 1926. But a hurricane in September wiped out the Miami boom, and the city took years to recover. After this the Leach family suffered financial reversals and was forced to turn over control to Publix. This approach of stepping in when owners or investors were financially weak and seizing control worked many times for Publix, throughout the state — until 1933.

By 1933 Publix was overextended, fighting the bottomed-out economy of the Depression, and near insolvency. At that point it entered voluntary reorganization. Thereafter Publix began spinning off its assets, selling theatres, and attempting to regain profitability during the worst years of the Depression. A 1940 Federal Court order finally wiped out Publix, and its assets were divided among regional companies.[42] Florida State Theatres came into being by inheriting former Florida Publix properties, but Florida State, though a giant, could not crush competition with the effortless aplomb of Zukor's former juggernaut. This opened the door to stronger regional operators. Miami's Wometco was one of these.

As Publix faded, Wometco became the dominant theatre chain in South Florida. Wometco was founded in 1924 by Colonel Mitchell Wolfson and Sidney Meyer — the name was an acronym for Wolfson-Meyer Theatre Company. Wometco had affiliated at first with Fox Studio, while also exhibiting Universal, United Artists, and Columbia releases. Eventually Wometco grew to operate eighty-nine theatres, with forty in Florida (concentrated in Dade, Broward, and Palm Beach counties), another twenty-five in Puerto Rico, eleven in the Caribbean, and thirteen in Alaska. Always ahead of its time, Wometco advertised its international aspirations for Miami in the 1940s by stressing that it had "Spanish-speaking attendants."[43] Under Wolfson's leadership, the company established the first television station in Florida, WTVJ, in 1949, converting the 1,234-seat Capitol Theatre (1926), in downtown Miami, into television studios (fig. 26).[44] Both the Capitol and the fourteen-hundred-plus-seat Biscayne Plaza (1926), the second theatre in Miami Beach, were designed by local architect E. T. Wells.[45] The Biscayne Plaza (fig. 27) was erected on the southern tip of the island, at Biscayne Street between Collins and Washington avenues, near Miami Beach's most famous restaurant, Joe's Stone Crab.

Thomas W. Lamb of New York City was among the nationally prominent architects who designed movie palaces in Florida. Lamb, considered the dean of American theatre architects, worked on two Miami Beach theatres late in his career: the Lincoln (1936) and the Cinema Casino (1938) (figs. 28 and 29). Like John and Drew Eberson, Lamb also successfully made the switch to the Art Deco style. Original work in both these theatres has been substantially destroyed in subsequent renovations. Lamb's celebrated Cinema Casino was named to tie into a well-advertised but short-lived prior name, the French

41. City of Miami building plans, microfilm roll 20: M.87.

42. MacCann, *The First Tycoons*, 181.

43. "The New Miami, Showplace of the Americas," inaugural performance souvenir program, 18 April 1947.

44. Dick Lehman, "From One Boom-Time Theatre to a Miami Entertainment Empire: A Reminiscence with Mitchell Wolfson," *Update: Historical Association of Southern Florida* 3 (April 1976): 6–7.

45. "Theatre Designer Leader in Field," *Miami Herald*, 26 June 1926, 14.

Fig. 27. E. T. Wells, Biscayne Plaza Theatre, Miami Beach, exterior facade with busts in niches, dome, arched entry, 1926. Photograph © Miami Herald, used by permission.

Fig. 29. Thomas W. Lamb with T. Hunter Henderson, Cinema Casino, Miami Beach, view of etched-glass decorative panels that flanked entrance, 1938. Photograph © Miami Herald, used by permission.

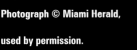

Fig. 28. Thomas W. Lamb with T. Hunter Henderson, Cinema Casino, Miami Beach, view of auditorium and sidewall murals from center of balcony, 1938. Photograph © Miami Herald, used by permission.

Fig. 30. Joseph Urban,
Paramount Theatre, Palm
Beach, aerial view of layout
of theatre, twin spires of
Breakers Hotel in background,
1927. Historical Society of
Palm Beach County.

Casino—a theatre and supper club opened in 1934 and advertised jointly with its famed counterpart of the same name in Manhattan. In both cases, the supper-club format failed quickly in the Depression. Miami Beach's Cinema began as a club, was converted to show films, and was renovated by Lamb in 1938 to become the twelve-hundred-seat Cinema Casino (later just the Cinema).[46] In the rear of the lobby was a panoramic mural and a forty-foot-long undulating, curved counter surfaced in mother-of-pearl, used as a refreshment stand (it originally served as an elegant bar in the supper club). Lamb's hand is quite obvious, and the design—with its etched glass, murals, the bar, and the fluid, sweeping lines of the lobbies and auditorium—is among the best interiors in Miami Beach.[47] T. Hunter Henderson, of Miami Beach, worked with Lamb on this project.

The Viennese-born, New York City architect Joseph Urban (1872–1933) designed the 1,235-seat Palm Beach Paramount (1927), one of the most unique and beautiful theatres ever constructed in the United States (figs. 30 and 31). Urban began his career by designing sets for the Ziegfeld Follies. He then became art director for Cosmopolitan Pictures (1920–1926), which was owned by William Randolph Hearst. With Lamb, Urban designed the New York Ziegfeld Theatre (1927), which opened one month after the Palm Beach Paramount. Urban is best known for New York City's New School Auditorium and for his designs

46. Today the Lincoln is home to the New World Symphony and the Cinema is a nightclub. In the face of a then-declining economy and poor attendance, its owners closed the Cinema in March 1977. When jackhammers began ripping out the floor of the lobby, a preservation battle erupted, with Barbara Baer Capitman leading the Miami Design Preservation League to "Save the Cinema." While the battle to save the original lobby was lost, Capitman was successful in getting the Art Deco district listed on the National Register in 1979. Soon thereafter, the lobby was reconstructed in a rough approximation of the original. The auditorium took on a new life as a successful nightclub; it is currently protected by strong historic preservation ordinances.

47. Based upon personal observation by the authors in site visits, 1977–1986.

(never executed) for a Metropolitan Opera House intended for Rockefeller Center—where instead the famed Radio City Music Hall was built. Some scholars believe Urban's designs for a proposed Rockefeller Center subtly guided the eventual design of the Music Hall.[48]

In Palm Beach, Urban capitalized on the temperate subtropical weather, including an open courtyard with several shops and an imposing gatehouse (not unlike the Paramount Studios gates in Hollywood). He specified a two-story auditorium of unusual proportion, shallow and fan-shaped. The resulting wide amphitheatre-type space left room for twenty-five private boxes — far more than a normal complement. These were finished with fine wood dividers and thick upholstery and were very popular with the Palm Beach society patrons, who paid high prices for their private redoubts. These boxes had excellent sight-lines, since they were not isolated along the sidewalls as was common, but spanned the entire rear of the auditorium, placing many of the 156 private seats dead center. The shallowness of the house kept them comfortably close to the screen. Other features of Urban's designs included exposed wood-beam ceilings, Art Deco Viennese chandeliers, wooden columns capped by German Expressionist busts (fig. 32), silk wall coverings, and auditorium murals of fantastic underwater scenes.[49] With its exclusive boxes and an expensive Wurlitzer pipe organ, the Paramount opened 8 January 1927. This was a theatre for the wealthy, selling one- and two-dollar tickets at a time when other theatres charged thirty-five cents. The boxes sold for $1,000 for the two-month season.

48. Gomery, "Paramount Palm Beach," 6.

49. The extensive murals, one of the most striking features of the auditorium, may have been the work of Joseph Urban's daughter, Gretl, who did mural work for him at Marjorie Meriwether Post's Palm Beach mansion, Mar-A-Lago, also considered among Urban's greatest accomplishments.

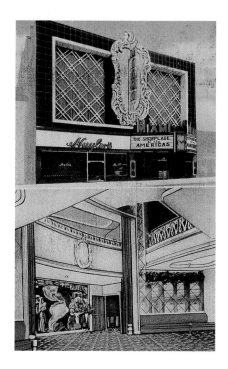

In the late 1940s the theatre, already in commercial decline, began marketing to the middle class. It closed and reopened several times, closing for good in 1980, later to be stripped and converted into offices.[50]

Another major theatre architect, S. Charles Lee, designed one of Florida's most beautiful and significant dream palaces. The Miami Theatre (1947) on Flagler Street (figs. 33 and 34) was designed for Wometco. Lee, who was based in Los Angeles, designed few theatres in the East, but designed more than one hundred in the West. His work included the Mayfair (1942) in New York City; El Capitán (1941), the Lido (1942), and others in Mexico City; and numerous theatres in Arizona, Ohio, Montana, Nevada, and Managua, Nicaragua. Much of Lee's work was done for the Fox West Coast chain in the 1930s and 1940s.

The Miami Theatre had many unique and beautiful features. Lee included a series of grand lobby spaces decorated in a tropical motif to match the Florida locale. In fact, as Lee explained, the lobby spaces and auditorium were translated into an over-scaled aquarium through which moviegoers "swam." There was a restaurant in the building with entry provided both from the street and from the theatre lobby.[51]

Lee designed the Miami Theatre in association with noted Miami Beach Art Deco architect Robert E. Collins, who had worked on several theatres. Collins was associate architect on Lamb's Lincoln Theatre, and designed four theatres himself, including the Cameo Theatre (1936) on Washington Avenue, Miami Beach. Other works included the St. John Theatre (1941) in Jacksonville, the Dixie Theatre (1948) in Miami, and Cinemorada (1956) on Islamorada, Florida Keys.

50. For national average of ticket prices, see Maggie Valentine, *The Show Starts on the Sidewalk, An Architectural History of the Movie Theatre, Starring S. Charles Lee* (New Haven: Yale University Press, 1994); Gomery, "Paramount Palm Beach," 4–6.

51. For a comprehensive discussion of S. Charles Lee's work, see Valentine, *The Show Starts on the Sidewalk*; Ibid., 174.

Another nationally known architecture firm, Kiehnel and Elliott, designed the Coconut Grove Theatre (now the Coconut Grove Playhouse) in 1926.[52] It has been a legitimate theatre for decades, but spent its early years as a movie palace operated by Paramount Publix, and later by Wometco. Kiehnel and Elliott also brought South Florida the Mediterranean Revival style in 1917 with El Jardin, a Coconut Grove mansion that is now the historic Carrollton School.

Regional architects did hundreds of theatres outside Florida, but seldom worked beyond their geographic area. This group included: Herbert J. Krapp, Armand D. Carroll, and William Harold Lee in the Northeast; Boller Bothers in the Southwest; B. Marcus Priteca, Timothy Pfleuger, and G. Albert Lansburgh in the West; Liebenberg and Kaplan of Minnesota in the Midwest; Emile Weil and Roy A. Benjamin in the South. Of these, Lee, Weil, and Benjamin worked in Florida.

New Orleans architect Emile Weil (1878–1945) designed Pensacola's seventeen-hundred-seat Saenger Theatre (1925) for the New Orleans-based Saenger Amusement Company, founded in Shrevesport, Louisiana in 1914 by Abe and Julian Saenger (fig. 35).[53] The family-owned Saenger chain grew rapidly. Saenger Amusement Company controlled three hundred theatres throughout the South before falling on hard times and being swallowed up by Publix in 1928.[54] Weil is also well-known for the atmospheric Saenger Theatre in New Orleans.

Pennsylvania's William H. Lee was commissioned to design the sixteen-hundred-seat Miracle Theatre (1948) in Coral Gables. He also designed the Art Deco-styled Norris Theatre (1929) in Norristown, Pennsylvania, which has been torn down, but whose massive terra-cotta entrance grille stands at the end of the main lobby atrium of The Wolfsonian, Florida International University, in Miami Beach.

Roy A. Benjamin, designer of St. Petersburg's Florida Theatre, was another regional architect, albeit one who dominated theatre design in Florida. An Ocala native, Benjamin moved to Jacksonville in 1902 and opened his own practice. His firm, still in business today as KBJ Architects, lists more than eighty theatre projects in Florida, many for Paramount Publix.[55]

Benjamin was known and respected nationwide, as indicated in the lavish display given his work in the 1927 edition of *American Theatres of Today*, which published eight sets of his plans.[56] He designed many theatres elsewhere in Southern states and was responsible for some of Florida's earliest theatres, many in Jacksonville.[57] Most notable are the Jacksonville Arcade (opened 1915), Crescent City's VIA (1916), Jacksonville's Imperial (1917), St. Petersburg's Pheil (1917), Winter Haven's Grand (1919), and Lakeland's Palace (1924). His largest early theatre was the Palace (1919) in Jacksonville, a classic Palladian-style house with 1,876 seats (fig. 36). Located on East Forsyth, The Palace was

Fig. 35. Emile Weil, Saenger Theatre, Pensacola, exterior facade with marquee and parapet, 1925. Saenger Theatre, Inc. collection.

52. Kiehnel and Elliott are best known in South Florida for their Carlyle Hotel on Ocean Drive in Miami Beach's Art Deco district.

53. The Saenger Theatre was listed on the National Register in 1979, the venerable movie palace was donated to the city of Pensacola in 1975, and underwent a $1,600,000 rehabilitation to reopen in 1981 as a performing arts center, operated by a non-profit corporation. Lucius and Linda Ellsworth, *Pensacola, the Deep Water City* (Tulsa: Continental Heritage Press, 1982), 125, 158, 161.

54. "The Strand, Shreveport, Louisiana," *Marquee* 18 (third quarter 1986): 13–15.

55. Wayne W. Wood, *Jacksonville's Architectural Heritage, Landmarks for the Future* (Jacksonville: University of North Florida Press, 1989), 8; KBJ Benjamin project list.

56. Sexton, *American Theatres of Today*, 1:2, 76–79, 83, 104–106, 108–109, 135, 139, 144–145, 174–175.

57. KBJ Benjamin project list.

the largest theatre in the state when it was built, and it remained so until 1926 when Publix opened the Florida in St. Petersburg and the Olympia in Miami.[58] In 1920 Benjamin was responsible for designing (or co-designing) six of the state's ten largest movie palaces. Eventually Benjamin designed theatres in twenty-two Florida counties, working steadily until retiring and selling his practice in 1946.[59]

Like all prolific theatre architects who wanted to stay in business, Benjamin stopped using classical, Moorish, Spanish, and Italianate designs by the early 1930s and adopted the simpler, sleeker Art Deco style. He left many prime examples of his design skills in Art Deco's streamline period, including the 850-seat Lake Theatre (1939) in Lake Worth and the 1,374-seat Florida Theatre (1940) in Tallahassee (fig. 37).[60]

Benjamin also remodeled many theatres, including his own. Most remodeling came in the 1930s, when the Colonial- and Adam-style buildings from earlier in the century typically received an Art Deco facelift. The historic 1915 Jacksonville Arcade was renovated by Benjamin in 1934 and renamed the Center; it was one of the longest-surviving theatres in Florida, remaining open and showing films until the 1990s. In 1941 Benjamin redesigned the Imperial (1917) and the Palace (1924), both in Jacksonville.[61]

Miami Beach's premiere 1930s architect, Henry Hohauser (1895–1963), designed a small theatre on Washington Avenue in the Art Deco district— still standing, but no longer a cinema. It opened as the Variety (1945) and closed as the Paris.[62]

Robert Law Weed (1897–1961) with William L. Pereira (1909–1985), then of Chicago, designed the Beach Theatre (1941), a project so spectacular it won an

58. The Palace was the fourth largest movie theatre in the state until 1950 when it was bumped to fifth. It is now demolished.

59. KBJ Benjamin project list.

60. The Lake was the Lannan Museum and is now the Palm Beach Community College Museum of Art.

61. KBJ Benjamin project list.

62. Hohauser is listed as architect on building card, City of Miami Beach building department. Keith Root, *Miami Beach Art Deco Guide* (Miami Beach: Miami Design Preservation League, 1987), 179.

Fig. 37. Roy A. Benjamin,

Florida Theatre, Tallahassee,

facade with upright, curved Art

Deco marquee and glass-block

corners, 1940. Florida State

Archives.

award as the nation's best theatre of the year at its opening (figs. 38 and 39).[63] Seating 1,604, it featured a lobby with glass atriums, anticipating by several years Morris Lapidus' (born 1902) similar spectacle in the Miami Beach Americana Hotel. The theatre even had a stairway at its entrance, like the Fountainebleau — only this one was not a stairway to "nowhere at all," as Lapidus called his at the hotel, but rather led to the balcony.[64]

Other noteworthy Florida theatres were: the Aladdin (1924), in Cocoa, designed by the firm of Thornton P. Mayre, which is best known for its subsequent design of the Atlanta Fox; the 350-seat Vero (1924), architect unknown, in Vero Beach; and in Sarasota, the 1,445-seat Edwards (1926), designed by Benjamin, with interior design by W. M. Holland. Built by local developer A. B. Edwards, it was leased by Carl Laemmle's Universal Studios organization.[65] The contractor, G. A. Miller, also built the Tampa Theatre (and many Florida Kress stores). The Edwards had a $25,000 Robert Morton pipe organ and was in a four-story steel-frame building with apartments and shops. The auditorium had a plaster and beamed ceiling, with ornamental plaster cartouches.[66]

It is important to note that the practice of racial segregation persisted in Florida throughout the golden age of the movie palace. Very few Florida theatres provided access for nonwhites. If a theatre allowed all races, the policy — even

top,

Fig. 38. Robert Law Weed with

William L. Pereira, Beach

Theatre, Miami Beach, main

lobby with grand staircase and

atrium terrarium, 1946. Arva

Parks collection.

63. William L. Pereira is famous for Chicago's landmark Esquire Theatre (1938) and later, after moving to Los Angeles, the flying-saucer-shaped central restaurant building at Los Angeles International Airport. Barbara Capitman, Michael Kinerk, Dennis Wilhelm, *Rediscovering Art Deco U.S.A.* (New York: Viking, 1994), 57–58; David Gebhard and Robert Winter, *Architecture in Los Angeles, A Complete Guide* (Salt Lake City: Peregrine Smith, 1985), 70; the Beach Theatre's design won first place, "bronze medallion," in the largest seat class. *The Theatre Catalog* (Philadelphia: Jay Emanuel Publications, 1942), 3:61–63.

64. Morris Lapidus, *An Architecture of Joy* (Miami: E. A. Seeman Publishing Inc., 1979), 164.

65. Florida site file #SO00410, Tallahassee: Division of Historic Preservation, Secretary of State's Office, State of Florida; "Extensive Program to Feature Opening of Edwards Theatre Here on Saturday Evening," *This Week in Sarasota*, 8 April 1926, sec. A, p. 7.

66. The Edwards was listed on the National Register in 1984 and renovated in 1985 to become home to the Sarasota Opera Association, Inc.

Fig. 39. Robert Law Weed with William L. Pereira, Beach Theatre, Miami Beach, auditorium with scrolling plaster work, 1941. Arva Parks collection.

opposite,

Fig. 40. Michael J. de Angelis with Roy F. France, Carib Theatre, Miami Beach, a map of the Caribbean above the entry, 1950. Photograph © Miami Herald, used by permission.

in Northern states —was to provide a separate side or rear entrance for African-Americans. In the largest palaces, this entrance would lead up many flights of stairs to a third- or fourth-floor vestibule tucked under the rear of the balcony. However, racial segregation policies did not stop the chains from seeking profits directly in the African-American communities. Several of the theatres surveyed were exclusively for "colored" patrons. Like all neighborhood houses, these were convenient to the patrons and usually profitable, though seldom showing first-run pictures.

At least nine such African-American theatres were built in Florida. The most historic of these is the 490-seat Lyric (1913) in Miami. It was built by one of the city's most successful African-American businessmen, Geder Walker.[67]

Designed by Benjamin, the nine-hundred-seat Strand (1919) in Jacksonville was also built for African-American patrons. The 970-seat Ritz (1929) in Jacksonville, designed by Jefferson Powell, is most intriguing: its style has been described as Egyptian-Mediterranean Revival with Art Deco touches.[68] It is actually closer to Vienna Secession, one of Art Deco's antecedent styles.

New York City architect Michael J. de Angelis, along with noted Miami Beach Art Deco district architect Roy F. France (1888–1972), working for Wometco, designed the last of Florida's dream palaces, thus bringing down the final curtain in the saga. Wometco commissioned De Angelis and France to design Miami Beach's twenty-two-hundred-seat Carib (1950) (fig. 40).[69] It was the second-largest theatre in the state until it was gutted for a shopping center in 1978. Even its outstanding facade depicting the Caribbean basin was destroyed during the renovation. France also designed the fifteen-hundred-seat Gateway Theatre in Fort Lauderdale (1952).

The early 1950s marked the end of the dream palace era in Florida. Few other theatres were built with single screens, as times changed and the movie theatre business faced deadly competition from television and cable television. Yet the legacy of Florida's dream palace era lives on in the four performing arts centers that have been founded in the former theatres, preserving for the public a glimpse of a fabulous and dazzling era, the likes of which we shall never see again. □

67. Gary Goodwin and Suzanne Walker, *Florida Black Heritage Trail* (Tallahassee: Bureau of Historic Preservation, 1991), 15; the Lyric was listed on the National Register in 1989, and has been in a process of renovation for many years.

68. Wood, *Jacksonville's Architectural Heritage*, 98.

69. New York architect Michael J. de Angelis' name appears on all drawings of the project. Roy F. France was his local affiliate. City of Miami Beach building department data and Mitchell Wolfson Jr. personal archives.

1.1 Theodore de Bry, engraving, based on a painting by Jacques Le Moyne, Timucans farming, c. 1564, Florida State Archives.

Edens, Underworlds, and Shrines: Florida's Small Tourist Attractions

By Margot Ammidown

Margot Ammidown writes on Florida history and architecture. She is former director of Metropolitan Dade County's Historic Preservation Office and is currently completing an M.Arch. at the University of Miami School of Architecture, Coral Gables, Florida.

The promoters of Florida real estate in the 1920s are sometimes credited with creating the mythic image of Florida as a place where anyone could buy a fifty-by-one-hundred-foot swath of paradise. Yet, as often as not, paradise turned out to be a barren, ready-to-build subdivision lot or a slice of wetland awaiting drainage. Nonetheless, the faithful flowed in on rivers of crude highways with cash in hand. The 1920s were neither the first nor the last time that people were lured to Florida by the siren song of an earthly Eden. The mythology of Florida is as old as the earliest written accounts of the New World.

Many of the natural areas of Florida were indeed beautiful, but they were no match for the hyperbole of the advertisements and real estate brochures published in the first decades of the twentieth century. Thus, the state's new arrivals had to create their own version of paradise, and how does one start to build paradise but as a garden? Because of Florida's warm climate and long growing season, a small patch of land could yield a profusion of flowers, exotic plants, and fruit-bearing trees. In relatively little time the illusion of a naturally fecund and life-sustaining garden could be coaxed from swamp muck or pine flat.

From the invention of the automobile in the beginning of this century to the opening of interstate highways in the 1960s, small roadside tourist attractions of almost every form were created. In part a response to the popular mythic image of Florida, they were frequently based on the native environment — the springs, the forests, the wildlife — and they were often intertwined with a narrative extrapolated from Florida history. Small attractions naively attempted to create what the tourist or prospective resident surely must have felt lacking: a glimpse of the extraordinary.

The small tourist attraction was distinguished from other attractions by size, intent, and design. Unlike Walt Disney World or Busch Gardens, small attractions generally were limited to a few acres and were without a public image or corporate resources. The owners frequently lived on or adjacent to the site, although that is not usually the case today. By necessity the small attractions differed from public gardens or parks in that they were not solely botanical displays or nature preserves, even though many of the small attractions of the 1920s and 1930s owed much of their design inspiration to the rustic architecture and planning style of national parks.

The garden alone could not sustain the family attraction. Reptiles, rare birds, and jungle boat rides became standard fare. Thematically, small tourist attractions were a hodge-podge of mixed metaphors evolved over time, as owners responded to visitor feedback and their own fertile imaginations.

Ultimately, small attractions were about the commerce of fantasy. Before corporate management and promotion, the attractions were relatively unknown to the travelling public. They had only seconds to present themselves on the roadside and lure passing travellers with the promise of something magical, exotic, or grotesque. The goal was to provide tourists with something they wanted, something that would compel them not so much to make a special trip as to step on the brake. Deliberately interpreted or not, it was often the mythic image of Florida that tourists wanted to see.

This image of the state had its genesis in the late Renaissance. At that time, the collective imagination began to focus on an earthly rather than a heavenly paradise. The New World expeditions of the sixteenth century, ostensibly quests for gold and territory, also were infused with the desire to find this earthly paradise. Published accounts of the explorations were popular in Europe, despite the fact that many were not much more than edited captains' logs and cartographic notations, while others were embellished descriptions and outright fabrications, with exaggerated representations of the landscape and indigenous people. Florida was mythologized based on the Judeo-Christian image of Eden as bountiful and temperate, enlivened by the noble savage standing naked in the garden.

The most notable of the Spanish New World legends were collected and published in 1530 in the seven-volume *Decades del Nuevo Mundo*, by Pietro Martiere d'Anghiera. It is through d'Anghiera's work that we know the story of the Fountain of Youth, derived from reports of Juan Ponce de León's explorations. It was one of many fanciful stories written as fact, published in part to promote further travel and settlement and thus help secure the territories. The legend of Chicora, spun from the accounts of the 1521 exploration of Pedro de Quexo and Francisco Gordillo, told of a "new Andalusia" that was plentiful in timber, fruit, and flowers and populated by a stately indigenous people wearing pearls, gold, and silver. The legend was known widely in Europe and spurred investment in future trips. Repeated accounts placed Chicora somewhere between the Carolinas and Florida's northeast coast.

French explorers Jean Ribaut and René Laudonnière, who established a short-lived colony near present-day Jacksonville, are believed to have been familiar with the legend.[1] From their 1564 expedition, Laudonnière's cartographer and artist, Jacques Le Moyne, produced the first images of Florida, and engravings based on his illustrations were distributed throughout Europe (figs. 1 and 2).[2] Le Moyne's illustrations depicted the native Timucans and the St. Johns River area in central Florida with a mythic grandeur that may have been influenced by the Chicora legend. However, his representations were not a total fabrication. The Timucans were, in fact, tall people who covered themselves with ornate tattoos, wore pearls, gold, and silver, and were prolific farmers. The landscape was depicted as fertile and idyllic. The St. Johns River area became the mythic heart of Florida and the focus of most of the travel writing about the state until the late nineteenth century.

Fig. 2. Theodore de Bry, engraving, based on a painting by Jacques Le Moyne, Timucan family crossing a river, c. 1564. Florida State Archives.

1. Paul E. Hoffman, "The Chicora Legend and Franco-Spanish Rivalry in *La Florida*," *The Florida Historical Quarterly* 62 (April 1984): 419–438.

2. Shortly after Le Moyne's death, Flemish engraver Theodore de Bry purchased Le Moyne's forty-two paintings and his written account of Florida and reproduced the images as engravings. They were then published in the second volume of *Brevis Narratio Eorum Quae in Florida Americae* (Frankfort, 1591), which was printed in Latin and German. An English-language edition was published in 1875 by James Osgood and Company, Boston. Ribaut and Laudonnière also published their own accounts of their Florida adventures.

Fig. 3. William Bartram,
alligators in the St. Johns
River, looking particularly
serpent-like. From *The Travels
of William Bartram* (1791).
Florida State Archives.

Other images more rooted in classical mythology emerged from early accounts of the state. Spanish, British, and French explorers frequently sent home vivid descriptions of the alligators inhabiting the swamps and rivers. William Bartram, son of the famed botanist John Bartram, visited Florida on a botanical expedition in 1773 (fig. 3). Bartram described his journey up the St. Johns River as generally Edenic, but his depictions of alligators evoked the terrors of the underworld beasts from classical myth:

> What expression can sufficiently declare the shocking scene that for some minutes continued, whilst the mighty army of fish were forcing the pass? During this attempt, thousands, I may say hundreds of thousands of them were caught and swallowed by the devouring alligators. I have seen an alligator take up out of the water several great fish at a time, and just squeeze them betwixt his jaws….The horrid noise of their closing jaws, their plunging among the broken bank of fish, and rising with their prey some feet upright above the water, the floods of water and blood rushing out of their mouths, and clouds of vapor issuing from their wide nostrils, were truly frightful.[3]

Bartram's passage is reminiscent of Virgil's description of the watery death of the Laocoon by serpents in *The Aeneid*: "Their eyes are drenched in blood and fire — they burn. They lick their hissing jaws with quivering tongues."[4] This is not to suggest a direct connection between Bartram's description and Virgil's writing; however, the explorers of these expeditions were educated men, familiar with the classics, and it was through their accounts that a full mythological context for Florida was created. Even the name "Florida" — a feast of flowers — conjured visions of paradise. That a terrifying underworld existed beneath the idyllic surface of the fish-filled rivers reinforced the notion of an earthly paradise with the implied threat of damnation.

By the late nineteenth century, with the Indian and Civil wars past, the state became more accessible to the travelling public. Feature articles on Florida

3. William Bartram, *The Travels of William Bartram* (1791), excerpted in Jack Lane and Maurice O'Sullivan, ed., *The Florida Reader: Visions of Paradise From 1530 to the Present* (Sarasota, Fla.: Pineapple Press, 1991), 57.
4. Allen Mandelbaum, trans., *The Aeneid of Virgil* (Berkeley: University of California Press, 1981), 36.

became commonplace in popular consumer publications such as *Scribner's Monthly*, *Harper's*, and *Frank Leslie's Illustrated*. The stories, generally written in the form of anthropological travelogues, were unabashedly promotional. An 1874 article in *Scribner's Monthly*, entitled "Pictures from Florida," makes reference to the Fountain of Youth in describing the state's first popular natural attraction, Silver Springs (figs. 4 and 5):

> What poet's imagination, seven times heated, could paint foliage whose splendors could surpass that of the virgin forests of the Ocklawaha and Indian Rivers? What "fountain of youth" could be imagined more redolent of enchantment than the "Silver Spring" now annually visited by fifty thousand tourists? The subtle moonlight, the perfect glory of the dying sun as he sinks below a horizon fringed with fantastic trees, the perfume faintly borne from the orange grove, the murmurous music of the waves along the inlets, and the mangrove-covered banks, are beyond words.[5]

The idea of the landscape as a source of wonder for travellers took hold in the United States in the 1820s and 1830s. Places like Niagara Falls and later the Grand Canyon and Yosemite were often described in quasi-religious terms by travel writers who frequently referred to themselves as "pilgrims."[6] The notion of recreational travel in association with a spiritual quest had its roots in religious pilgrimage. The idea can be traced to the Church in medieval Europe, which encouraged travel to sacred sites that were enshrined with religious buildings or other symbolic structures. Shrines are "believed to be places where miracles once happened, still happen and may happen again," according to pilgrimage scholars Victor and Edith Turner.[7] When holy sites were formalized with a "sacralizing structure," they completed the accepted definition of a shrine.

5. "Pictures from Florida," *Scribner's Monthly* (November 1874): 3.

6. John Sears, *Sacred Places: American Tourist Attractions in the Nineteenth Century* (Oxford: Oxford University Press, 1989), 5.

7. Victor and Edith Turner, *Image and Pilgrimage in Christian Culture* (New York: Columbia University Press, 1978), 6.

Among the most common architectural form marking these shrines was the gateway, an ancient symbol which, even in archaic cultures, expressed the possibility of transcendence.

As society became more secularized, travel was still propelled by the desire to be transported, perhaps more physically than spiritually, from the mundane to a state of wonder. Yet religious overtones remained, as Mircea Eliade, a scholar of myth and ritual, wrote, "To whatever degree he may have desacralized the world, the man who has made his choice in favor of a profane life never succeeds in completely doing away with religious behavior…even the most desacralized existence still preserves traces of a religious valorization of the world." Eliade called this "crypto-religious behavior."[8] If Eliade's thesis is true, a relatively mundane activity such as a family road trip might inspire associations with a pilgrimage — especially if the destination is paradise.

Small attractions proliferated as automobile use increased and the first North-South highways were completed. Florida became one of the most popular destinations in the United States. Americans took to the road in staggering numbers, and the nomadic family motor vacation was written about in terminology that might describe a spiritual quest. A 1924 *Saturday Evening Post* article noted, "This year something less than 15,000,000 Americans will indulge in the motor tour. They are the Argonauts, the Argonauts of the automobile. Their nightly haunt is the motor tourist camp. They are more or less remodeling our civilization."[9] Although they were often written about as "pilgrims" or "argonauts," it is unlikely that these travellers thought of themselves in any mythic context. Quickly labeled "tin-can tourists," they were courted for their dollars, which often transformed small towns into busy commercial centers, but they were discriminated against for their unsightly habits of roadside camping and hunting. Publicly run tourist camps — forerunners of the motel — were established by local governments. The nomadic tin-can tourists formed an association, "The Tin-Can Tourists of the World," and held annual camp meetings in several small towns along U.S. Route 27. Also known as the Orange Blossom Trail, Route 27 ran from Ohio down through the central part of Florida and was the principle conduit for campers. Perhaps it is just an amusing coincidence that the tin-can tourist association chose the Florida town of Arcadia as the place to hold their annual Christmas meetings and homecoming.

The tin-can tourists were the primary patrons of many of the new roadside businesses — including the attractions. In the 1920s and 1930s numerous attractions were opened on or near U.S. Route 27, the Dixie Highway (U.S. Route 1), and on the outskirts of towns and cities. Naive, occasionally eccentric, and rarely designed by trained landscape architects, there is little evidence that these attractions, with rare exceptions, were conceived with the deliberate intent of drawing on mythic subtexts. Nonetheless, the imagery and symbols incorporated are evidence that the subtext was there.

Indeed, the attractions that flourished were the ones that best came to embody the mythological landscapes and ideas of the supernatural first described by the explorers and later transmitted to the popular imagination by writers, artists, and advertisers. The small attractions can be separated into thematic categories: Florida as a magical source, or shrine (the springs); Florida as Eden (the garden attractions); Florida as the underworld (the alligator and reptile attractions).

8. Mircea Eliade, *The Sacred and Profane: The Significance of Religious Myth, Symbolism and Ritual Within Life and Culture* (New York: Harcourt Brace and World, 1959), 23.

9. Earl Chapin, "The Argonauts of the Automobile," *The Saturday Evening Post*, 9 August 1924, 25.

Seeing Silver Springs in Glass Bottom Boats.

Fig. 6. View of Silver Springs, showing the original glass-bottom boats. From a postcard, Curteich-Chicago, c. 1915. Author's collection.

Beautiful Silver Springs, Florida

Fig. 7. View of Silver Springs. From a postcard, c. 1935. Author's collection.

Florida's most unique natural wonder, Silver Springs, was one of its first small tourist attractions (figs. 6 and 7). Hubbard Hart, the owner of a stagecoach line that ran between Palatka, Silver Springs, Ocala, and Tampa, originally brought steamboats to Silver Springs in 1860 via the Ocklawaha River, a tributary of the St. Johns River. The trip up the Ocklawaha's dark, tannin-stained, and alligator-infested waters was two days of steamy discomfort through a dense jungle. The river was shrouded with a gray beard of Spanish moss, which added a lugubrious sense of mystery. The boat was clammy, cramped, and bug-ridden, causing numerous patrons to refer to it as a "coffin." Among the writers who made that analogy were Harriet Beecher Stowe in her 1873 Florida book, *Palmetto Leaves* and Lady Duffus Hardy in *Down South*, published in 1883.

However, by most accounts the Ocklawaha steamboat ride was worth enduring because eventually it arrived at the Silver Run, a stretch of river where the water turned light blue and crystal clear, before proceeding into a clearing in the forest where the spring — or actually a grouping of individual springs — was located. The transformational experiences described by visitors were noteworthy for their consistent yet seemingly unwitting references to spiritual metaphors. Take, for example, the letters of George McCall, who was serving in Florida during the Third Seminole Indian War when he visited Silver Springs on patrol. He described the canoe that brought him into the spring as an "eggshell" gliding over water "so pellucid that looking at it is like looking into the air." When the motion of the boat gradually ceased he described a strange sensation: "We were stationary...In a moment all was still as death. The line of demarcation between the waters and the atmosphere was invisible. Heavens! What an impression filled my mind at that moment! Were not the canoe and its contents obviously suspended in mid-air like Mahomet's coffin?"[10]

Many of the written descriptions of the early trips to the springs seemed to equate the journey with a spiritual transition to the afterlife, or to refer to the time-honored notion of the river as a metaphor for a spiritual journey to the source, which, with the advent of tourism, became a regular mini-pageant acted out on the Ocklawaha. Another early visitor, anthropologist and archeologist Daniel Brinton, described it as "one of the most dramatic transitions from darkness into light that a traveler can make anywhere on the continent."[11] Designated a Registered National Landmark by the United States Department of the Interior in 1925, Silver Springs is the largest natural artesian well formation in the world. It is only one of many springs in north and central Florida, which has seventeen of the country's seventy-five first-magnitude springs.[12]

As the springs became popular tourist destinations, hotels were built on their banks. Some of the springs were promoted as having restorative powers and catered to invalids and those seeking health benefits. Others, Silver Springs especially, were popular with more hardy tourists. A two-hundred-room hotel (which later burned) was constructed there in 1881, and a gateway and ticket booth (the secular versions of sacralizing structures) provided access to boats that took visitors down the river. On the glass-bottom boats invented by Hullam Jones in 1878, tourists could watch alligators and other aquatic life swim underneath as guides regaled them with stories of miracles, Indian rituals, and

10. Maj. Gen. George A. McCall, *Letters from the Frontiers* (1886; reprint, Gainesville: University Presses of Florida, 1974), 145–152.

11. Richard A. Martin, *Eternal Springs: Man's 10,000 Years of History at Florida's Silver Springs* (St. Petersburg, Fla.: Great Outdoors Pub. Co., 1966), 107.

12. First magnitude springs are those which discharge from ten to one hundred cubic feet of water per second. Charlton W. Tebeau, *A History of Florida* (Coral Gables: University of Miami Press, 1971), 6.

Fig. 8. The Florida Burning Spring Museum, St. Augustine, c. 1915. St. Augustine Historical Society.

ill-fated maidens drowning themselves for lost loves. It seems likely that most visitors did not perceive their Silver Springs excursions to be spiritual pilgrimages, but that it was the mystical beauty and the lore that drew people and informed their perceptions of the experience.

The springs became so popular that counterfeit versions began appearing. One of Florida's first contrived attractions, if not the first, was the Burning Spring Museum, founded in 1893 in St. Augustine by Everette C. Whitney (fig. 8). The "burning spring" was actually a natural artesian well, but Whitney, intent on separating tourists from their dollars, added gasoline to the sulfuric water and ignited it, causing a "mysterious" blue flame.[13] The Burning Spring Museum was moderately successful. Not long after the "museum" opened, however, it was observed that tourists were more interested in the alligators crossing the road than in the burning spring. The alligators promptly were corralled and put on display, and the Burning Spring Museum became the Burning Spring Museum and Alligator Farm and eventually the St. Augustine Alligator Farm. An immediate and enduring success that encouraged many similar operations, the St. Augustine Alligator Farm is the oldest continuously operating commercial alligator attraction in the state. Another early alligator attraction was Alligator Joe's, located both on the Miami River and in Palm Beach (figs. 9 and 10).

One of Florida's legendary themes is that of the Fountain of Youth, and there were several purported fountains of youth in the state. One, the Fountain of Youth Park in St. Augustine, founded in the early 1900s, claimed to be the original landing place of Ponce de León (figs. 11 and 12). Charles Reynolds, a local historian who in the 1930s set about debunking a rash of what he believed to be fraudulent attractions in St. Augustine, thought the "spring" on the site was actually a well from an early homesite and that Ponce de León's association was a deliberate fabrication by an early owner of the property.[14] But the fact that

13. William R. Adams and Carl Shiver, *The St. Augustine Alligator Farm: A Centennial History* (St. Augustine: Southern Heritage Press, 1993), 4–5.

14. Charles Reynolds, "Fact Verses Fiction for the New Historical Saint Augustine" (self-pubished, 1937), Florida Room, Otto G. Richter Library, University of Miami.

"*Young Alligator Joe*" GIVING AN EXHIBITION OF CATCHING AND HYPNO-
TIZING A WILD ALLIGATOR. Daily exhibitions are given at
THE FLORIDA ALLIGATOR FARM, Jacksonville, Florida. The Largest Alligator Farm in the World.

Fig. 10. Tourists reached Alligator Joe's on the Miami River on the tour boat *Sallie*, c. 1910. Author's collection.

Fig. 11. St. Augustine's Fountain of Youth Park, showing the entrance. From a postcard. Author's collection.

S. A. 112—Entrance Drive to "Fountain of Youth," St. Augustine, Fla.

Fig. 12. St. Augustine's Fountain of Youth Park. From a postcard, c. 1935. Though no actual claims of youth-restoring powers were made, the possibility was suggested. Author's collection.

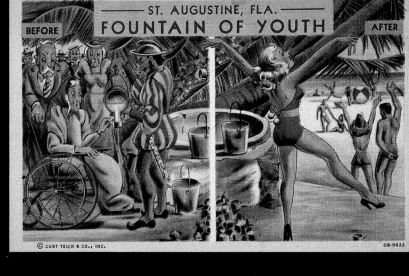

ST. AUGUSTINE, FLA.
FOUNTAIN OF YOUTH
BEFORE AFTER
© CURT TEICH & CO., INC.

Fig. 13. St. Petersburg's Fountain of Youth. From a postcard, c. 1926. The message on the back of the postcard reads, "This is where we get our drinking water every day. Mame is getting better already." Author's collection.

there was no evidence that the waters restored eternal youth didn't seem to dissuade visitors, and still doesn't — the Fountain of Youth Park remains a popular attraction. Another Fountain of Youth attraction was a municipal fountain at an artesian well in St. Petersburg (fig. 13). Here, crowds of winter visitors stood in line to fill containers of water. As it turned out, the faithful had good reason to feel better after drinking the water there. When the Pinellas County Health Department tested the water in 1971 it was found to contain an unusually high percentage of the trace element lithium.[15]

Most of the spring attractions survived very well with nothing more than glass-bottom boat rides, wildlife displays, and swimming areas. However, at the still-popular Weeki Wachee Springs, north of Tampa, "home to the Florida mermaid," the audience can look into the spring and watch women in neoprene mermaid outfits perform underwater routines referencing mythological themes ranging from Poseidon to Pocahontas. Weeki Wachee was founded by Newton Perry, a stunt coordinator who developed the concept for the attraction while working as a technical advisor on one of the *Tarzan* movies filmed at Silver Springs. Perry designed a breathing apparatus for star Johnny Weissmuller that allowed him to be filmed underwater without any visible attachments. It was a system of free-floating hoses, which proved quite successful and provided the possibility for a permanent underwater attraction. In 1946 Perry purchased Weeki Wachee Springs and built what the attraction claimed was the "first underwater theater."

To enter the Weeki Wachee Springs attraction, the visitor passes a gauntlet of cast-concrete parking-lot statuary of semi-nude mermaids that provides a dramatic and kitschy processional to the gateway (fig. 14). Inside, a cheerful garden area divides into paths that lead either to a jungle-boat ride, petting zoo, gift shop, or underwater amphitheater (fig. 15). Although mermaids embody the ideas of youth and eternity that traditionally are associated with the springs, they are not an element of Florida lore; the inspiration for them is more likely to have come from Perry's work in films.

15. Judy McKnight, "Curative Pinellas?" *St. Petersburg Times*, 20 October 1971.

Fig. 16. Florida Chambers of Commerce brochure, cover, c. 1920. Nymphs and fairies were popular icons in the paradisiacal image of Florida. This brochure described the state as, "an emerald kingdom…fanned by zephrys laden with ozone." University of Florida, Lee Harrison Collection.

Most of Florida's garden attractions were designed landscapes. If, as Leo Marx and other landscape scholars suggest, the image of the garden in general is representative of paradise, the Florida attraction gardens are interesting to look at in terms of the various interpretations of paradise that they offer (fig. 16).[16] A brochure for tourists that appears to have been published in the late 1930s contained a list of Florida's outstanding roadside garden attractions that included Dupree Gardens, north of Tampa, where twenty-five acres of flowers were "set to music"; Rainbow Tropical Gardens in West Palm Beach, lit by floodlights and open until midnight; Oriental Gardens on the St. Johns River, with oriental plants and "monastery chimes"; Turner's Sunken Gardens outside of St. Petersburg, built in a large solution hole; and Sarasota Jungle Gardens, where geese, cranes, and flamingos roamed freely in a native jungle and former banana plantation.[17]

In some gardens, the references to Eden were particularly direct. Mountain Lake Sanctuary in Lake Wales was built in 1929 as an admission-free retreat and bird refuge. Bok Tower, the carillon tower where its founder and benefactor

16. Leo Marx, *The Machine in the Garden* (Oxford: Oxford University Press, 1964).
17. "Florida's Finest Attractions" (Ocala, Fla.: n.d.), Historical Museum of Southern Florida.

Edward Bok was later entombed, was embellished with images of Adam and Eve. The grounds were an idyllic picturesque setting on top of central Florida's highest hill.

Another garden attraction, which no longer exists, actually was called "The Garden of Eden." Although no landscape plan has been found for this Palm Beach site, which was a private residence, at least one postcard view shows a cactus garden labelled as "The Garden of Eden" (fig. 17). Other garden attractions had Garden of Eden displays, including Silver Springs, which in one of its later incarnations had an underwater Garden of Eden. There is no specific landscape plan that literally identifies this type of garden as an Eden. The common thread is that of Eden as a garden transformed, rather than a found garden.[18] What the garden is transformed into is the individual choice of its human creator.

Sarasota Jungle Gardens, listed as a five-star attraction by the popular motor tour guidebook published during the 1930s and 1940s, *Kim's Guide to Florida*, is a still-existing attraction that was built as a private garden in the early 1930s by a local journalist, David Lindsay (fig. 18). His neighbor, Pearson Conrad, who owned a nursery, provided many of the plants and designed much of the plan. Lindsay reportedly found so many people peering through the fence that in 1936 he began admitting visitors for a fee. According to the historical information compiled by the garden, the land was originally "an impenetrable swamp."[19] This description was typical, reflecting a disappointment in the native landscape. The intent of gardens in general was to organize nature and make it pleasantly accessible and understandable. Many of the attraction gardens employed a quasi-scientific approach to their displays by carefully identifying most plant species by their Latin and common names and place of origin, which was a practice of botanical exhibition that began during the Enlightenment as a way of making nature quantifiable and manageable. While the symbolic importance of the garden was its connection to the divine, it was man's dominance over the landscape that transformed the threatening wilderness into a welcoming garden. That idea of transformation, whether from wilderness

---

18. This insight is based on author's interview of Rocco Ceo, Coral Gables, Florida, 14 March 1997. Ceo, an associate professor at the University of Miami School of Architecture, has documented many Florida gardens.

19. "Sarasota Jungle Gardens Information Sheet" (Sarasota: Sarasota Jungle Garden, 1997).

THE PRAYER OF THE WOODS
"I am the heat of your hearth on the cold winter nights,
the friendly shade screening you from the summer sun,
and my fruits are refreshing draughts quenching your
thirst as you journey on. "I am the beam that holds
your house, the board of your table, the bed on which
you lie, and the timber that builds your boat. "I am
the handle of your hoe, the door of your homestead,
the wood of your cradle, and the shell of your coffin.
"I am the bread of kindness and the flower of beauty.
"Ye who pass by, listen to my prayer: harm me not.

S-45—Sarasota Jungle Gardens,
Sarasota, Fla.

Fig. 18. Sarasota Jungle Gardens. From a postcard, c. 1940. Author's collection.

to order, from ordinary to extraordinary, or as a result of the actual experience of the garden itself, was a common, if naively interpreted, theme shared by many garden attractions, particularly the "jungle" gardens.

The jungle gardens were among the earliest of the roadside attractions. Among the jungle gardens developed during the mid-1920s and 1930s were McKee Jungle Garden, Monkey Jungle, Orchid Jungle, Sarasota Jungle Gardens, and Parrot Jungle. Florida's garden attractions in general offered an assemblage of beneficent wonders that soothed rather than threatened. However, the more familiar their wonders became, the more necessary it was to add other sources of amusement. In the case of Cypress Gardens, founded in 1936 in central Florida's "lake country," women in antebellum costumes with huge, brightly-colored hoopskirts were added to the exhibit after a 1940 freeze devastated the garden and left conspicuous gaps in the foliage (figs. 19 and 20). The idea was the desperate inspiration of Julie Pope, wife of the owner, who happened to have the costume on hand. Visitors seemed to respond favorably, so other women were added and the temporary remedy became a permanent fixture. Other responses to circumstance were incorporated through the years, so that today antebellum beauties stroll in a Japanese garden cruised by jungle boats, as stunt skiers suspended from hang-gliders land over a prehistoric native cypress swamp. Seemingly contradictory assemblages of imagery and activities were not unusual in many of the garden attractions. Jungle gardens, however, tended to present a more unified interpretation of the landscape.

The jungle gardens were as prevalent as the spring and alligator attractions. Some jungle attractions, as their names implied, were simply carved out of existing hammocks and their trails supplemented with added wildlife or botanical features. McKee Jungle Garden, which comprised eighty acres in Vero Beach designed by landscape architect William Lyman Phillips, was a sophisticated, planned landscape, but it was not typical. Its plan, however, did make use of transformational imagery; its "jungle trail," for example, led to a "cathedral of Royal Palms."

One of the most enchanting jungle attractions, Parrot Jungle, still one of Miami's most popular attractions, was opened in 1936 by Franz Scherr, an

C G-9—Clubhouse at Florida Cypress Gardens

Fig. 20. Cypress Gardens. Photograph by Michael Carlebach, 1996.

PARROT JUNGLE. MIAMI. FLORIDA

Fig. 21. Parrot Jungle, original entrance. From a postcard, c. 1936. Author's collection.

Austrian immigrant with an interest in exotic birds. Parrot Jungle was located on five acres of a native cypress stand that was formerly the site of a nudist colony.[20] According to Scherr's son Jerome, who still lives in Miami, Scherr was homesick for the physical terrain of Austria.[21] The original entrance to Parrot Jungle was a log cottage constructed from Florida pine, with a steeply pitched palmetto roof, which, except for its materials, was reminiscent of an Austrian architectural vernacular (fig. 21). Scherr lived in the structure's attic while he was getting the garden up and running. Later, he built a home next-door to the attraction. Parrot Jungle remained in the Scherr family until 1988. During the years of the Scherr's ownership, the attraction was expanded gradually to twelve acres, but it retained a cohesive design representative of Scherr's vision.

The garden plan of the Parrot Jungle continues to offer an interesting transformational experience. A large arched limestone gateway designed by architect Tony Sherman in 1954, which replaced the cottage as the main entrance (fig. 22), provides a traditional gateway onto an outdoor "foyer" rife with lush greenery and colorful birds. There a winding path leads into a dense tropical jungle (fig. 23). The trail winds around and back on itself, which was typical of jungle attractions, where limited acreage had to be maximized. The almost immediate effect is of being lost. In the effort to find the way out, or the way to the next event, visitors occasionally find themselves on stretches of trail where they have been before, wandering past sandy pits of alligators or giant tortoises, free-flying parrots, and exotic plants, all added to enhance the native jungle. From this rather safe and charming chaos the trail eventually reaches a straight stretch, which leads to an elevated point. Walking up to it, visitors are delivered to a shady pergola, a beautifully ordered vista of flamingos around a landscaped, manmade pond and fountain — and a refreshment stand (fig. 24). In short, a paradise has been reached via a (minimally) dark journey of the soul.

20. Metropolitan Dade County, Historic Preservation Division, "The Parrot Jungle and Gardens," Designation Report, 19 December 1990.

21. Jerome Scherr, interview by the author and Teresa Lenox, Miami, Florida, 24 October 1990.

Fig. 22. Parrot Jungle, current entrance. Photograph by Michael Carlebach, 1996.

Fig. 24. Parrot Jungle, Flamingo Lake promontory at the end of the jungle trail. Photograph by Michael Carlebach, 1996.

Fig. 23. Parrot Jungle, trail. Photograph by Michael Carlebach, 1996.

above,

Fig. 25. Henry Coppinger Jr.,
the first alligator wrestler,
and a few of his opponents.
Photograph by Gleason W.
Romer, c. 1928. Romer
Collection, Miami-Dade
Public Library.

right,

Fig. 26. Henry Coppinger Jr.
in the swamp. Photograph by
Gleason W. Romer, c. 1928.
Romer Collection, Miami-Dade

Following a "jungle trail" to an ordered environment is a typical format of the jungle attraction.

Monkey Jungle, which opened near Homestead, Florida several years before Parrot Jungle, offers a similar and equally inadvertent testimony to man's ability to tame a threatening environment, which is often the implication of an earthly Eden. There one walks through a native hammock, past solution holes, gator pits, and free-roaming "wild" monkeys, to a rustic but pleasing arena where animals perform tricks in response to the directions of their human trainer. Orchid Jungle, which opened in 1925 and closed after Hurricane Andrew in 1992, was also located outside of Homestead. It conveyed a similar message. There the visitor followed a winding jungle trail, where exotic orchids appeared to grow naturally from the dense vegetation. The trail led to an enclosed laboratory, with large picture windows, where people in white lab coats plucked orchid spores from test tubes. It was a sight suggesting that the whole previous "natural" experience was in reality the product of man's design.

At the other end of the mythological spectrum were the underworlds, embodied in the alligator and reptile attractions. Alligator "farms" were familiar sights along the North-South highways. Physically, the gator farms tended to be barren landscapes of boardwalks and fenced gator pits that emphasized the dangerous environment the visitor had entered. Although the success of the Alligator Farm in St. Augustine and Alligator Joe's in Miami and Palm Beach inspired many similar attractions, it was Coppinger's Tropical Gardens, Alligator Farm, and Indian Village, which opened in 1914 on the Miami River, that had the greatest influence on how the alligators' "ferociousness" was demonstrated to the public. Commercial alligator exhibitions tended to conform to a distinct plan of ponds and sand pits visible from protected and often barren walkways. In these attractions, vegetation was minimal, native, or relegated to a separate adjoining garden. Additional animal exhibits typically featured reptiles or birds of prey. In South Florida the alligator attractions often were linked to displays of Native American culture. Some of the alligator attractions were — quite literally — farms, where the primary business was breeding alligators for hides and meat, and little effort was put into exhibiting the reptiles. However, where tourists were the main focus the experience was of a threatening and slightly uncomfortable environment. This was also true of the shows intended to frighten audiences or demonstrate the alligators' lethal potential. Alligator Joe's proprietor Joe Campbell (also known as Warren Frazee) may have been the first exhibitor to capture alligators by hand and put them to sleep by rubbing their bellies, but it was the handsome and athletic Henry (Sonny) Coppinger Jr., son of the founder of Coppinger's Tropical Gardens, who gained celebrity status around Miami for capturing wild alligators in the Everglades single-handedly and incorporating their display in the attraction as the act of "wrestling alligators" (figs. 25, 26, and 27).[22] Coppinger taught the skill of alligator wrestling to the Miccosukee Indians, who camped at the attraction during tourist season, and although Miccosukees never wrestled alligators at Coppinger's, they did so at a nearby Miami River attraction, Musa Isle. Sonny Coppinger — South Florida's version of Saint George wrestling the dragon — became so popular with tourists that he was asked to perform the act in the pool of Henry Flagler's Royal Palm Hotel. Coppinger eventually travelled around the country performing until he was injured by an alligator and gave it up. Today almost all alligator attractions include a wrestling exhibition.

Fig. 27. Henry Coppinger Jr. with alligator. Photograph by Gleason W. Romer, c. 1928. Romer Collection, Miami-Dade Public Library.

22. Dorothy Downs, "Coppinger's Tropical Gardens," *The Florida Anthropologist* 34 (December 1981): 225–231.

None of the currently existing alligator attractions makes a more dramatic first impression than Gatorland in Kissimmee, just outside of Orlando. A relative latecomer in the small attraction business, Gatorland opened in 1949 as the Florida Wildlife and Reptile Institute. It was owned by Owen Godwin and his son Frank, who designed the attraction. The two men built the initial attraction themselves. A cypress log and palm-thatched hut with a sawdust floor stood at the original entry and led to sand trails and a bridge that spanned a manmade lake containing alligators. Like many small attractions, it was molded through the years by customer demand, and eventually the staid Reptile Institute was transformed into Gatorland. The entrance structure, built by Frank Godwin in 1962, is an open-jawed stucco alligator the size of Jonah's whale: one must literally walk through the jaws into the belly of the beast to enter the attraction (fig. 28). The story of Jonah is the story of resurrection after a trial. The implication is that the visitor too, must endure and then triumph by being spit back out of the open jaw, which conveniently serves as the exit, via a gift shop full of now-submissive alligators in the form of belts and handbags. In discussing the attraction, Frank Godwin said that when it was started, "tourists came to Florida to see three things — palm trees, flamingos, and alligators." The alligator's mystique for tourists was in its exaggerated image as a "man-eater" and a "prehistoric beast." The illusion of danger was desired and expected in a gator attraction.[23]

A handful of Florida's small attractions are still owned and operated by succeeding generations of the founding families, but many were sold to large corporations. Some of the surviving attractions have subsequently been sold back to mid-size, Florida-based management corporations. The American Broadcasting Company bought Weeki Wachee in 1959 and Silver Springs in 1962 and later sold them both to Florida Leisure Management. Harcourt Brace Jovanovich acquired Cypress Gardens in 1985, and later sold it to a Florida-based management group. Parrot Jungle was purchased by P. J. Birds, Inc., which is abandoning the original site designed by Franz Scherr and moving to a larger location closer to downtown Miami.

Small attractions began to fade from the Florida roadside landscape in the 1960s as interstate super highways diverted vehicular tourists away from the back roads where the small attractions were usually established. In some of the remaining attractions, market surveying has replaced entrepreneurial vision. Typically, professional designers are now responsible for additions. In the case of animal exhibits, state regulations dictate how wildlife must be displayed for the health and safety of the animals as well as the visitors. Company representatives frequently claim that operational costs have dictated the addition of such elements as shopping complexes and corporate-sponsored displays. To some degree the need to meet rising costs is indistinguishable from the desire to maximize profits, but running a successful attraction these days seems largely beyond the scope of a traditional family business.

Yet, despite the extravagance, corporate precision, and promotional resources of Walt Disney World, which has made it difficult for small attractions to compete, a significant number continue to flourish precisely because they offer something unique. To varying degrees fanciful, naive, and grotesque, small attractions are the embodiments of regional myth. Whether they satisfy any deeper, however unconscious, spiritual quest seems unlikely. The roadside attractions are often disparaged as tacky pseudo-events, pale reflections of what

23. Frank Godwin, telephone interview by author, 11 March 1997.

Fig. 28. Gateway to Gatorland, in which tourists are swallowed into the belly of the beast. Photograph by Michael Carlebach, 1996.

media-manipulated tourists expect to see.[24] This notion seems a harsh indictment given the surprising charm and beauty of some of the small attractions. As landscape scholar Simon Schama writes in *Memory and Landscape*:

> For if…our entire landscape tradition is the product of a shared culture, it is by the same token a tradition built from a rich deposit of myths, memories and obsessions. The cults which we are told to seek in other native cultures — of the primitive forest or the river of life, of the sacred mountain — are in fact alive and well and all around us if only we know where to look for them.[25]

As naive interpretations of myths, crass and commercial as they are, the appeal of the small attractions may be that they address the human longing for the mystical. In our secular culture, where taking to the highway in some way serves as a pop surrogate for a more complex journey, the mythic quest as pseudo-experience for tin-can pilgrims is still available via the small attraction. The revelations are small, but they may be had for no greater trial than the price of admission. □

24. Daniel J. Boorstin, *The Image: A Guide to Pseudo-Events in America* (New York: Harper Colophon, 1961), 40.
25. Simon Schama, *Landscape and Memory* (New York: Alfred Knopf, 1995), 14.

Fig. 1. William Lyman Phillips, Somerville Latin School portrait, Somerville, Massachusetts, 1904. The William Lyman Phillips Papers of the Charlton W. Tebeau Research Center, Historical Museum of Southern Florida.

The Memorable Landscapes of William Lyman Phillips

By Joanna Lombard

Joanna Lombard is a graduate of Tulane University School of Architecture and Harvard University School of Design. She is a registered architect and an associate professor at the University of Miami School of Architecture, Coral Gables, Florida. A 1996 University of Miami Max Orovitz Award supported research on William Lyman Phillips.

The landscape of Florida is integral to its culture. Fantastic architecture may have conjured up the storybook legend of the state, but it was the invented landscape — with its profusion of imported exotic plants and trees — that led to the clichéd image of the state. The coconut palm that has graced both beaches and postcards for generations, almost as a synonym for tropical Florida, was first cultivated in the state after W. J. Matheson imported it from the Federated Malay States for his Biscayne plantation in the early years of the century.[1] Yet many of Florida's tourists and a large portion of its residents consider the coconut palm to be native to the Florida beach. Florida's landscape has a lengthy history of inspiring imaginative reinterpretations, most of which depended on a transformation that virtually eliminated the native condition; witness developer Carl Fisher's creation of the resort of Miami Beach from an untamed sandy barrier island. One might term it the remaking of the state as Shangri-la.

Still, one landscape architect, William Lyman Phillips (1885–1966), successfully argued through his work that the native landscape has a significant place in the designed landscape (fig. 1). His work took on increasing importance as he designed parks and gardens across Florida, both in private practice and on behalf of the United States government's Civilian Conservation Corps. Phillips' creations in Florida reveal the unified relationship that is possible when designed and native landscapes are artfully arranged in a single vision so powerful that it becomes nature to successive generations. Indeed, many of the landscapes Phillips designed, especially Mountain Lake Sanctuary in Lake Wales (fig. 2) and Fairchild Tropical Garden in Coral Gables (fig. 3), came to epitomize an image of nature.

Much as Capability Brown (1716–1783) is known to have "improved" the English landscape, Phillips enhanced the prospect of the Floridian wilderness by creating both open spaces and smaller "garden rooms" from which to view the native condition. Though he did not totally shun imported species, Phillips employed a varied palette of indigenous materials in his compositions, both in landscape design and architecture, bringing together those plants and trees he thought most appropriate to the site. Often he would use found materials from the site, such as rock, to construct benches, walls, pavilions, and bridges. He composed the landscape around ordered spaces and axes, and directed vistas to include long views over the land. Phillips arranged the landscape to achieve both picturesque and naturalistic effects, guided at all times by an abiding sense of unity achieved from disparate elements. Like a painter, he

---

1. James C. McCurrach, *Palms of the World* (New York: Harper and Brothers, 1960), 55.

Fig. 2. Tower design by Milton B. Medary; landscape by Olmsted brothers, William Lyman Phillips, Bok Tower and reflection, Mountain Lake Sanctuary, Lake Wales, Florida, c. 1929. The William Lyman Phillips Papers of the Charlton W. Tebeau Research Center, Historical Museum of Southern Florida.

would create a composition that relied on a variety of contrasting characteristics — enclosed and open, sunlit and shadowed, reflective and absorptive, textured and smooth — in order to achieve that harmony.

The compositional principles Phillips employed were fundamental and unchanging. The source of those principles lies in the historic traditions of landscape and architecture and a design process that coupled a deep knowledge of human history with an immediate, thorough, and analytical understanding of site and context. Phillips was endowed with both curiosity about and insight into the relationship between native plants and their context. He created parks and gardens that have now become significant historic sites as well as places that teach about possibilities for the future.

Phillips' genius in the arrangement of materials to greatest effect can be seen in a wide range of landscapes, from the grand gesture of the axis of Fairchild Garden's Overlook (in which architectural historian Vincent Scully has noted the same driving force, linking the individual to the horizon, that inspired

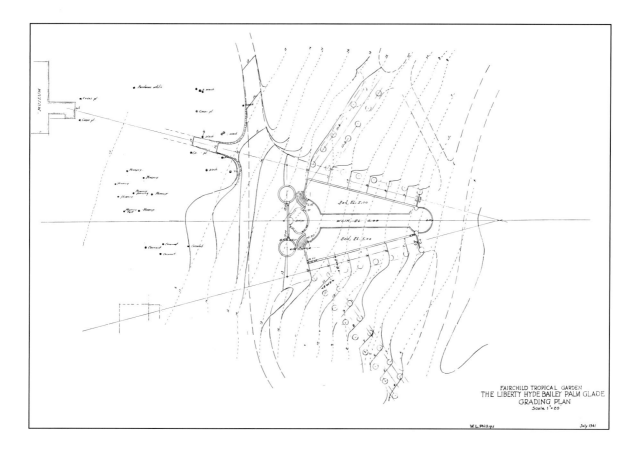

FAIRCHILD TROPICAL GARDEN
THE LIBERTY HYDE BAILEY PALM GLADE
GRADING PLAN
Scale 1"=20

W. L. Phillips   July 1941

André Le Nôtre [1613–1700] at Versailles) to the careful carving of a singular path joining the woods to the sea at Matheson Hammock. The intertwining of the universal and the particular rearranged the natural landscape to reveal not only its specific beauty and unique condition but also its ability to connect the present day through time and memory to the places humans have always cherished.

Landscape design is often described as formal or informal, depending on whether a particular garden is symmetrical with distinct rectilinear edges or asymmetrical with curvilinear edges. A more accurate understanding is that all gardens are formal, because informality is itself a design principle; in fact, it is one of the leading concepts guiding modern design of both landscape and architecture. All gardens are also geometric, since geometry is the basis for design and is used to determine not only clearly perceptible patterns in the landscape but seemingly random patterns of planting. The principles of landscape design have governed such apparently opposite works as the formal French gardens of André Le Nôtre and the seemingly uncultivated English countryside of Capability Brown.

Phillips was a member of the first generation of landscape architects educated at Harvard, just after the turn of the century, in a course of study that provided an intellectual foundation of the legacy of landscape architecture. These landscape architects were disciples of Frederick Law Olmsted Sr. (1822–1903), whether directly or indirectly. Olmsted was the United States' premier landscape architect of the nineteenth century. He believed that the goals of the profession involved organizing ideas such as a unity of vision or a variety of experience into a specific design. Based in Brookline, Massachusetts,

Olmsted and his firm designed parks and gardens that were to spread his philosophy throughout the United States. Though Olmsted is best known for his naturalistic landscape designs, such as the Ramble in New York City's Central Park, he also designed more obviously ordered spaces such as the Central Park Promenade, and his success with the picturesque has often overshadowed the totality of his legacy.

Olmsted's ideas took hold in the new generation of landscape architects after Charles Eliot (1859–1897), an Olmsted partner, began to advocate for a professional program in landscape architecture at Harvard. Eliot, himself largely self-taught, strongly believed that landscape architecture belonged in "a School of Design rather than a School of Horticulture," saying in a letter to Charles Francis Adams of the Harvard Board of Overseers that "the popular notion that my profession is chiefly concerned with gardens and gardening is utterly mistaken." [2]

On 17 March 1897 after an outing to determine the best grades and vistas for a roadway, Charles Eliot remained home with a cold. A week later, he died of cerebrospinal meningitis. Eliot's death inspired his father, Charles W. Eliot, then president of Harvard University, to establish Harvard's landscape architecture program in 1900, and in 1903 to award Frederick Law Olmsted Jr. (1870–1957) the Charles Eliot Professorship.[3] President Eliot noted that his son had defined landscape architecture to be "the art of arranging land and landscape for human use, convenience, and enjoyment."[4] Those words reappear almost verbatim on the first page of William Lyman Phillips' notebook from Professor James Sturgis Pray's course, Landscape Architecture I, offered at Harvard in the fall of 1908.[5] Olmsted's concepts were a major influence as the first generation of young Harvard-educated landscape architects began to design parks, gardens, and towns across the country.

Writings from Eliot, Olmsted, and the curricula at Harvard in those early years reveal a unified philosophy that led to several powerful precepts for landscape architecture. Among those principles was the consensus that the goal of the profession was to arrange the landscape for human purposes.[6] A second principle was the opinion, held by Olmsted and Eliot, that landscape architects were responsible for what Eliot called the main lines of the project.[7] Eliot noted that landscape gardening was "but a secondary part of the profession: the devising of general schemes which shall combine convenience with preserved, increased, or created beauty is the most important part of our work," a view that reinforced the concept of the landscape architect as orchestrator and visionary.[8] A third principle emerged from Eliot's contention that "the site, the scene, the 'landscape,'" and the building must be studied as one design and composition.[9] The concept of a unified experience derived from a long tradition in landscape design. In Eliot's era Andrew Jackson Downing, an important nineteenth-century writer on the American landscape, espoused

2. Charles W. Eliot, *Charles Eliot, Landscape Architect* (Boston and New York: Houghton and Mifflin Company, 1902), 630.

3. James Sturgis Pray, "The Department of Landscape Architecture in Harvard University," *Landscape Architecture* 1 (January 1911): 54–56.

4. Eliot, *Charles Eliot*, 274.

5. *Official Register of Harvard University* 6 (September 1909), 40:10–12.

6. Eliot, *Charles Eliot*, 274.

7. Ibid., 367.

8. Ibid., 273.

9. Ibid., 366.

"unity" as his first "leading principle." In 1841 Downing elucidated the principles of unity, harmony, and variety that should guide landscape design, and explained that "Unity, *or the production of a whole*, is a leading principle of the highest importance."[10]

Although Downing's popular text, *A Treatise on the Theory and Practice of Landscape Gardening*, was not on Eliot's list of "books and papers which influenced or recorded, the beginnings of the modern art of landscape gardening,"[11] Frederick Law Olmsted Sr. had been an associate of Downing's, and Downing's collaborator, Calvert Vaux, joined Olmsted in the design of Central Park. In his "Description of a Plan for the Improvement of the Central Park, 'Greensward,' 1858," Olmsted explained that "The idea of the park itself should always be uppermost in the mind of the beholder."[12] The principle of unity is repeated throughout Phillips' Harvard class notes, which recorded that "the goal of landscape architecture is a complex, but unified impression."[13]

Born 11 June 1885 in Somerville, Massachusetts, William Lyman Phillips graduated from Somerville Latin School in 1904 and earned his A.B. at Harvard in 1908. He completed the graduate program in landscape architecture at Harvard in 1910, and then worked in Montreal on the design of several parks. In 1911 Phillips joined the Olmsted Brothers firm as an assistant with responsibility for site work on the Boston Common. In 1913, after four months of extensive European travel, Phillips began work on "the design and construction of the new town of Balboa," for the Isthmian Canal Commission.[14]

Phillips returned to Cambridge in 1914 to find very little work. For the next several years he moved around the country. In 1919 he landed at Camp Bragg, South Carolina and began working on layouts for Army establishments. During the following five years Phillips worked in Brookline, spent a year based in Paris, where he worked on American military cemeteries, continued his travels in Europe and the United States, and finally wound up in Boca Grande, Florida, where he developed an island town for a chemical company. When the company decided to abandon real estate development in 1925, Phillips moved to Lake Wales, Florida, and began work on Mountain Lake Sanctuary with Frederick Law Olmsted Jr., who had become the senior partner in the family's landscape firm.

Phillips' collaboration with the junior Olmsted was to continue for the rest of Olmsted's life and led to Phillips' long career in Florida, during which he designed private, public, commercial, and institutional landscapes. Phillips' work was recognized by his peers, although he often commented that his isolated circumstances left him working in obscurity. The landscapes he made, however, were never obscure, and his public parks at Crandon, Greynolds, and Matheson Hammock, as well as the great botanical garden at Fairchild Tropical Garden, have defined Florida for generations of residents and tourists.

10. Andrew Jackson Downing, *A Treatise on the Theory and Practice of Landscape Gardening* (New York: A. O. Moore and Company, 1841), 64.

11. Eliot, *Charles Eliot*, 219.

12. Frederick Law Olmsted Sr., *Forty Years of Landscape Architecture: Central Park*, ed. Frederick Law Olmsted Jr. and Theodora Kimball (1928; reprint, Cambridge, Mass.: The M.I.T. Press, 1973), 222.

13. Notes by William Lyman Phillips, 1908, File 23–5, William Lyman Phillips Papers, Charlton W. Tebeau Research Center, Historical Museum of South Florida, Miami, Florida (hereafter cited as Phillips Papers).

14. William Lyman Phillips, letter to Frank Albert Waugh, 30 October 1915, File 14–5, Phillips Papers.

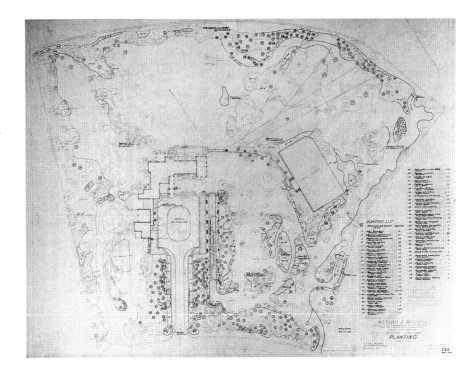

Early among these many influential landscapes was Mountain Lake Sanctuary in Lake Wales, Florida (fig. 4). Olmsted's and Phillips' work at Mountain Lake Sanctuary was characterized by Eliot's idea of orchestrating many disciplines toward a unified effort in service of human use, convenience, and enjoyment.[15] The Sanctuary was owned by Edward Bok (1863–1930), an immigrant from the Netherlands who for thirty years edited *The Ladies' Home Journal*. Bok was known for admonishing his readers to avoid wearing the feathers of exotic birds in order to stop the slaughter of Florida's species. He established the Sanctuary in 1922 near his home in Lake Wales to create a landscape for his own use that would "be open and accessible to his friends and neighbors of the Mountain Lake Colony."[16] The original Sanctuary site was the wooded northern slope of Iron Mountain, the only such hill in central Florida, just outside Fred Ruth's two-thousand-acre citrus groves and his five-hundred-acre resort community of Mountain Lake Colony (figs. 5 and 6).

Phillips represented the firm in Lake Wales from the project's inception in 1924 through its completion in 1931. He was responsible for all of the site work and collaborated with Olmsted on the siting of the tower, plateau, moat, and oak grove, as well as the construction of the reflecting pool. Phillips also designed a number of residential gardens for Mountain Lake Colony homeowners.

To understand Phillips' role in the creation of a landscape image for Florida, it is necessary to review Olmsted's notes and correspondence. The thinking reflected in these writings is as much that of Phillips, whose attention was focused solely on Mountain Lake, as of Olmsted, who was overseeing numerous jobs. Mountain Lake, too, establishes many of the landscape ideas that were to follow.

15. Eliot, *Charles Eliot*, 274.
16. "The Mountain Lake Sanctuary, Mountain Lake, Florida: A Report," Olmsted Brothers, Landscape Architects, Brookline, Massachusetts and William Lyman Phillips, Landscape Architect, North Miami, Florida, 2 July 1956, File 8–4:1, Phillips Papers.

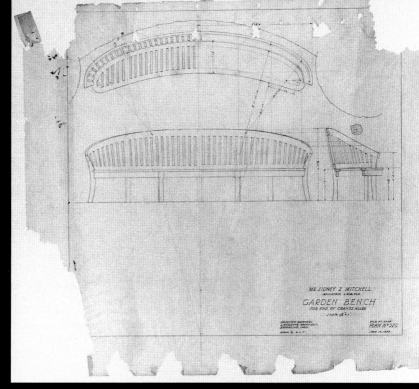

Fig. 5. William Lyman Phillips for Olmsted Brothers, plan and elevations of the "Sidney Z. Mitchell Garden Bench for End of Orange Allee," Mountain Lake, Lake Wales, Florida, pencil on tracing paper, 24 x 24", 1939. The William L. Phillips Papers, Archives and Special Collections, Otto G. Richter Library, University of Miami, Coral Gables, Florida.

MR. SIDNEY Z. MITCHELL
MOUNTAIN LAKE FLA.
GARDEN BENCH
FOR END OF ORANGE ALLEE

Fig. 6. William Lyman Phillips for Olmsted Brothers, view of Mitchell bench on site, Mountain Lake, Lake Wales, Florida, c. 1940.

The William Lyman Phillips Papers of the Charlton W. Tebeau Research Center, Historical Museum of Southern Florida

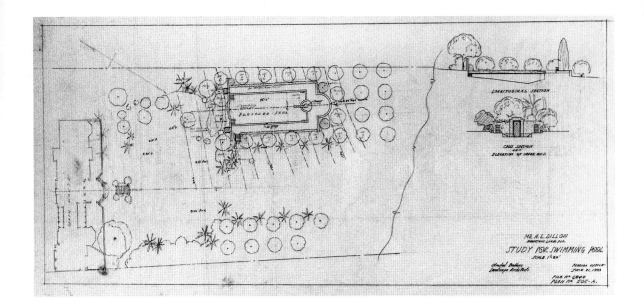

Fig. 7. William Lyman Phillips for Olmsted Brothers, plan and sections of Mr. H. L. Dillon swimming pool, Mountain Lake, Lake Wales, Florida, pencil on tracing paper, 16 x 32", 1933. The William L. Phillips Papers, Archives and Special Collections, Otto G. Richter Library, University of Miami, Coral Gables, Florida.

Olmsted wrote to Bok while travelling by train on 4 July 1922 to propose and explain his design for the Sanctuary. Olmsted imagined a wooded walk across the hillside with several lookout points along the way. The walk would culminate in a plateau that would be selectively cleared and planted to frame views of the panoramic vistas at the top of the climb. Olmsted's description captivated Bok.

Olmsted described the initial approach by road, which would start in the "flattish, shady grove for parking," from which the visitor would advance toward the entrance to discover "the glorious western view" by "having it burst upon him."[17] The parking area would be surrounded by orange groves, and the home sites of the Mountain Lake Colony would begin within a quarter-mile or so of the groves (figs. 7 and 8). Olmsted imagined a variegated wood, beginning with the native pine landscape and adding live oaks, laurel oaks, and other broad-leaved evergreens.

Olmsted considered the parking grove "a sort of antechamber to the Sanctuary."[18] The actual Sanctuary entrance would be:

> a rather narrow passage, at least one or two hundred feet in length, rising gently through a dense wood, completely overarched by trees and flanked on either hand by a seemingly impenetrable thicket of undergrowth. It should be just long enough and just sufficiently indirect in its easy curvature for one to shake off his impressions of the road and of the automobiles and of the orange groves as roadside companions, and to feel that he is penetrating into something different.[19]

Olmsted then described a rapid but not arduous rise diagonally across the hill toward the northwest, in which the thickets would begin to clear and "would merge into patches of low bushy growth over which the eye would range." The thicket would be similar to the New England "bushy pastures studded

17. Frederick Olmsted Jr., letter to Edward Bok, 7 July 1922, File 7–22, Phillips Papers.
18. Ibid.
19. Ibid.

Fig. 8. William Lyman Phillips for Olmsted Brothers, view of completed Dillon swimming pool, Mountain Lake, Lake Wales, Florida, 1941. The William Lyman Phillips Papers of the Charlton W. Tebeau Research Center, Historical Museum of Southern Florida.

with junipers, blueberries…" To the northeast would be distant views across the pine ridges to Lake Pierce.

The climb would proceed through trees and evergreen shrubs such as wax myrtle, with fern and floral ground covers, to a small plateau that Olmsted planned to enlarge to create a level plane. The plateau would recreate the hammock typically found along the shoreline between the mangrove and the pineland. This plateau of hammock scenery "would be the heart of the Sanctuary, completely self-contained and shut off from the rest of the world, —a little sunlit forest glade surrounded by dense shadow." Rising further would be a "narrow belt of undergrowth" and then:

> an open grove of Live Oaks and Long Leaf Pine, not over forty or fifty feet wide east and west but a couple of hundred yards long north and south, nearly level and backed on the east by the dense "hammock" growth much as that growth backs the beach of many a Florida lake. On the west the ground would drop away, more precipitously for the first ten or fifteen feet of drop than it does at present, as precipitously indeed as would seem at all natural in this sandy soil.[20]

The drama of the sequence of the climb would enhance the whole experience. The return trip would amble along the plateau. The southern hollow would hold "a winding dumbbell-shaped pond, perhaps a hundred and fifty feet long, with characteristic water-side vegetation and likely to become a happy haunt of the birds." Finally, Olmsted suggested that a caretaker's cottage might become a gate-lodge between the parking grove and the Sanctuary.[21]

After Olmsted's initial design, a carillon tower was added to the composition. It was designed by Milton B. Medary of Philadelphia, who also designed the Lincoln Memorial in Washington, D.C. The tower was set within a moat, and connected to the proposed pond through a new pond along its northerly axis (figs. 9 and 10). A path leading down the hill to the east was added with new

20. Ibid.
21. Edward Bok, letter to Frederick Olmsted Jr., 10 July 1922, File 7–22, Phillips Papers.

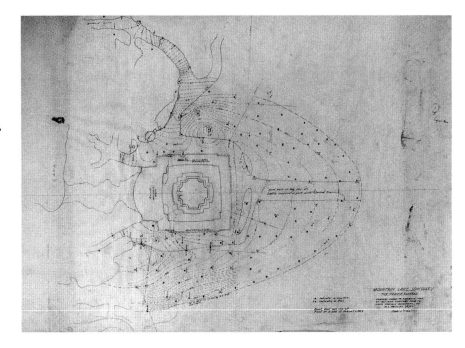

Fig. 9. William Lyman Phillips for Olmsted Brothers, plan of Mountain Lake Sanctuary Tower plateau, Lake Wales, Florida, pencil on tracing paper, 24 x 30", 1956. From a 1956 report. The William L. Phillips Papers, Archives and Special Collections, Otto G. Richter Library, University of Miami, Coral Gables, Florida.

Fig. 10. Tower design by Milton B. Medary; landscape by Olmsted Brothers, William Lyman Phillips, view of Bok Tower, Mountain Lake Sanctuary, Lake Wales, Florida, c. 1929. The William Lyman Phillips Papers of the Charlton W. Tebeau Research Center, Historical Museum of Southern Florida.

parking for the residents and guests of the Colony. The twenty-story tower and garden were dedicated by President Calvin Coolidge in 1929. Bok commented that he

> wanted to present to the American people for visitation…a spot which would reach out in its beauty through the plantings, through the flowers, through the birds, through the superbly beautiful architecture of the Tower, through the music of the bells, to the people and fill their souls with the quiet, the repose, the influence of the beautiful, as they could see and enjoy it in the Sanctuary and the Tower.[22]

Although the Sanctuary ascent originally was conceived for the enjoyment of Bok, his friends, and the residents and visitors of Mountain Lake Colony, the carillon concerts attracted many more visitors than Phillips and Olmsted had anticipated. Despite the fact that the original concept of the ascent did not account for crowds, the open areas were capable of holding the increased number of visitors.

In 1956 Phillips and the Olmsted office prepared a report noting that the tower "dominated the composition" not only in its physical form, set in a grove at the top of Iron Mountain, but also

> in public understanding. For unfortunately the words "Bok Tower" were considered by makers of road signs and writers of press notices to be preferable to any longer and more comprehensive designations, and this title has become so universally used that to mention the Mountain Lake Sanctuary is ordinarily to utter an enigma. The Tower has the fame, the carillon concerts are what one has to attend. Yet the Sanctuary as a whole is still valid in the concept of its founder. It is the part of the world that he left more beautiful than he found it. Regardless of the motives by which

22. Edward W. Bok, "A Personal Foreword," *The Sanctuary and Singing Tower* (Mountain Lake, Fla.: The American Foundation Incorporated, 1929).

people are drawn there, the Sanctuary, once entered, affects the senses of the visitor gratefully, creates a poetic mood, induces feelings of reverence, stirs the mind to rapt admiration. Here voices are hushed as in a church, and decency for the moment takes possession of the vulgar. A more striking example of the power of beauty could hardly be found, better proof that here beauty exists could not be asked for.[23]

Frederick Olmsted Jr. died on Christmas day in 1957, and the following spring Phillips wondered whether "F. L.O., confronted by the problem of providing a setting for a carillon to be visited by hundreds of people at a time, would have come up with what we see now, speaking more especially of the old Sanctuary area. The Tower had been completed, the moat and reflection pool made, when E. Bok decided to open the place to the public."[24] It was upon the basis of more than thirty years of work that Phillips pondered the best way to accommodate the gardens' numerous visitors and still preserve what Phillips said was the place where he felt "more satisfaction of being than in any other piece of humanized ground."[25]

In May 1958 Judge Curtis Bok, the founder's son, agreed to greater maintenance of the paths and thickets to maintain Olmsted's original principle of contrasts between open and closed spaces, and Phillips agreed that new magnolias might be planted along the western edge to start to build new areas of interest that would not conflict with the original intent of the Sanctuary. The adherence to the ideas that governed the Sanctuary for its first thirty years represented a decision to honor the project's history. While architects, engineers, horticulturists, and many others participated in the Sanctuary, Olmsted and Phillips were responsible for the character and detail that made the Sanctuary a memorable landscape — a landscape where a person could form an idea of a place that would stay with him, as the senior Olmsted said of Central Park. That characteristic was also evident in other landscapes Phillips designed.

In April of 1932 Olmsted asked Phillips to conclude his work at Mountain Lake and to supervise work the firm had in Houston, Texas. Phillips immediately wrote to Olmsted explaining that his wife, Simone Guillot, had just given birth to baby Mary in January and that she very much needed him to assist her with young Juliette, who was not yet three years old, and the tasks of daily life.[26] Olmsted responded with the suggestion that Phillips take the train to Houston and leave Simone the car so that she might be able to get around Lake Wales without Phillips' assistance.[27] On 15 April Phillips agreed to go to Texas, leaving his young family behind in Lake Wales. Shortly after the conclusion of that job, however, Phillips and Olmsted determined that Phillips would be best suited to work as a consultant to the firm rather than as an employee. Phillips moved his family to Palm Beach and then to Miami, where he began working as the project superintendent of the U.S. Department of the Interior's National Park Service construction of Greynolds Park in North Miami on behalf of the Civilian Conservation Corps. (CCC). He later worked on Matheson Hammock, and eventually, Fairchild Tropical Garden in southern Dade County.

23. "The Mountain Lake Sanctuary," 4–5.

24. William Lyman Phillips, letter to William Bell Marquis and Edward Clark Whiting, 14 April 1958, File 5–7, Phillips Papers.

25. William Lyman Phillips, letter to William Bell Marquis, 12 April 1958, File 5–7, Phillips Papers.

26. William Lyman Phillips, letter to Frederick Olmsted Jr., 7 April 1932, File 13–12, Phillips Papers.

27. Frederick Olmsted Jr., letter to William Lyman Phillips, 12 April 1932, File 13–12, Phillips Papers.

Greynolds Park (fig. 11) is significant in many ways. The project shows Phillips' grand ambitions at work, especially in his design of the "Mound" as both a focal point for the park and a place from which the landscape could be surveyed (figs. 12 and 13). In addition, the park's buildings have an organic quality, demonstrating Phillips' talent for using materials found on site.

Phillips supervised a crew of CCC workers in the design and building of Greynolds Park, named after the quarry owner on whose land the park was built. Phillips organized the park around a central axis that leads to the Mound and then provides numerous spaces for views and woodland experiences that relate to individual buildings and bodies of water (fig. 14). The interweaving of land and water is a concept that describes the overall plan of the park. Responses to the park were enthusiastic. Olmsted wrote to Phillips in January of 1935 to congratulate him on the success of the Observation Mound and Tower. Olmsted found that the "silhouette of the main body of masonry reminds me strikingly of the Chateau of Murols in Puy-de Dome or thereabout, though of course on a very much smaller scale…the thing itself seems to be a fine piece of constructive design; suitably theatrical and arresting but very refined in line and composition."[28] The public flocked there — from the first week of the park opening in 1936, it "became an overcrowded, overused facility."[29] The support facilities and amenities were later expanded (fig. 15). Phillips' inventiveness in dealing with the numerous challenges of construction and the varied experience of his work crew prepared him to address the mangrove of Matheson Hammock.

Matheson Hammock was named for W. J. Matheson, a successful chemical engineer who donated land for several public parks in Florida (figs. 16 and 17). Phillips, in a 31 March 1936 report, described the objectives of his work at Matheson Hammock as to "protect the valuable natural forest reservation for

28. Frederick Olmsted Jr., letter to William Lyman Phillips, 16 January 1935, File 7–5, Phillips Papers.

29. A. D. Barnes, "History of Dade County Park System 1929–1969, The First Forty Years," 1986, File 5–23:174, Phillips Papers.

Fig. 14. William Lyman Phillips, oolitic limestone bridge, Greynolds Park, North Miami, Florida, c. 1936. Photograph by Gleason W. Romer. Romer Collection, Miami-Dade Public Library.

Fig. 15. William Lyman Phillips, beach along lagoon with shelter and boathouse in the distance, Greynolds Park, North Miami, Florida, c. 1936. Photograph by Gleason W. Romer. Romer Collection, Miami-Dade Public Library.

left,

Fig. 16. William Lyman Phillips,

"improved vista" through ham-

mock, Matheson Hammock,

Coral Gables, Florida, c. 1937.

Photograph by Gleason W.

Romer. Romer Collection,

Miami-Dade Public Library.

right,

Fig. 17. William Lyman Phillips,

waterfront of Biscayne Bay,

Matheson Hammock, Coral

Gables, Florida, c. 1937.

Photograph by Gleason W.

Romer. Romer Collection,

Miami-Dade Public Library.

which the Park was primarily established," and "to gain access across a wide swamp to the bayshore for the purpose of developing the exceptionally good water recreation possibilities."[30] In the context of beach development Matheson Hammock holds a special significance. Phillips chose to save the natural environment, instead of the more usual approach of clearing and filling the mangrove. At Matheson Hammock he did this brilliantly, letting the beach become a prize at the end of a process of discovery, an encounter with Florida as the first settlers might have found it. Phillips asserted that the "amount of natural surface modified for use and visitation will be relatively very slight. The park is primarily a nature preserve."[31] One of the most challenging projects at Matheson Hammock was clearing the road to the beach. Phillips, in his report of October and November of 1935, marveled at the sense of accomplishment as the road moved forward yard by yard:

> To the outsider, to those who later use the road, there is presumably nothing marvelous about it at all — there are so many miles of road in Florida built through marsh and swamp lands that the thing is commonplace.... But if it happens in a case like this that qualities of scenery somewhat commonplace have nevertheless aesthetic significance of a definite nature, though not obvious to everyone, it is worth while to call particular attention to them. The qualities here are the properties of a foil, of a contrasting element…The swamp is silent, windless, monotonous. Suddenly one comes out into the open of a quiet cove where low dark forest walls are reflected in still water, and the illimitable Bay is seen past a headland of high wind-moulded trees. It is as if one had passed through a dim chamber into a bright and splendid hall. The swamp crossing has provided a few minutes of quieting detachment from humanized scenes, from any scene which would particularly attract the eye, so that the terminal incident comes with a freshness and vigor which would have been lacking if this special

30. William Lyman Phillips, letter to National Park Service, 31 March 1936, Research Group 79, Box 15, National Archives, College Park, Maryland (herafter cited as National Archives).

31. Ibid.

preparation had not been made. A different sort of contrast, and a stronger one, can be experienced where the road reaches the Bay shore. There the dead silence of the mangrove forest is suddenly broken by the "many-voiced tongue of the Sea," by the incessant lapping of wavelets on the beach and that rattle of wind in foliage which is peculiar to tropical strands. The breeze is fresh and bracing, and the views seaward through the screen of fantastically contorted mangrove trees have a dramatic quality. It is a fine effect, one could almost say an exciting effect, and yet it must be dependent largely on the contrasting prelude, for if one came to this beach by the way of an ordinary bayshore boulevard he would scarcely experience any emotion when he arrived.[32]

Phillips called his superiors' attention to the vital role of the mangrove that was being eliminated rapidly from the South Florida shoreline. Phillips noted that:

> The mangrove swamp is to most humans a hateful, hostile growth. Their first and only desire is to do away with it, preferably by a fill which replaces wet ground with dry and kills the trees. The growth is somehow incompatible with human habitation. It is a vanishing type of forest; the swamps year by year are pushed further away from the City. Yet, as a forest type, mangrove is unique; and where, in a given situation such as this, the swamp can be assigned an important role in a total park effect, and can be regarded and managed sympathetically, the preservation and passing down of it to posterity would seem to be an act of considerable cultural significance.[33]

Fig. 18. William Lyman Phillips, oolitic limestone shelter, Matheson Hammock, Coral Gables, Florida, c. 1937. Photograph by Gleason W. Romer. Romer Collection, Miami-Dade Public Library.

The bay road acts as a unifying device in the design of the park, linking the many and varied landscape experiences to a unified whole. Once again, Phillips drew upon principles of variety and contrast to heighten the differences of the park elements within an overall composition that is carefully orchestrated to produce a grand effect (fig. 18). The principles he employed at Matheson and earlier at Greynolds, which drew upon such ideas as approach and contrast, would be refined during the next thirty years in his composition of Fairchild Tropical Garden.

Phillips' association with Fairchild Tropical Garden began in 1938 (figs. 19 and 20). Marjory Stoneman Douglas in her *Dedication of the Fairchild Tropical Garden, March 23rd 1938*, explained that "Colonel and Mrs. Robert H. Montgomery had acquired and had given to the Garden eighty-three acres of land situated in the City of Coral Gables adjoining and immediately south of Matheson Hammock and Dade County Park, east of Cutler road. Combined with the Dade County Property the land runs to and has a frontage of one mile on Biscayne Bay." Dade County combined the entire Matheson Hammock development of several hundred acres with the Fairchild acquisition.

Colonel Montgomery and a group of friends had decided in 1934 to start a botanical garden in honor of David Fairchild, the renowned plant scientist, explorer, and collector. In order to accommodate county regulations prohibiting the expenditure of public funds on private property, fifty-eight acres adjoining Matheson Hammock were donated to Dade County to develop as part of Fairchild Tropical Garden. The remaining twenty-five acres, formerly a

32. William Lyman Phillips, letter to National Park Service, October–November 1935, Research Group 79, Box 15, National Archives.

33. Ibid.

Fig. 19. William Lyman Phillips, with Noel Chamberlin, consulting, Fairchild Tropical Garden plan. From *Dedication of the Fairchild Tropical Garden, March 23rd 1938*. The William L. Phillips Papers, Archives and Special Collections, Otto G. Richter Library, University of Miami, Coral Gables, Florida.

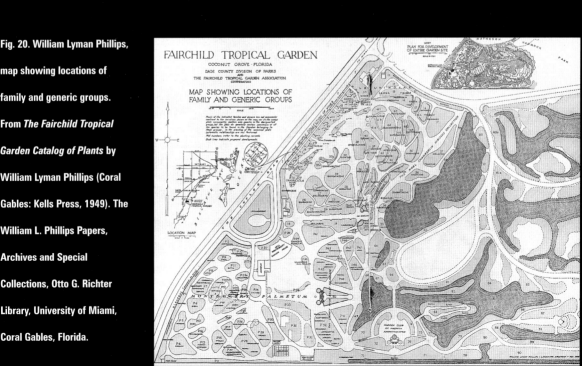

Fig. 20. William Lyman Phillips, map showing locations of family and generic groups. From *The Fairchild Tropical Garden Catalog of Plants* by William Lyman Phillips (Coral Gables: Kells Press, 1949). The William L. Phillips Papers, Archives and Special Collections, Otto G. Richter Library, University of Miami, Coral Gables, Florida.

mango, avocado, and citrus grove, were retained by the Garden and referred to as the Montgomery Palmetum. The Montgomerys' donations also included two hundred species of palms and flowering trees as well as the funds to improve the twenty-five acre tract.[34]

Charles Crandon, a Dade County Commissioner, pledged that the county would "cooperate 100% in this very meritorious enterprise."[35] Elmer D. Merrill, of Harvard's Botanical Collections and the acting supervisor of the Arnold Arboretum in Massachusetts, reminded the audience gathered for the dedication of the importance of plants in civilization and predicted a bright future for Fairchild.

What was not discussed at the 1938 dedication was the landscape architecture of the Garden, nor the design intent of Phillips, its chief landscape architect. The skeletal structure of what the site would become is shown in a preliminary plan by Phillips and Noel Chamberlin, a landscape architect who was a friend of Colonel Montgomery's. The main overlook extended from what was then the Garden's entrance, establishing the central vista. An axis of secondary importance was outlined in the vista from the director's house to view out over a smaller lake. The two parallel vistas were linked through smaller paths and occasional views between them, with a garden room north of the overlook and a smaller clearing at the south end.

Phillips did not fully explain his ideas and intentions for the project to a national audience until a 1963 article in *Landscape Architecture,* entitled "Developing A Tropical Garden." However, his reports and correspondence during the development of Fairchild Tropical Garden reveal much of his design goals. Phillips compared the botanical garden to the architecture of a museum. He explained that since "a museum consisting entirely of large salons" was not possible, "corridors and long galleries" were the practical result. Phillips believed, though, that the garden could afford, "as most museums can afford, a few large rooms in which large and particularly fine pieces can be viewed from a distance…even if they are only 50 or 75 feet in diameter."

Phillips identified the overriding design principle at Fairchild as "the principle of contrast, as expressed by the opposition of solids and voids and of relative degrees of solidity and vacancy — using contrast to attain variety." His elaboration of the voids expanded from an open lawn, or the turf floor of a garden room, to the use of water, low-profile plantings, and generally any concavity which would contrast with the vertical profiles of the major trees (fig. 21).

Phillips worked on Fairchild through the early 1940s, communicating with Colonel Montgomery to discuss design possibilities. Phillips appreciated the Colonel's enthusiasm for the design of the Palm Glade, and he continued his supervision of the CCC crew in the building of the amphitheatre.[36] In 1942 Phillips informed Montgomery that the "Dade County Park Division has now been cut back to within an inch of the ground," and that he, Phillips, was "among the severed portions."[37] Montgomery retained Phillips to continue developing the overall design structure as well as numerous details of the project.

34. Marjory Stoneman Douglas, *Dedication of the Fairchild Tropical Garden, March 23rd 1938* (Miami: Fairchild Tropical Garden, 1938), 2.

35. Ibid., 3.

36. William Lyman Phillips, letter to Robert Montgomery, 17 July 1941, File 13–11, Phillips Papers.

37. William Lyman Phillips, letter to Robert Montgomery, 3 June 1942, File 13–11, Phillips Papers.

Fig. 21. William Lyman Phillips, overlook at Fairchild Tropical Garden. Courtesy of Bertram Zuckerman, from the Fairchild Tropical Garden collection.

In July of 1943 Phillips proposed a new approach to the Palm Glade that would frame the view out over the little lake with a cycad collection (figs. 22, 23, and 24). He suggested that "at the easterly corners of the flared opening, sitting places could be provided with appropriate ground form and a backing and a canopy of small palms....It is a pleasant, advantageous place to sit."[38]

Phillips subsequently began to explore with Montgomery the possible opportunities for a memorial to Noel Chamberlin, who had just died. That exchange is significant because Phillips took the opportunity to identify areas of Fairchild for future projects. His comments offer a closer understanding of how essential the formal organization and structure of the landscape were to him. Phillips also explained, through his resistance to change, the precise role of certain aspects of the Garden. Regarding the amphitheatre, for example, he resisted the idea of adding a "shell," explaining that the role of the amphitheatre in the garden was functionally "collateral" (figs. 25 and 26). The amphitheatre was not designed for numerous, actual assemblies. Instead, Phillips explained, the amphitheatre was a formal element whose purpose was to establish a "contrast to the general informality, but existing and justified mainly as a garden. Hence the arrangements for speaking would be relatively unassertive, gardenesque in character." Phillips conceded, however, that the dais might "be built by subscriptions to a Noel Chamberlin fund."

Phillips also suggested that the Garden "might build and dedicate various typically gardenesque structure — exedras, belvederes, arbors, alcoves, terraces," noting that "such things are good and desirable in moderation, if purposefully placed and interestingly done." Two possibilities that Phillips said were already marked on plans were the benches on his proposed new approach to the Palm Glade, "which could be treated as exedras, and a shore terrace terminating

---

38. William Lyman Phillips, letter to Robert Montgomery, 23 July 1943, File 13–11, Phillips Papers.

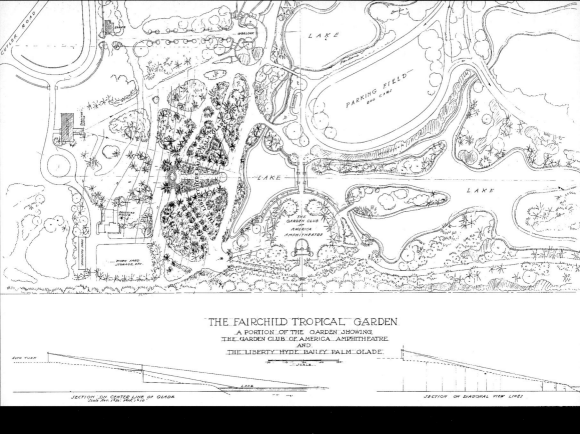

THE FAIRCHILD TROPICAL GARDEN
A PORTION OF THE GARDEN SHOWING
THE GARDEN CLUB OF AMERICA AMPHITHEATRE
AND
THE LIBERTY HYDE BAILEY PALM GLADE

SCALE

SECTION ON CENTER LINE OF GLADE
Scale Nov. 1 Sn. Sept. 1910

SECTION ON DIAGONAL VIEW LINES

Fig. 22. William Lyman Phillips, plan and section of Garden Club of America Amphitheatre and Liberty Hyde Bailey Palm Glade, Fairchild Tropical Garden, Coral Gables, Florida. From a 24 x 36" mylar reproduction in the Fairchild Tropical Garden collection, original drawing in the Metro-Dade Parks and Recreation Department collection.

Fig. 23. William Lyman Phillips, detail of Liberty Hyde Bailey Palm Glade pool and grotto, Fairchild Tropical Garden, Coral Gables, Florida, 1942. From a 24 x 36" mylar reproduction in the Fairchild Tropical Garden collection, original drawing in the Metro-Dade Parks and Recreation

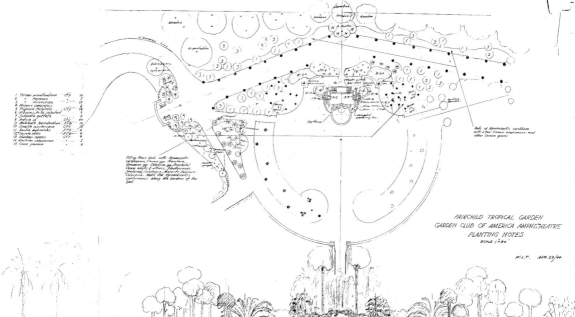

Fig. 25. William Lyman Phillips, planting notes for Garden Club of America Amphitheatre, Fairchild Tropical Garden, Coral Gables, Florida, 1944. From a 24 x 36" mylar reproduction in the Fairchild Tropical Garden collection, original drawing in the Metro-Dade Parks and Recreation Department collection.

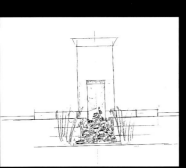

Fig. 26. William Lyman Phillips, detail of podium of Garden Club of America Amphitheatre, Fairchild Tropical Garden, Coral Gables, Florida, c. 1944. From a 24 x 36" mylar reproduction in the Fairchild Tropical Garden collection, original drawing in the Metro-Dade Parks and Recreation Department collection.

the Royal Palm Avenue which borders the amphitheatre on the south." If, Phillips continued, the proposed items were of too little cost or significance, then he believed that "a high-walled court garden attached to the museum on the east side," would be useful and would fulfill an idea he had long contemplated, since "such courts, as demonstrated by the walled rubber experiment plots at Chapman field, provide the best outdoor conditions we have for difficult tropical plants, and one or more of them would, for that reason alone, be a most valuable addition to the Garden."[39]

Although the discussion raised many design opportunities for Fairchild, the memorial to Chamberlin ended up as a hibiscus collection. Originally, Phillips located the collection at the east end of the south lake with stone posts to mark the entrance, "but the famous high-water hurricane of Sept 15 1945 knocked down the entrance posts and left the plantings in a ruinous state." That inspired Phillips to move the memorial to the upland "as an underplanting to whatever trees might be there, and possibly to move it back to the original site in a few years."

In September of 1958, at the request of Director Nixon Smiley, Phillips wrote a report on his experience with Fairchild Tropical Garden, a document that Smiley and others would later call Phillips' memoir. Phillips discussed several of the significant design concerns in this memoir. He recalled that his first decision was to choose the "principle families" to be exhibited, having already determined the tropical basis of the collections as well as the decision to exhibit large shrubs and trees in families. The dimensions of the property, 1320 feet wide along Old Cutler Road and 2700 feet deep, "divided into a northerly half under one ownership (Dade County) and a southerly half under another" then began to set design parameters.

Phillips explained that the uplands, "a strip about 500 feet wide on the northerly half and 800 feet wide on the southerly half," was at an elevation of about eighteen feet above sea level with "a strong slope or escarpment face 100–200 feet wide joining it to the lowland."[40] He described the upland as "the edge of an ancient marine terrace which appears as an abrupt cliff at other points along the Biscayne Bay shore. The escarpment was the boldest topographical feature and strongly influenced the planning." Phillips defined the fundamental challenge to be the evolution of "a unified plan." [41]

Phillips believed that an informality of the garden plots "offered the utmost freedom in the choice of vegetation," and that other than the original overlook axis, the Garden's later formal elements, such as the Palm Glade and amphitheatre, "demonstrate the use of particular species for compositional purposes." The site's existing plant material of pines and live oaks did not exert significant influence on Phillips' thinking, although he said the presence of "a number of old mango, avocado, and sapodilla trees on the Palmetum site did affect the layout to some extent, as did three sink holes, one in the Palmetum and two on the County side." Phillips explained that the escarpment's bare rock face inspired a system of terraces with "stone walls retaining earth fills, forming plots elongated along the sidehill," which, when planted, would "form a windbreak" on the north side of the overlook.

39. William Lyman Phillips, letter to Robert Montgomery, 15 September 1943, File 13–11, Phillips Papers.

40. William Lyman Phillips, "The Fairchild Tropical Garden: A Memoir," 3 September 1958, File 13–1:3, Phillips Papers.

41. Ibid., 5.

Phillips' plans for the lowland were based on his reliance upon the flat open space to extend the axial views from the overlook and later the Palm Glade to the horizon. "The entire plan," said Phillips, "is essentially an articulated complex of openings."[42] Phillips explained that the need for open spaces "was obvious, for without well defined openings no sense of organization, no scenic effects, would be possible."[43] Phillips recognized the narrowness of these vistas in relation to broader views but believed that "in Florida small landscape units and close views of vegetation are apt to be more attractive than wide views, and walks in the shade more agreeable than walks in the sun."

Phillips further distinguished the formal principles that governed the design to be: "Variety," which he felt dictated the relationships of the major openings and the garden plots; "Consistency," the unity, or harmony, achieved by the participation of the individual parts in a designed whole; and "Contrast," which established the interaction between the large vistas and the "close, intimate views on the upland," the sunny openings and the shady passages, as well as the contrast of the expansive panorama of the overlook, the Palm Glade, and the connecting views linking the Garden's narrow and shaded pathways.[44]

At Fairchild, as he had at both Greynolds and Matheson Hammock, Phillips extended his supervisory role to include architecture. He proposed an orchid house, which he termed "fanciful." But by the time that the Garden had raised funds for additional buildings, Phillips' role had diminished, and in 1952 Russell Pancoast was awarded the commission for the office building and director's house, as well as the public bathrooms, which were sited northwest of the gift shop Phillips designed.[45] Robert Fitch Smith was the architect of the museum in 1939–1940 and the Garden House in 1946. Phillips was not pleased with the resulting architectural and functional shift of the entrance to what he considered a service area, a condition that remains in the Garden today.

He was happier with the results of the Palm Glade. He explained that "the narrow east end of the trapezoid would not let in much of the unwanted northeast wind, and the broad upper end would make possible a standing place where people could take in the view down the lake." Phillips was concerned that the sunken garden below should not become filled with large palms, "without invalidating the viewing purpose." His concept of the Palm Glade required "cutting through the woods two diagonal avenues centered on the viewing position," so that "the whole plot would acquire a certain integration and might then be regarded as a palmglade." He recommended planting the sides of the trapezoid with palms and underplanting the oak woods "with shade-demanding species of palms," and felt that his revised approach of 1943, with its curving avenue of cycads, would complete the composition.[46]

In the memoir, Phillips also discussed the pergola of Mrs. Semple's vine collection (fig. 27). Clarence Dean, the architect of the Fairchild home (the Kampong), and Noel Chamberlin consulted with Phillips on the pergola's design.[47] Phillips felt that the pergola had not solved "the problem of displaying

42. Ibid.,7.
43. Ibid.
44. Ibid., 8.
45. Ibid., 10.
46. Ibid., 12.
47. Ibid., 18.

Fig. 27. Ladies of the Vine Pergola Committee under the Semple Vine Pergola, Fairchild Tropical Garden, Coral Gables, Florida, 1941. From *The Dream Lives on: A History of the Fairchild Tropical Garden 1938-1988* by Bertram Zuckerman (Miami: Fairchild Tropical Garden, 1988), 50. Original photograph in the Fairchild Tropical Garden collection.

vines in all of their potentialities — some of them being capable of almost unlimited growth."[48]

Regarding the surface of the ground, Phillips explained that the forest floor was the ideal floor for the tree plots. He believed that grass should be restricted to specifically designed lawns in order to heighten the contrast between the dense plots and the open spaces.[49] In addition to his concern that the lowlands upon which the overlook and palm glade vistas rely be preserved as open space, Phillips considered a more tropical forest-like development for other lowland areas. His description of the tropical plantings is strong with compositional concepts, such as contrast and variety. He explained, for example, that one might find "light-toned trunks rising from a bushy cover, or seen against a solid green background."[50]

Phillips felt that the upland relationships of alternating strips of lawns with the mulched, wooded plots would be impractical in the lowland where high water would wash the ground away. Instead, Phillips proposed consideration of "herbaceous and shrubby ground covers," which would lead to "a wilder,

48. Ibid., 14.
49. Ibid., 17.
50. Ibid., 20.

more natural place than the upland." This strategy would allow "dense growth," which Phillips believed "would attain a stability similar to that of the dune hammocks for that matter where maintenance in any ordinary sense is out of place."[51]

Phillips also expressed concern for the future. He suggested that "for the upland, it would seem desirable to search for plants of low or moderate growth suitable for underplantings, and for small shrubs and trees suitable for outside positions in the plots."[52] He believed that "the first concern of any administration" is the maintenance of "the integrity of the open spaces." Given the Garden's location in the hurricane belt, Phillips recommended plans that would acknowledge the susceptibility of large mature trees to wind damage and proposed that the Garden consider "a system of replacement, starting young trees to replace eventually the older ones."[53]

In 1937, before Phillips began his work at Fairchild, he wrote to George Merrick, the founder and developer of Coral Gables, explaining that he had "been working for the National Park Service in the superintendence of CCC park projects in Dade County, a not uninteresting occupation, but a very obscure one that has continued long enough."[54] It wasn't long before Phillips' work within the system of public park design was recognized, published in professional journals, widely enjoyed by the public, and awarded the attention of his professional colleagues. Ironically, his successful integration of formal principles and native landscape elements contributed to his current obscurity, as the results of his work are so powerfully believable that only the cognoscenti are aware of the designer's hand.

The intersection of Phillips' personal travail and professional ambition rooted him to South Florida in a way that was unlikely for his peers from his Harvard and Olmsted Brothers' days. A number of Phillips' letters refer to his isolation, which was considerable. However, it may have been this very isolation that allowed him to focus intently on the goals he developed over a lifetime, rather than being absorbed by trends that swept the rest of the professional world. In addition, working in isolation from his peers may have been the appropriate choice due to Phillips' ability to hone his focus so precisely on the issues of interest to him. Regardless of whether it was fate or choice, Phillips pursued his vision of landscape architecture in South Florida's wilderness in many projects with several key design principles, especially his regard for unity of effect. Phillips worked in Miami on institutional landscapes, such as the University of Miami; cemeteries, such as Woodlawn and Inman; private clubs, such as the Indian Creek Country Club and the Biscayne Bay Yacht Club; hundreds of private residences and businesses; numerous roadways and bridges, including the Venetian and Rickenbacker causeways; as well as projects throughout Florida, including McKee Jungle Garden (fig. 28), a Riverfront Promenade for St. Augustine, and the Overseas Highway to the Keys. His work at Fairchild, however, which spanned his professional career, synthesizes many of his ideas into a cohesive vision and reveals the manner in which Phillips developed an iconic public landscape.

51. Ibid., 21.
52. Ibid., 22.
53. Ibid., 23.
54. William Lyman Phillips, letter to George Merrick, 6 August 1937, File 1–12, George E. Merrick Collection, Charlton W. Tebeau Research Center, Historical Museum of Southern Florida.

Fairchild Tropical Garden is at once specific and original to its site, geography, and material, while at the same time universal in its connection to leading ideas in landscape tradition. Phillips drew the mangrove, hammock, and native building materials into the composition of the Garden through the grand axis of the overlook and the smaller but also expansive vista of the Palm Glade. This ability to both magnify the qualities of a particular place and simultaneously engage larger historical tradition is the great gift that Phillips applied to his work. Through his use of indigenous materials in historic compositional principles, Phillips preserved native landscapes that others were eager to erase. Phillips, however, was not a strict conservationist; he was a designer whose larger goals respected the context. Rather than simply cordon off the native material, Phillips engaged the natural landscape in a design that owed as much to André Le Nôtre at Versailles as to Henry Thoreau at Walden Pond.

Three fundamental aspects of design emerge from consideration of Phillips' notes from his days at Harvard and the projects he shaped from the Florida wilderness: his dedication to the proposition that the purpose of landscape architecture was the use, convenience, and pleasure of people within a context that gave identity to native landscapes; his commitment to the role of the landscape architect as the primary supervisor under whom all other professionals took their direction; and his fervent belief in the foundational role of such formal principles as unity and variety in the determination of a landscape's structure and disposition of parts.

Phillips was in a unique position to be able to design and execute both landscapes and buildings. It is not a coincidence that his buildings are made of the oolitic limestone found on the site; Phillips thoughtfully engaged all aspects of his sites, including its materials for building. The details he designed, such as the use of wood in a natural state, refer to the special qualities of each site, interweaving universal, compositional principles with the immediate context of materials and site. This may be Phillips' most important, yet still unexplored, legacy.

William Lyman Phillips was adept and expansive in his use of symbols. The great avenue he designed for Crandon Park, for example, was composed of the coconut palms that recall the Matheson plantation. Phillips drew upon the native landscape as well as the designed and cultivated landscapes to make all the world his palette. The result of his education, travel, and work was a broadly informed vision that generated a legacy of extraordinary and unique places. □

A Guide to the
Southernmost State

FLORIDA

FLORIDA

Federal
Writers Project

Oxford

AMERICAN GUIDE SERIES

Fig. 1. Artist unknown, *Florida: A Guide to the Southernmost State*, dustjacket, 21 x 19.5 cm, 1939.

Touring Florida Through the Federal Writers' Project

By James A. Findlay and Margaret Bing

James A. Findlay is director of Broward County Library's Bienes Center for the Literary Arts, The Dianne and Michael Bienes Special Collections and Rare Book Library, Fort Lauderdale, Florida. An art and rare-book librarian since 1975, he has curated and authored numerous exhibitions and catalogues. He is the author of *Modern Art of Latin America: A Bibliography* (Westport, Conn.: Greenwood Press, 1983).

Margaret Bing is cataloguer and curator of The Dianne and Michael Bienes Special Collections and Rare Book Library, Fort Lauderdale, Florida. Her research and curatorial activities have focused on the writings of the Works Progress Administration and the New Deal.

The United States has always been a society of travellers and explorers. An undercurrent of wanderlust has pervaded the country's culture since well before the founding of the Republic, and due largely to the automobile, it persists in modern times with an exuberance little imagined or anticipated by our forefathers. The Wall Street Crash of 1929 brought the country's booming economy to a sudden halt, and the Depression that followed ended — at least temporarily — the nation's zeal for recreational travel. Instead, as a result of massive unemployment, poor families took to the road in search of work. The government recognized that it would be necessary to apply extraordinary measures to jump-start the economy. In 1935 President Franklin Delano Roosevelt did so by creating the Works Progress Administration (WPA) and its subsection, "Federal One."[1] The establishment of the WPA was a revolutionary act; it was the first time in United States history that the federal government used public monies to put writers and artists to work.

Roosevelt summarized the WPA's objectives as:

> To bring together the records of the past and to house them in the buildings where they will be preserved for the use of men living in the future, a nation must believe in three things. It must believe in the past. It must believe in the future. It must, above all, believe in the capacity of its people to learn from the past so that they can gain in judgment for the creation of the future.[2]

Federal One was the umbrella organization for the government's artistic and professional work-relief programs. Several subagencies fell under the aegis of Federal One. The Federal Arts Project (FAP) employed artists, art education specialists, and art researchers; the Federal Music Project (FMP) employed, retrained, and rehabilitated unemployed musicians; the Federal Theater Project (FTP) produced live theatre pieces across the country, employing actors, stagehands, technicians, playwrights, and administrative workers; the Historical Records Survey (HRS) employed clerks, teachers, writers, librarians, and archivists to catalogue and analyze public records and to provide inventories of materials; and the Federal Writers' Project (FWP) was created to put to work writers and publication-experienced, unemployed white-collar workers.

1. James S. Olson, *Historical Dictionary of the New Deal* (Westport, Conn.: Greenwood Press, 1985), 182–183.
2. *American Portraits (1645–1850), Found in the State of Maine (Preliminary Volume)* (Boston: Massachusetts Historical Records Survey, 1941), verso of first preliminary page.

During the years 1932–1943 many aspects of American culture, government, and society were scrutinized and recorded by WPA researchers. The publishing output of the WPA and related agencies included guidebooks, entertainment handbooks, instructional manuals, style manuals and methodologies, statistics, and information. The United States' ethnic diversity was recorded and celebrated in the travel literature of the *American Guide Series*, as well as in other publications (fig. 1). Working together, agencies and individuals produced a huge amount of material, both published and unpublished.

The FWP's primary goal was the compilation and publication of the *American Guide Series*, a collection of travel guides modeled on the well-known and popular *Baedeker* series of travel books. The decision to compile a guide series took into account many factors. Not only was the series a way of providing work for unemployed white-collar workers, but during a time of rising international tension the project helped promote patriotism by formally documenting the nation's accomplishments and culture. In addition, in a country of vast distances, with a rapidly developing nationwide highway system, the series promoted travel and tourism. The *American Guide Series* was the crowning achievement of the FWP. As one study of the FWP pointed out:

> In 1935 alone, 35 million vacationers took to the nation's highways. The guides would serve the rapidly growing number of visitors to national parks, as well as the newly emerging youth hostel movement, the American Camping Association, and the Scouts. They would also help in the rediscovery of historic landmarks and scenic wonders.[3]

Henry Alsberg (1881–1970) was appointed National Director of the Federal Writers' Project on 25 July 1935. A New Yorker trained in journalism and law, Alsberg decided early in his tenure that rather than produce large and cumbersome guides to regions of the country, as was originally planned, a more useful and practical approach would be to publish titles for all forty-eight states and two territories.

The state guidebooks were not the only titles to be published. The FWP also produced a wide range of other works, including local guides and folklore studies.[4] Many city and local guidebooks were written and published because they provided the FWP with "community support for the project, which might increase the sales of larger guides when they finally appeared."[5] The subjects commissioned included transcontinental tour books, trail books, black studies, folklore, school bulletins, agriculture pamphlets, gazetteers of place-names, an encyclopedia of Idaho, local newspaper indexes, and map inventories.[6] However, many of these works were never printed because the local sponsoring agencies lost confidence in the projects, often due to controversial passages. For example, a guide to Tampa was rejected because the text

---

3. Monty Noam Penkower, *The Federal Writers' Project: A Study in Government Patronage of the Arts* (Urbana, Ill.: University of Illinois Press, 1977), 25.

4. Ibid., 157–158.

5. Ibid., 136.

6. Examples include: *The Intracostal Waterway: Norfolk to Key West* (Washington, D.C.: U.S. Government Printing Office, 1937); *The Ocean Highway: New Brunswick, New Jersey to Jacksonville, Florida* (New York: Modern Age Books, 1938); *U.S. One: Maine to Florida* (New York: Modern Age Books, 1938); *The Florida Negro: A Federal Writers' Project Legacy* (Jackson and London: University Press of Mississippi, 1993); *Palmetto Country* (Tallahassee: Florida A and M University Press, c. 1942, c. 1989); *Birds in Florida* (Tallahassee: State of Florida, Department of Agriculture, c. 1941); *Tropical Fruits in Florida with Commercial Possibilities* (Tallahassee: State of Florida, Department of Agriculture, 1941).

"mentioned a red-light district, the illegal 'Little Chicago' gambling area, and the fact that Cuban Negroes did not speak English in their homes."[7]

Approximately twenty thousand writers worked for the FWP during its lifespan, earning anywhere from $93.50 to $103.50 per month in New York and other urban states while their counterparts from rural states such as Georgia and Mississippi earned as little as thirty-nine dollars.[8] In Florida, Stetson Kennedy (born 1916), who went on to become a professional writer after his involvement with the FWP, earned seventy-five dollars per month working as a junior interviewer.[9] Being unemployed or on the "dole" was the main criterion for employment in the FWP, and with few exceptions, anonymity was deemed essential. Not permitting individual writers to sign their pieces helped to ensure stylistic uniformity and, in an age of socialist ferment, emphasized society's accomplishments rather than those of the individual.

Administrators of the FWP decided that each state warranted its own director. Carita Doggett Corse (1892–1978), one of the few women in the project, was named head of the Florida Writers' Project in October 1935.[10] Her interest in recording Florida history was reflected in her master's thesis, *Dr. Andrew Turnbull and the New Smyrna Colony of Florida* and later manifested itself in publications including *The Key to the Golden Islands* and *Story of Jacksonville*.[11]

Corse was responsible for the organization of units throughout the state and for developing ideas for Florida researchers and writers. It was through her efforts that the Florida Negro and folklore units were formed. Early in her career she developed a profound appreciation for the colorful folklife of Florida's diverse cultures, and she worked diligently to record them before they were lost to the forces of modernization. She dispatched teams of researchers to interview and document Greek sponge fishermen in Tarpon Springs, Bahamian Conchs in Riviera Beach, Portuguese fishermen in Fernandina, Native Americans in the Everglades and Dania, and African-Americans throughout Florida.[12]

Traversing the state, Corse personally interviewed and selected every writer and researcher hired. She was also responsible for finding sponsors to cover the publication costs of each title, including the state guide. One of the more productive sponsors with whom she collaborated was Nathan Mayo (1876–1960) of the Florida Department of Agriculture. Together they published a wide variety of small books and pamphlets for the FWP.[13]

7. Penkower, *The Federal Writers' Project*, 137.

8. Ibid., 62.

9. Charles C. Foster, *Conchtown USA: Bahamian Fisherfolk in Riviera Beach, Florida* (Boca Raton: Florida Atlantic University Press, 1991), 46.

10. Born and raised in Jacksonville, the daughter of Judge John Doggett, Carita Doggett Corse attended Vassar College where she was active in the women's suffrage movement. She received a B.A. degree in 1913 and went on to Columbia University where she received an M.A. degree in 1916.

11. Carita Doggett Corse, *Dr. Andrew Turnbull and the New Smyrna Colony of Florida* (Florida: Drew Press, 1919); Corse, *The Key to the Golden Islands* (Chapel Hill: University of North Carolina Press, 1931); Corse, *Story of Jacksonville* (Jacksonville: Woman's Club, 1937).

12. Foster, *Conchtown USA; Seeing Fernandina: A Guide to the City and Its Industries* (Fernandina, Fla.: Fernandina News Publishing Co., 1940); *The Seminole Indians in Florida* (Tallahassee, Fla.: Florida State Department of Agriculture, c. 1941); *The Florida Negro: A Federal Writers' Project Legacy* (Jackson: University Press of Mississippi, 1993).

13. *Birds in Florida* (Tallahassee: State of Florida, Department of Agriculture, c. 1941); *Tropical Fruits in Florida with Commerical Possibilities* (Tallahassee: State of Florida, Department of Agriculture, 1941).

Fig. 2. Zora Neale Hurston at the Federal Writers' Project booth, The New York Times, Book Fair, Rockefeller Center, New York City, 1937. WPA photographer. Photographs and Prints Division, Schomburg Center for Research in Black Culture, The New York Public Library, Astor, Lenox and Tilden Foundation.

The Florida Writers' Project hired unemployed residents to write chapter-by-chapter analyses of the social, economic, and artistic history of the state. The results were self-guided tours of well-known tourist attractions and intimate, down-to-earth descriptions of little-known small towns and back roads of Florida's hinterland. In its heyday the Florida Writers' Project employed up to two hundred writers, although today almost all of them remain anonymous. Addressing the question of who worked on the project, Evenell Powell-Brant, a WPA book dealer and collector, stated, "There never was a master list. No local lists survive — indeed if there ever were any. Only by grapevine reports and recollections do we know who did work."[14]

There were notable exceptions, however. Zora Neale Hurston (1901–1960) was already a published author when she joined the Florida Writers' Project as a field researcher and writer (fig. 2). She travelled the state collecting stories

14. Evenell K. Powell-Brant, *WPA Federal Writers' Project with Emphasis on the Florida Writers and Carita Doggett Corse* (Lake Panasoffkee, Fla., 1990).

for *The Florida Negro*, which was eventually published in 1993 using the original manuscripts.[15] Hurston was also responsible for writing the section on her hometown of Eatonville (one of the first towns in the United States incorporated by African-Americans, in 1886), and the guide quoted two long excerpts from her 1937 novel *Their Eyes Were Watching God*.[16] In her day, Hurston's writing enjoyed little commercial or literary success. As Claudia Roth Pierpont pointed out in a recent reexamination of the writer's life: "Against the tide of racial anger, she wrote about sex and talk and work and music and life's unpoisoned pleasures, suggesting that these things existed even for people of color, even in America; and she was judged superficial. By implication, merely feminine."[17] It has only been in the last two decades that Hurston's writing has been reappraised and reevaluated. The new recognition of Hurston "has to do with her use of her native place and her cultural traditions as the main stuff of her work."[18]

Stetson Kennedy, a native Floridian, was twenty years old when he was hired to work as a junior interviewer in the Florida Keys. Shortly thereafter, he was transferred to the Jacksonville state office where he headed the unit on folklore, oral history, and social-ethnic studies. He was one of the project's half-dozen state editors who worked at converting raw copy submitted by some one hundred field workers into finished chapters for the Florida guide. Kennedy later became a founding member of the Florida Folklore Society and wrote *Palmetto Country*, a book on Florida folklore.[19] He is best known for his crusading civil rights' work in his book *The Klan Unmasked*.

Another writer on the Florida project was Albert C. Manucy (1910–1997) of St. Augustine, who was director of the Key West Unit and went on to write many books on St. Augustine's archeology and architecture. His secretary in Key West was Mario Sánchez, internationally known for his bas-relief carved and painted murals of Florida Hispanic folklife in Key West and Ybor City.

The *pièce de resistance* of the Florida Writers' Project was its travel guide, *Florida: A Guide to the Southernmost State*, published in November 1939. Print reviews from the era were somewhat mixed. *The Saturday Review of Literature* praised the work: "Only such a set-up as a WPA Writers' Project could compile so thoroughgoing a treatise on an entire state as is this latest addition to the American Guide Series. The added achievement of being not only exhaustive, but largely interesting, fresh, authoritative, and at moments even entertaining, is unique for a guidebook."[20] A less enthusiastic reviewer considered the guidebook to be "useful for its contemporary and historical information, and its generalized comments are reasonably restrained in the main. There is some excess of color here and there, and some statements should have been checked more carefully."[21]

15. *The Florida Negro: A Federal Writers' Project Legacy* (Jackson: University Press of Mississippi, 1993).

16. *Florida: A Guide to the Southernmost State* (New York: Oxford University Press, 1939), 362, 475.

17. Claudia Roth Pierpont, "A Society of One: Zora Neale Hurston, American Contrarian," *The New Yorker* 73 (17 February 1997): 80–91.

18. Steve Glassman and Kathryn Lee Seidel, *Zora in Florida* (Orlando: University of Central Florida Press, 1991), ix.

19. *Palmetto Country* (c. 1942; reprint, Tallahassee: Florida A and M University Press, c. 1989).

20. *The Saturday Review of Literature* 21 (20 January 1940): 16.

21. *Springfield Republican*, 30 December 1939, 6.

Florida: A Guide to the Southernmost State was the first of thirteen state guides published by Oxford University Press. It was a quirky, unusual, and informative examination of the state as it existed up to 1939. Combining a "blend of history, legend, myth, gossip, and nature lore," its purpose was to equip the traveller with a portrait of Florida that was simultaneously educational, insightful, revealing, and entertaining.[22] The authors involved in the project strived to write a guide that wasn't "touristy" and yet conveyed "as accurately as possible the quality of life in Florida without glossing over its more sordid aspects."[23] According to Stetson Kennedy, "they won some and we won some, so it is fairly well balanced."[24] The finished product conveyed the essence of small-town rural Southern culture, yet at the same time promoted the trendy, sophisticated, and expensive elite coastal resort communities of Palm Beach and Miami.

Fig. 3. Robert Delson (the Florida Art Project), seascape, pen and ink sketch, 5 x 5 cm, 1939. From *Florida: A Guide to the Southernmost State*, 206.

The six-hundred-page guide contained illustrations (fig. 3), maps, and 101 black-and-white photographs taken by several photographers, including Gleason Waite Romer, a local Miami photographer, and photographers from the Farm Security Administration (FSA) (figs. 4, 5, and 6). The book was bound in green cloth; a small image of an alligator appeared inside the dark blue lettering. On the front of the dustjacket were a photograph of a palm tree, an unidentified body of water, and a sailboat printed in green. The dustjacket's back had a small ink drawing of a Florida shack shaded by a tree dripping with moss and an Oxford University Press announcement for other guidebooks in preparation.

The beginning section of the guide, "General Information," provided practical advice for travellers regarding railroads, bus lines, highways, passenger steamships, airlines, accommodations, recreational areas, fishing and hunting regulations, climate, equipment, information for the motorist, and a calendar of annual events. That advice included cautions to tourists, such as: "Do not enter bushes at sides of highway in rural districts; snakes and redbugs usually infest such places. Do not eat tung nuts; they are poisonous. Do not eat green pecans; in the immature stages the skins have a white film containing arsenic."[25]

"Florida's Background," the 173-page history in part one of the guide, distinguished this publication from others of the time. An examination of its various sections illustrates how the traveller was outfitted with vital information on topics such as the "Contemporary Scene":

> The pioneer settler…knew little of life beyond his own small clearing and saw only a few infrequent visitors, until a network of highways left him exposed to many persons in motorcars. This traffic affected his economy and aroused his instinct to profit. He set up a roadside vegetable display, then installed gasoline pumps and a barbecue stand, and finally with the addition of overnight cabins he was in the tourist business.[26]

Other section topics included nature; archeology; history; transportation; agriculture; education; and sports. Folklore was also represented, as in the following example describing the lifestyle of a "cracker," a typical rural Florida pioneer resident: "The cracker's wants are simple — his garden plot, pigpen, chicken coop, and the surrounding woods and near-by streams supply him

22. *Florida: A Guide to the Southernmost State*, xxii.

23. Ann Banks, *First-Person America* (New York: Knopf, 1980), xxii.

24. *The American Guide Series: Works by the Federal Writers' Project* (Pittsburgh: Arthur Scharf, Bookseller; Schoyer's Books, c. 1990), 21.

25. *Florida: A Guide to the Southernmost State*, xxxviii.

26. Ibid., 4–5.

Fig. 4. Burgert Brothers, *University of Tampa (formerly Tampa Bay Hotel)*, photograph, 15 x 13 cm, 1939. From *Florida: A Guide to the Southernmost State*, between 254–255.

▼

Fig. 5. Artist unknown, *Rehearsal—Circus Winter Quarters, Sarasota*, photograph, 5.5 x 13 cm, 1939. From *Florida: A Guide to the Southernmost State*, between 254–255.

and his family with nearly all the living necessities. Fish is an important item of diet, and when the cracker is satiated with it he has been heard to say: 'I done et so free o'fish, my stommick rises and falls with the tide.'" [27]

Sections on the arts discussed literature, music, theater, art, and architecture, offering an evaluation of Florida's cultural achievements by that time. The guidebook even included the very recent work of the FAP:

> Under the Federal Art Project…much permanent art has been produced in Florida buildings. Project work includes bas-relief designs of Florida fauna, carved in native stone on the Coral Gables Library; murals in the Orlando Chamber of Commerce; over-mantel decorations in the student union building at the University of Florida; seven murals in the Tony Jannus Administration Building at the Tampa airport; and many murals in school buildings. An outstanding piece is the memorial monument on Matecumbe Key to those who lost their lives in the 1935 hurricane, a rectangular shaft of Key limestone bears a carved panel, showing in simple lines palm trees streaming in a high wind (fig. 7). [28]

The second part of the guide, "Principal Cities," provided factual information about Daytona Beach, Jacksonville, Key West, Greater Miami, Orlando, Palm Beach, Pensacola, St. Augustine, St. Petersburg, Sarasota, Tallahassee, and Tampa.

In addition to practical information, the guide reported on oddities, introducing readers to such idiosyncratic places as the "Hen Hotel" in Miami: "The 'Hen Hotel,' NW 27th Ave. and NW 34th St., a huge unfinished building begun as a hotel in 1925, was named the 'million-dollar hen hotel' when a hatchery was established here during the early 1930's. The floor space accommodated more than 60,000 laying hens, 20,000 fryers, and 50,000 incubator chicks." [29] Sarasota's unique "Tourist Park" also fit this category: "In past years this park has been the site of the Tin Can Tourists of the World, an organization of trailer

27. Ibid., 128.
28. Ibid., 161.
29. Ibid., 219.

Fig. 7. Arthur Rothstein (the Farm Security Administration), *Memorial to Hurricane Victims, Matecumbe Key*, photograph, 17.5 x 12 cm, c. 1941. From *A Guide to Key West*, 17.

and house-car owners with membership of 30,000. A giant parade of 'tincanners' and the showing of new model trailers, house cars, and equipment were integral parts of the convention."[30]

At the time of the Depression, much of Florida remained comparatively undiscovered. Land was inexpensive, especially in the rural areas inland from the coasts. These isolated spots were ideal settings for some of society's marginal or disenfranchised groups to establish settlements in which to put into practice

30. Ibid., 272.

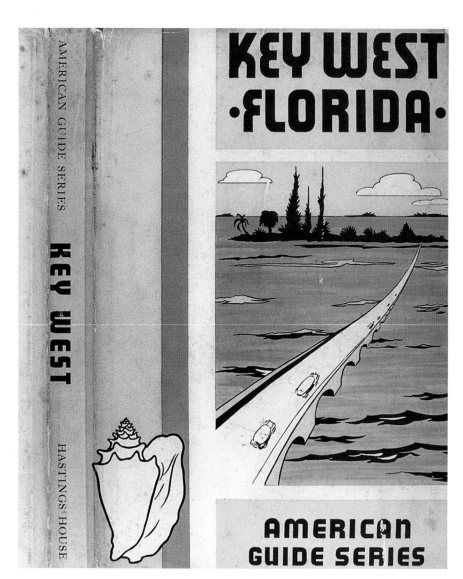

Fig. 8. F. Townsend Morgan
(the Florida Art Project), *A
Guide to Key West*, dustjacket,
21 x 17 cm, 1941.

their theoretical ideas and philosophies. Several examples of how these groups established themselves in Florida were described in part three of the guide, "The Florida Loop," a section of twenty-two automobile tour routes that traversed the state. Tour Four, for example, took the adventurer on U.S. Route 41 from the Georgia border to Naples, a distance of 381.9 miles. Masaryktown was located 71.5 miles into the tour. The driver was told that the town of fifty inhabitants was: "named for Thomas G. Masaryk (1850–1937), the first President of Czechoslovakia, [and] was founded as an agricultural colony in 1924 by Joseph Joscak, editor of a Czech newspaper in New York City....Characteristic of the colony are the half-dozen windmills that stand against the horizon."[31]

In Tour Four-A, the visitor was directed to the village of Ruskin (population six hundred) at mile marker 23.2, where he would find:

> a co-operative tomato-growing settlement at the mouth of the Little Manatee River, founded in 1910 as a socialist colony by George M. Miller, Chicago lawyer and educator, and named for John Ruskin, English author

31. Ibid., 391.

Fig. 9. F. Townsend Morgan,

***Old Bahama House*, etching,**

16.5 x 12 cm, c. 1941. From

***A Guide to Key West*, 61.**

Fig. 10. Artist unknown,

Florida: [Facts, Events,

***Places, Tours]*, pamphlet cover,**

21.5 x 14.5 cm, 1941.

and critic. Of the 6,000 acres purchased, 600 were set aside for a proposed Ruskin College, its curriculum to be modeled somewhat on that of Oxford University. Students were to have four hours of schooling and, quite unlike Oxford, four hours of farm work a day.[32]

In Tour Two from Jacksonville to Punta Gorda along U.S. Route 17, Zora Neale Hurston's *Their Eyes Were Watching God* was quoted extensively: "Joe Clarke, the founder and first mayor of Eatonville…sold groceries and general merchandise, while Lee Glenn sells drinks of all kinds and whatever goes with transient rooms."[33]

"Appendices," the final part of the guide, contained a ten-page chronology beginning with the entry for 1513: "April 3, Juan Ponce de Leon lands on coast in vicinity of St. Augustine site and names land *Florida*, claiming it for Spain." The entry for 1763 stated: "Spain cedes Florida to England, in exchange for Cuba." The last entry, for 1939, reported: "WPA relief rolls are cut from 1938 peak of 55,000 persons to 37,000 on September 1."[34] The volume concluded with an extensive bibliography, a list of consultants, and an index.

Among the other titles produced by the Florida Federal Writers' Project was *A Guide to Key West* (fig. 8). It was a simpler version of the Key West section of *Florida: A Guide to the Southernmost State*. The Florida Art Project in Key West, a forerunner to the Federal Art Project, grew out of the dire economic conditions the town endured in the early 1930s. As a result, in 1934 Key West was declared bankrupt by the State of Florida and Julius Stone (1901–1970), head of the Florida Emergency Relief Administration, was dispatched to attempt to revive the economy.

Stone's efforts were aimed at reshaping the city's image in order to attract tourists, and he is frequently credited with the seemingly superficial suggestions that residents use bicycles and wear Bermuda shorts. He encouraged citizens to clean and beautify the town. At the same time, he selected ten artists from more than three thousand applicants to the Public Works of Art Project to create art works of Key West scenes for booklets and postcards that were used to advertise the area as a tropical resort. F. Townsend Morgan, the director of the Key West WPA Community Art Center, was one of the ten artists brought to Key West to produce art work. *A Guide to Key West* included eleven photographs by renowned FSA photographer Arthur Rothstein and ten of Morgan's etchings (fig. 9).

Florida: facts, events, places, tours, one of a series of booklets from the *American Recreation Series*, followed an established format consisting of a brief introduction, short chapters on facts, tourist information, annual events, seasonal sports and recreation, and a description of recreation areas arranged in a series of tours (fig. 10).

The Ocean Highway: New Brunswick, New Jersey to Jacksonville, Florida, published in 1938, was written in a format similar to the tour sections in the other *American Guide Series* books (fig. 11). This mile-by-mile description of the Ocean Highway also covered some of the short routes that were accessible from it. The one-thousand-mile Ocean Highway, which branched off from U.S. Route 1 in the industrial area of New Jersey, was the shortest route between

32. Ibid., 403.

33. Zora Neale Hurston, *Their Eyes Were Watching God* (Philadelphia: J.B. Lippincott, 1937), quoted in Ibid., 362.

34. Ibid., 541–542, 551.

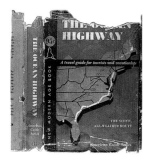

Fig. 11. Artist unknown,

The Ocean Highway: New

Brunswick, New Jersey to

Jacksonville, Florida,

dustjacket, 20 x 17 cm, 1938.

▶

Fig. 12. Politzer, *Planning Your*

Vacation in Florida: Miami and

Dade County, Including Miami

Beach and Coral Gables, dust-

jacket, 22 x 19 cm, 1941.

New York City and Florida. The introduction claimed that the route was ice-free in the winter, due to its proximity to the Gulf Stream.

Planning Your Vacation in Florida: Miami and Dade County, Including Miami Beach and Coral Gables contained chapters on a variety of subjects including fishing, the Gulf Stream, the Seminoles, and points of interest in Miami, Miami Beach, Coconut Grove, Coral Gables, and other parts of Dade County (figs. 12 and 13). History, general information, and a calendar of events rounded out the coverage of the region. This book was also issued in a special edition as a "Souvenir of the United States Brewer's Association" at the United Brewers' Industrial Convention held in Miami in 1942.

The city of Fernandina was described in *Seeing Fernandina: A Guide to the City and its Industries* (fig. 14). Part of the *American Guide Series* and co-sponsored by the City Commission, this booklet described the city's history from 1564 to 1940 and discussed thirty-two points of interest.

Seminole Indians in Florida was written to provide the general public with an introduction to the history, lifestyle, and customs of the Seminole Indians (figs. 15 and 16). The eighty-seven-page work contained photographs by the

Fig. 13. Miami Beach News Service, *Ocean Promenade… Miami Beach*, photograph, 18 x 15 cm, 1941. From *Planning Your Vacation in Florida*, between 60–61.

Fig. 14. Artist unknown, *Seeing Fernandina: A Guide to the City and Its Industries*, pamphlet cover, 23 x 15.5 cm, 1940.

Fig. 15. Florida Art Project,

Seminole Indians in

Florida, pamphlet cover,

23 x 15 cm, c. 1941.

Fig. 16. *Map of Everglades*

Section of Florida, map,

5 x 26 cm, c. 1941. From

Seminole Indians in Florida,

inside back cover.

Florida Art Project and a list of "Indian Place Names in Florida." The publication used as its guide a 1932 report produced by the Indian Affairs Commission entitled *Survey of the Seminole Indians in Florida.*

Similar in concept to *The Ocean Highway*, the volume *U.S. One: Maine to Florida* provided a mile-by-mile description of U.S. Route 1 from the Canadian border to Key West, using the same tour-guide format as the state guides (fig. 17). A glossary-cookbook section on regional delicacies, called "Special Foods from Maine to Florida," included recipes and trivia, such as the history of hush puppies.

In addition to the Florida Writers' Project titles discussed above, The Bienes Center for the Literary Arts of Broward County Library, Fort Lauderdale, Florida, houses one of the most complete collections of Federal Writers' Project

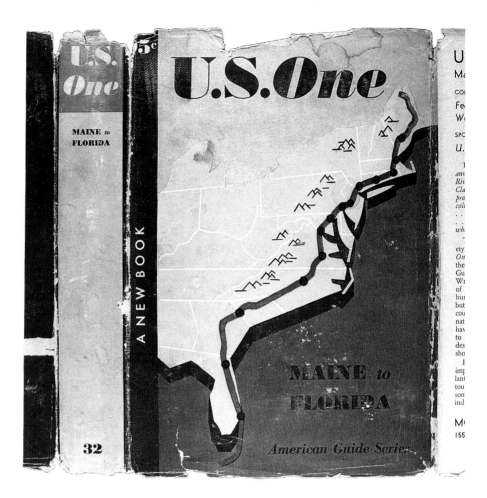

Fig. 17. Artist unknown, *U.S. One: Maine to Florida*, dust-jacket, 20 x 18 cm, 1938.

literature in the United States. Furthermore, the Bienes Center's Works Progress Administration collection, which grew out of an initial gift of more than six hundred Federal Writers' Project titles donated by Jean Fitzgerald in 1986, includes numerous printed books, archives, and ephemera from most of the other New Deal agencies.[35]

The titles compiled by the Florida Writers' Project provide a comprehensive portrait of the state as it existed up to 1943. For perhaps the first time, writers, artists, and other researchers recorded for the nation's collective memory a detailed, balanced historical overview of Florida that has stood the test of time.

The New Deal gave the American people a well-documented and intimate view of the country at a time when it was attempting to lift itself out of severe economic depression and poverty. It was a unique era in United States history and it endowed the nation with governmental traditions and social models that will be difficult for future generations to equal or surpass. □

35. Jean Fitzgerald is a former Broward Public Library Advisory Board member and a founder of the Broward Public Library Foundation.

Note

The Florida Federal Writers' Project travel and related titles in The Dianne and Michael Bienes Special Collections and Rare Book Library include:

Birds in Florida / Compiled by Workers of the Writers' Program of the Work Projects Administration in the State of Florida.—Tallahassee: State of Florida, Department of Agriculture (Printed by Florida Grower Press, Tampa), [c. 1941].—213 p.—Color illustrations.

Florida: A Guide to the Southernmost State / Compiled and written by the Federal Writers' Project of the Work Projects Administration in the State of Florida.—New York: Oxford University Press, 1939.—xxvi, 600 p.—(American Guide Series).—In dustjacket.

Florida: [Facts, Events, Places, Tours] / [Compiled by Workers of the WPA Writers' Project in the State of Florida; Florida State Planning Board].—Northport, N.Y.: Bacon and Wieck, Inc., 1941.—28 p.—(American Recreation Series; 1).

A Guide to Key West / Compiled by Workers of the Writers' Program of the Work Projects Administration in the State of Florida.—New York: Hastings House, 1941.—122 p.—(American Guide Series).—In dustjacket.—Maps on endpapers.—Cover design and many illustrations by F. Townsend Morgan and the Florida Art Project. Sponsored by the Florida State Planning Board.

History of Broward County / Frances H. Miner.—Miami, Fla.: Federal Writers' Project, 15 July 1936.—16 typescript leaves. (Unpublished).

History of Jefferson County Florida / [Federal Emergency Relief Administration, Civil Works Administration].—Monticello, Fla.: Ocala Star-Banner, 1958.—144 p.—(Compiled in 1934–1935, published in 1958).

The Intracoastal Waterway: Norfolk to Key West / Compiled by Federal Writer's Project of the Works Progress Administration.—Washington, D.C.: U.S. Government Printing Office, 1937.—143 p.—(American Guide Series). Fold-out map in back.

The Ocean Highway: New Brunswick, New Jersey to Jacksonville, Florida / Compiled and written by the Federal Writers' Project of the Works Progress Administration.—New York: Modern Age Books, 1938.—244 p.—(American Guide Series). In dustjacket. Sponsored by Charles L. Terry Jr., Secretary of State of Delaware.

Pensacola Recreation Handbook / [Compiled by Workers of the Writers' Program of the Work Projects Administration in the State of Florida, in cooperation with the WPA Recreation Program; University of Florida, State-wide sponsor of the Writers' Project].—Pensacola, Fla.: Escambia County Commission, October 1941.—19 p.

Planning Your Vacation in Florida: Miami and Dade County, Including Miami Beach and Coral Gables / Compiled by Workers of the Writers' Program of the Work Projects Administration in the State of Florida; sponsored by the Florida State Planning Board.—Northport, NY: Bacon, Percy and Daggett, 1941.—202 p. (American Guide Series).—In dustjacket.—Foreword by Marjory Stoneman Douglas.

Seeing Fernandina: A Guide to the City and Its Industries / Co-sponsored by the City Commission, Fernandina; [Compiled by Workers of the Writers' Program of the Work Projects Administration in the State of Florida; sponsored by the Florida State Planning Board].— Fernandina, Fla.: Fernandina News Publishing Co., 1940.— 84 p.— (American Guide Series).

Seeing St. Augustine / Compiled and written by the Federal Writers' Project, Works Progress Administration; sponsored by City Commission of St. Augustine.— St. Augustine, Fla.: The Record Company, 1937.—73, v, p.— (American Guide Series).

Seminole Indians in Florida / [Compiled by Workers of the Writers' Program of the Work Projects Administration in the State of Florida; University of Florida, State-wide sponsor of the Florida Writers' Project].—Tallahassee: Florida State Department of Agriculture, [c. 1941]. — 87 p. — (Fold-out color map in back).— (Photos by the Florida Art Project).

The Spanish Missions of Florida / [Compiled by Workers of the Writers' Program of the Work Projects Administration in the State of Florida; sponsored by the Florida State Planning Board]. — [S.l.: s.n., c. 1940].— 51 p.— (This account of the early Florida missions was compiled by Zelia Sweett and Mary H. Sheppy).

Stetson Kennedy's WPA Archive. Papers, correspondence, photographs and publications from the Florida Federal Writers' Project and the Florida Federal Music Project. (Unpublished).

Tropical Fruits in Florida with Commercial Possibilities / [Compiled by Workers of the Writers' Program of the Work Projects Administration in the State of Florida].—Tallahassee: State of Florida, Department of Agriculture, 1941.— 43 p.

U.S. One: Maine to Florida / Compiled and written by the Federal Writers' Project of the Works Progress Administration.— New York: Modern Age Books, 1938.—344 p.—With thirty photographs. (American Guide Series). Sponsored by the U.S. No. 1 Highway Association.

Later Florida Federal Writers' Project publications include:

Conchtown USA: Bahamian Fisherfolk in Riviera Beach, Florida / Photographed and written by Charles C. Foster; folk songs and tales collected by Veronica Huss.— Boca Raton: Florida Atlantic University Press, 1991.— 176 p.— (33 1/2 record in back cover.— *The voices of Wilbur Roberts and Mary Jane Roberts* / recorded January, 1940, by Stetson Kennedy).

The Florida Negro: A Federal Writers' Project Legacy / edited, with an introduction, by Gary W. McDonogh.—Jackson and London: University Press of Mississippi, 1993.—177 p.— (In dustjacket… an annotated version of the completed manuscript…now in the possession of the Florida Historical Society…).

Palmetto Country / Stetson Kennedy.—Tallahassee: Florida A and M University Press; c. 1942, reprint c. 1989.—354 p.

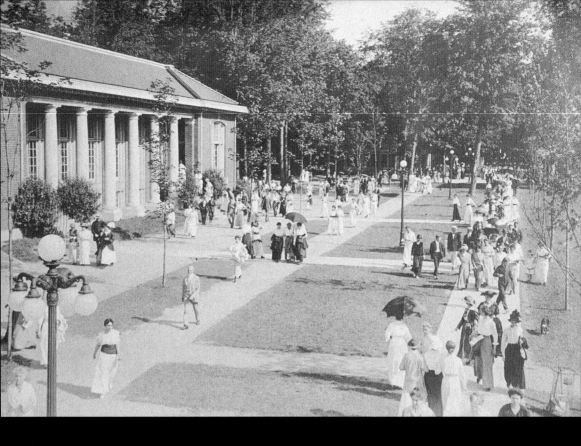

above,

Fig. 1. A Chautauqua green, photograph. John Nolen Papers, Department of Manuscripts and University Archives, Cornell University Library.

opposite,

Fig. 2. Early-twentieth-century United States Geographical Survey map of the town of Chautauqua on Chautauqua Lake, New York. John Nolen Papers, Department of Manuscripts and University Archives, Cornell University Library.

The Chautauquans and Progressives in Florida

By Thomas E. Low

Thomas E. Low heads the Charlotte, North Carolina office of Duany Plater-Zyberk and Company Architects and Town Planners. He lectures on town planning and is completing a book on the planning techniques of John Nolen.

The lofty dreams and aspirations of the nineteenth-century Chautauqua movement, though born in New York State, both directly and indirectly helped shape some of Florida's most interesting and important towns. Among the most significant was DeFuniak Springs, the southern outpost of the movement. In the early twentieth century, Chautauqua provided an intellectual framework for town planner John Nolen (1869–1937) as he designed such Florida cities as Venice, San Jose, and Belleair. These places sprang from a philosophical premise that the physical environment and healthy life of both mind and body were linked. Research consistently points to late-nineteenth-century Chautauqua and early-twentieth-century Progressive movement towns as models sharing attributes of social philosophy and community form. By exploring how town designers of the latter era learned from their predecessors, the similarities become clear.

Chautauqua was founded by the industrialist Lewis Miller (1829–1899), manufacturer of the buckeye mower, and the theologian John Heyl Vincent (1832–1920), under a charter of the Methodist Episcopal Church in 1869. Originally it was a two-week retreat for Sunday school teachers, musicians, and artists. The program included lectures, "normal" lessons, sermons, devotional meetings, conferences, illustrative exercises, and recreational elements. Eventually the program extended to the entire summer. Chautauqua, located on Lake Chautauqua in western New York, flourished in the late nineteenth century and is still very active today (figs. 1 and 2). A large part of the organization revolved around the Chautauqua Institution (fig. 3). Chautauqua was well-known as a "College in the Home, the Summer City in the Woods, and Vacation Schools" and included winter home-correspondence courses.

Chautauqua's intention, according to Vincent, was that "The full-orbed 'Chautauqua Idea' must awaken in all genuine souls a fresh enthusiasm in true living, and bring rich and poor, learned and unlearned, into neighborship…, helpful and honorable to both….It exalts education,— the mental, social, moral, and religious faculties…"[1]

Vincent described Chautauqua as having rude beginnings with narrow quarters, hard beds, and poor fare in rough and rural surroundings. But this was considered appropriate for the "out-of-doors movement" in which nature played a major role. "At Chautauqua," he wrote, "Nature is our text-book, Nature our laboratory, Nature our teacher. We study Nature in her material

---

1. John Heyl Vincent, *The Chautauqua Movement* (Boston: Chautauqua Press, 1886), 2–4.

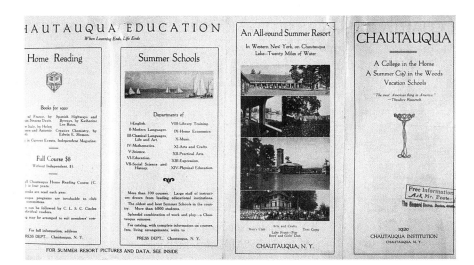

manifestations, in her mental and moral manifestations."[2] The first housing consisted of simple tents on platforms. But Vincent had a very clear vision of its potential: "I see among the trees of our groves stately halls, grand museums, lofty observatory, and delightful homes….Models of cottages and farmhouses will illustrate architectural possibilities within the reach of the humblest people."[3] As families returned year after year, the canvas walls and roofs were replaced by more permanent structures, with some still using the original tent platforms for foundations. These intimately scaled buildings now form the most charming and picturesque streets in Chautauqua.[4] The lanes ultimately became paved streets and the lots well defined. From those humble roots, Chautauqua communities were established throughout the country—including DeFuniak Springs in Florida's Panhandle (fig. 4).[5]

Thirty years after Chautauqua's conception, the trustees decided to commission a plan to remodel it as a more permanent community. At that time, 1902, the summer-camp meeting site comprised some five hundred dwellings and twenty public buildings on two hundred acres, with summer residents numbering about ten thousand. A competition in 1902 awarded the commission to the design team of architect Albert Kelsey of Philadelphia, landscape architect Warren H. Manning of Boston, and sculptor J. Massey Rhind. Kelsey was an active member in the American League for Civic Improvement and the American Art and Outdoor Art Association. The St. Louis Fair adopted his plans for a "Model City" exhibition. Manning had worked in the office of Frederick Law Olmsted Sr. (1822–1903) and John C. Olmsted of Brookline, Massachusetts, which was responsible for the design and execution of the planting plans for more than 125 projects in twenty-two states, including the World's Columbian Exposition of 1893 in Chicago and the Biltmore House in Asheville, North Carolina.

2. Ibid., 220.

3. Ibid., 234–237.

4. Daniel Cary, lecture to Suburb and Town Design graduate studio, University of Miami, Coral Gables, Florida, spring 1990.

5. There are several books on the Chautauqua communities describing the many locations, including Theodore Morrison, *Chautauqua: A Center for Education, Religion and the Arts in America* (Chicago: University of Chicago Press, 1974) and Harry P. Harrison, *Culture Under Canvas: The Story of Tent Chautauqua* (Westport, Conn.: Green Wood Press, 1978).

Fig. 4. DeFuniak Springs, aerial view. Photograph by Alex B. Maclean, Landslides, Boston, 1993.

In a 1903 article from *The Chautauquan*, Kelsey declared the designers' intention to turn Chautauqua into a model town, saying that "neither in public edifices or private houses has there ever been during thirty years of building that conscious appreciation of or regard for the picture value of the place as a whole, which is the essence of the modern civic improvement creed."[6] The design was skillful. It interfered with the position of only three houses but proposed readjusting approaches, driveways, park areas, and lakes, as well as regrouping public buildings, and subdividing the grounds into quarters. The four sections were the Intellectual Quarter, the Athletic Quarter, the Arts and Crafts Village, and the College Department. Residential dwellings were purposefully scattered throughout the entire property. The original intent was that Chautauqua be richly landscaped. Consistent with that goal, the team proposed extensions of the plantings, including trees placed on built-up mounds or set in depressions to conform to the proposed grading changes so that when the future phases were funded and undertaken or the older trees fell or died, the new trees would be as mature as possible. As for the sculptural elements, both functional and inspirational pieces were proposed. Stone stair treads were carved with quotations; drinking fountains were surrounded by carved benches, each with representations of one of the cardinal virtues; and the Chautauqua seal was set in gilded metal for the four clock faces of the campanile. A "Fountain of Triumph" with figures of youth and old age was designated by the Hall of Philosophy on the circle; a towering obelisk was to be placed at the end of the high elevation of the main avenue; and the finial of the grand dome was to be embodied with a strong-winged female figure poised on a winged wheel representing

6. "Making Chautauqua a Model," *The Chautauquan* 37 (April–August, 1903): 449–458.

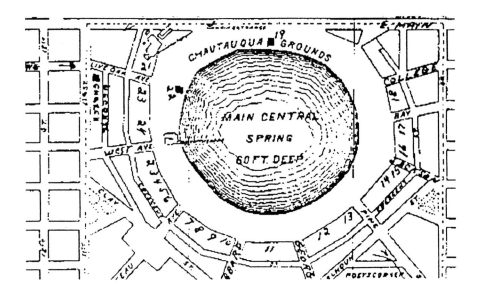

"Progress." In addition, Kelsey recommended erecting two statues of Chautauqua's founders, Vincent and Miller, at the approach from the lake to the Hall of Philosophy.[7]

DeFuniak Springs, also called Florida's Chautauqua, is located approximately thirty-five miles north of the Gulf of Mexico in Florida's Panhandle. First known as Lake DeFuniak, the town was named in honor of Colonel Fred DeFuniak, first president of the Pensacola and Atlantic Railroad. Colonel W. D. Chipley, who engineered the project, is credited with the decision to route the railroad past the beautiful lake destined to become the centerpiece of the community. Chipley's decision came after he had camped overnight beside the lake with a group that included Colonel T. T. Wright and Major W. J. Van Kirk while the railroad survey was being taken. The men decided that their community should be developed as a winter resort and educational center.[8]

The town was planned around a body of water from a sinkhole called Round Lake (fig. 5). The gentle sloping bank surrounding the lake was reserved as a continuous linear park shaded with trees. Public buildings were located within the park, including a large auditorium building (no longer existing except for the entrance gallery). The remaining structures and residences were built fronting the lake across from the lakeside drive, with additional homes located on radiating streets and blocks. A town center developed at the railroad junction within walking distance of the lakefront.

Records show that early settlers, some of them attracted from Northern and Midwestern states, included such leaders as Professor W. C. Eddy, Jevi Plank Sr., C. C. Banfill, and Colonel Wright. Banfill, hearing that Dr. A. H. Gillett was with a group in Florida looking for a site for a winter Chautauqua, headed a delegation to Jacksonville to induce Gillett to visit DeFuniak Springs. Gillett and Reverend C. C. McLean returned with Banfill and the first session of the Florida Chautauqua was announced for 10 February to 9 March 1885.

7. Ibid.

8. "DeFuniak Springs," *The Iron Horse in the Pinelands* (n.p., n.d.), 60.

An auditorium and a hotel were rushed to completion to accommodate the program and visitors. Annual sessions, some of them six weeks in length, were held thereafter. Classes in art, cooking, music, hygiene, home economics, and drama were offered, as were entertainment and lectures. A resident orchestra provided outdoor concerts.

The railroad operated Saturday excursions from River Junction and Pensacola, bringing hundreds of visitors. The railroad featured trips from such cities as Chicago and New York, for a round-trip rate of $15.50. During World War I the railroad excursions were discontinued, but the Chautauqua sessions were still held. Without the support of the railroad, however, the buildings deteriorated and interest waned. The Chautauqua buildings were restored and renovated by Works Progress Administration (WPA) labor in the early 1930s, and the Women's Club sponsored a free ten-day Chautauqua in 1931 and 1932, but for the most part, the Chautauqua sessions at DeFuniak had died out.[9]

Still, in Florida, the impact of Chautauqua lived on. The physical form of the Chautauqua communities helped shape town planning work during the following generation and emerged as an influence in the formative years of the planning profession during the Progressive Era. "In this vast work the incentive has not been chiefly the improvement of property but the betterment to human life,"[10] John Nolen wrote, almost as a manifesto for the town planning movement in the early years of this century.

At the turn of the century, the United States experienced rapid industrial growth. Giant businesses were formed and fortunes were made. The population, desiring to take advantage of this industrial boom, shifted away from the countryside and came flooding into the cities. Building and land speculation became rampant in both newly opened sections of the cities and in the older preexisting areas. But as the economy slowed in the first decade of the twentieth century, a portion of the populace grew increasingly discontented with the state of living conditions. New reform parties as well as educational and civic organizations were formed in reaction to the growing ills associated with the mechanization of industry. This call for broad reform is collectively identified as the Progressive movement. In architecture the growing interest in human scale and simple handwrought objects found expression in the Arts and Crafts movement. Extended into land development, the movement took broader form, into what planner Elbert Peets termed "civic art." The city planning profession was founded during this period.

The Progressive Era—dated by most as 1900–1930—was a time of unprecedented civic enlightenment. It was also truly the pinnacle of city planning in terms of civic design initiatives. When John Nolen opened his town planning practice in the early twentieth century, he found many sources to reinforce the civic ideals of the Progressives.[11] These sources included Camillo Sitte's book *Der Städtebau* (City Planning According to Artistic Principles) from Germany and the new towns of the English Garden City movement. For sources in the United States, Nolen looked to the New England colonial towns, but he also had a personal interest in the town of Chautauqua.

9. Ibid.

10. John Nolen, *Replanning Small Cities: Six Typical Studies* (New York: B. W. Huebsch, 1912), 24.

11. John Nolen is part of a larger group of Progressive Era town planners, including Frederick Law Olmsted Jr. and John C. Olmsted, Harlan Bartholomew, Hegeman and Peets, Stein and Wright, Russell Black, Earle Sumner Draper, and others.

As historian John Hancock has noted, Nolen was an international giant in the field of modern city and regional planning in the early-twentieth-century United States. He was a Renaissance man in the profession—a path-breaking visionary, innovative practitioner, widely informed educator, prolific author, and an eloquent, forceful speaker. Nolen wrote a half-dozen books and many articles on planning. He helped establish the first planning degree programs in the country at Harvard University and Massachusetts Institute of Technology. Nolen was one of the founders of the professional organization that later evolved into the American Planning Association. In the course of his professional career he worked on more than four hundred planning projects.[12] By understanding his background, one can understand why Chautauqua had such a strong influence on his town planning. Nolen's work shows a commitment to and an understanding of the relationship between mind and body, in the broadest sense.

Nolen was born into a lower-middle-class Philadelphia family in 1869. He worked from early childhood and graduated with honors from Girard College in 1884 and from the University of Pennsylvania in 1893.[13] Prior to his decision to attend the newly formed School of Landscape Architecture at Harvard in 1903, with the specific intent of going into large-scale civic improvement work,[14] Nolen served as director of the Philadelphia-based Society for the Extension of University Teaching, or the People's University, as it was sometimes termed.[15] Like Chautauqua, the Extension was an example of the rising popularity of

12. John Hancock, "John Nolen: New Towns in Florida," *The New City* 1 (fall 1991): 71.

13. John Lorentz Hancock, *John Nolen and the American City Planning Movement: A History of Cultural Change and Community Response, 1900–1940* (Ph.D. diss., University of Pennsylvania, Philadelphia; Ann Arbor, Mich.: University Microfilms, 1964), 5, 8. While research material on Nolen's career is becoming more accessible, John Lorentz Hancock remains an important resource.

14. Ibid., 21.

15. Ibid., 17.

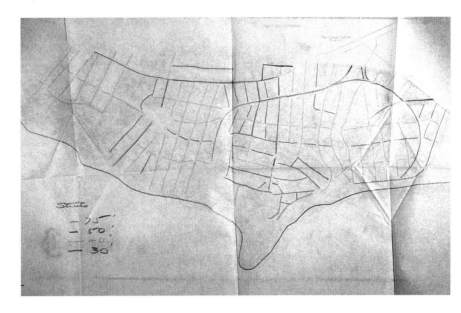

Fig. 7. John Nolen's overlay sketch study of the street network on the plan of Chautauqua. John Nolen Papers, Department of Manuscripts and University Archives, Cornell University Library.

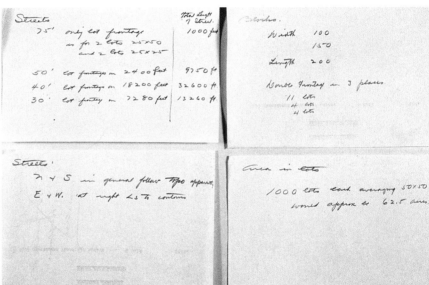

Fig. 8. Examples of John Nolen's index card statistics for the Chautauqua plan. John Nolen Papers, Department of Manuscripts and University Archives, Cornell University Library.

adult education in late-nineteenth-century England and America. The Extension was structured somewhat like the old Lyceum, the later Redpath Bureau, and the nationally popular Chautauqua Institution Lecture Series. It had a direct and permanent influence on Nolen's belief that informed public opinion was the first and most important basis of broad social reform.[16]

Nolen may have been the first to clearly understand the connection between the physical design of Chautauqua and its relevance to the social issues of the Progressives. Several Chautauqua Institution booklets, including the *Civic Improvements Number* and the *Tree Number* were part of Nolen's office reference material (fig. 6). His office records show that he obtained a detailed site plan of Chautauqua and sketched over the plan (fig. 7). He produced tissue overlays to analyze the city's physical composition, including street

16. Ibid., 15.

Fig. 9. Plan of Chautauqua. John Nolen Papers, Department of Manuscripts and University Archives, Cornell University Library.

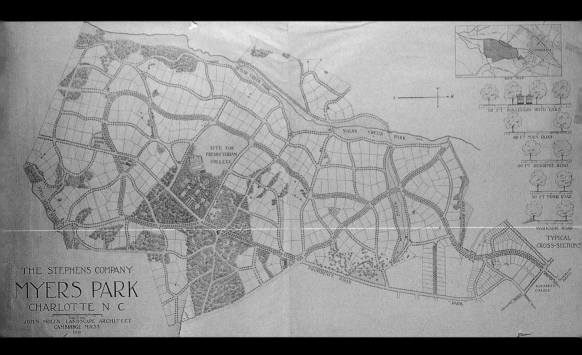

Fig. 10. John Nolen, general plan of Myers Park, Charlotte, North Carolina, 1911. Architectural Archives, University of Pennsylvania.

types — identifying each by their width and the total land area to the proportion of open space. Nolen's index cards show that he also examined the perimeter block sizes, linear feet of street types, and percentages of public to private uses (fig. 8). These records reveal the amount of time and the extent of research that Nolen's office conducted in order to understand every detail of a good physical design model.

The influence of Chautauqua (fig. 9) can be seen in John Nolen's design for Myers Park in Charlotte, North Carolina, which was planned in 1911 as a "high-class Residential Suburb" situated about one-and-one-half miles from the center city of Charlotte (fig. 10). Nolen compared Myers Park to one of a small number of characteristically beautiful suburbs including Roland Park, Baltimore; Forest Hills, New York; the Country Club district, Kansas City; the Twin Peaks district, San Francisco; and Palos Verdes, California. He also compared Myers Park to the newer developments in Florida including San Jose, Jacksonville, and the town of Venice.[17]

The physical layout of all these towns share design elements, but the plans of Chautauqua and Myers Park are especially similar. Both towns have a looping avenue for public transit, a variety of streets, centrally located institutions, abundant public open space, and street frontages bordering natural corridors. In both towns nature has been brought into the most urban conditions, reflecting Nolen's belief in the importance of the relationship between man and nature.

Nolen's involvement in Florida was during the 1920s boom era from 1922–1927. His first and only branch office was located in Jacksonville (1925). Nolen's Florida practice produced city plans for West Palm Beach (1922), Sarasota (1924), Clearwater (1925), and St. Petersburg (1926); regional plans for St. Petersburg (1922), Sarasota (1925), Clearwater (1925), and Venice Farms (1925); plans for new towns and suburbs including Clewiston (1922), Belleair (1924), Venice-Nokomis (1924), Bay Point, Venice (1924), Maximo Estates, St. Petersburg (1924), St. Augustine Beach (1924), San Jose Estates, Jacksonville (1925), Venice (1925), University Park, Gainesville (1925), Alturas (1925), and Orangewood, Fort Myers (1925); and landscape architecture for the Thomas A. Edison Estate, Fort Myers (1927).[18]

His commissions came from city governments, labor unions (such as the Brotherhood of Locomotive Engineers for Venice), national corporations, and private individuals. The initial impetus for the Florida development was the opening of new railway lines, new state and federal highways, canals, and filled shorelines.

Even though these plans did not come with the high aspirations of the Chautauqua movement, the civic design objectives of the Progressive movement were the underlying driving principles. Nolen's projects were generally laid out on the "Neighborhood Unit" developed by Clarence Arthur Perry (fig. 11). The planning principles of the Perry model include a mixed-use neighborhood where every residence is within walking distance of the center, which generally has a school, church, or community center. Businesses and shopping are usually located at the edge, where the transit is accessible.

17. John Nolen, *New Towns for Old: Achievements in Civic Improvement in Some American Small Towns and Neighborhoods* (Boston: Marshall Jones Co., 1927), 100.

18. John Nolen and Justin R. Hartzog, brochure, "Selected examples of Public Planning Work," *John Nolen, City and Regional Planner, Cambridge, Mass., 1935*, 1–8.

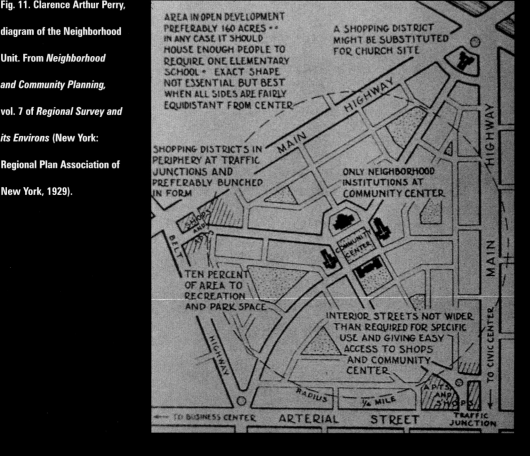

Fig. 11. Clarence Arthur Perry, diagram of the Neighborhood Unit. From *Neighborhood and Community Planning*, vol. 7 of *Regional Survey and its Environs* (New York: Regional Plan Association of New York, 1929).

The text within the diagram reads:

AREA IN OPEN DEVELOPMENT PREFERABLY 160 ACRES •• IN ANY CASE IT SHOULD HOUSE ENOUGH PEOPLE TO REQUIRE ONE ELEMENTARY SCHOOL • EXACT SHAPE NOT ESSENTIAL BUT BEST WHEN ALL SIDES ARE FAIRLY EQUIDISTANT FROM CENTER

A SHOPPING DISTRICT MIGHT BE SUBSTITUTED FOR CHURCH SITE

SHOPPING DISTRICTS IN PERIPHERY AT TRAFFIC JUNCTIONS AND PREFERABLY BUNCHED IN FORM

ONLY NEIGHBORHOOD INSTITUTIONS AT COMMUNITY CENTER

TEN PERCENT OF AREA TO RECREATION AND PARK SPACE

INTERIOR STREETS NOT WIDER THAN REQUIRED FOR SPECIFIC USE AND GIVING EASY ACCESS TO SHOPS AND COMMUNITY CENTER

GENERAL PLAN
MAXIMO ESTATES
ST PETERSBURG
FLORIDA

Fig. 12. John Nolen, general plan of Maximo Estates, St. Petersburg, Florida, colored engraving, 71.8 x 41.2", 1925. John Nolen Papers,

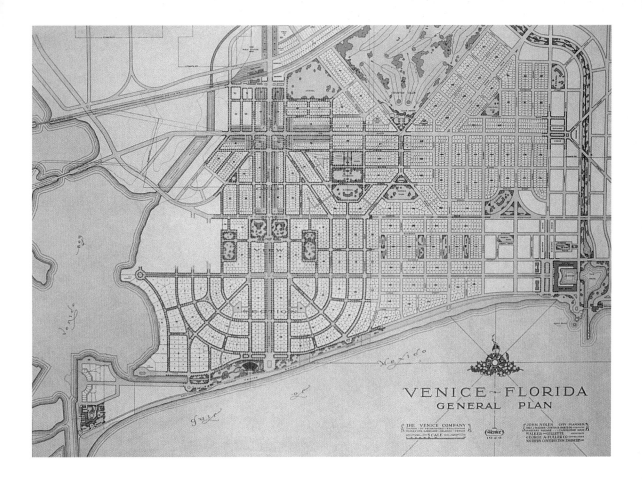

VENICE ~ FLORIDA
GENERAL PLAN

Fig. 13. John Nolen, general

plan of Venice, Florida,

colored engraving, 70.8 x 52.4",

1926. John Nolen Papers,

Department of Manuscripts

and University Archives,

Cornell University Library.

A network of streets provides various ways for pedestrians and cars to get around, and parks and playgrounds are abundant.[19] The plan for Maximo Estates, St. Petersburg (1925) is a prime example of a well-laid-out town with all the attributes of the neighborhood unit, incorporating physical forms of the waterfront and bay (fig. 12). The waterfront property to a great extent has been retained for the enjoyment of all the citizens rather than privatized.

While Chautauqua influenced planning projects in general, Nolen's plans for Florida's new towns share characteristics with DeFuniak Springs. Comparisons between DeFuniak Springs and the Florida towns of Venice (fig. 13), San Jose (fig. 14), and Belleair (fig. 15) show that all have streets radiating from civic and commercial centers with concentric rings of cross streets interconnecting to form a complete street network. Public open space has been reserved along the waterfront, and natural features and civic sites are in prominent locations.

The planning work of both the Chautauqua movement and the Progressive Era aimed to enhance and carefully integrate environmental, social, economic, and political conditions and needs to serve all segments of society fairly.[20] Just as the Chautauquas provided inspiration for Progressive Era communities,

19. Clarence Arthur Perry, "The Neighborhood Unit," *Neighborhood and Community Planning*, vol. 7 of *Regional Survey and its Environs* (New York: Regional Plan Association of New York, 1929), 25–30.

20. Hancock, "John Nolen," 78.

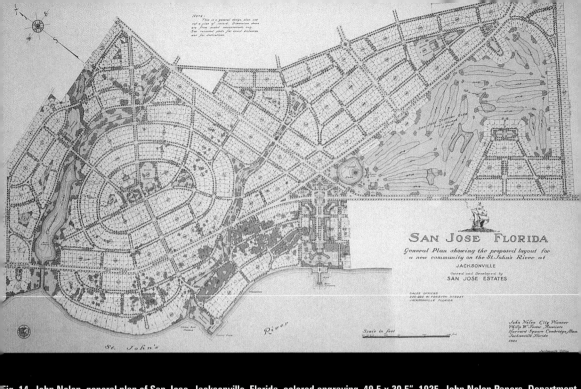

Fig. 14. John Nolen, general plan of San Jose, Jacksonville, Florida, colored engraving, 49.5 x 30.5", 1925. John Nolen Papers, Department of Manuscripts and University Archives, Cornell University Library.

Fig. 15. John Nolen, general plan of Town of Belleaire, Florida, hand-colored engraving, 35.6 x 29.6", 1924. John Nolen Papers, Department of Manuscripts and University Archives, Cornell University Library.

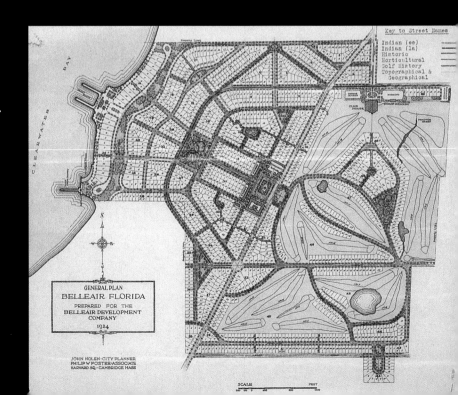

Fig. 16. Aerial view of Seaside, Florida. Photograph by Alex B. Maclean, Landslides, Boston, 1993.

the planning attributes of both the Chautauquas and the Progressives are being successfully emulated today. Architectural historian Vincent Scully points to DeFuniak Springs and Venice, Florida as inspirations for developer Robert Davis and architects Andres Duany and Elizabeth Plater-Zyberk in forming the social ideology and creating the physical form of the recently designed town of Seaside (fig. 16).[21] A similar example is a 1920 plan that Nolen used as an illustration of a model Progressive community in his book *New Towns for Old* (fig. 17). When comparing this Progressive Era plan to Seaside, similar design characteristics become clear (fig. 18).

As we examine the characteristics of these eras we can begin to understand that in order for the United States to satisfy its ongoing quest for community, there is a growing need to reattach the thread of historical continuity that has been broken for the past two generations. The plans of Belleair, Florida and Round Lake at DeFuniak Springs show these shared ideals turned into physical form. As with traditional neighborhoods today, they were developed for people who hold a general appreciation for the well-ordered social life. Nolen summarized this in *New Towns for Old*, writing about Myers Park:

---

21. Peter Katz, *The New Urbanism: Toward an Architecture of Community* (New York: McGraw-Hill, Inc., 1994), 226; Vincent Scully, Architectural History lectures, University of Miami, Coral Gables, Florida, 1993–1994.

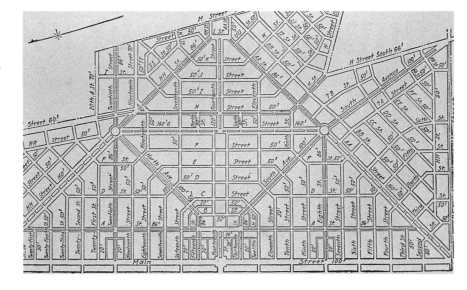

Fig. 17. Plan example of a Progressive Era town. From John Nolen's book *New Towns for Old* (Boston: Marshall Jones Co., 1927).

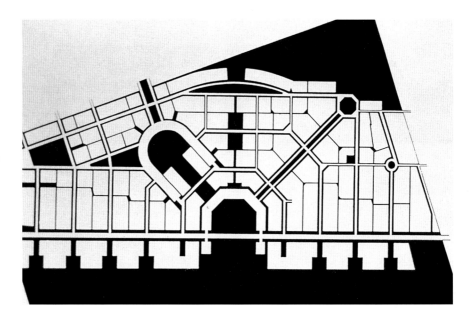

Fig. 18. Andres Duany and Elizabeth Plater-Zyberk, plan of Seaside, Florida, 1981. Courtesy of Duany Plater-Zyberk and Company Architects and Town Planners, Miami office archives.

Only in settled communities where a sense of personal responsibility among the people prevails can a genuine social life manifest itself. The seclusion of the private house may be understood to represent the personal qualities of the individual and family. But the street and the great out-of-doors assuredly stand for the brotherhood of man and its unity with all of nature. Family life is spontaneous and Primæval; social life is cultivated and typifies the progress of the race.[22]

Nolen's belief that informed public opinion is the primary basis for broad social reform tells us it is important not only to learn from the projects but also to understand their significance as a part of our history and heritage (fig. 19). □

22. Nolen, *New Towns*, 110.

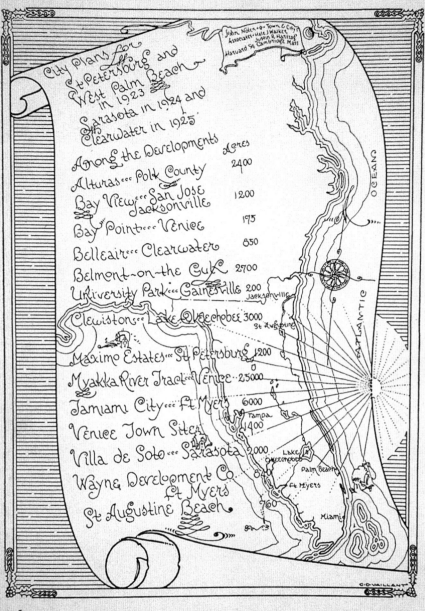

City Plans for
St Petersburg and
West Palm Beach
in 1923
Sarasota in 1924 and
Clearwater in 1925

Among the Developments   Acres
Alturas ••• Polk County   2400
Bay View ••• San Jose
           Jacksonville   1200
Bay Point ••• Venice   175
Belleair ••• Clearwater   850
Belmont-on-the Gulf   2700
University Park ••• Gainesville   200
Clewiston ••• Lake Okeechobee   3000
Maximo Estates ••• St Petersburg   1200
Myakka River Tract ••• Venice   25000
Tamiami City ••• Ft Myers   6000
Venice Town Site   1400
Villa de Soto ••• Sarasota   2000
Wayne Development Co
              Ft Myers   840
St Augustine Beach   760

John Nolen • Town & City
Associates • Hale J Walker
           Justin R Hartzog
Harvard Sq   Cambridge Mass

OCEAN
ATLANTIC
Jacksonville
St Augustine
Tampa
Lake Okeechobee
Palm Beach
Ft Myers
Miami

C. D. VAILLANT

FLORIDA ✦✦✦ AND LISTED
"IN THE MAKING" SOME OF THE
WORK IN THE
STATE BY •••••
John Nolen

Fig. 1. Procession in front of Greater Bethel AME Church, c. 1915. The Lyric Theatre is visible in the background.

Tracing Overtown's Vernacular Architecture

By Dorothy Jenkins Fields

Dorothy Jenkins Fields, a native Miamian, is an educational specialist in the Office of Multicultural Programs, Dade County Public Schools. She is the founder and archivist of the Black Archives, History and Research Foundation of South Florida, Inc. Jenkins Fields holds a Ph.D. in Public History from The Union Institute, Cincinnati, Ohio.

That the railroads, the highways, the architecture, and the towns made Florida is recorded in its history. Less amply documented is the world of those who built them, the "after-hours" culture and legacy of the black laborers who settled in the state. Nowhere is this legacy more evident than in Miami, in what is now called Overtown, but was originally referred to as Colored Town.[1]

From the 1890s through the 1930s, black men who emigrated from the Bahamas and migrated to Florida from other Southern states were the primary work force for the state, building the railroads and highways that opened Florida to tourists and residents. Black men constructed James Deering's bayfront estate, Vizcaya (1914–1917), in Miami, were integral to building the city of Coral Gables in the early 1920s, and erected many other grand mansions and ambitious new towns and cities throughout Florida. In the early decades of this century, black laborers would work during the day on the construction of railroads and resort towns, then gather in the evenings to help build their own residences, shops, hotels, and churches (fig. 1).

The locations of the black communities at the beginning of the twentieth century were not chosen places; they were assigned by law. By custom, they were restricted to individuals defined by the Florida legislature as "Negro," "Colored," "mulatto," "persons of color…," "every person having one-eighth or more African or Negro blood."[2] The governance was the same for all "colored" settlements in the state, including Lincolnville near St. Augustine, Gifford near Vero Beach, "The Styx" in West Palm Beach, Rosewood near Tampa, and the Bahama Village in Key West. Public policy and local ordinances assigned black people to specific areas. As a result of these limitations, the communities of color drew on their own resources — financial and emotional — and created places of significance. For example, "The Styx" in West Palm Beach, now the Northwest Historic District, was settled in 1894 by black laborers who followed the railroad to work on pineapple and vegetable farms and in the tourist industry. The black residents created a community of their own with schools,

Images are courtesy of the Black Archives, History and Research Foundation of South Florida, Inc., Miami, Florida, except where noted.

1. The original boundaries within the city limits were and to this day remain northwest of the downtown business district, Cherry Street (now known as Flagler Street): North—First Street (now Northwest Eleventh Street; Second Street (now Northwest Tenth Street); Third Street (now Northwest Ninth Street); Fourth Street (now Northwest Eighth Street); Fifth Street (now Northwest Seventh Street); South—Sixth Street (now Northwest Sixth Street); East/West—Avenue G (now Northwest Second Avenue); Avenue H (now Northwest Third Avenue); Avenue I (now Northwest Fourth Avenue).

2. Florida Legislature, Rev. Gen. St. 1920, Sec. 3939, Comp. Gen. Laws, 1927, sec. 5858. Over time, people defined themselves as Black, Afro-American and African-American. These terms are used interchangeably depending upon the era being discussed.

Fig. 2. Northwest Second Avenue, c. 1915. This street later became known as "Little Broadway."

residences, businesses, churches, social clubs, and civic groups. The majority of the homes and businesses were constructed by black builders and often designed by Hazel Augustus, who most likely was the first black architect in Florida. Augustus' buildings included the Payne Chapel (1925), his house on Division Street (1921), and the residence of Joseph and Sally Johnson on Ninth Street (1924), all in the Northwest district.[3]

In 1896, Henry Morrison Flager (1830–1913), anticipating the development of a tourist city similar to Palm Beach but prior to the construction of the Florida East Coast Railway tracks to Miami, sent black workmen with a white foreman to build hotels and cottages for the tourists who would come to Miami. There, Flagler's black workers had separate lodgings. Julia Tuttle's land deeds specified the west side of town as the location for factories and for blacks, hence the name Colored Town. The neighborhood grew and flourished as the center of economic activity, education, and culture for Miami's growing black community, and Colored Town became the oldest black community located in the original city limits of Miami.

Although Colored Town began as an accommodation for the white tourist industry, it soon began to develop on its own (fig. 2). By 1905 Colored Town's Avenue G was emerging as the main business block. It evolved as Colored Town's downtown, with an equal mix of commercial and residential structures. The residences were two- and three-room frame houses, while commercial structures were primarily masonry. In later decades, buildings with two stories often combined facilities for boarders and businesses in a single masonry structure. For nearly five decades, most of the houses, businesses, and churches were built by Colored Town resident H. S. Braggs. As contractor, Braggs prepared the drawings, hired skilled laborers in the neighborhood as subcontractors, and supervised the work. Braggs and builder J. R. Knowles, also a resident of Colored Town, are credited with building most of Colored Town's pioneer structures.

---

3. The Northwest District of West Palm Beach was listed on the National Register in 1992.

Many of these buildings were nondescript; they were simple handmade vernacular houses or imitations of the various architectural styles of the day. Nonetheless, a few stood out, and serve as eloquent reminders that architecture transcends the boundaries of law and cultural restrictions. In recent years, six of Colored Town's buildings have been listed on the National Register of Historic Places.

A fine early commercial building was Geder Walker's Lyric Theatre. It opened in 1913, and was a major center of entertainment. Regarded as one of the most beautiful buildings in the area, it was an example of the masonry vernacular style. It included a stage and orchestra pit for theatre and later for movies, and it also provided meeting spaces in its comfortable, well-furnished interior. Still located on its original site, 819 Northwest Second Avenue, the theatre shows signs of its former elegance through the three-part composition of the facade and the applied classical details.

Walker, who owned and operated the Lyric Theatre, moved to Colored Town from Georgia. According to oral histories, Walker travelled to Europe and had been fascinated with the opera houses. Upon his return he built the Lyric Theatre, along with an adjoining ice-cream parlor. Beginning with vaudeville acts, eventually the theatre was equipped with everything needed for modern theatrical performances as well as motion pictures.

Roberta Thompson, a Colored Town resident who attended high school at Tuskegee Institute in Tuskegee, Alabama during the early 1920s remembers feeling this way about the Lyric:

> I was attending school in Alabama because there was no high school available for 'colored' students in Miami before the 1920s. When we arrived at the theater downtown [in Tuskegee] we were told to go upstairs to sit in the balcony. Downstairs was for white people only. I was shocked and disappointed. I told my classmates that in Miami, we have our own theatre, the Lyric, with red velvet seats and a beautiful stage. It is ours and we can sit anyplace we wish.[4]

Fig. 3. Rebecca Dorsey, wife of D. A. Dorsey, in front of their frame vernacular house, c. 1920s.

Two years after the Lyric opened, D. A. (Dana Albert) Dorsey, who also moved to Colored Town from Georgia, built an imposing residence at 250 Northwest Ninth Street (fig. 3). Dorsey, a carpenter by trade, designed and built the two-story frame structure. The exterior drew on three architectural prototypes: the Bahamian or Conch, the frame vernacular, and the Flagler cottage. Unlike the Flagler cottage, however, which was painted Flagler's favorite hue of yellow, Dorsey painted his house white. There was a bathroom on each floor and a walk-in closet on the second floor. The living room had French doors and dark furniture upholstered in maroon velvet with beige trim. The second floor included three bedrooms. D. A. Dorsey paved the area in front of his house and was forced by the city to pay for the remaining sidewalks on the block.

Although his formal education ended with fourth grade, D. A. Dorsey became Colored Town's first millionaire. After arriving in Dade County in 1897, he was involved in many businesses — he was an independent carpenter for Flagler's railroad, the keeper of the Cape Florida Lighthouse, and a truck farmer. In 1905 he initiated and organized the Miami Industrial Mutual Benefit and Savings Association, Colored Town's first savings bank, loan, and insurance company. In 1912, he was one of the founders of the Ocean View Investment Company. Later he was appointed chairman of Dade County's Colored School Board.

4. Roberta Thompson, interview by the author, Miami, Florida, 25 December 1995.

Fig. 4. The D. A. Dorsey Memorial Library, c. 1940s.

Fig. 5. The Chapman residence, c. 1920s.

Dorsey made his fortune in real estate and became one of the wealthiest men in Dade County. It is said that with twenty-five dollars he purchased a parcel of land from which he developed a business empire that included properties in Dade and Broward counties, Cuba, and the Bahamas. He acquired Fisher Island, where he established a public beach for blacks, and he sold land to the city for a park.[5] He was also a generous benefactor, donating land for the Dorsey Memorial Library (fig. 4) in Colored Town and for the Dorsey Senior High School in Liberty City (now the Dorsey Skills Center).

On New Year's Eve, the Dorseys traditionally hosted a party at their home following the midnight church service. It was an open-house affair enjoyed by the community—professional people, laymen, tenants, and neighbors. Dorsey's wife, Rebecca Dorsey, was an accomplished pianist who attended the Boston Conservatory of Music. She encouraged Dorsey to learn to play the violin, and he played well enough to accompany her. For their first anniversary he gave her a baby-grand piano.

William A. Chapman Sr., a physician, built a seventeen-room house for his family of four at 513 Northwest Thirteenth Street (fig. 5). This house, constructed in the masonry vernacular style, contained a formal living room and dining room, a breakfast nook, four bedrooms, and a library. Chapman's medical office was added to the first floor and an upstairs sleeping porch was also added. Built in 1923, the original structure had shutters stamped with the family's initial.

In 1920 the Cola-Nip Bottling Company was established. In 1925 its owners, Osborne Jenkins and William Sampson, relocated the business to the newly constructed building at 227 Northwest Ninth Street, which the company occupied until 1940. The Cola-Nip Bottling Company was one of Colored Town's major businesses, and the first black manufacturing company there. It bottled carbonated drinks, including Cola-Nip, Orange Smile, and Peach Whip. The building was of the commercial masonry vernacular style, and the first letter of each last name appeared on a front panel that read, "J & S Bldg. 1925." After the Cola-Nip business closed in the 1940s, the Atlanta Life Insurance Company

5. City of Miami Planning Department, "D. A. Dorsey House," Designation Report, prepared 14 January 1983, 5.

Fig. 7. Thurgood Marshall in a

meeting inside the x-ray clinic,

c. 1940s.

Fig. 6. The x-ray clinic of

Dr. S. H. Johnson. Photograph

by Mario Ramos, 1996.

Courtesy of the Barbara Baer

Capitman Archives, Miami,

Florida. (Address: 171

Northwest Eleventh Street,

Miami.)

occupied most of the space before the building became a rooming house on the second floor, with individual businesses on the first floor.[6]

Samuel Johnson, a prominent physician and the first black radiologist in Miami, opened an x-ray clinic in Colored Town in 1939. The building was significant for both its place in history (in the days of segregation and Jim Crow laws, blacks were not allowed to be x-rayed or treated at Miami's City Hospital) and for its architecture (figs. 6 and 7). The clinic was a Streamline Moderne building with rounded corners, horizontal banded windows, and glass block trimmed in pink-tinted keystone, with a decorative screen door and detailed bas-relief ornamentation. Located at 171 Northwest Eleventh Street, it was designed by Mr. Barker, a mechanical drawing instructor at Booker T. Washington School.[7] Much later, Dr. Johnson recalled, "I decided to build a clinic that would be self-contained, comfortable, and affordable and welcome the people of Colored Town for treatment and anyone else who came to the door."[8]

Booker T. Washington Junior/Senior High School was the first public high school to provide a recognized twelfth-grade education for black children in Dade County. It opened in Colored Town in 1927, nearly thirty-one years after Miami became a city (fig. 8). Students came from as far north as Dania in Broward County and as far south as Key West in order to complete twelfth grade. Often parents would ask relatives and friends in Colored Town to allow their children to board with them so that they could complete a high-school education.

The original Booker T. Washington School was a masonry vernacular building of simple design with some classical details.[9] The structure was comfortable,

6. City of Miami Planning Department, "Cola-Nip Bottling Co.," Designation Report, prepared 6 January 1984.

7. City of Miami Planning Department, "X-Ray Clinic," Designation Report, prepared 6 January 1984, 6.

8. Dr. S. H. Johnson, interviewed by the author, Miami, Florida, June 1983.

9. Booker T. Washington School's original structure was razed and rebuilt in 1985. In 1997 the Dade County School Board voted to reinstate its high school status.

Fig. 8. Booker T. Washington School, c. 1926. (Address: 1200 Northwest Sixth Avenue.)

Fig. 9. Program cover for event featuring Langston Hughes at the Mount Zion Baptist Church, 1947.

light, and airy, with large windows arranged in groups. The school's courtyard was a favorite meeting place for community groups. Two colorful murals in the school auditorium, painted in the 1940s by a parent, the Reverend Louis H. Portlock, provided the only known visual art in a public building in Colored Town prior to the 1950s. Matinees were held frequently in the auditorium and showcased poets, dancers, singers, and other performing artists. Poet Langston Hughes, classical pianist Phillipa Schyler, and singer Roland Hayes all performed there. Etta Motten, an international singer, displayed African artifacts in the auditorium after her concerts.

For many years, the spiritual, cultural, and intellectual growth of the community revolved around the school and the churches. The churches were the anchors of Colored Town. Many of the original congregations began in private homes and then moved to one- and two-room frame vernacular temporary church structures. In subsequent decades, permanent buildings were erected. Greater Bethel African Episcopal (AME) Church, Mount Zion Baptist Church (fig. 9), Saint Agnes Episcopal Church (fig. 10), and St. John's Baptist Church were among the first organized congregations.

The oldest black church in the city's original boundaries, Greater Bethel AME, was organized in March of 1896, several months before the city of Miami was incorporated. It is now located at 245 Northwest Eighth Street, in a Mediterranean Revival-style building with stained-glass windows. Construction on the site began in 1927 and was completed in 1943. St. John's Baptist Church, at 1328 Northwest Third Avenue, was an Art Deco building with Gothic massing. It was designed by the black architectural firm of McKissak and McKissak of Nashville, Tennessee and was completed in 1940. The Mount Zion Baptist Church, a Mediterranean Revival-style building at 301 Northwest Ninth Street, was designed by architect William Arthur Bennet. Construction began on the Mount Zion Baptist Church in 1928 and was completed in 1941.

During the Depression, Colored Town experienced extreme poverty and overcrowding. This was particularly the case in Good Bread Alley, an area that began evolving prior to 1920 and was so-named because some of the women baked and sold bread in their homes (fig. 11).[10] In the "alley" there were more than

10. Good Bread Alley, located between Northwest Twelfth and Fourteenth Street and between Third and Fourth Avenues, was eventually demolished to make room for the expressway.

Fig. 10. Vacation Bible school outside the parish hall of St. Agnes Episcopal Church, c. 1930s.

Fig. 11. Good Bread Alley

ew houses, c. 1930s

three hundred shot-gun houses with less than five feet between them. The front porch of one house was directly in front of another, divided only by a path or alley.

In 1934, the Reverend John E. Culmer, a priest at Saint Agnes Episcopal Church and a member of the Negro Civic League, initiated a clean-up campaign of Good Bread Alley. Annie M. Coleman and the members of the Friendship Garden and Civic Club were asked to survey the area's residents. The results, published in a study called "Housing and Sanitation," documented the squalid living conditions.

Culmer then enlisted the support of Frank Stoneman, the editor of the *Miami Herald*. Stoneman sent a reporter to Good Bread Alley, which resulted in the community's plight being explored on the front pages of the newspaper in banner headlines for nearly two weeks during September 1934. The newspaper wrote about the sordid state of Good Bread Alley, documenting everything from the high infant mortality rate to the prevalence of crime.

As a result of this exposure and other efforts, improvements were made through Franklin D. Roosevelt's Works Progress Administration (WPA). Liberty Square, a 243-unit planned community, was built in a park setting, and became the fourth public-housing project in the United States. The development included a central building with a recreation hall, a nursery school, a doctor's office, and a cooperative store.

Like many projects of the time, the housing project was the work of many, rather than a single architect. Liberty Square was designed by a consortium of Miami architects, including Phineas E. Paist, Harold Steward, Sheldon Tucker, Walter De Garmo, E. L. Robertson, and V. E. Virrick. It was progressive in its social aspirations, if less so in its architecture. The May 1937 *Architectural Record* described it this way:

> The site plan calls for a community building, centrally heated with accommodations for a day nursery to care for children of working mothers, a large auditorium, and several stores. Behind the community building is an open terrazzo-paved dance floor. The swimming and wading pool are flanked on either side by large grass plots. The arrangement of the buildings allows court space for children's playgrounds and garden areas for adults.[11]

In later years, Colored Town began to attract tourists. During this time, Colored Town boomed; it was alive and busy all the time. There was constant motion, day and night, and the offerings of exotic food, popular music, and gospel music lured white tourists and residents as well as blacks. Indeed, Colored Town developed into quite a celebrity hangout for both the famous and the infamous.

In addition to standard goods and services, there were many fine restaurants, a privately owned tennis court, and several first-class hotels in the neighborhood. The Dorsey, the Marsha Ann, the Lord Calvert (renamed the Sir John), and in later years the Carver hotels became favorite stopovers for tourists. One hotel, the Mary Elizabeth, with three floors, was the tallest building in Colored Town and the first hotel in the community to install an elevator (fig. 12). It was a favorite retreat for such well-known personalities as the first black

11. "Miami's Liberty Square Project," *Architectural Record* (May 1937).

Fig. 12. Mary Elizabeth Hotel, c. 1950s.

United States Supreme Court Justice, Thurgood Marshall; Congressman Adam Clayton Powell; labor leader A. Phillip Randolph; and Dr. Mary McLeod Bethune, president of Bethune Cookman College and the National Council of Negro Women. The author and journalist, W. E. B. DuBois, vacationed there on his way to and from conferences in Cuba and the West Indies.

World-famous boxer Joe Louis came to Colored Town for an extended stay. In fact, he became a fixture in the neighborhood and hosted other boxers including Jersey Joe Walcott and Sugar Ray Robinson. When Jackie Robinson and Roy Campanella broke into major league baseball, they played with a team that practiced in Cuba. On their way to and from Cuba they would stay in Colored Town.

Nearly all of the arts were available continuously through touring music, dance, and theater performances. Singers Paul Robeson and Marian Anderson were among the artists featured (fig. 13). Colored Town's Northwest Second Avenue, known both as "the strip" and "Little Broadway," which developed into the "Great Black Way," offered popular music and entertainment.

Black entertainers who performed on Miami Beach could not stay there because of racial segregation laws. As a result, after their last performances, they headed back across the railroad tracks to Colored Town's hotels and nightclubs. They often held jam sessions for the local residents, sometimes until daybreak. Count Basie, Ella Fitzgerald, Cab Calloway, Josephine Baker,

Fig. 13. Paul Robeson arriving

in Miami, c. 1940s.

Billie Holiday, Sammy Davis Jr., the Inkspots, Louis Satchmo Armstrong, Nat King Cole, B. B. King, and many others performed year-round (fig. 14).

Entertainment promoter Clyde Killens brought the black stars who were performing on Miami Beach, along with some who were just being discovered, to Miami to perform in Colored Town. Born in Valdosta, Georgia, Killens relocated to Miami in 1924, when he was in his teens. His first job was at the Lyric Theatre, playing drums during silent movies and vaudeville shows. In the late 1920s, he and Georgette Campbell, a friend from Waycross, Georgia, opened a confectionery store, the Ramona Inn. Located on Northwest Second Avenue across the street from Artemus Brown's blacksmith shop, it became a hangout for waiters, waitresses, and chauffeurs.

Killens is best-known for managing hotels and nightclubs and promoting entertainment. The nightclubs he managed were located on Northwest Second Avenue from Northwest Sixth Street to Tenth Street. They included the Nut Club, the Elks Club, the Fiesta Club, the Fiesta Club across the street from the Mary Elizabeth Hotel, the Fiesta Club located in the Mary Elizabeth Hotel, the Lord Calvert Hotel, the Night Beat located in the Sir John Hotel, and the Island Club located in the Harlem Square Club.

Black and white residents and visitors were enticed to the area by word of mouth and by continuous advertising in the *Miami Times* and the *Miami Herald*. Active in civic affairs, Killens was one of the first residents in Colored Town to register and vote in the 1920s, and he encouraged others to do the same. These were brave acts in the era of Jim Crow, when black people were intimidated. Killens, who is now retired, still lives in the Art Deco-style house he shared with his late wife, Ova, for more than forty years.

One hundred years ago black people were the primary work force in South Florida. They helped create Miami's major industry — tourism. They were ambitious. Collectively and individually they came to the wilderness and helped make it a tourist mecca. Their ambition and courage resulted in significant accomplishments, including thriving cultural and business communities, despite the limitations of racially motivated customs and laws. □

Fig. 14. Billie Holiday at Georgette's Tea Room, c. 1950s.

Fig. 1. Igor B. Polevitzky, Michael Heller residence number two, the "Birdcage House," 1949. Photograph by Ezra Stroller, Pictorial Services, Inc.

Igor Polevitzky's Architectural Vision for a Modern Miami

By Allan T. Shulman

Allan T. Shulman is a practicing architect who teaches at the Florida International University School of Architecture, Miami, Florida and the University of Miami School of Architecture, Coral Gables, Florida. He currently is working on monographs on Morris Lapidus and L. Murray Dixon. He received his B.Arch. from Cornell University and his M.Arch. in Suburb and Town Design from the University of Miami.

Between 1934 and 1978 Igor Polevitzky (1911–1978) designed more than five hundred buildings in South Florida and the Caribbean. He explored the gamut of Florida building types, taking into account the most significant aesthetic and functional architectural issues of the emerging tropical city of Miami. The breadth of his work is impressive in that Polevitzky rejected repetition — each project was a complex initiative responding to the particular client, climate, and site. He did not subscribe to an established architectural doctrine, preferring to develop a creative and personal style. Polevitzky had a thematic interest in spatial elements suitable to the tropics such as courtyards, loggias, porches, terraces, raised galleries, and patios. He experimented with the theme of the building envelope, which he progressively distorted and reduced from the white planar masses of the Bauhaus until the envelope itself became little more than a frame. He investigated the possibilities of movement and the corollary implications of the progression of spaces in his designs. Finally, he delved into the innovative programming and iconography critical to the emerging resort structure of Miami. The significance of Polevitzky's work lies in his consistent intent to make architecture appropriate to living in Florida and responsive to Florida's developing urban and suburban landscapes (fig. 1).

Polevitzky was an important transitional figure in the development of South Florida's architecture. He realized the intrinsic value of vernacular and traditional building elements such as the patio, porch, and loggia, yet came to view these not as fixed elements but as spatial themes. Combined with the open plan in his early work, these elements began to take on new forms, often becoming part of the structure itself. Polevitzky developed techniques governing the gradation of space from indoor to outdoor, with nuanced levels of partial protection in between. This progression became thematic, establishing the logic of the entire structure. By adapting the climatic necessities of Florida to the language of Modernism, abstracting, and finally amplifying these elements to define the whole structure, Polevitzky explored the Florida house in ways it had never been seen before and has not been seen since.

Igor Boris Polevitzky was born in St. Petersburg, Russia, in 1911, the son of Boris Polevitzky, an electrical engineer who at one time was mayor of the Russian port city of Murmansk. Cast out during the Russian Revolution in 1918, the Polevitzky family took refuge in Finland until 1922, when they moved to the United States and settled in Philadelphia. Igor studied engineering at the University of Pennsylvania in 1929 but later switched to the prestigious department of architecture. The excellent reputation the university enjoyed at the time was partially due to the presence of Paul Philippe Cret (1876–1945), the architect and critic most associated with Modern Classicism, whose works

Photographs and drawings from the Historical Museum of Southern Florida, except where noted.

and writings engaged issues of functional planning and up-to-date styling. Under the tutelage of Cret and others, the school remained officially Beaux-Arts, but the cutting edge of the Modern movement was never far from the surface.[1]

Polevitzky graduated with honors in 1934 and moved to Miami. He was part of the first group of architects to give a Modernist face to Miami and Miami Beach. This group included Robert Law Weed (1897–1961) and Thomas Triplett Russell (born 1910), a classmate from the University of Pennsylvania with whom Polevitzky formed a partnership in 1936. Isolated from the lingering effects of the Depression, Miami's population was growing at a rate of ten percent per year by 1935, and tourism was increasing as well. Architect Richard Kiehnel (1870–1944) wrote in *Florida Architecture* in 1935 that "prosperity is no longer just around the corner, but is actually facing us on all sides."[2] After the Depression, between 1934 and 1941, Miami and Miami Beach saw an unfolding transition to an architectural vocabulary that increasingly embraced Modernism. Modernism was an important link between distant Miami and contemporary American ideas and practices. This connection nurtured a regional style in Florida as local architects used the style to focus attention on the functional and aesthetic implications of climate and landscape. This symbiosis of Modernism and regionalism in Miami provides the background against which Polevitzky's work must be viewed.

World War II interrupted the pace of construction in Miami and Miami Beach, ending Polevitzky's partnership with Russell. Polevitzky remained in Miami Beach, working as the chief engineer for the Army Air Force. In the postwar era, as national prosperity once again thrust Miami into another important wave of development, Polevitzky opened his own office. He practiced alone until he formed a partnership with Verner Johnson (born 1916) in 1955.

Indeed, postwar Miami was changing from a seasonal resort city into a permanent year-round metropolis, intensifying the necessity of creating a livable environment in Florida's most severe summer weather. Polevitzky — along with such architects as Robert Little (born 1903), Marion Manley, Rufus Nims (born 1913), and Alfred Browning Parker (born 1916) — developed a vision of Florida in which finding the appropriate architecture for the tropical environment led deeper into pure functionalism. Polevitzky's designs evolved in an almost scientific progression of experiments aimed at defining comfort in the tropics. This intense interest was partly a by-product of his personal struggle with Florida's climate, a result of a chronic skin allergy. Polevitzky's numerous projects during this period developed around a central theme: defining an "envelope for living."

By the 1950s Polevitzky was a confirmed, if regional, figure of American Modernism. His work was seen as innovative and functional because it addressed issues considered central to the Modern movement in the United States: contextualism, a responsiveness to environmental factors, and a creative use of materials and techniques. His personal dialectic of regional Modernism, which he adapted to Florida, earned Polevitzky recognition outside Miami. His work was extensively published in *Architectural Record* as well as in *Architectural Forum*, the "major distributor of International Style

1. Thomas Triplett Russell, interview by author and Jean-Francois Lejeune, at Russell's home in Punta Gorda, Florida, February 1997.

2. Richard Kiehnel, *Florida Architecture and Allied Arts* (Miami: February 1935). *Florida Architecture* was in effect a promotional yearbook of projects organized under the headings of Miami's architectural firms.

Fig. 2. Robert Law Weed,

Florida Tropical Home, rear

elevation. From *The Florida*

Tropical Home at A Century

of Progress 1933 (New York:

Kuhne Galleries, 1933). The

Mitchell Wolfson Jr. Collection,

The Wolfsonian, Florida

International University,

Miami Beach, Florida.

values among magazines."[3] Although Miami had no architectural school at which Polevitzky could express his vision, his growing fame in the 1950s resulted in invitations to teach at the University of Illinois, Cornell University, Syracuse University, University of Florida, Washington University, and elsewhere.

The emergence of a Modernism tempered to the tropics was one of the great creative forces in Miami, making the city an important architectural laboratory. However, the first tangible example of this style, and arguably the most influential one, was not built in Miami. It was Robert Law Weed's 1933 Florida Tropical Home, featured in the Home and Industrial Arts group at the 1933 Century of Progress Exposition in Chicago (fig. 2). The exhibit home illustrated and advocated the Modern style as useful and appropriate to "modern living" in general, and more importantly, as uniquely conditioned to the landscape and climate of Florida. The point was emphasized by Earl Brown (1890–1963), the manager of the exhibit home, in the accompanying brochure: "Nowhere in America has architecture been so thoroly [*sic*] adapted to local conditions as it has in Florida, and the Florida Tropical Home is the last word in the small home architecture of Florida."[4]

The elements of the Florida Tropical Home helped define Florida's regional Modernism — airy two-story living spaces; the idea of living on rooftops expressed in nautical roof decks; porches and loggias covered by thin concrete slabs supported on pipe columns or cantilevered concrete beams; windows protected by projecting concrete canopies (termed "eyebrows"); and a smooth appearance, which veiled a building's structural logic.

Polevitzky and Russell absorbed the lessons of the Florida Tropical Home and built in a Modern style that rejected excessive stylism. Within the synthesis of Miami Beach Moderne, they defined for themselves a position closest to the principles of the Bauhaus and International Style. Their early commissions

3. Terry Smith, *Making the Modern* (Chicago: University of Chicago Press, 1993), 399.
4. Earl W. Brown, "Florida—Where Summer spends the Winter," *The Florida Tropical Home at A Century of Progress 1933* (New York: Kuhne Galleries, 1933).

Fig. 3. Igor B. Polevitzky and Thomas Triplett Russell, J. A. Benson residence, exterior, 1937. Photograph by Samuel H. Gottscho.

Fig. 4. Igor B. Polevitzky and Thomas Triplett Russell, J. A. Benson residence, double stair, 1937. Photograph by Ernest Graham.

were a series of residences built in Miami Beach. The Benson residence (1937) illustrates the composition of these early houses (figs. 3 and 4). Like the Florida Tropical Home, it was an assemblage of two-story and one-story volumes topped with roof decks, but it was composed in a pinwheel fashion. Smooth and white, the house was kept narrow to promote ventilation, and had a projecting concrete roof plane that shaded the terrace. The play of verticals and horizontals in the design was punctuated by a freestanding chimney. The juxtaposition of interior and exterior, seen in the solid-void contrast of this composition, extended to the central feature of the house: the stair. This winding concrete stair was mirrored on the outside wall of the house. The two stairs — divided by nothing more than a glass window wall — foreshadowed the ambiguity between interior and exterior spaces typical in Polevitzky's later work.

Like the Benson residence, the Alvin Greif residence (1938) was composed of two-story and one-story volumes, but here the two-story block was sheltered by a gently sloping roof with broad overhangs, a solution much more appropriate to South Florida's sun and rain. The house had a cruciform plan. At the intersection of the two volumes Polevitzky and Russell placed the stair hall. In the Greif residence, the shifts of level and orientation created by the stair were critical to the sequence of movement through the house. These shifts animated its open plan layout. The entry sequence began on axis with the fireplace, which also provided the focus of the living room. The front entrance led into a paved forecourt enclosed by the garage, low walls, and planting. At that point, a new axis led from the front door into the two-level entry hall, the back corner of which was entirely cut away and sheathed in glass. A shift at the stair landing led to the dining room, an exedra that penetrated the back of the house as an almost purely transparent screen of glass and metal running from the floor to the cantilevered roof slab. Such spatial themes (the closed forecourt, the cut-away volume of the stair hall, and the dissolution of the building envelope at the dining room) echoed throughout Polevitzky's work.

Located on a narrow lot, the Greenwald residence (1939) was developed along the lot's depth (figs. 5 and 6). The main body of the house was organized like a Venetian palazzo, a tripartite scheme with rooms around a central hall forming a long living/dining space running directly from the front to the back of the house. The vista into the house was dominated by a drive court formed by the placement of the garages and by a cutaway corner of the stair hall through which a winding staircase made a dramatic appearance. From the glass front door and two-story entry hall to the living room and finally the dining room, a visual trajectory was established directly through the house. The back wall of the ground floor faced the southeast trade winds and was slit horizontally by a continuous ribbon window. To reach the backyard terrace, one turned sideways into the screened porch and then back again to the rear terrace. The sequence of spaces that progressively unfolded toward the environment — from the enclosed living room to a well-lit dining room to a screened porch and finally to the outside — introduced what Polevitzky would later describe as the "four stages of indoor-outdoor living."

At the same time that he designed these rather elaborate houses, Polevitzky developed the "Tropotype" house model — so named because it was devised specifically to suit the Florida tropics. In the Tropotype, Polevitzky gave the plantation house a Modernist face, constructing it largely of concrete and articulating it in cubic and planar terms. The Tropotype shows Polevitzky's early interest in creating a home appropriate for Miami. Architect Steven Holl has

left,

Fig. 5. Igor B. Polevitzky and

Thomas Triplett Russell,

Jay and Florence Greenwald

residence, exterior, 1939.

From *Architectural Forum* 71

(October 1939): 294.

right,

Fig. 6. Igor B. Polevitzky and

Thomas Triplett Russell,

Jay and Florence Greenwald

residence, winding stair, 1939.

From *Architectural Forum* 71

(October 1939): 294.

shown that although the raised cottage was explored by such twentieth-century architects as Le Corbusier and Frank Lloyd Wright (1867–1956), in the Southeastern United States it was a common response to the problem of dampness, promising second-story living in shaded galleries, improved views, and air circulation.[5] Polevitzky designed his first Tropotype house as a model home for the Seaway Corporation and built it in 1935 in Surfside. The idea certainly was borrowed from the plantation-house model and perhaps even from Miami's historic Barnacle (1891), the home of Ralph Munroe on Biscayne Bay in Coconut Grove. The kitchen, dining room, and parking were on the ground floor; the living room and bedrooms were located upstairs and had access through wide French doors to a broad wrap-around gallery.

The gallery was not recessed into the structure but cantilevered out from it. The tapered concrete beams supporting the balcony were plainly visible. The thin-slab roof was similarly cantilevered to completely shelter and de-emphasize the volume of the house. The stark white cantilevers floating above the Florida landscape were an assertion of uncompromised modernity. The scheme was reflected at the ground level, where a smooth parterre of grass and paving corresponded with the cantilevered balcony above.

The Tropotype house had rich progeny in the years between 1935 and 1941 and was even reiterated in the postwar years. The Sailing Baruch residence on DiLido Island (1938) formalized the scheme with an almost Palladian four-directional equilibrium in the organization of the plan and a frontal double stair and porte-cochere (fig. 7). A 1950s variation on the same scheme, the Yount house project, reduced the gallery to planar slabs enclosed by diaphanous screens.

By the mid-1930s the southern portion of Miami Beach was evolving into an urban landscape with hotels and businesses built in close proximity. Restaurants, commercial buildings, and hotels designed by Polevitzky and Russell during this period illustrate the firm's contextual approach to the city. Economics

5. Steven Holl, "Plantation House," *Pamphlet Architecture* 9 (1982): 23.

Fig. 7. Igor B. Polevitzky and

Thomas Triplett Russell, Sailing

Baruch residence, the

"Tropotype" house, 1939. From

Architectural Record/Building

News **87 (March 1940): 74.**

would play an important role in shaping these buildings. The rising value of land and the restricted size of most building lots meant that even the most complex building had to be carried out in compact spaces, thus fostering new urban types. Combined with the modern imagery of the 1930s, these buildings helped establish a new monumentality and urban dimension for commercial resort architecture.

One such project was the Gulf Service Station and Hotel (1936) at the MacArthur Causeway entrance to Miami Beach, which blended the ill-matched elements of gas station, hotel, and restaurant, effectively merging the realms of commerce and leisure. The centerpiece of this project was a lighthouse containing a restaurant at its base as well as a radio room, with an operational beacon above (figs. 8 and 9). On a symbolic level it was an entrance monument to Miami Beach; its beacon (visible from Miami) was perhaps inspired by the nearby Flamingo Hotel, which had a celebrated dome of colored glass that served largely the same purpose. The lighthouse also functioned as a hinge between the ground-floor service station and second-floor hotel. A composition of intersecting canopies — one covering the office, service areas, and a bait-and-tackle concession, the other reaching out dramatically towards the causeway entrance — made the service station seem to float, an impression reinforced at night when it was illuminated. On its waterfront edge, a stair and terrace wrapped the base of the lighthouse, leading to the hotel lobby. The cantilevered roof of the gas station provided a gallery entrance to the hotel units above. A ground-floor loggia composed of arches (a curious reference to Miami's Mediterranean Revival style) connected the restaurant with a parking lot located in back of the complex. The success of the scheme came not only from the separation of the various tourist facilities but also from the integration of those facilities around the theme of the lighthouse beacon.

The Lincoln Center Hotel and Office Building (1938) epitomized the approach that Polevitzky would employ in several projects on Lincoln Road, Miami Beach's famed shopping street. The layout coupled an ordinary commercial block containing ground-floor shops and two additional floors of offices

Fig. 8. Igor B. Polevitzky,
Gulf Service Station and
Hotel, 1936. Photograph by
Samuel H. Gottscho.

Fig. 9. Igor B. Polevitzky,
Gulf Service Station and Hotel,
1936. Photograph by Samuel H.
Gottscho. Russell Partnership,
Inc. collection.

▼

(never built) with a hotel that wrapped the other three sides of the property to form a shared patio court. The commercial block faced Lincoln Road, while the entrance of the hotel fronted Euclid Avenue, a residential side street. The synthesis of commercial and hotel buildings paid homage to Miami's legacy of courtyard buildings, but the Lincoln Center was a new mixed-use building type.

The patio was an amenity for hotel guests and also invited shoppers and other passersby to enter, thus functioning as an extension of the street. The patio was neither isolated nor inward-focused. It was connected to Lincoln Road by a narrow commercial arcade. A second arcade, at a right angle to the first, linked the glass-enclosed hotel lobby to the residential side street. The mass of the hotel was lifted on Corbusian "pilotis," with shop spaces below. The resulting arcade incorporated the hotel lobby while affording some separation between public and private spheres. The entire scheme was extremely austere, except for an azure- and gold-tiled fountain in the center of its landscaped patio and a projecting canopy over the hotel entry topped by the cast-concrete hotel sign. These features punctuated the flow of the ground-floor spaces between the patio and street. This connection of the landscaped patio with the surrounding streets characterized Polevitzky's "patio" solution at the Lincoln Center.

The Albion Building, designed two years later, was an even more ambitious exploration of the same hybrid patio scheme (figs. 10, 11, and 12). Designed for Harry Sirkin, the developer of the Lincoln Center and a lifelong patron of Polevitzky, the Albion was located just off Lincoln Road. It was a seven-story, 110-room hotel tower facing a residential side street, a commercial block of offices and stores facing Lincoln Road, a restaurant, and an elevated pool structure, all composed around a patio court. These four elements revolved around the courtyard in a way that emphasized its centrality. The building occupied its whole site and was a self-contained resort, not unlike a cruise ship. The imagery of smokestacks, portholes, streamlined corners, the roof deck, and above all, the rooftop sign reinforced that analogy.

As in the Lincoln Center, two major axes connected from the surrounding streets into the complex. The first, originating on Lincoln Road, arrived at the patio through an arcade and ended in a long and narrow terrace. A curious feature of this terrace was that its wall was pierced with portholes that allowed viewing into the elevated pool from the patio. The second axis was completely transparent: it incorporated two-story glass window walls on both sides of the lobby to connect the street to the patio visually, a trajectory that rested at the facade of the restaurant block beyond. The patio with its terrazzo dance floor and surrounding landscaped buffer therefore linked the lobby and the restaurant. On the mezzanine level a series of "decks" wrapped around the patio, ending in an artificial sandy beach and cabanas constructed over the roof of the restaurant. All the elements of Florida as a resort were thus swept into one structure — shopping, dining, social activities, swimming, and even the beach.

The facade of the Albion used a syncopated rhythm. Continuous horizontal detailing contrasted with punctured openings that offered a counterbalancing vertical emphasis. The commercial block's facade was composed of continuous projecting eyebrows and an uninterrupted band of zigzag windows slit into the wall. Horizontal window bands wrapped around the streamlined corner, interrupted at intervals by porthole windows and other features. Giant channel letters perched on concrete pylons capped the corner. It is worth noting several features that can be seen as quotations from the International Style. First, the vertical blue glass Vitrolite band on the Lincoln Road facade of the hotel structure imparted the idea of a curtain wall. Second, the alternating

Fig. 10. Igor B. Polevitzky and Thomas Triplett Russell, Albion Building, 1939. Photograph by Samuel H. Gottscho. (Address: 1650 James Avenue, Miami Beach, Florida.)

Fig. 11. Igor B. Polevitzky and Thomas Triplett Russell, Albion Building, courtyard view, 1939. Photograph by Samuel H. Gottscho.

Fig. 12. Igor B. Polevitzky and Thomas Triplett Russell, Albion Building, private rooftop solarium, 1939. Photograph by Samuel H. Gottscho.

projections and recesses of the building mass on the top floor implied a habitable roof deck. The impression was reinforced by the cantilevered roof slab pierced at intervals with round holes, perhaps inspired by Philip Goodwin and Edward D. Stone's Museum of Modern Art building completed the year before.

Their restrained architectural approach earned Polevitzky and Russell the commission to design a new store on Lincoln Road for Saks Fifth Avenue. The facade was designed in an austere planar fashion of highly polished oolitic limestone veneer with one-inch strips of stainless steel and an abstracted cornice of fluted limestone as its only articulation. The windows were small and set flush in the plane of the facade. Polevitzky repeated the themes of reducing a commercial facade to a planar slab or counterbalancing the facade with a slab-like signage pylon in almost all his commercial projects. For instance, at the Just Gas Station (c. 1955), the structure and the sign became, in effect, one.

Polevitzky used diverse building elements with a central spatial focus in two small restaurant projects where he volumetrically inverted the atrium to create a large, enclosed dining room. Fan and Bill's Dining Place (1936) in Miami Beach was essentially a central dining room surrounded by subsidiary spaces, including the kitchen and a famous icebox where the restaurant's prize-winning beef was stored (and was visible through a plate-glass window). An especially dramatic feature was a nautical dining gallery supported on pipe columns attached to the front facade. The dining room was connected to the street by an open stair, emphasizing indoor-outdoor dining. The 7 Seas Restaurant (1945) followed roughly the same scheme (fig. 13). A lozenge-shaped double-height dining room, encrusted with ornamental aquatic features, was in the center. Around it were clustered private dining rooms, a bar, a sidewalk cafe, an upper-level deck, a banquet room, and kitchens. At one end, a circular stair led to the second-floor banquet hall. From the street the hall was plainly visible, a dominant sight. An enormous pylon on top announced the restaurant to downtown Miami's central shopping district, Flagler Street.

Polevitzky and Russell's first oceanfront hotel was the Triton (1938). The narrow, three-story building was typical of South Beach's smaller hotels yet exhibited a monumentality quite different from the "skyscraper" and Art Deco motifs of its neighbors. Against a backdrop of brown-glazed terra-cotta tiles, a window wall exposed the full lobby. The cast-concrete "sky-sign" was fused to the top of the facade, as an element of the cornice. Most significant, however, was the dramatic relief of a sculptural element placed in front of the building. Following the Modernist premise that "ornament, if used, should be in scale, original and relevant to its setting," a statue of Triton riding a dolphin and blowing a conch shell was designed for the site by Trip Russell's brother, William Russell (fig. 14).[6]

The thirteen-story Shelborne Hotel (1940) represented a more profound evolution of the oceanfront-hotel type (figs. 15–19). Built on a narrow site, the hotel was located at the center of a sequence of spaces leading from the street to the Atlantic Ocean. The approach swept from the street to the glass front of the lobby underneath a concrete canopy on steel columns. A drive court bordered the canopy, and the shape of the canopy was in fact defined by the automobile circulation. For the first time in Miami Beach, arrival by car was treated as the equal of pedestrian approach.[7] The glass entry wall, reflecting the Modernist concern for maintaining the panorama of the view, was designed to allow a straight view of the distant ocean from the entry. The voluminous lobby led into the pool and cabana colony in back. A dramatic winding stair leading to the mezzanine punctuated the lobby space. The main axis was actually diagonal, toward the irregularly shaped dining room. The dining room faced southeast to catch the breezes and was designed on two levels to give a maximum of diners a commanding view.

If the Albion was introverted, the Shelborne was extroverted. The front-to-back hierarchy of the hotel acknowledged that eastern views and breezes were desirable but the western sun was problematic. The schism between east and west was elaborated in the conflicting imagery of each facade. The tower largely turned its back on the west (street) side, which was partly occupied by stair towers. In the fashion of Miami Beach's Moderne hotels, the Shelborne's west facade hinted at a periphic development while remaining fundamentally frontal. It was inherently compositional, mitigating the building's apparent volume with a combination of projecting canopies and decorative tile treatment and articulated further by eroded corners. The windows were an assemblage of projecting horizontal and vertical elements. At the northwest corner a dramatic sky-sign bore the hotel's name. Engineered and cast in concrete, the S was twenty-eight feet high and ten feet wide.

On the east facade the solid mass of the tower was stepped back to provide an ocean view and balconies for a maximum of rooms. Though the Shelborne was one of the few steel-frame structures on Miami Beach at the time, the facades were actually block curtain walls with Miesian balcony trays and continuous horizontal window treatment. The composition was symmetrical and extremely horizontal. In contrast to the west facade, the articulation of the east facade was rendered in the idiom of the International Style.

Polevitzky and Russell described the Shelborne through the prism of the International Style: "Running counter to the currently prevailing design trend, which was Art-Deco, with its mediocre planning and its meretricious decoration,

Fig. 14. Igor B. Polevitzky and Thomas Triplett Russell, Triton Hotel, 1938. Photograph by Samuel H. Gottscho.

---

6. *The Work of Polevitzky and Russell 1936–1941*, typed, from the collection of Thomas Triplett Russell. The date of compilation is unknown, but is presumed to postdate Igor Polevitzky's death in 1978.

7. "The Shelborne Hotel, Miami Beach, Polevitzky and Russell Architects," *Architectural Record* 90 (July 1941): 41–46.

Fig. 15. Igor B. Polevitzky and Thomas Triplett Russell, Shelborne Hotel, 1940. Photograph by Ernest Graham. (Address: 1801 Collins Avenue, Miami Beach, Florida.)

this building was designed in the simple Bauhaus manner, devoid of useless ornament and planned to take maximum advantage of its fine site."[8] Considered locally to be "Florida modern design," it drew the praise of both architects and architectural magazines. Morris Lapidus (born 1902), visiting Miami prior to his hotel work in Miami Beach, recalled that he considered the Shelborne "the finest hotel in Miami Beach."[9] Lapidus later built an extension to the Shelborne, an addition he remembered executing with extreme modesty and respect for the details of Polevitzky and Russell's original masterpiece. One may speculate that perhaps Lapidus considered the dramatic lobby space, with its winding stair, in the formulation of his own ideas of hotel design; such theatrical staircases were to become a Lapidus trademark in hotel lobbies.

The Center Hotel and Office Building project of 1945 (for Harry Sirkin) was never built, but it represented the culmination of Polevitzky's interventions on

8. *The Work of Polevitzky and Russell 1936–1941.*
9. Morris Lapidus, interview by author, Miami Beach, Florida, 9 March 1997.

Fig. 16. Igor B. Polevitzky
and Thomas Triplett Russell,
Shelborne Hotel, view from
drive court, 1940. Photograph
by Ernest Graham.

Fig. 17. Igor B. Polevitzky
and Thomas Triplett Russell,
Shelborne Hotel, detached
glass lobby enclosure, 1940.
Photograph by Ernest Graham.

Fig. 18. Igor B. Polevitzky and

Thomas Triplett Russell,

Shelborne Hotel, lobby, 1940.

Photograph by Ernest Graham.

Fig. 19. Igor B. Polevitzky

and Thomas Triplett Russell,

Shelborne Hotel, lobby, 1940.

Photograph by Ernest Graham.

Fig. 20. Igor B. Polevitzky,

Center Hotel (project),

rendering, 1945.

Lincoln Road and offered a fascinating glimpse of the world to come (fig. 20). Incorporating a blend of commercial and residential uses around an open space, the design seemed to reiterate all of the earlier Lincoln Road themes. Yet in the five years since building the Albion, the terms of both function and style had changed. The project was more akin to the pedestal-tower structure of contemporary buildings. The ground-floor retail component of the scheme grew to the proportions of a multilevel shopping center, the increase in its mass partially accounted for by the requirement for parking. The hotel block was turned to better receive the southeast trade winds. The west-side rooms had a sawtooth configuration, allowing each room to have a balcony facing north. The lobby of the unbuilt Center was to be entered on an angle from Lincoln Road, and was the central focus of the scheme. Its grand, multistoried space was to be enlivened by the amoeba-shaped cutout that revealed an upper mezzanine.

In an area now known as "Motel Row," at the northern end of Collins Avenue, north of Miami Beach, Polevitzky built two projects using a mix of hotel and bungalow types. At the Golden Strand Hotel (1947), two five-story hotel structures built along the coastal highway were designed to provide ocean views over the rooftops of a complex of cottages. The scheme created a microcosm of a tourist environment, with the promenade between street and ocean as its central feature. The two-part hotel structure was joined at the roof, creating a framed entry to the complex. The path, sheltered by a concrete canopy supported on pipe columns, soon forked. The scale was immediately reduced to that of a residential complex. At the end, one descended a pedestrian "street" framed by the cottages, each consisting of a two-bedroom unit with a terrace. One arrived finally at a private beach and boardwalk from which one could look back at the cottages and towers. The scheme had the character of a planned community but was informal in its layout and articulation. The Golden Gate (1950), now demolished, expanded the theme of the Golden Strand to include a swath of land between the ocean and Biscayne Bay. Here the hotel was located on the narrow beach, while the rest of the complex was to its west, moving toward the bay in a mix of cottages and low-rise hotels structures. Polevitzky returned to the use of the signage pylons in this area, placed symmetrically across the highway to frame the road.

After World War II Polevitzky's attention shifted more directly to the challenges of Florida living, of which the house appeared to be the unequivocal statement. To Polevitzky and his contemporaries in Miami, the design of the house was inseparable from the issue of indoor-outdoor living. Thus, his Florida houses were shaped by the gradation of space from inside to outside, and such concerns as shade, insects, and breezes took on primary importance. Polevitzky codified this response to the environment into a series of basic rules: wide overhangs, second-floor living, the big-screened patio, and exposure to the southeast trade winds. Though these issues figured prominently in his prewar architecture, in the postwar era Polevitzky looked upon them as thematic, form-giving issues.

Polevitzky's postwar architectural experiments connecting house and environment can be seen as belonging to two categories: explorations of the patio type and the porch type. Polevitzky investigated the patio through the technique of the screened enclosure. The porch type was explored as a space enclosed by a significant roof and the ability to fully open the house, primarily in one direction; the porch was an indoor space, but it was flexible and adaptable to various weather conditions, as well as loosely zoned for function. Polevitzky's work in both areas led to his idea of a Florida-tempered envelope for living, or "atmospheric envelope."

Between 1947 and 1949 Polevitzky designed two adjacent houses in Miami Beach for Michael Heller. The earlier is notable for the elaboration of the screened patio as an extension of the living space (figs. 21 and 22). The screened patio was not a new element, but here it was, as *Architectural Forum* remarked, "extended to its logical conclusion, an airy large (nineteen-by-thirty foot) cage, framed in aluminum, screened in stainless steel mesh and 'roofed' with a sliding aluminum awning which is parked under the eaves when not in use."[10] The screened patio, almost as large as the house itself, has been renamed the "Outdoor Living Area" and comprises changes in level, a pool, and landscaping, creating a quasi-natural environment. The patio

10. "Tropical House with Aluminum Screened Porch for Outdoor Living," in "40 Houses: Architectural Forum Special House Issue No. 14," *Architectural Forum* 88 (April 1948): 119.

punched directly through the mass of the house, terminating in an angled window wall. It is particularly interesting because here Polevitzky assembled the essential features of year-round living—kitchen and living room—as an extension of the patio. The bedroom was separated from the living room by a louvered wall, yet these rooms could be closed with sliding-glass doors on cold nights.

In the later Heller house, dubbed the "Birdcage House," the screened enclosure expanded to become the main formal volume of the house, enclosing almost everything (figs. 23 and 1). Perhaps there was no more direct expression than this of the first underlying principle of the International Style: architecture as volume. The "birdcage" itself was a simple frame of plain wood and steel trusses supporting a flat roof. The indoor elements of the house were mainly at ground level, tucked under the concrete upper-level deck and set back from the slab edge to allow its enclosure by the screens, which came down to the ground. This effectively inverted the relative importance of house and screened patio, with the patio literally forming a multilevel stage on which life was acted out.

The "Birdcage House" was a tempered environment for living, without the protective features of the traditional house. It was, as much as possible, invisible and transparent to its surroundings—where the aluminum screen of the first Heller house was expressive, the "Birdcage House" was neutral. The partially covered environment was large enough to include a swimming pool and full-size black olive trees. The connection between interior and exterior was softened by the extensive use of glass and the overall rusticity of the house; enclosed portions of the house were rendered in exposed and waterproofed concrete block, which, though expensive, allowed the "satisfaction of exposed craftsmanship."[11] The house was considered relevant enough to the discourse on modern architecture to be included in Museum of Modern Art's 1952 exhibition and catalogue *Built in the USA–Post War Architecture*, the influential survey of postwar American architecture curated by Henry Russell Hitchcock and Arthur Drexler.[12]

11. "Bird-cage House," *Architectural Forum* 92 (May 1950): 138–141.

12. Henry Russell Hitchcock and Arthur Drexler, *Built in the USA–Post War Architecture* (New York: Museum of Modern Art, Simon and Schuster, 1952).

Fig. 24. Igor B. Polevitzky, Gibbs residence (project), c. 1955.

A series of houses that probed the tectonic possibilities of the "Birdcage House" followed. The Phillips' residence (1952) sat completely on the ground. It had a shed-type roof and sloping screen walls. The simple screen envelope intersected an L-shaped house layout to enclose a pool area. Because the house was at ground level, a baffle wall provided privacy. At the Braznell residence (1958) the screen was a large shed, where screened areas and enclosed areas meshed seamlessly within a common structure, and where the living area was lifted off the ground, reversing the scheme of the Heller residence. At the Gibbs residence (c. 1955), a never-built project, the experimental use of the traditional A-frame structure in forming the volume of the screen enclosure is notable (fig. 24).

The Houck residence (1950) was one of Polevitzky's porch-type houses. It was composed of elements that pinwheeled dynamically around a central living area. The exposed timber structure and screened walls transmitted the impression that the room was a large porch. The Schulman house (1951), also dubbed the "Porch House," crystallized the porch idea much as the "Birdcage House" did the indoor-outdoor patio (figs. 25 and 26). The porch spanned the full width of its suburban lot, and the entire living area of the house was subsumed by the roof of the porch. The house was almost entirely open on the side facing Biscayne Bay, closed only by a screen of vertical sash windows, which disappeared into pockets in the floor. The opposite long facade was a screen wall of wood jalousie louvers. The organization of the interior created total openness under the roof. In this layout, elements such as fireplaces and partition walls were the devices to achieve a spatial zoning. In effect the house was transformed into a porch for the contemplation and enjoyment of views and nature.

The well-adapted Florida houses that Polevitzky designed in the postwar era were both numerous and influential. Although one might infer that his practice was dominated by the domestic program, the breadth of his work was in fact extraordinary. Unlike many architects of his time, Polevitzky did not specialize, but rather took pride in addressing the range of building types. He was the consummate architect, giving form to everything. His work included shopping centers, gas stations, water-treatment plants, stores, schools, dance studios, and auto showrooms. These projects often revealed a crossover of ideas

Fig. 25. Igor B. Polevitzky,
Samuel E. Schulman
residence, the "Porch House,"
rendering, 1950.

Fig. 26. Igor B. Polevitzky,
Samuel E. Schulman residence,
the "Porch House," 1950.
Photograph by Rudi Rada,
RADA Photography.

Fig. 27. Igor B. Polevitzky,

Arthur Murray Dance Studio,

1948. Photograph by Ezra

Stroller, Pictorial Services, Inc.

(Address: 767 Arthur Godfrey

Road, Miami Beach, Florida.)

from Polevitzky's domestic work, especially in the treatment of the building skin and the progressive opening of spaces toward the environment. The Arthur Murray Dance Studio (1948), for instance, had a ballroom with a convertible roof that could be retracted, exposing the dance floor to the stars (fig. 27).

It was in the familiar realm of the hotel that Polevitzky built one of his most important designs of the postwar era: the Havana Riviera (figs. 28 and 29). Designed in 1957 for Meyer Lansky, and built on Havana's Malecón during the last boom days of pre-revolutionary Cuba, the Riviera belonged to the group of hotels that Polevitzky had earlier pioneered, including the Shelborne Hotel and Center buildings.

The exposed structure of the sleek Y-shaped hotel was emphasized by the concrete structural floor slabs that exceeded the volume of the walls in all directions. Polevitzky emphasized the plasticity of the structure by scalloping the slabs on the leg of the Y, giving the entire building a sculptural quality. The exterior walls, set back behind the slab edge as well as behind the exposed structural columns, were expressed as nothing more than light infill panels, an impression reinforced by the alternating pattern. The relationship was repeated, although somewhat overstated, in the entry porte-cochere of the hotel, where a concrete slab was cantilevered over a skewed diagonal wall.

The Havana Riviera Hotel block was lifted off the ground floor on columns, allowing an open-plan sequence of hotel facilities to run completely through the structure, from the entry drop-off to the extensive pool and cabana deck with its elegant and multistoried diving platform. Like the Albion of twenty years earlier, the lobby was completely transparent, with views to the Malecón and

Fig. 28. Igor B. Polevitzky and Verner Johnson, Havana Riviera Hotel on the Malecón, Havana, 1958.

Fig. 29. Igor B. Polevitzky and
Verner Johnson, Havana
Riviera Hotel on the Malecón,
Havana, 1958.

Fig. 30. Igor B. Polevitzky and Verner Johnson, Havana Biltmore Hotel (project) in Havana, c. 1958.

Fig. 31. Igor B. Polevitzky and Verner Johnson, Sea Tower Apartments, 1959. Photograph by Bill Hedrick, Hedrich-Blessing. (Address: 2840

North Ocean Boulevard, Fort Lauderdale.)

Fig. 32. Igor B. Polevitzky and

Verner Johnson, Seaview

Realty, ground level, 1959.

the water beyond. Polevitzky also designed the hotel's interiors, which were largely austere, though set off by rich use of materials and elements of relief applied to the walls. The Riviera was a gambling hotel, and the casino formed the most important element of the ground-floor plan. It was a circular domed hall, with gilded, sculpted walls.

For a second Havana hotel that was never realized, the Biltmore (c. 1958), Polevitzky designed a low-rise serpentine block with its lobby expanding beneath a concrete shell (fig. 30). The shell undoubtably was influenced by the concrete vaults of the airport terminals by Eero Saarinen (1910–1961) and Minoru Yamasaki (born 1912). The exterior walls of the hotel block were to be screened with a rustic precast screening system, a device that would be explored in the Sea Tower Apartments (1959), one of two oceanfront towers in Fort Lauderdale (fig. 31). There, the oceanfront facade was articulated by ribbons of decorative precast-concrete railing containing the balconies behind which the building walls were entirely glass. The western exposure was solid, punctured only by small windows. Decorative precast-concrete screens alternated in a pattern, shading the front doors and providing a striking impression from the street.

Screens were used again in one of Polevitzky's last commissions, the Seaview Realty Building (1959) (figs. 32, 33, and 34). This project brought together many of the themes of his career. It was a composition of two elements: a cylindrical office block and a wedge-shaped lobby block that faced Biscayne Bay. The office tower was internalized, opening through corridors and plate-glass walls to a "hole." In a reversal of the traditional atrium scheme, this hole was roofed with a dome punctured by colored lights in order to create atmosphere. The entire office block was lifted on pilotis, allowing a landscape of discus-shaped

Fig. 33. Igor B. Polevitzky and Verner Johnson, Seaview Realty, view across atrium, 1959.

Fig. 34. Igor B. Polevitzky and Verner Johnson, Seaview Realty, plastic dome covering atrium, 1959.

bowls and circular planters and pools to flow underneath, closed above but opened below, and thus continuous with the landscape. Although the exterior of the cylinder was substantially glazed, it was sheathed in knobby precast-concrete "solar-screens" used to shroud the building from the surrounding commercial avenue. In contrast, the wedge-shaped lobby framed open terraces and glassed-in spaces designed for viewing the bay. Here the structure was exposed, the skin of glass alternating with colored panels. The combination of doughnut and wedge formed a bipolar scheme, effectively reversing inside and outside, and the opposites of enclosure and openness were experienced repetitively in the process of moving between floors.

In the mid-1960s Igor Polevitzky left Miami. Years earlier, he bought and remodeled a ranch in the drier climate of Estes Park, Colorado. Increasingly ill and in search of relief from his worsening skin allergies, he permanently left Miami and the practice he built. Later confined to a wheelchair, he died in 1978.

For a variety of reasons, Polevitzky's legacy in Florida has remained comparatively obscure. In spite of his responsibility for the influential Albion and Shelborne hotels, Polevitzky did not play a major role in the formation of the Art Deco character of Miami Beach. Furthermore, his postwar buildings belong to a regional Modernist language that has not, in general, won the worldwide appreciation that prewar Moderne architecture or a more universally expressed International Style can claim. Cosmopolitan, well-educated, analytically minded, but somewhat diffident, Polevitzky was among the most respected but least appreciated of Miami architects. His work was considered intellectual and avant-garde, and although he was well published, he seems to have made little effort to explain or popularize his approach. Thus, his adventure in evolving an architecture for Florida was an inherently personal one.

Sadly, Polevitzky's patrimony in South Florida is severely diminished. Although the Albion Hotel, one of the most significant structures in Miami Beach and one of his greatest buildings, has been reopened, many other structures have been demolished or otherwise severely transformed. Ironically, the architectural style Polevitzky chose contained the seeds of its own demise. He interpreted Modernism as a mechanism of symbiosis between man and the natural environment. Future interpretations would otherwise view Modernism as a tool for perfecting man's environment, a direction that would lead to the wide use of air conditioning by the 1960s. Air conditioning dead-ended Polevitzky's experiments in Florida living, and caused the obsolescence of his houses, which were not easily adaptable to the sealed boxes required by mechanized climate control. One wonders whether the irony was clear to Polevitzky, whose allergies forced him to work and even live in the air conditioned environment of his office.

Polevitzky's vision of Florida living can still inspire an architecture of connection with the environment. For him the magic of the tropical landscape and climate were not in their representational or associative qualities; rather he emphasized the gentle, embracing qualities of a tropical atmosphere that allowed individuals to live in the outdoors. The central focus of his architecture was to reduce the distinction between inside and outside. His work never succumbed to the creation of fantasy. Polevitzky always preferred to remain rooted in the realities of client, site, and environment. In this sense his vision transcends Modernism as a vision unique to Florida. □

Note

Preliminary research for this essay was a joint project of the author and Jean-Francois Lejeune.

Fig. 1. From *left to right*, Wilho Anderson, Corrine Anderson, Alison Kay Silverthorne, and Paul Silverthorne. Photograph taken in the main dining room of Lou Walter's club, The Latin Quarter, Miami Beach, 1945.

Pragmatism Meets Exoticism: An Interview with Paul Silverthorne

By John A. Stuart

John A. Stuart is an assistant professor in the School of Architecture at Florida International University, Miami, Florida. He earned his M.Arch. at Columbia University and is a recent recipient of grants from the Graham Foundation for Advanced Research in the Fine Arts and the National Endowment for the Humanities.

Paul Silverthorne was one of the most successful of a small group of mural painters and interior designers active in South Florida in the 1940s (fig. 1). Born in 1914, Silverthorne left his native Toronto for New York in 1939. Shortly thereafter he moved to Miami Beach, where he lived until 1953. At that time he returned to Toronto, where he continued to practice as an interior designer (fig. 2). While in South Florida, Silverthorne won several of the most competitive bids for murals and interior design projects and worked with the most productive architects and builders of his day. This interview explores Silverthorne's experiences and discusses his insights on issues that are largely ignored in traditional accounts of Miami history — issues of building and business practices, professional negotiations within the design profession, patronage, gender, and race relations.

An innovator and businessman, Silverthorne purportedly introduced the first pink neon to Miami Beach (the start of a long and illustrious history) in the outdoor signage of the Sherry Frontenac Hotel and challenged paint makers to introduce new tints reflecting those that occurred naturally in the aquatic life of South Florida. His greatest innovations, however, were in the creation of complete interior environments that brought together color, light, painting, and sculpture. In the Fu Manchu Restaurant, for example, Silverthorne and his collaborators enhanced the two-dimensional wall with the unusual addition of an enormous red lacquer sculpture of a Buddha. Female customers were notified by a sign on the statue that rubbing the Buddha's belly would ensure the birth of male children. Although a joke, this is an example of Silverthorne's characteristic desire to promote interaction between visitor and design.

All photographs are from the Mitchell Wolfson Jr. Collection, The Wolfsonian, Florida International University, Miami Beach, Florida.

Silverthorne's muralistic style and the content of his wall paintings before World War II were similar to the work of other muralists in South Florida at the time, including May and Sherwood Allen, Kenneth De Garmo, Howard Hilder, and Cora Parker. After the war (and the invention of a glue and wallpaper system that would hold up under the sometimes brutal South Florida humidity), he revealed his talent for the creation of the complete interior experience. The best examples of this include his designs for the cocktail lounge at the President Madison Hotel (fig. 3) and the Sapphire Room at the Belmar Hotel. In the latter project, Silverthorne created one of the most outrageously lavish entertainment spaces in postwar Miami Beach, using an ornately crumpled fiberglass ceiling to conceal lights that changed color with the flip of a switch, pink glowing lights in the settee, padded walls with mirrored rosettes, white plaster ornament, a dance floor, and reflective tubular steel chairs and tables.

top,

Fig. 2. Club One Two in Toronto,

Ontario, Canada, 1953.

top,

Fig. 2. Club One Two in Toronto,

Ontario, Canada, 1953.

below,

Fig. 3. The cocktail lounge at

the President Madison Hotel,

Miami Beach, c. 1948.

PRESIDENT MADISON
-COCKTAIL LOUNGE-
COMPLIMENTS,
RUBY & WALLY

Two major ironies arise in considering Silverthorne's work. First, although he was a very successful mural painter and designer, the record of his work is contained almost entirely within the Silverthorne archives in The Wolfsonian, where he has deposited a large collection of the photographs, drawings, and newspaper accounts that remained in his possession. Archival research in Toronto and Miami, the two cities he lived and worked in longest, did not yield significant additional information. The reasons for this are many. Silverthorne's career was based on his ability to produce new designs and create spectacular effects as efficiently as possible for a demanding social elite. This same clientele of club and hotel owners ruthlessly covered Silverthorne's murals and had his interiors redesigned to keep up with the latest trends. Combined with the popular notion that interior design and mural paintings were a "secondary" art form, this economy of newness has left only photographs and drawings. No remaining Silverthorne interiors are to be experienced in South Florida. In the late 1970s Silverthorne again became a prominent figure in the Miami Beach design community and worked closely with the newly formed Miami Design Preservation League. Unfortunately, preservation efforts came too late to save his own work. When the El Chico Club fell to the wrecker's ball in 1980, it took with it his last remaining murals from the 1940s (fig. 4).

The second irony involves Silverthorne's pragmatic discussions of his projects in light of their fantastic iconography. His murals were windows into faraway dream worlds based on images of such places as Mexico, Norway, and the Far East. Likewise, many of his club interiors were executed as complete works of art, with ceilings, walls, furniture, and lighting offering the visitor a fantasy within the fantasy that already defined the experience of South Florida in the 1940s. Silverthorne, however, rarely discusses the iconography of his work. Instead, he emphasizes the importance of the savvy business practices and high levels of efficiency closely associated with the successful creation of these evanescent environments. As indicated by his closing remarks on his two favorite parts of a project—"Collecting the money!" and "Opening night!"—Silverthorne combined pragmatism with exoticism in the culture of design emblematic of the phenomenal growth experienced by South Florida in the 1940s (fig. 5).

This interview with Paul Silverthorne was conducted in Miami Beach on 29 March 1997 and is the second of two undertaken in February and March of 1997. Throughout the interview Silverthorne examined archival photographs of his projects.

JS: How did you get started in your career as a muralist and interior designer?

PS: I was born on 24 April 1914. I was born in Toronto, Ontario, Canada, where I grew up, went to school, went to art school, and spent most of my life until I was about twenty-five. I am mostly self-taught. I went to high school and was there until the third month of the third year, when I decided that I wanted to be an artist. I transferred from the Jarvis Collegiate High School in the beginning of my third year to Toronto Central Technical Institute where they had a four-year art course. I took the four-year art course and was only able to complete two years. All of my work is based on those two years in the art course. The teacher I had in my second year for floor-plan layout and perspective was an Englishman we used to call "Mr. Orthographic Projection." He was a marvelous teacher. The basic ingredients that I derived and took from this man were the foundation for me becoming a top designer later in Miami Beach. I could bid against the best in America. This man contributed to my financial

Fig. 4. Page one newspaper article. From the *Sun Reporter* (Miami Beach), 3 April 1980.

Fig. 5. Sapphire Room at the Belmar Hotel, Miami Beach, opening night, 1946. Standing in back are from *left to right*, Paul and Alison Kay Silverthorne. Seated in front, *second from left*, is Wilho Anderson.

and competitive welfare more than any of my other teachers. I owe him a great deal.

JS: After Toronto, you took one of your first jobs with the Eugene Dunkel Studios in New York City, working on sets for the 1939 World's Fair. What was your experience with that project?

PS: That was amazing. They [Eugene Dunkel Studios] hired me. But at that time I was lucky. They were under pressure because they had so much work, and they could not get qualified people, even in those days. They gave me a chance. I worked as an assistant to the owner's son. He was the main scenic artist. And I had experience with that from working at the Loew's Uptown Theatre [in Toronto]. My father used to make the uniforms and tuxedos for the orchestra leader, and I met the scenic artist for the theatre chain. My father used to make his clothes, too. Red McLean was his name. He liked me. I showed an interest in his work. And he started me off as a paint boy. He showed me how to scale things up from a drawing this big [six-by-twelve inches] to the size of a prop on a theatre stage. I learned all that from this man. When I went down [to New York] I had a pretty good background. They saw that I knew what was coming next, and they loved that. I got paid thirty-five dollars per week and thought I was a millionaire. I worked on Billy Rose's Aquacade, *Streets of Paris, Little Old New York*, and there were several others I do not recall. I worked on about a half-dozen [projects]. Once the flats were painted at the studio and trucked out to the World's Fair, I went out to supervise the installation and touch-up. I was going back and forth for about five or six weeks on the subway. And that was very good experience for me. When I got through, I could handle anything.

JS: After working in New York, what drew you to Miami?

Fig. 6. Mural at the Sunny Isles Casino by Wilho Anderson and Paul Silverthorne, Miami Beach, 1939.

PS: I moved after a ten-week summer job up in the mountains as a scenic artist and stage manager taking care of a recreation hall. I ran the dances and the shows. I lined up the entertainment for the weekends and the parties. It was an all-around scenic artist and stagehand kind of job. It was after Labor Day when I came down to Miami. I am a chronic sinus sufferer. And the fall came on and the wet weather, and I got an infection. A doctor, who knew my background as a champion swimmer and diver, said, "Why don't you go down to Miami for the winter, down to the nice warm sunshine. Spend a winter there. The weather here affects your sinuses." I thought this was a pretty good idea. I decided to hitchhike to Florida. I started at the Holland Tunnel and in forty-eight hours I was in Miami. I landed at Biscayne Boulevard and the MacArthur Causeway. I took a jitney across to the beach. I got out at Eighth Street and Washington Avenue at the turn-around. I walked over to the beach opposite the Avalon Hotel just as the sun was going down. The sun was on top of all these cumulus clouds with pinks and roses…brilliant colors…they just took my breath away. I stood there looking around in amazement at the turquoise sky, the sea, and the sand. And it just mesmerized me. I said, "This is for me." And I crossed the street and there was a clapboard two-story building. This kid who was travelling with me and I hired a hotel room for five dollars per week — split it $2.50 each. That's where I started. That was on a Friday, and the next day, Saturday, there was a penny-ante poker game on the living-room table with a half-dozen young guys there and loose change. I met the artist Wilho H. Anderson. I told him who I was and what my background was. I asked him where I could get some work. He said he had a mural job. That was the first job I worked on.

JS: What job was that?

PS: That was at the Sunny Isles Casino (fig. 6). He had the job to do a panel up there. And I asked him if he could hire me. He said he could, but he couldn't pay me much. I said, "What can you pay me?" He said, "Fifteen dollars per week." I said, "Sold!" I grabbed anything to get started. I didn't know a soul. I had come two thousand miles and had to earn my keep, pay my way. That was on a Saturday night. On Monday morning I went up to the Sunny Isles Casino on 163rd Street on the fishing pier up there. I started to work with him on this job.

JS: What was Wilho Anderson's reputation up to that point?

PS: I had only met him. But from what I could gather, he was a Pratt Institute graduate, and he had gone out to Hollywood to paint portraits of the stars, pastel and oil portraits. He travelled around the country to resorts where the money was. That was during the height of the Depression, and he was doing pretty well for himself as a young man. He was confident and drove a big Buick. He was doing fine.

JS: How would you characterize the Miami Beach you discovered when you arrived?

PS: When I got here, as I understood it at that time, this seemed to be a place where only wealthy people could afford to come, in those years, during the height of the Depression. Poor people couldn't afford to come to Florida. They didn't have the cars, they didn't have the highways. This was a little pocket of moneyed people who had their winter homes here and their clubs where they could party behind stone walls and have their fun and games and look at everybody's clothes as they came in. This is the background and the reason I was able to find work. Because I happened to be an artist, and a good one at that, I was able to fulfill their artistic needs. I was hired for that talent. And that's the way I made my living.

JS: What was it like for you and other young artists in Miami Beach in 1939?

PS: It was brutal. It was the survival of the fittest. Andy [Wilho Anderson] and a few others of us survived. There were about six of us all told: Andy and I, Earl LePan, he was there about ten years before we were and was older. Then there was Gustav Poland, a sculptor, and Paul Simone lived right next-door to me. His work was up on the Beach. He was a fine artist. The last one was the Russian, Raymon Chatov. His work is in the Nautilus Hotel. That was the extent of it. We competed against each other. There was enough work at that time to go around. Andy and I did a major part of it. We did the biggest, most important jobs.

JS: Could you tell me about the residential projects you completed on Miami Beach?

PS: Well, while working on the Sunny Isles Casino job, we met the owner, Joe Stehlen. Through him, we met his wife, Dorothy White Hoover. She had just come back from a round-the-world cruise. She had stopped at Bali and picked up these Balinese batiks and brought them home. There were hand-painted figures on these things. She had built a twelve-by-fifteen-foot addition onto the west side of her house and had built herself a little cocktail lounge that could seat ten, twelve, maybe fifteen people. She asked us what we could do…and we proceeded with the work.

JS: What was involved in creating a mural like this?

PS: The batiks were about eighteen-by-twenty-four inches or something like that. The figures were no bigger than three or four inches high. I had to scale them up.

JS: How did you scale them up?

PS: I just did them by eye. Whatever fit in a certain place, I fit in there. It was all freehand. All done with a number two brush.

JS: What were the colors?

PS: Reds and…the background in a flesh tone, a tan, a neutral all the way around.

JS: Why were murals so popular in the residential interiors of the time?

PS: It wasn't a question of being popular at that time. It just so happened that I was lucky enough to get the finest home in Miami Beach to set an example of the kind of work I could do. She [Dorothy White Hoover] knew about it because she was a member of the Surf Club, and she knew of the sets and scenery I was doing there. That's why she invited me to her house to see if I could do something for her. When I saw what she had brought back from Bali, I realized the importance of it and how beautiful it would look.

JS: Did you produce a set of drawings as a proposal for her?

PS: No, there were no drawings! She furnished me with it and told me that this is what I was going to transfer and add it like wallpaper. I explained to her what I was going to do. She knew the kind of work I did and just said go ahead and do it. She figured it would come out all right. And it did (fig. 7).

JS: Why were people doing murals at the time?

PS: Well, it was just her up until that time. She was the one who started the pattern. She set the style. When she opened and had her first cocktail hour or a party like that, all these people from the Surf Club and the Bath Club came down…and, well, it was the talk of Miami Beach. Everybody wanted to go to Dorothy's house for a private party among her hand-painted murals. It sold itself.

JS: Would you say that the murals were first painted in the clubs before they became popular in residences?

PS: I had to paint sets and scenery for parties there [the Surf Club and Bath Club], for Christmas parties, Valentine's parties, the "Way Down East" party, Thanksgiving parties. I painted the sets and scenery for the dining and other rooms as the background for these dress-up parties at the Surf Club and the Bath Club. It created a sensation. So all these people came up to me and gave me their name, address, and telephone number and asked me to come do something for them. She [Dorothy White Hoover] was a style-setter, a trailblazer. That's the way one thing led to another. She was the best advertisement I had in Miami Beach. I was lucky, as an artist. I took advantage of it, and I made a living at the height of the Depression when most artists were starving to death.

JS: Were you doing this with Andy?

PS: Yes, while I was working on this, he was working on other things. He'd come in and help me with the partnership, then he'd go off and line up another job. Andy was lining up the Surf Club and the Latin Quarter and other places.

JS: From what I understand, you painted many of these murals while the clubs remained open. How did you find your role as both artist and entertainer?

PS: We didn't mind it. We weren't actors. But we didn't mind it because it was the opening wedge to people who had the money and could afford the hand-painted murals in their homes. Ordinarily we would finish a job in three or four weeks, but this one [the El Chico Club] we spread out over the fall into November, December, and January, during the height of the season. This was so we could meet the people who had the homes and had the money, who could afford to have this thing done. That's why we were so successful. I danced with the wives, I drank with them. There were two of us there. I'd be up on the scaffold painting, while Andy would be discussing a job. And that's the way we survived.

JS: Can you describe the colors?

PS: Well, the El Chico Club was done in a monotone royal blue and white. It looked very photographic. There were ten panels, five on one side of the room and five on the other with a big scene of Guadalajara, Mexico across the bandstand that was about fifteen feet wide (fig. 8). They had a Cuban band, a rumba band, and a circular dance floor in front of the bandstand. Tables and settees were placed around the perimeter of the room. And people would come in for cocktail hour at four o'clock, sit and drink there and eat all the way through the whole evening until twelve, one, or two o'clock in the morning. Andy and I would be painting and drinking and the owner of the club would offer us the best of food and that's the way we got along.

JS: Did you work with architects in Miami Beach?

PS: Yes, architects would come in for dinner or drinks and we met them: Igor Polevitzky [1911–1978], Trip [Thomas Triplett] Russell [born 1910], Roy France [1888–1972], Robert Swartburg [1895–1975]. This was the main hangout for the crowd, the "in" crowd.

JS: How would you describe the architectural community on Miami Beach at the time?

Fig. 8. From *left to right*, Paul Silverthorne, Corrine Anderson, and Wilho Anderson in the El Chico Club, Miami Beach, 1940.

PS: It was all Art Deco-style buildings that the architects had designed and built. It was not as colorful as it is today. We were a lot more conservative in our taste and what we did…[today] they go one step further, let's put it that way. I mean, in their outlandish color schemes.

JS: Did you have a favorite architect to work with?

PS: Igor Polevitzky was the best. He did the biggest and most important jobs. When he put us in the Clover Club, I mean, that was an important job. And he put us in the Club Bali and those were important places. We stuck pretty close to whatever he wanted.

JS: What was Polevitzky's reputation?

PS: He was the top Modern-style architect in the whole Beach. His work created the most attention, like the Shelborne Hotel. He was written up all over. We were very fortunate to be able to tie in with him and also with Roy France and, occasionally, Robert Swartburg. Of course, I worked with Henry Hohauser [1895–1963] on the Sherry Frontenac. We got these architects because they saw our work and when you work with some of the architects we worked for, you must know your business. And that would help us get jobs.

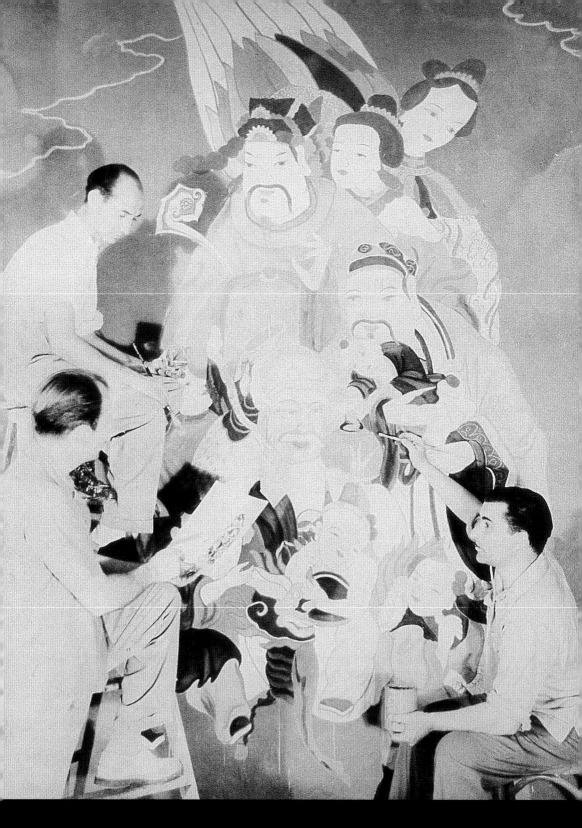

Fig. 9. From *left to right*, Paul Silverthorne, Wilbo Anderson, and assistant in the Fu Manchu Restaurant, Miami Beach, 1940.

Fig. 10. From *left to right*, Paul Silverthorne, assistant, and Wilho Anderson sculpting the Buddha in the Fu Manchu Restaurant, Miami Beach, 1940.

JS: The Buddha sculpture in the Fu Manchu Restaurant is a very interesting project. Were there any other large-scale interior sculptures in Miami at that time?

PS: No. There were a lot of attempts to copy it later. That was actually the very first one of that size in a restaurant in the country (fig. 9). It weighed a ton. It had a steel armature, chicken wire all built up to within a few inches of the top and covered with concrete. We hired a sculptor to mix the concrete (fig. 10). We scraped, polished, and sanded down the concrete so that it could take a lacquer paint job. We then sprayed it with Chinese red lacquer. It sat up on a two-foot dais that led down to a temple that was on the back wall that was about twenty to thirty feet long.

JS: Had you already left the monochrome blue and white behind?

PS: It just happened that this job was in full color. There was another, Sun Hoy Restaurant, where we did four panels, two eight-by-fifteen-foot panels and two four-by-twelve-foot panels. These were done in a monotone blue. One was the scene of Yangtze River with all the boats done in a monotone blue and white. It was on Fifth Street, between Washington and Collins [Avenues] on the north side of the street. That was a very popular place that was torn down. It's a parking lot now. But most of our jobs were done in full color.

JS: You were an active GI in World War II from 1941 through 1945. When did you work on the murals for the Hopkins Potter residence?

PS: This was the very first job that I did after the war. I got out 11 August 1945. I don't remember where I found Mrs. Hopkins Potter, but I think it was through Dorothy White Hoover. She invited me up there. This was the very first money I earned after the war, and she gave me this job to do on her back patio where she used to sit in the evenings. She had a photograph of her home in Grandview, Illinois. It showed a picture of her garden out in the back of her

home. It was a gorgeous garden. She asked me if I could transfer the garden onto the walls of the patio so she could sit on her sofa and look out on her garden at home that she missed so much. And that's what I did for her, and I got $1,200 for that little work around there (fig. 11). That was August, September, and October 1945.

JS: Were most of your residential clients women?

PS: Yes.

JS: Why?

PS: Most of them were rich women who controlled the money. This is what they wanted, and this is what they had because they could pay for it themselves. That's why it sold. Most of these guys were kept men!

JS: Would men be involved in the interior design of their homes?

PS: Very rarely. I can't remember anybody offhand in the male department. Clem Levine, I think was one, just a couple hundred yards down the street from Dorothy's house. But he was the only one. And all he wanted me to do was a copy of what Dorothy had. He had been invited to one of the parties, and he was one of the guys who pulled me aside and asked me to do something at his house, and I copied some of Dorothy's…I went from house to house.

JS: Then there was a chain of women who knew each other?

PS: That's right. One would recommend me to the other. That is the only way you could get in the door. I couldn't walk up to the front door and say, "I'm a mural painter." They would have thrown me out and sent the police after me. But I started with Dorothy White Hoover, and she made my reputation. She [Mrs. Hopkins Potter] came to her house, and they both came from Grandview, Illinois, by the way.

JS: How did the mob activity on Miami Beach at that time affect your work?

PS: It only provided more work. I had a good rapport…They relied on me heavily to get things done for them…They were my best customers. I was well paid by them. I only had trouble with one during the 1945–1946 season. It was called the Riptide, right across the street from the Grand Hotel where my partner lived. I did a $12,000 or $15,000 alteration. He paid me completely up until the last $1,200. I used to call on him once a week, on a Saturday night. We'd go out and have some drinks, and I would try to collect a payment on what he owed me. One Saturday I went down there to see him and demanded my money. I met him in the back kitchen. He got real hot. Threatened me. Threw a cleaver at me. I ran out of there and didn't know what the hell to do. This hood was threatening me. I had worked for Sam Cohen who was head of the bookie syndicate at the Island Club and Gray's Inn. I had never had trouble with him. He was a beautiful customer, a good payer. I decided I'd go down and tell Sam my troubles. He had his office in the Mercantile National Bank Building. He said, "Young man, you meet me at Gray's Inn at supper time, seven o'clock tonight. Come and see me there. We'll see what we can do." That night I went to Gray's Inn, and he waved me in. There were about eight of them sitting there at a big round table. He stood up and pulled a wad of money out of his pocket. He peeled me off twelve one-hundred-dollar bills. "There's your money kid, we don't go for that crap around here," he said. "You go back there anytime you want to. If he raises a finger to you, you just let me know." I never had any more trouble. That's the way I got my money. I didn't go to court. I went to the father.

JS: The next season you worked on the Sapphire Room in the Belmar Hotel. This seems to be an important moment in your career.

PS: Yes, that was the 1946–1947 season. This was after we had done several other jobs. This pair of brothers, Al and Paul Pollack, called us up to look at this big bare room. The room was just concrete floors, high, twenty-foot ceiling. It was used as a warehouse. And they came to us and asked us what we could do for them. This was a couple of weeks before New Year's. They wanted to get it ready based on a contract that said that we would be paid half the cash in advance, and half when we completed the job. If we didn't complete the job on time, we would forfeit the balance of our payment. This was a bare room — no plumbing, no electric, no air conditioning. Everything that went in there was installed in ten days. It was incredible. It was impossible. It was all padded walls with fiberglass blocks and Baroque plaster ornament. And there was a fireproof drop ceiling hung on wires with clips. It was all made in a special factory in New York by an expert who did festooned ceilings. His name was Joe Dobish. He was famous for this kind of ceiling. We had to give him a design and size. He would make it and send it down. It arrived in pieces and all we had to do was string the wires we had prepared. Our shipment caught the last train out of New York before the railway embargo. We were lucky to get [our supplies] on that thing. Otherwise, we would have lost all our money. There was a shortage of materials and a strike! We searched around eleven or twelve o'clock at night with flashlights on a seventy-five- or a hundred-car freight train to find that car, open it up, and haul all this stuff out so we could get it strung up on time. It was insane. I was a skinny little toothpick of a guy, and I don't know where I got the energy to do this. In the meantime the other guys were stripping the walls and putting stuff up. People were coming up to the big windows in the club, which were open to the boardwalk on the ocean side, and tourists in the hotel were walking by, and when they heard it had to be done in ten days, they would bet fifty-to-one or ten-to-one that I would never make it. And I kept grabbing these people…I took thousands of dollars into the safe in the manager's office. I got twenty-five hundred-dollar bets that it couldn't be done! But it got done (fig. 12).

We were going twenty-four hours a day. If we needed any sleep, we laid out a sheet of plywood and took a little nap. It was on the eighth day when he [Andy] collapsed. We laid him out on a sheet of plywood. And he stayed there while I ran around checking on the subcontractors, keeping them lined up. You had to have people you could trust to put the particular features of this nightclub together — like the carpet, the dance floors, the bars, the bar equipment, stainless steel, all the padding, all the brackets coming down from New York. Nobody could do that here. It had to come down from New York. To get that all timed and put together, so that we could have that nice New Year's party in the hotel for all those people.

JS: Was this project the last you completed in partnership with Andy?

PS: Yes, Andy was also a portrait painter, as fine a painter as they came. And he could make beautiful money just painting portraits — sitting on his fanny a few hours a day, then going out and playing golf. Come cocktail hour, he would be smoking his cigars, drinking booze, and talking with the people in the lobby. He had an easel set up in the corner. He was making money hand-over-fist. He made a lot of money and would get so busy I would go help him at night. I made extra money myself that way. He'd line up people and get so much business he couldn't handle it. I would do the preliminaries for him. I would take the photographs, blow them up, and transfer them to the paper. This was after the war, when all that war money was coming. We were charging seventy-five to ninety dollars for just a head and would complete seven to ten portraits a night. We were making a lot of money.

JS: Then you continued working for him in that capacity?

PS: Off and on. He would go away for the summer. I had a wife and kids; I couldn't leave. He would follow the tourists, go up to the tourist resorts in Maine and New Hampshire and come back after Labor Day and work Miami Beach for the winter. He had a good racket.

JS: What was your first "solo" project in Miami Beach?

PS: That was the Baroque Room at the Albion Hotel (fig. 13). As a matter of fact, they just finished redoing it. A new person took it over. I saw it the last time I was here. It was all gutted.

JS: How did you get the commission?

PS: Well, two guys came down from Philadelphia and took over the Albion Hotel. I took them around and showed them the Sapphire Room and one or two of my previous jobs and they hired me. This was right after the war. I found this beautiful piece of fabric. It had a white background with multicolored greens, blues, reds, and it had accents…gorgeous. Then I got "Schwarzy" [Robert M. Schwarz] to come over. I gave him a layout of these groups [of plaster sculptures] for this wall and that wall. Then we used pink, flesh-toned lights to throw out a pink glow on the white plaster. In other words, it was gorgeous, a hot pastry kind of an atmosphere. It was lavish, let's put it that way. When people would come in the door, their eyes would open with the color of the design. And it made a hit! It became a popular place. They would line up outside waiting to get in there.

JS: Were places that were lavish like the Albion more popular than simple modern spaces?

Fig. 12. The Sapphire Room at the Belmar Hotel, Miami Beach, 1946.

Fig. 13. The Baroque Room at the Albion Hotel, 1946. (Address: 311 Lincoln Road, Miami Beach.)

Fig. 14. The Sherry Frontenac

Hotel, front view, 1947,

Henry Hohauser, architect.

(Address: 6565 Collins Avenue,

Miami Beach.)

PS: The more lavish, the better. It was very hokey. But this is what they wanted, and this is what they liked. And when you went into a space with all that pink light flaring up, well, that was really something to see. It gained a reputation. When some people started to come, others wanted to come there too. This was the headquarters for the hoods. They would meet in the back.

JS: Had you worked with Schwarz before this project?

PS: Oh, yes. We started out and worked together right after the war. After the war we did a lot of this stuff. It was very popular. We didn't know he existed until after the war. Examples of his work can still be seen around Miami Beach, statues and other items are still here. He had a studio on Southwest 8th Street.

JS: Your largest project on Miami Beach was the Sherry Frontenac Hotel (figs. 14, 15, and 16). Can you describe how you managed to win the bid?

PS: It was the late summer of 1946–1947. I think it opened on New Year's, 1948–1949. I drove by [the Sherry Frontenac] every day, and as they got closer to deciding who was going to design it, I paid daily visits on the way home to see what was happening. Of course, at that time everybody on Miami Beach in the design business who was big enough to do a project of this size, like Maxwells, Eden Strauss, Fort Lauderdale decorators, Palm Beach decorators, and others from around the country, came down in droves to try to get this job. It was the biggest job to go up since the boom. It was really a feather in anybody's cap. I never thought I had a chance of ever getting it. But I had a good background, a good reputation for getting things done. People with whom I had worked before highly recommended me. These were things that paid off for me. When the owners went around town to check the jobs I had

Fig. 15. The Sherry Frontenac Hotel, ocean terrace, 1947.

Fig. 16. The Sherry Frontenac
Hotel, cocktail lounge, 1947.

done and the people I had worked for, that is what pushed me to the fore-front. They called me. And it went on for several months, this back and forth, this dickering with competition. People would come and make offers and pre-sentations. But they waited right up to the last minute before they made a final decision. It was the largest design and decorating order in the history of hotels in that area and that time. This included a lot of back-stabbing and underhanded dealing, bribery, and everything went on in the preliminaries to get that job. Maxwells was after me and said that if I would get it for them, they would pay me and put me in charge.

JS: How did this affect your relationship with your competitors?

PS: They could see from the owners that I was there, and as they eliminated the others I still remained alive. They would question these people about me and they would give them word back, either good, bad, or indifferent, but mostly bad if they could. When they [the owners of the Sherry Frontenac] would say that I had never seen a three-hundred-and-fifty-room hotel, I replied that there had never been one built in that place since the boom, so neither had they! So when I put it to them that way, they nodded that that made sense. When it got down to right before the final decision, they were eliminating people right and left and I had gone over all the derogatory things people were saying against me. I took two bankbooks, one from Miami Beach, and one from Miami, and I threw them on the table. I said, "There, that's the kind of business I do as an interior designer every year. That represents five, six, maybe seven jobs a season. And all that work, I could concentrate on one job. I don't have to do all that. It would be much easier for me. But I want you to know that I do that kind of business on my own around this town. This is over $150,000 of business." They took a look at that and went into the back room, the three of them. I could hear them mumbling to one another and a few minutes later they came out and told me, "You got the job."

JS: Were there any special innovations of design in this hotel?

PS: This was the first colored outdoor [neon] sign in Miami. Everything else was in white. We used pink there. Mickey Kraus got it done for me from the sign people. And it's there to this day. I picked the French Provincial lettering. I picked the rosette placard on the front and hand-painted it myself. It's also still there. That was extra money. I got several thousand dollars. I started out small, but eventually made over $20,000 that season. I wasn't there every day. I was working on other projects at the same time.

JS: What other projects did you work on during this time?

PS: The Mary Elizabeth Hotel.

JS: How did you get that project?

PS: I was working at my table in the Sherry Frontenac when these two black men came up onto the platform and asked for Sam Cohen. Sam Cohen went over and talked to them. I could see him turn around and point in my general direction. He sent them over to me. They explained that they were Dr. William Sawyer, the first black pediatrician in Miami, and his son, Bill, and that they had a fifty-room hotel in Overtown. They asked me if I would come and give an estimate on a redecoration. They had heard about this job [The Sherry Frontenac] and me and explained that they had had difficulty getting people to do the job. They had asked Decorator Row [41st Street, Miami] decorators to come to Overtown, but nobody ever showed. I didn't know if I wanted to go over there either, because it didn't have a very good reputation then.

I happened to drive by there on Monday morning. I stopped and walked into the lobby. There was just a guy tending the desk and a few other people. It was in pretty bad shape. But I thought it could make a nice job. I went into the bar and saw what had to be done there. I didn't say anything to anybody, and I turned around and walked back on out. As I got to the door, Bill Sawyer came running out of his office and called me back in. I was the first decorator that had showed up. That had ever showed up! He took me around and explained to me what he would like done and asked me if I would present him with a proposal. I looked it over. I said I could do something. I got it done before the Christmas–New Year season (fig. 17). It got to be so busy, so lined up with people, that they decided to break through the wall and take over an eighteen-by-sixty-foot addition on the other side. He loved this design. What that little kitchen did for the money he made! I could do no wrong. He would give me anything I wanted. He would lend me anything I wanted. He made a lot of money. This was the best contract I ever had. The best cash I ever had in my life. They would pay me in cash, one-hundred-dollar bills.

JS: Did you paint the murals in the Mary Elizabeth yourself?

PS: Yes, I painted them myself.

JS: How did you choose the theme of the Zebra Lounge?

PS: I forget. I came upon it somewhere. I had to take the layout of the Zebra to my friend Schwarzy to see if he could do that relief for me. He said sure. So once I had that guy on my side, I was off to the races. The rest of the stuff was just furniture, tables, chairs, and design layout, stuff like that. I needed two zebras, one on either side of the door. He made them up for me and came in and installed them. I hand-painted all the stripes on them (fig. 18).

JS: What was the Mary Elizabeth like?

PS: Joe Lewis bought me lunch there. Cab Calloway drank with me. Count Basie played music for me. I met everybody there, Marion Anderson, Lena Horne…All the entertainers that entertained at the Cope Cabana and the Clover Club had to stay here. They couldn't stay on the Beach because segregation wouldn't allow them.

It also had a ballroom, or a dance pavilion, with a black orchestra. Oh geez, the lines and the screaming, the fights. People were fighting to get in. Everybody wanted to get in there. One night when Count Basie was there, after the show, they set up a little upright piano. He sat down and started tinkling his introduction to "The One O'Clock Jump," my favorite number. I won a contest dancing to that number. And, my God, the trumpet player, Bruce Sanders, came over, then the bass player came over, and they took their parts. They played music together. From the heart! Music that you never heard anywhere else. There were less than one hundred people in there and it was a privilege to be there! It was a most unusual experience for a white man!

JS: When did you leave Miami?

PS: In 1953. It was after I worked on the Jockey Bar and a number of projects downtown. After this the downtown contractors ganged up on me.

JS: In summary, what was your favorite part of a project?

PS: Collecting the money!

JS: And your second favorite part of a project?

Fig. 17. Paul Silverthorne with presentation board for the Zebra Lounge in the Mary Elizabeth Hotel, Miami, 1950.

PS: Getting it done! Opening night!

JS: Do you have a favorite project in Miami?

PS: The Sapphire Room.

JS: What made that space so special for you?

PS: Completing it in ten days! Look at what had to be done from a bare room in ten days and you'll understand. The pressure and tension, the force and drive that was required to keep that thing going and on track and making sure that nothing would go wrong…for the want of a nail, as the saying goes, the whole thing could have been destroyed.

JS: Do you have a summary statement about your career?

PS: I got the jobs done. And no one else could do what I could do. □

Note

The author wishes to thank Paul Silverthorne and his daughters, Andrea and Jeanne, for their cooperation, patience, and enthusiasm.

**Not everything in the
Museum of Modern Art
has earned a place
in our collection.**

But walking through Luminaire
you might think you are in the
Museum of Modern Art. Our
showrooms are an exquisite
curated collection of timeless design—

everything from a teaspoon to a
sofa—tended by intelligent
associates who will help make
Luminaire part of your environment.
So, if you want to visit one of the
great collections of
contemporary
furnishings, the
Museum of Modern Art will
do. But if you want to buy
from a great collection,
come to Luminaire.

LUMINAIRE®

Brilliant European Design. At Home. At Work.

Miami   2331 Ponce de Leon Blvd.
        (305) 448-7367   (800) 645-7250
Chicago 301 West Superior
        (312) 664-9582   (800) 494-4358

Charles Cowles Gallery

420 West Broadway
New York 10012
Tel (212) 925-3500
Fax (212) 925-3501

Charles Arnoldi	Patrick Ireland
David Bates	Harry Kramer
Howard Ben Tré	Doug Martin
Stephanie Borns	Wilhelm Moser
Marsha Burns	Manuel Neri
Dale Chihuly	Beverly Pepper
Gene Davis	Skrebneski
Elizabeth Enders	Toshiko Takaezu
Vernon Fisher	Peter Voulkos
Tom Holland	Darren Waterston

Bertha Lum "Mother West Wind" Woodblock 1918

The Arts & Crafts Movement
Twentieth Century Design: 1870 to Present
Furnishings . Studio Ceramics . Latin American & American Modernist Paintings

Bryce Bannatyne Gallery
2439 Main Street . Santa Monica . CA 90405 . 310.396.9668

LATIN AMERICAN ART

Miguel Covarrubias
(1904–1957)
*George Gershwin,
An American in Paris*
Oil on canvas
Painted in 1929
29⅞ by 39 in.
(75.9 by 99.1 cm.)
Sold for $244,500

SOTHEBY'S

FOR MORE INFORMATION ABOUT LATIN AMERICAN ART, PLEASE CALL ISABELLA HUTCHINSON or Cristina W. Vicinelli at (212) 606-7290 or fax (212) 606-7558. For a local representative in your area call Stefanie Block Reed at (305) 448-7882. To purchase illustrated catalogues, call (800) 444-3709; outside the continental U.S. call (203) 847-0465; http://www.sothebys.com Sotheby's, 1334 York Avenue, New York, NY 10021

LATIN AMERICAN ART

Amelia Peláez
(1896–1968)
Marpacífico
Gouache on paper
41 by 28⅜ in.
(104.1 by 72.1 cm.)
Signed and dated *1943*
Sold for $68,500

SOTHEBY'S

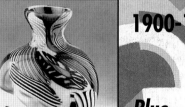

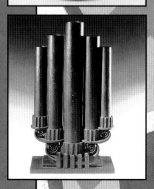

American Express

Cards

Establishment
Services

Travel

Travelers
Cheques

Corporate
Services

Small
Business

Financial
Advisors

Telecom

...we help people

do more

INVOLVED, CONCERNED, COMMITTED.

At Colonial Bank we believe that it's our duty to be *involved* in the communities that we serve. We are also *concerned* about the issues that are important to the people that live and work in these communities. Finally, we are *committed* to making things better, by improving the quality of life for this and future generations.

COLONIAL BANK
MEMBER FDIC

Dade: Miami Beach Main Office (305) 535-9100, Miami Beach Giller Building (305) 535-9140, Key Biscayne (305) 361-6451, Sunny Isles (305) 949-2121, North Miami Beach (305) 935-6911, Mystic Pointe/Aventura (305) 933-1516, **Broward:** Downtown Fort Lauderdale (954) 462-6093, Hollywood (954) 920-2265, **Palm Beach:** Boca Raton (407) 368-6900

MEMBER FDIC AND

EQUAL HOUSING
LENDER

small table
maple, ebony, glass

classically designed furniture, flatware, and china

bissell & wilhite co.

3875 Wilshire Boulevard, 12th floor Los Angeles, California 90010

213.380.2027 Fax 213.380.4037

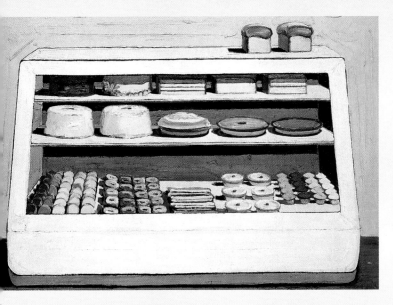

Miami Design Preservation League (MDPL) is a non-profit historic preservation group and arts organization founded in 1976 by the late Barbara Baer Capitman. It was the first of many Art Deco societies, and has led the worldwide movement to educate the public about early 20th Century architecture and design — and to protect it. MDPL has fostered appreciation of South Florida history, emphasizing the art, music, dance, fashion, photography and typography from the period between the two world wars. In 1996 the Society of American Travel Writers (SATW) awarded MDPL the prestigious PHOENIX AWARD in recognition of the role the League has played in reviving tourism in Miami Beach through the use of historic preservation.

MDPL's efforts gained stature because of the unique "Art Deco District" of Miami Beach, which members identified, surveyed and nominated to the National Register of Historic Places. The District was listed in the National Register in 1979, becoming the first 20th Century historic district. Today, twenty years after its founding, MDPL continues to sponsor activities which educate the public about the District, promoting it throughout the world. Most successful among the many activities are the guided walking and bicycle tours, the self-guided audio-cassette walking tour available daily throughout the week, and the world famous Art Deco Weekend® festival which takes place each January.

The 21st annual Art Deco Weekend® will take place January 16-19, 1998. This year's theme, ART DECO . . . ALWAYS IN FASHION, will celebrate the haute couture of the Deco era and the hot and sizzling fashions of South Beach today. The event, produced by the Miami Design Preservation League, begins January 12 with the week long film and lecture series by renowned historians, curators and educators from all over the world. The celebration culminates in a four day street festival on Ocean Drive, January 16 through 19 featuring an antique auto parade, Deco music, entertainment, antique and collectible vendors and artists. Not to be missed are the educational programs featured by walking, bike and trolley tours, as well as an extensive children's area.

For more details about Art Deco Weekend,® the lecture & film series, vendor applications and the movement to preserve the Miami Beach Art Deco District, call (305) 672-2014, Fax (305) 672-4319, or write to:

Miami Design Preservation League
P.O. Box 190180
Miami Beach, FL 33119-0180

FLORIDA INTERNATIONAL UNIVERSITY

proudly announces the establishment of the

SCHOOL OF ARCHITECTURE

Fifteen years in the making, the FIU School of Architecture is dedicated to becoming the premier accredited architecture program at a public university in south Florida. The new school currently offers a Bachelor's Degree in Architectural Design and Interior Design as well as a Master's Degree in Architecture.

This year we are increasing the size of our facility to accommodate our plans for the Master of Interior Design and Bachelor of Landscape Architecture Programs. We also invite you to celebrate with us our new association with the Wolfsonian Museum.

FIU SCHOOL OF ARCHITECTURE
UNIVERSITY PARK CAMPUS
MIAMI, FLORIDA 33199
TEL: (305) 348 3181

Founded in 1986, The Journal fosters scholarship in the period 1875–1945, exploring the role of art and design in the modern world.

For further information on current and back issues, contact The Journal office:
The Wolfsonian–Florida International University
1001 Washington Ave., Miami Beach, FL 33139 USA
Phone: 305.532.2612, Fax: 305.531.2133

The Journal of Decorative and Propaganda Arts

THE WOLFSONIAN
FLORIDA INTERNATIONAL UNIVERSITY

1001 WASHINGTON AVENUE   MIAMI BEACH   FLORIDA   33139

The Wolfsonian–Florida International University promotes the collection, preservation, and understanding of art and design of the period 1885–1945. Located in the heart of Miami Beach's Art Deco District, the exhibition and research center houses more than 70,000 artifacts and provides rich evidence of the changes that swept the world from the late nineteenth century through World War II.

Through exhibitions, academic activities, and public programs, The Wolfsonian–Florida International University investigates the ways in which design has reflected and shaped the human experience.

1998 EXHIBITION SCHEDULE

Art and Design in the Modern Age	Ongoing
Pioneers of Modern Graphic Design	October 16, 1997 – April 26, 1998
Public Works	January 11, 1998 – April 26, 1998
Drawing the Future: Designs for the 1939 New York World's Fair	May 15, 1998 – November 1, 1998
Leading "The Simple Life": The Arts and Crafts Movement in Britain, 1880–1910	October 1998 – February 1999

TRAVELING EXHIBITION SCHEDULE

The Arts of Reform and Persuasion, 1885–1945 Indianapolis Museum of Art	January 25, 1998 – April 5, 1998

The Wolfsonian–Florida International University
is open to the public Tuesday – Sunday.
For general information call (305) 531-1001 or fax (305) 531-2133.
For membership information call (305) 535-2631.

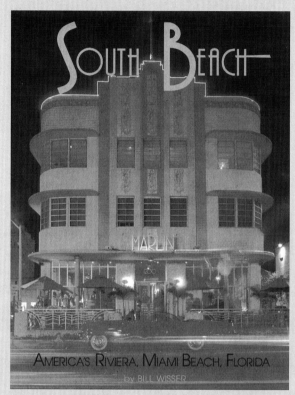

From a talented group of craftsmen who built the Florida Exhibit at the 1939 World's Fair...

Envelope
detail, 1930's

EXHIBIT BUILDERS
INCORPORATED
POST OFFICE BOX 1320 - - - DELAND, FLORIDA

Letterhead, *ca.* 1955

Letterhead   *detail, ca.* 1961

PHONES RE 4-3196 -

Letterhead   *detail,* 1959

Business card, 1965

Business card, 1970's

Business card
1997

...ebi now offers a compelling diversity of services based on the most modern technology.

EBI is proud to have our archive collection displayed at the Wolfsonian.

South Florida Historian
Cesar Alejandro Becerra proudly presents . . .

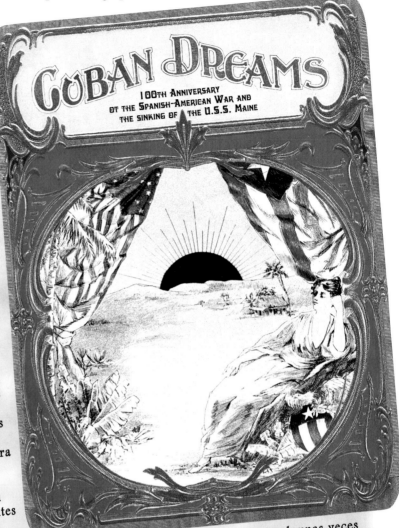

"For 113 days during the spring and summer of 1898, the United States was at war with Spain. It happened because forces set in motion decades before had become too powerful to resist. It happened because some were indifferent to the suffering of the world's wretched and others were not. And it happened because history is sometimes the plaything of chance."

"Por 113 días durante la primavera y el verano de 1898, los Estados Unidos estuvieron en guerra contra España. Sucedió porque fuerzas puestas en acción décadas antes se volvieron muy poderosas para resistir. Sucedió porque algunas personas eran indiferentes a los sentimientos de los pobres del mundo, mientras que otras sí las notaron. También ocurrió porque la historia algunas veces queda al azar."

—George O'Toole, 1984
The Spanish War

A one-year only, weekly (50 issues), full color, bilingual newsletter commemorating the 100th Anniversary of the Spanish-American War, the sinking of the U.S.S. Maine and exploring the historical links between the island of Cuba and the Florida peninsula.

William H. Johnson

William H. Johnson. *Lame Man,* c. 1939

Coming soon…

A major traveling exhibition and publication on William H. Johnson (1901-1970).
The exhibition will span Johnson's entire career and the catalogue will be fully
illustrated including photographs of Johnson never before published.

ECHOES

THE MAGAZINE OF CLASSIC MODERN STYLE & DESIGN

The **Fifties in France:** an overview
Finn Juhl's Scandinavian modern | **Vintage Fashion** première
Italian designer jewelry by **Coppola e Toppo**
Dominick Labino and Studio Glass of the 1960s
Charles Haertling's tribute to **1950s organic architecture**

Summer 1997
USA $4.95
Canada $6.00

0 74470 84175 3

TURN YOUR FINANCIAL PLANS INTO
A UNIQUE WORK OF ART

An artist chooses from the raw colors on a palette to turn a blank canvas into an
individual work of art. At SunTrust, our skilled financial managers help you
identify financial goals and select from a diverse palette of investment opportunities.
And then, we create a personal investment and trust program that fits your specific goals.
We're one of Florida's oldest and largest trust and investment managers, and our
skill and experience have allowed us to achieve superior investment performance for
our clients. So you can be sure your individual plan will be a timeless work of art.
Call a financial manager in our Trust and Investment Services group at (305) 579-7150.

SUNTRUST

Be Ready For Life℠

Visit our web site at www.SunTrust.com.

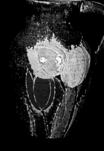

AMBROSINO GALLERY

The venue in Miami for Contemporary Art

3095 S.W. 39th Avenue Miami, Florida 33146
Tel (305) 445.2211 Fax (305) 444.0101

THE **NATIONAL** HOTEL
MIAMI BEACH

A N   A R T   D E C O   C L A S S I C   R E S U R R E C T E D

1677 COLLINS AVENUE, MIAMI BEACH, FL 33139
TEL 305-532-2311   800-327-8370   FAX 305-534-1426
WWW.NATIONALHOTEL.COM   E-MAIL: SALES@NATIONALHOTEL.COM

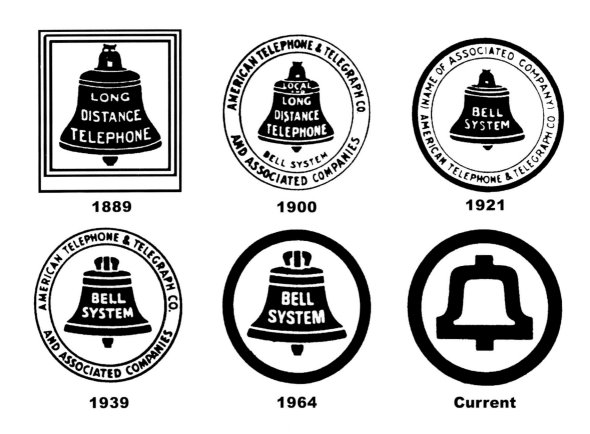

1889   1900   1921

1939   1964   Current

BELLSOUTH

We've been in the neighborhood a long time.

Give Art a Call!

THE LOUIS WOLFSON II MEDIA HISTORY CENTER

A State of Florida designated moving image center and archive

is one of the largest film and video archives of its kind in the United States. Important to Florida, and part of a broader national effort, its mission is to collect, preserve, and make accessible film and video materials which document history and culture. The Center's collection spans eight decades and contains millions of feet of film and thousands of hours of videotape, encompassing everything from 1920s home movies to last night's news.

The collection is accessible through a wide range of public activities and programs including screenings, seminars, workshops and exhibitions; it is an invaluable resource for researchers, historians, students, educators, history buffs, film, video makers, and the general public.

For more information about the Wolfson Center, to help in our preservation efforts, or to donate film and video materials call (305) 375-1505 or write to the Center at: Miami-Dade Public Library, 101 West Flagler Street, Miami, Florida, 33130

You never really

leave this place.

You just go home

for a while.

For your FREE Florida Vacation Guide, call toll free 1-888-7-FLA-USA.   www.flausa.com

DON'T MISS THESE EXCITING EVENTS!

Angel, 18th Century, Spain, Wood, San Antonio Museum of Art Collection, San Antonio, TX

EL ALMA DEL PUEBLO: SPANISH FOLK ART AND ITS TRANSFORMATION IN THE AMERICAS

January 23 - March 21, 1998

The first major exhibition devoted to the folk culture of Spain and its impact on the Americas. Featuring more than 350 objects from 25 museums and private collections in Spain and the Americas, it will open a window onto the Soul of Spain, its people, and its lasting impressions on the New World.

Opening Reception:
Friday, January 23, 1998 in PC 110 *following lecture*

Robert Hughes
© Joyce Ravid

STEVEN AND DOROTHEA GREEN CRITICS' LECTURE SERIES XVIII
featuring

ROBERT HUGHES

Art Critic for *Time* magazine and Host and Scriptwriter of PBS documentary series *American Visions*

Friday, January 23, 1998, 8:00 p.m. in AT 100

The 1997-98 Critics' Lecture Series is sponsored by Steven and Dorothea Green and Christie's, Inc.

Tony Rosenthal, *Marty's Cube*, 1983, Painted steel, 168" x 137" x 137", On loan from the Margulies Family Collection

ARTPARK AT FIU

F.I.U.'s University Park and North Miami campuses are home to The Art Museum's *ArtPark at FIU*, outdoor sculpture park, which includes works from the Martin Z. Margulies Sculpture Collection. This world renowned collection includes over 50 works by some of the most celebrated sculptors including, Jean Dubuffet, Joan Miró, Alexander Calder, Willem de Kooning, Louise Nevelson, and Richard Serra.

Open year-round, free of charge.
Guided educational tours available!

The Art Museum
AT FLORIDA INTERNATIONAL UNIVERSITY

University Park Campus • PC 110 • S.W. 107th Ave. & 8th St. • Miami, FL 33199
(305) 348-2890 • FAX (305) 348-2762

MARCIO ROITER

20th century decorative arts

Rua Pacheco Leão, 110
Tel/fax : 294-4845 / 239-5503
CEP 22460-030

Jardim Botânico
Rio de Janeiro
BRASIL

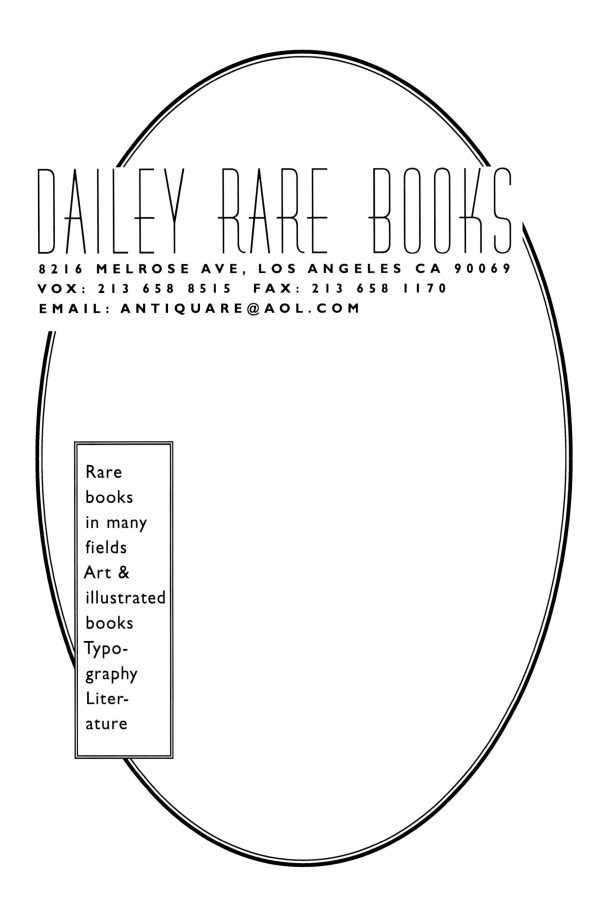

DAILEY RARE BOOKS

8216 MELROSE AVE, LOS ANGELES CA 90069
VOX: 213 658 8515   FAX: 213 658 1170
EMAIL: ANTIQUARE@AOL.COM

Rare
books
in many
fields
Art &
illustrated
books
Typo-
graphy
Liter-
ature

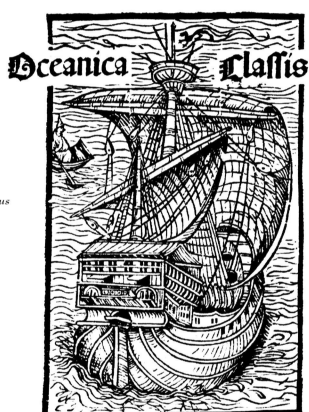

MODERNISM GALLERY
FINE AND DECORATIVE ART OF THE 20th CENTURY

Rug Fragment from Design by Ruth Reeves for Radio City Music Hall 1932.
Bookshelf by Donald Deskey for Widdicomb 1930's. Three Vases by Loetz 1920's.
Center Vase by Deque, France 1930's. Hunt Champagne Set by Bimini Werkstatte 1920's.

RIC EMMETT
305/442-8743   FAX: 305/443-3074
1622 PONCE DeLEON BOULEVARD / CORAL GABLES, FLORIDA 33134

Featuring fine American Impressionist, Regionalist and Modern
paintings, prints and sculpture. Now representing the Estate of
John Storrs.

New 1997 catalogue available for $18.00 postpaid.

ROBERT HENRY ADAMS FINE ART

715 N. FRANKLIN • CHICAGO, IL 60610 • 312/642-8700 • fax 312/642-8785

LYNNE GOLOB GELFMAN

blastone, oil & acrylic on canvas 15 x 13 in. 1997

Fredric Snitzer Gallery

3078 SW 38 COURT MIAMI, FLORIDA 33146 305 • 448 • 8976 FAX 305 • 448 • 0711